INTRODUCTION TO METAPHYSICS

JEAN GRONDIN

TRANSLATED BY LUKAS SODERSTROM

INTRODUCTION TO METAPHYSICS

From Parmenides to Levinas

COLUMBIA UNIVERSITY PRESS   NEW YORK

COLUMBIA UNIVERSITY PRESS

Publishers Since 1893

NEW YORK   CHICHESTER, WEST SUSSEX

cup.columbia.edu

Introduction à la métaphysique © 2004 by Les Presses de l'Université de Montréal
Published under arrangement with Les Presses de l'Université de Montréal, Québec, Canada

English translation © 2012 Columbia University Press

Library of Congress Cataloging-in-Publication Data

Grondin, Jean.
[Introduction à la métaphysique. English]
Introduction to metaphysics : from Parmenides to Levinas / Jean Grondin ; translated by Lukas Soderstrom.
p. cm.
Includes bibliographical references (p.).
ISBN 978-0-231-14845-0 (cloth : alk. paper)–ISBN 978-0-231-14844-3 (pbk. : alk. paper)–
ISBN 978-0-231-52723-1 (ebook)
1. Metaphysics—History. I. Title.
BD112.G7613 2012

110–dc22   2011012094

Columbia University Press books are printed on permanent and durable acid-free paper.
This book is printed on paper with recycled content.

Printed in the United States of America

References to Internet Web sites (URLs) were accurate at the time of writing. Neither the author nor Columbia
University Press is responsible for URLs that may have expired or changed since the manuscript was prepared.

To all my students

There is a science which investigates Being as Being.
ARISTOTLE, *METAPHYSICS*, IV, 1

Thus, all philosophy is like a tree, of which Metaphysics is the root, Physics the trunk, and all the other sciences the branches that grow out of this trunk, which are reduced to three principal, namely, Medicine, Mechanics, and Ethics.
RENÉ DESCARTES, PREFACE TO THE *PRINCIPLES OF PHILOSOPHY*

Metaphysics is without a doubt the most difficult of all things into which man has insight. But so far no metaphysics has ever been written.
IMMANUEL KANT, *INQUIRY CONCERNING THE DISTINCTNESS OF THE PRINCIPLES OF NATURAL THEOLOGY AND MORALITY*

A people without any metaphysics is like a temple without a "Holy of Holies."
G. W. F. HEGEL, PREFACE TO THE FIRST EDITION OF *THE SCIENCE OF LOGIC*

Metaphysics belongs to "human nature." It is neither a division of academic philosophy nor a field of arbitrary notions. Metaphysics is the fundamental event of our existence. It is our existence itself.
MARTIN HEIDEGGER, *WHAT IS METAPHYSICS?*

CONTENTS

This book hopes to introduce the reader to the intellectual discipline called "metaphysics." If quotation marks are called for, it is because metaphysics is not a science that is taught today in any significant way. Even though some once considered it to be the queen of the sciences, there are no faculties of metaphysics like there are, say, departments of physics, mathematics, or theology. In fact, there never were any such faculties or departments. Nowadays, and for quite some time now, metaphysics is more often than not used as a foil for so-called postmetaphysical thought as though being nonmetaphysical were some kind of philosophical virtue. Indeed, most major trends in contemporary philosophy—phenomenology, analytic philosophy, and deconstruction—generally agree on the urgency of overcoming metaphysics. But what is thereby overcome? Is it always known? And, are these new postmetaphysical trends even thinkable without the insights of their metaphysical forbearers?

The author of this book belongs to a generation that was not schooled in metaphysics and was taught instead that it represented an illusory, inherently repressive, and even tyrannical form of thought from which one had to be freed. This was proclaimed, and quite autocratically at that, in the name of the philosophies of Heidegger and Kant. But as any impartial reader will not fail to notice, both Kant and Heidegger's philosophical projects were not only profoundly influenced by metaphysics, they were metaphysical to the core. To be sure, Kant faulted traditional metaphysics for laying claim to a form of knowledge that would go beyond experience, but he himself laid the groundwork of a metaphysics of nature and a metaphysics of morals, which culminated in a proof of the existence of God and of the immortality of the soul. Quite a feat for a gravedigger of metaphysics. As for Heidegger, he stigmatized metaphysics because it aimed at a rational, theological and totalizing account of Being. But he was himself seeking a new understanding of "Being" (for which he unearthed indicative names, like *Ereignis* or *Seyn*), obviously set forth "reasons" and arguments for doing so, and did so in the hope of preparing a new experience of the "divine" in a modern world which has been "abandoned" by the gods. As with Kant, all his basic terms (Being, essence, truth, existence, ground, foundation, identity) were borrowed from the metaphysical tradition, to which his major interlocutors (Parmenides, Heraclitus, Plato, Aristotle, Augustine, Descartes, Leibniz, Kant, Hegel, Schelling, and Nietzsche) belonged. Indeed, one does not need an advanced degree to know that Kant's ultimate goal was to make metaphysics possible and Heidegger's was to reawaken the question of Being, which is undoubtedly one the most important themes of all metaphysics. Why was this overlooked in the rush to "overcome" metaphysics?

Moreover, when did metaphysics ever exert its purported "hegemony"? Certainly not during Antiquity. Since the term metaphysics was not coined until the twelfth century, the Ancients can hardly be called metaphysicians.[1] Now the thinking of Being and its reasons we call "metaphysics" did indeed first appear during Greek Antiquity, and it may be considered one of the greatest achievements of classical thought. But it only appeared in highly elliptical and difficult texts of authors like Parmenides, Plato, and Aristotle, who ceaselessly emphasized the fact they were leaving behind the well-beaten paths of mortal discourse when they spoke of Being. And their new way of thinking always and immediately raised the same problem: What was the real object of their new discourse? What did they mean by Being, the Ideas, or Being as Being? So even as early as Antiquity any explanation of the world oriented by the question of Being has been met with puzzlement. Thus the immobility of Parmenides' Being was countered by the evidence of movement. And Aristotle famously stigmatized the Platonic theory of ideas for its useless "metaphysics" (in which he saw a vain duplication of our world with little or no practical use), despite having himself put forth the idea of an enigmatic "first philosophy," which would later come to be identified with metaphysics. In fact, "metaphysical" thought was of so little importance during Antiquity that neither the post-Aristotelian Hellenistic schools (Stoicism, Epicureanism, Skepticism) nor the Romans really prolonged its first halting steps in any meaningful fashion (at least until Neo-Platonism).

What about the Middle Ages? The image of a Middle Ages completely beholden to metaphysics is an unfortunate myth. Since the medieval world encountered metaphysical thought rather belatedly and, since it strongly relied on a revelation which came from another source than feeble human reason, metaphysics was never dominant or uncontested. In fact, the average reader will be hard-pressed to name even a single medieval author who presented his own thought as metaphysics.

As for modernity, it has, since Descartes, sought to oppose and overcome metaphysics in the name of another "first philosophy," but it has only done so on the basis of a more rigorous conception of reality and a better account of Being, its principles, and reasons. But this new attempt to better explain the Being of things, and thus to go beyond the inherited and erroneous discourses, reiterated the fundamental hope of metaphysical thought—that is, that of an accurate account of Being and its reasons. It is indeed very difficult to overcome metaphysics without presupposing it or putting it into practice.

Thus this book wishes to recall, against all odds, that metaphysics is the insurmountable presupposition of all thought insofar as it carried and supported the project of a universal understanding of the world that inquires into the Being and reason for things.

For some time now, I have deplored the absence of a historical introduction to metaphysics in English. Those that do exist are either old or thomistic, in an outdated and caricatured understanding of the term. It is true that metaphysics has long been the affair of Thomists. In this tradition, which is really more Scotist than Thomist, general metaphysics, also called ontology, was viewed as the fundamental discipline of philosophy to the extent that it pertained to Being as Being, and relegated the study of its specificities (Being as this or that) to the other parts of philosophy. This conception of philosophy is perhaps old-fashioned, but its logic has not been superseded (Heidegger certainly adopted it in *Being and Time*).

The need for an introduction to metaphysics has not disappeared, however. In fact, it may be even more pressing now that metaphysics is regarded with such suspicion, but also with a certain degree of ignorance. It is a most common occurrence to run into an undergraduate student, or even the holder of a chair at a prestigious university, who will readily equate metaphysics with an outdated form of thought, if not with violence altogether.[2] Is metaphysics really violent? If that were the case, it should be prohibited by law and our

declarations of human rights. It could be that one falls prey here to a very inef-
fectual understanding of violence. Violence occurs when someone invades
your country or your home, rapes your children, murders, harms or robs someone, but where is the violence when someone like Parmenides or Plato writes a
poem or dialogue about Being? Are the sermons of Meister Eckhart or the lectures of Plotinus or Schelling particularly brutal? Isn't it this equation between
violence and metaphysics which is in itself quite violent, in the precise sense
that it does not do justice to what metaphysics has been?

Some allege it is the thinking about Being that would be inherently "violent." Really? But if that is the case, it is an argument one has to leave to those
who defend it. What else should one be thinking of? In any case, it would
have to be another being (say, alterity, society, the good, the human being, the
earth, linguistic structures) which one holds to be more fundamental and worthy of attention. But this claim must be justified, and it can only be justified by
arguing that this or that reality (or Being) is more fundamental than this one.
Whether one likes it or not, this is a metaphysical claim.

Metaphysics, with its universal breadth, is often faulted in recent times
for having disregarded "alterity" and difference, an argument made by Lévinas, Derrida, and their many followers. But is that true? As such, the notion
of alterity is one about which many metaphysical thinkers have spoken, such
as Plato in his *Sophists*, Hegel in his *Logic* or even Lévinas in *Totalité et infini* (a
book generally hostile to "ontology," but, lest one forget, amenable to metaphysics). Yet most of these authors recognized that alterity was a concept of
relation. An alterity is always the other of something else. This is why it is
arduous to praise it as such. The alterity of peace is war, that of the good is the
bad, and one doesn't readily see why one should put a premium on them. The
issue is not whether alterity should be exalted, but *which* alterity and *why*. And
if Levinas praises the alterity which shines in the face of the other, it is certainly because this other is endowed with a certain metaphysical distinction.

This book will argue that it is thus impossible to surpass metaphysics without presupposing it. Since they are largely forgotten, its immediate aim will
be to recall the important moments and principal steps in the somewhat subterranean history of metaphysics. This book's goal is not to review metaphysics' "great systems" in all their incommensurable diversity. Rather, through
its diversity, it hopes to bring to light the continuity of a question and a discipline of thought that is perhaps constitutive of philosophy itself. One need
not adopt a particular doctrine (like one joins a political party or a religion)
to practice metaphysics. One simply needs to realize what one is doing when
one attempts to understand our world and the meaning of one's experiences.

Toward a Concept of Metaphysics

"Metaphysics" has today lost much of its former luster. The term is often only understood in a pejorative sense, of which there are two varieties. In the first instance, "metaphysical" is used to describe empty reflections having little to do with the concrete facts of life. Metaphysical here is synonymous with the abstract, nebulous, or abstruse. Although this is a quite common understanding of metaphysics, and of philosophy as well, it has no place in this book, which will never discuss abstruse, obscure, or useless things. On the contrary, it will deal with the best of our metaphysical heritage and recall how it is impossible to think without abstraction. Even all that is called concrete must be thought of as part of a more general perspective, one which the concrete seeks to illustrate.

The second pejorative sense of metaphysics, although related to the first, is more precise. "Metaphysical," in the second widespread usage, designates what lies beyond the physical, or what is separate from the sensible and perceptible material world. In addition to the physical world that surrounds and stifles us but in which we live, there is what Nietzsche derisively called a metaphysical backcountry (*Hinterwelten*), a world inhabited, it would seem, by nonphysical beings such as gods, angels, souls, and thinking beings. In this second sense, "metaphysical" is synonymous with "transcendent," "theological," and "supernatural."

But is this the world to which this book is an introduction? No, or, rather, not directly. The main topic here is Western metaphysical thought, whose foundation is indeed metaphysical but is not necessarily related to thinking about the supersensible or to nebulous reflection. Such distinctions are indeed possible, sometimes even necessary, but most often excluded yet later reintroduced in other guises. That said, metaphysics will only be used here to designate the undercurrent of western philosophy that has from the time of Ancient Greece until now inquired into *that which is*—that is, into Being and its reasons. Such an inquiry need not be nebulous since Being is perhaps what is most immediate and visible. Nor must it necessarily focus on the supernatural because precisely what metaphysics does is to inquire into that which is: Being, such as it is given. Nevertheless, metaphysics is aware of its association with some form of transcendence. As its prefix *meta* suggests, metaphysics endeavors to overcome both overly particular perspectives and too restrictive ones, in order to consider Being in general, as a whole, thus developing an understanding of it that goes beyond any particular perspective.

As Parmenides' fourth century BCE discourse on Being demonstrates, philosophical thought, and with it scientific thought, began with Being. Plato and Aristotle carried on this tradition in extraordinarily halting texts where they argued that true Being (Plato) or Being as Being (Aristotle) had to be the favored object of knowledge. This inquiry into Being was perceived as universal and therefore as the most rational of inquiries. It was to bear on the most substantial Being—"the most being," as Plato put it—and therefore the most fundamental of all. This hope of a universal and fundamental discourse on Being is the basis of the philosophical discipline called "metaphysics."

Aristotle, writing before the invention of the term "metaphysics," named the discipline "first philosophy" because its object, Being, was to be considered first, and more importantly, because to discuss Being was also to inquire into the underlying principle of all that is. Since then, all really significant philosophical thought has been defined by an understanding of Being and its foundation, and can only be considered philosophy in this regard. Even though Being is not always the main theme—thank goodness!—all philosophical thought is necessarily metaphysical insofar as it discusses a being, a subject or an object it considers more important than all others (nature, reason, God, the subject, values, history, humanity, happiness, justice, meaning).

The philosophical importance of the question of Being is therefore greater than its place in the history of thought. This question has been important since the Greeks because Being, in one single word, defines the universe as a whole along with our own ephemeral existence in it. Fragile and fortuitous as it is, Being, including our own, might well have never come into existence. Yet Being is and we are, at least for a time. It is this mystery and our perplexed relation to it—to us—that is the origin of philosophy, of metaphysics—that is, of the thought of Being.

There are two noteworthy, but not necessarily exclusive, reactions to this mystery. The first attempts to explain *why* there is something—such as ourselves for example—rather than nothing. This is the meaning of a "principle of reason" in the works of philosophers such as Leibniz who sought reasons explaining why things are as they are.[1] This principle, or faith in rationality, has been the single most important impetus to scientific inquiry, which has been understood since Plato—and even since Parmenides—as a rational discourse (*logos*) on what is (the *on*, or beings).

The second reaction has, since Parmenides, always accompanied this attempt at understanding. This second attitude towards Being attempts to go beyond the explanatory approach of reason, which can never be discarded, and marvels at the fact there is something rather than nothing. Although it may appear irrational, this second position in relation to Being is no less rigorous than the first. Indeed, it observes that all explanations can only explain Being from Being. Although one may derive Being from another principle, the ensuing explanation does not really explain why there is something rather than nothing. Thus the following paradox: Being, which calls for an explanation, in a way resists all meaning and explanation. Even philosophy, which in its most scientific vein always seeks explanations, can be astonished at the immensity of all that is. Both Plato and Aristotle in fact claimed that philosophy was born out of astonishment, even admiration. It may be that the great works of philosophy, like those of art, are born of this astonishment, unceasingly renewing itself for more than two millennia.

While it embodies one of the most rigorous manifestations of metaphysics, the astonishment before the immensity of Being also renders the metaphysical project—the rational discourse on Being—all the more difficult. Indeed, what can be *said* about Being? Can a discourse on Being be anything other than halting and uncertain? Can it ever be a scientific discourse? Can philosophy ever measure up to what it wishes to express? Philosophy's embarrassed perplexity has at times led to skepticism (nothing certain can be said about Being) and to mysticism (Being is ineffable). It has also led to the clear and resolute rejection of the question of Being (it is not an object worthy of attention). If nothing can be said of Being because it is too general a concept, one must settle for predictable and explainable things. Nevertheless, such a resigned dismissal of the question of Being is itself the result of a metaphysical decision. One should be aware that all three of these attitudes towards Being (skepticism, mysticism and the rejection of the question of Being) are coherent and real attempts at philosophy despite the fact that Being is scientifically ineffable and its elusiveness can be somewhat exasperating. A philosophy devoid of mysticism and skepticism would not live up to its name because it would not measure up to the mystery of Being itself. One is tempted to respond to all these objections with Galileo's words: *eppur si muove!* "but it moves!" Being is indeed moving: it emerges and moves us. We never cease speaking of it and we are of it. To inquire metaphysically is therefore to strive to express Being which embraces and envelops us.

Its Origins

As we have just seen, the thought of Being began with Parmenides, of whom we know very little. In the three pages of contiguous text of his that remain, Being is held to be the favored, even sole, object of knowledge. Parmenides merely says, albeit tautologically, that Being is and Nonbeing is not. A rather simplistic claim, one may say, but the theme of Being emerged along with "rational" thought which seeks to overcome idle talk or unfounded opinions and can only grasp Being as something permanent that has not become. Plato would later be the first to call the thinking of a permanent and fundamental Being *philosophia*.

The term "metaphysics" appeared much later, however. Although usually dated to the twelfth century CE, it was coined in the first century BCE when Adronicus of Rhodes sought a title for fourteen short unclassifiable studies attributed to Aristotle. According to a possibly fictional account,[2] Aristotle's manuscripts rotted away in a cellar for almost two centuries after his death until they were edited by Adronicus, the tenth scholarch of the Peripatetic school founded by Aristotle. Andronicus began by arranging the rediscovered manuscripts according to specific headings, which corresponded to a doctrinal *curriculum*. Drawing his inspiration from the Stoic division of philosophy into logic, physics, and ethics, Andronicus organized Aristotle's manuscripts into four groups:[3]

1. Logical writings (later called the *Organon*)
2. Ethical, political, and rhetorical writings (including the *Poetics*)
3. Physical writings (including what we would today call biology and psychology)
4. "Metaphysical" writings

His use of the term "metaphysics" seems to designate "that which comes after the physics" (*meta ta physika,*) and would therefore only have had a bibliographical function. But it also indicates a problem that Andronicus faced. As he could not include the fourteen small and dissimilar treatises under any of the other headings because they were neither logical, ethical nor physical in the limited sense of the terms, he called them "metaphysical."

Yet the term "metaphysics" may also designate their content. It would then astutely include everything that is situated "beyond the physical." It is tempting here to cite Kant's well-known text on the origin of the term metaphysics:

> As for the name metaphysics, it is hard to believe that it was born out of chance since it fits this science so well: if we call nature *phusis* and if we can only arrive at the concepts of nature by experience, then the science that follows after it is called metaphysics (from *meta*, *trans*, and *physica*). It is, in a way, a science that is beyond the physical realm.[4]

In fact, this conception of metaphysics as a science of the supersensible corresponds much more to Kant's own understanding of metaphysics (which, to be possible, had to justify its claim to supernatural knowledge), than to the subject of Aristotle's texts. Indeed, the texts of the *Metaphysics* do not solely discuss things "beyond" the physical, nor do they give such matters any priority. Book V, for example, is a compendium of definitions that could have been classified along with the logical writings. Books VII, VIII, and IX all deal with substance in general and not in any "metaphysical" sense of the term. Nonetheless, some of the manuscripts do evoke the project of a universal science, or first philosophy. This science would pertain to what Aristotle called "Being as Being." Although the meaning of the expression is far from obvious, its main idea—that of distinguishing a universal reflection on Being from the topics of the individualized sciences concerned with particular objects—is easier to understand. Aristotle makes this distinction in the opening of Book IV of the compilation of his so-called metaphysical texts:

> There is a science which investigates Being as Being and the attributes which belong to this in virtue of its own nature. Now this is not the same as any of the so-called special sciences; for none of these others treats universally of Being as Being. They cut off a part of Being and investigate the attribute of this part, this is what the mathematical sciences for instance do.[5]

Any introduction to metaphysics must start from this important passage taken from Aristotle's *Metaphysics*. It defines the science that considers Being as Being by its claim to universality. While the other sciences deal with well-delimited domains of objects, there could be another more encompassing science, which Aristotle left nameless. To use the more recent terminology, of Husserl and Heidegger, one could say that all the sciences are "ontic" insofar as they pertain to one of the already determined *beings* or an object. Philosophy alone would be "ontological" in that it is centered on the consideration of Being itself, or Being as Being. The expression remains obviously enigmatic, and all the more so since Aristotle never explained it straightforwardly. It does imply, however, that metaphysics' subject, if one may speak of such a thing, is not only more universal than that of the other sciences, but is also more fundamental. A reflection on Being and its essential traits must seemingly *precede* the special sciences in which Being is specifically understood as being such and such, mathematical, physical, or the like. Although this conception may today appear hierarchical and accordingly obsolete, it remains essential to philosophy, if the latter must be credibly differentiated from the individual sciences and their specific objects. It is certainly possible to define philosophy without any recourse to the question of Being, but it would be difficult for it to remain what it is were it to forsake the universal and fundamental questions that are of no concern to the individual sciences. This is the level of inquiry the expression used in *Metaphysics* IV uncovers and reveals.

The history of metaphysics can be read as the history of Aristotle's expression, which was itself oriented by questions that Parmenides and Plato had raised. As we shall see, an important part of late medieval thought developed under the sway of the Aristotelian idea of a first philosophy tied to the problem of Being, understood in an un-Hellenic fashion as the creation of Being as a whole. Although modern philosophy called into question parts of the foundation of classical metaphysics, it did so in the name of a *new* metaphysical discourse. Indeed Descartes, in his *Meditations on First Philosophy* (1641), opened modernity to philosophical reflection, which abandoned the question of Being for a more universal and fundamental subject it found in thought itself. This *redefinition* of philosophy was but a reorientation of *metaphysics*, understood as a universal and fundamental discourse on what is. Authors such as Leibniz, Kant, Hegel, and Heidegger attempted to redefine its topic, but always in the name of a new and more radical conception of Being.

The most serious misinterpretation would be to turn metaphysics into a reflection on the most dignified and important "object" of all. The metaphysical tradition has always been aware that all meditation on Being must be accompanied by a conversion of one's perspective. Plato spoke of *metanoia*, of metamorphosis, or *epimeleia*, a concern of the soul. To consider Being is always to question oneself as to the meaning, or lack of meaning (the one presupposes the other), in our experience of Being. Even as early as Parmenides, the thought of Being was associated with an elevation and transformation of the mind. Plato then carried on this motif and incited the soul to turn away from shadows and idle chatter (*doxa*) that enchant the multitude, in order to better turn towards more fundamental realities. This is the first meaning we can give to metaphysical "transcendence."

Although obvious to ancient thinkers and not forgotten by all moderns, it was Pierre Hadot who rediscovered the idea that philosophy aspires less to a theoretical or doctrinal form of discourse, than to introspective deliberation and its actualization of a way of life worthy of the name wisdom.[6] The term "conversion" (*metanoia*) may have become obsolete, but the urgency of a concern of the soul (*epimeleia*) will never cease to be important as long as humans ponder the meaning of their short and accidental sojourn in Being.

Metaphysics is thus driven by ethical or existential concern. But the question of the priority of ethics over metaphysics, or of the latter over the former, need not be asked here. All ethics presupposes metaphysics or ontology—that is, some understanding of who we are. And all metaphysics is aware that it is directed by an ethical questioning into the meaning and possibilities of our existence. Does not Hamlet's famous "ethical" question *to be or not to be?* use the vocabulary of Being?

An introduction to metaphysics is thus our reintroduction to the fact one is always an enigma to oneself, or to use Augustine's expression: *quæstio mihi factus sum.*[7] Since it springs from this question, metaphysics is a reminder of this fundamental concern that is the root of all understanding. And although essential, this question is also one that ordinary existence tries to avoid, as Heidegger recalled. To cite Plato: All philosophy is reminiscence.

The following introduction is meant as a reminder of the important periods that have formed the core of metaphysics. Although the author has not chosen one over the other, the philosophies that are discussed here are those that have made the most rigorous contributions, both conceptually and historically, towards defining metaphysics. My only hope is that the choices made appear to be neither too arbitrary nor overly determined by a canon that others may regard—as is their right—as less constraining. It is, as we have just stated, up to each of us to introduce ourselves to metaphysics.

INTRODUCTION TO METAPHYSICS

CHAPTER I

PARMENIDES

The Evidence of Being

The Fragmentary and Almost Incomprehensible
Character of Pre-Platonic Thought

Just as we usually know very little about beginnings, we know very little about the beginning of the thought of Being. Since what we know about something is always based on its relation to something else, a point of departure or a previously known principle, what follows thereafter appears as its consequence. So how are we to understand the beginning itself? It is with this perplexity, which need not be dispelled, that we encounter Parmenides' *Poem*. Since it is easier to understand what follows from it, the beginning itself remains unprecedented and consequently unexplainable. As we shall see, Parmenides likens his discourse on Being to a revelation, and it thus squares awkwardly with what we already know, or claim to know. A warning is thus given to all those who hope to understand Parmenides through his "context."

Points of reference do exist, however. It is generally agreed that Parmenides lived between 515 and 440 BCE, founded a school at Elea in the south of the Italian peninsula, and belonged to what is called the "Presocratics." And yet, this classification, which has existed only since the nineteenth century, does not contribute to our understanding in any significant way since it characterizes a group of philosophers through reference to another philosopher, in this case Socrates (470–399 BCE) who did not write anything (one increasingly uses the term "pre-Platonic" to designate thinkers from the Greek archaic period, as if it made more sense). The other major characteristic of the Presocratics is that we only know about them through the remaining fragments of their texts and thought. But even the term "fragment" is overly generous. The only reason we are aware of these "texts" is because they were cited, invoked, and used by later authors, and they are accordingly always tainted by those who quoted them. In some cases, this can be quite obvious as when we easily recognize the telltale traces of the person who quoted them. But sometimes it is less obvious, especially when we unconsciously ascribe to them the use of now familiar "concepts." Generally such concepts—or translations, which amounts to the same—are those of recent commentators whose use of modern terminology in their reading of the Presocratics is not always forthright. Such is the case when, for example, they use terms like "theory of knowledge," "cosmology," or speak of Presocratic "thought" or "philosophy." If one is to speak of the Presocratics, or quote them, in any rigorous way, one should always use double quotation marks. The first pair to indicate that the texts are already quotations, and the second to remind the reader that the terms employed should be used with the utmost caution. One cannot really hope to understand their archaic and tragically lost writings without a critique or a "destruction" of the available sources—in the positive sense of the term, that is, an explication of the prejudices belonging to the sources that made our knowledge of the Presocratics possible. Ingratitude is, in a way, the prerequisite to the study of the Classics.

The complete Presocratic fragments—those that are judged to be authentic—would probably fit into a hundred-page book, and even then not all are of equal importance. For example, aside for some unverifiable anecdotes, all we know about Thales is that (according to Aristotle) he claimed water was the principle of all things (but the term ἀρχή [archè] cannot be the term Thales himself used). As for Heraclitus, whose ideas appear diametrically opposed to those of Parmenides, whom he may have never met, only a collection of some 130 insightful "aphorisms" remain, which easily lend themselves to a modern but inaccurate reading. As a point of comparison, let us consider a hypothetical situation where all the philosophical works of the last two centuries disappear after a nuclear catastrophe. All that is left of the knowledge of the last two centuries is an anthology of heterogeneous fragments that is passed on from generation to generation. After two millennia, all that remains of our civilization are a page from Einstein, three from Nietzsche, and twenty pages from Lenin's commentary on Hegel's *Logic*. All sorts of associations would then be made between Lenin and Einstein, questions of whether one had borrowed the other's terminology would be raised, and arguments would be made about the real object of Hegel's *Logic*. We are in a similar situation when it comes to the Presocratics: We have some strikingly interesting fragments that are nevertheless difficult to understand and others that are completely insipid.

In Parmenides' case though, the sources are better. Although we only have some eight or nine pages of his, he is the only Presocratic author of whom we have an authentic text with a relatively continuous line of argumentation. We owe the text to a sixth-century CE commentary on Aristotle written by Simplicius, in which he quoted the first 148 verses of Parmenides' *Poem* in their entirety. The circumstances of Simplicius's commentary are noteworthy. The quoted text appears in his commentary on Aristotle's *On the Heavens*, which discusses the Eleatics' purported argument against the possibility of generation and corruption.[1] Then, noticing that the original text was already hard to find, Simplicius had the happy idea, and the patience, to include large excerpts of Parmenides' text along with his commentary. All of this took place in the sixth century, a millennium after Parmenides. Yet, Parmenides' text was itself never discussed directly after the sixth century. So had we not conserved Simplicius's commentary on Aristotle, we would know little about Parmenides (or at least very little since we do have other sources, but these are even less "complete" than the one handed down to us by Simplicius).

The Context of Presocratic Thinking on Nature

What do we know of the general character of Presocratic thought? According to a widely accepted reading, Presocratic thought was characterized by reflections on nature and an inquiry into its principles. That may be, but one would be hard pressed to find this sort of reflection in the texts of its two greatest representatives—Heraclitus and Parmenides. This conception of pre-Platonic thought is not unsubstantiated, however. It comes from Aristotle, who was not only the first historian of philosophy, but also one of our main sources on the Presocratics. Nevertheless, while Aristotle is an invaluable source, it is well known that he tended to present his predecessors as so many steps leading to his own philosophy and its most important concepts. Aristotle's real intention in claiming that all thinkers concentrated on seeking the principles of nature until Socrates turned philosophy's attention to human affairs,[2] was simply to show how their search for principles led to the ambitious synthesis he proposed in his *Physics*.

Aristotle's presentation makes sense in light of our understanding of knowledge that associates science with an attempt to explain nature and discover the laws that make it comprehensible and predictable. According to Aristotle, the first thinkers initially sought a "material" principle of nature because it is both a basic principle, and because they were themselves rather primitive. Although this characterization is widespread, one must not forget that the notions "principle" (ἀρχή / *archè*) and "matter" (ὕλη / *hulè*) are themselves Aristotelian notions and were probably not used in any philosophical sense by Presocratic authors.

It is true though that the Presocratics' material principles appear quite rudimentary. This is the case of Thales of Miletus, the founder of the Ionian school and the first philosopher, according to Aristotle who says that Thales identified water as the principle of all things. Although it may appear primitive to us, the principle is nevertheless philosophically significant insofar as it brings all things back to some primordial source. We do not know what led Thales to this idea. Was he a forerunner of modern biology and perceived that all forms of life on earth require water to survive? Aristotle does seem to suggest this when he says:

> He perhaps came to acquire this belief from seeing that the nourishment
> of everything is moist and that heat itself comes from this and lives by this
> (for that from which anything comes into being is its first principle)—he
> came to his belief both for this reason and because the seeds of everything
> have a moist nature, and water is the natural principle of moist things.[3]

It may be difficult to say what is thereby "explained," but it was a beginning. Aristotle also tells us that the main point of disagreement in the Milesian school was precisely about the nature of this beginning.[4] Anaximander of Miletus, the first author of whose writings we still have a conserved sentence fragment,[5] and which should accordingly be quoted in its entirety, claimed that the principle is the infinite (or the undefined, ἄπειρον / *apeiron*):

> Of those who hold that the first principle is one, moving, and infinite,
> Anaximander, son of Praxiades, a Milesian, who was a successor and pupil
> of Thales, said that the infinite [*apeiron*] is principle and element of the
> things that exist. He was the first to introduce this word *principle*. He says
> that it is neither water nor any other of the co-called elements but some
> different infinite nature, from which all the heavens and the worlds in
> them come into being. And the things from which existing things come

into being are also the things into which they are destroyed, in accordance with what must be. For they give justice and reparation to one another for their injustice in accordance with the arrangement of time (he speaks of them in this way in somewhat poetical words).[6]

This principle is obviously subtler than Thales's. However, one should be wary of understanding "the infinite" in the theological and vaguely transcendent sense it acquired in the Middle Ages and which it still has today. Rather, "infinite" here designates something like "unlimited" (as one might say "infinite matter"); all things would then be its limitations. Anaximander argues that everything follows from this, in accordance with a certain justice that corresponds to time's implacable order. Undoubtedly, it is a profound text even though its precise meaning is difficult, if not impossible, to understand. But it is hardly a rational, or even a crudely material, explanation of the universe.

The next Milesian and successor to Anaximander was Anaximenes. He argued that it is air, which breathes life into all things, that is accordingly the principle of reality. Quite obviously the first "school," which, according to Aristotle, inquired into the material principle of things, did not agree on the nature of this "principle."

As a Presocratic, Parmenides is often classified in the tradition of "physiologists" of the Milesian school. One tradition says that he was a student of Anaximenes.[7] Another states that he was a student of Xenophanes, a "theologian" well known for his quite modern critique of anthropomorphic representations of divinity. One must bear in mind that the issue of philosophical lineages is an historian's reflex, sometimes influenced by the latest fad but sometimes just the product of the best of intentions, which attempts to understand an author by explaining who was his teacher. Thus Aristotle, in *Metaphysics*, A, 6, tries to show how Plato was more of a Pythagorean than a student of Socrates, which, historically speaking, is hard to believe. As for Parmenides, it is difficult at first to see how he could be related to Xenophanes' critique of anthropomorphism. Nonetheless, his rather "rational" conception of Being and his critique of popular opinions do in fact connect him with Xenophanes. The title of his poem, "On Nature," also seems to connect him with the Milesian school, and the Presocratics in general. And yet, it is Sextus Empiricus, writing during the second century CE, who is the first to tell us that the poem had such a name.[8] The title is a common one for Presocratic texts, and one must not forget that these titles appear to have been ascribed to the works at a later date.

Can we really identify Parmenides with the Presocratic physiological tradition? Some modern interpreters,[9] influenced by Aristotle (but then, who is not?), and by the modern scientific explanation of nature as well, have read Parmenides as a philosopher attempting to understand the structure of the universe. But one must recognize that he probably also opposed the Milesian physiological tradition by arguing against their attempts at a *genetic* explanation of nature. According to Parmenides' *Poem*, there is no becoming because this would imply a passage from Nonbeing to Being and therefore the existence of Nonbeing. And since Nonbeing is unthinkable, there can only be Being and therefore no becoming. Thus, briefly summarized, is the doxographical content of Parmenides' disconcerting *Poem*.

An Oral, Therefore Poetic, Culture

The only reason we speak of this work of Parmenides as a "poem" is because it is written in hexameter. But, that said, it would be a mistake to let modern science's nominalism and objectifying discourse label its poetic composition as simply ornamental. Such would be the case if verse were only an embellishment on an otherwise prosaic or descriptive discourse and if prose had a primordial importance over verse. A glance at Greek literature shows, however, that poetry appeared before written prose. This can be seen in the earliest texts we have, namely, those attributed to Homer. The texts ascribed to Homer, of whom we know next to nothing, were initially tales told by a culture without an alphabetical writing system, which only started to appear in eighth century BCE. Homer's epic poems, *The Iliad* and *The Odyssey*, were probably composed over more than a century and were first recited, memorized, and chanted before being written down. Early Greek culture was an oral one that was only later adapted to the written word.

In this context, texts worthy of recitation were poetic. Some philologists claim that this was because poetry is easier to memorize (even today it is much easier to remember songs or rhymes than prose). Again, such specialists presume the primacy of scientific and descriptive discourse and only give poetry a decorative or mnemonic purpose. In fact, according to the early Greeks, the only real discourse was poetry. It was only later and with great difficulty—both Parmenides and Plato can be indicted on this offense—that prosaic discourse became separated from this primary form of expression (although it still holds that anything worth saying should be said well—although, sadly, that happens less and less frequently).

The spread of the written word profoundly transformed Greek culture previously dominated by the spoken word. But this transformation happened progressively and the habits of oral civilization were preserved for many centuries in ancient Greece. The first Presocratic texts, those of Heraclitus and Xenophanes, were composed in hexameter.[10] Moreover, in Ancient Greece, reading was still done aloud. In fact, the first testimony of silent reading appears much later in the writings of Augustine.[11] The supremacy of the spoken word was so evident for Plato, whose teacher Socrates never wrote a line, that even though he lived a few centuries after the invention of writing he was still reticent to fully endorse it. After all, can one adequately understand a text if its author is not there to answer for what he had written? And more importantly, can essential knowledge be entrusted to writing?[12]

A Goddess's Revelation

Translated into English, Parmenides' *Poem* loses much of its poetic energy, but it does conserve some of it in its 32-verse-long prologue. It lyrically depicts a hero's ascension leading him to a deity who reveals to him the "way of truth," that of Being. This "revelation" is the poem's doctrinal core. But this ascension is more than an accessory element to the poem because it is the sign of the ascension of the discourse itself. The medium is here part of the message. This is important for understanding the poem. Although some speak of a "Parmenidian" conception of Being, the poem speaks of a *goddess's* perspective on Being. From her lofty vantage point, the goddess presents her perspective on Being, which is expressed in the doctrinal part of the poem (a tad less lyrical for us than it is in Greek). She knows quite well that the human perspective is very different. For those she calls mortals, reality is made up of opposites, of night and fire, of hot and cold, of clarity and light, of men and women,[13] and even of Being and Nonbeing. Such is *our* perspective on what is. But it is not that of the goddess who simply says that there is only Being, and becoming is just an expression that makes poor mortals giddy.

The text's first level of meaning marks the dramatic *contrast* between divine and mortal discourse. But this contrast is not meant to give a religious sense to the poem, it aims rather to set the limits of human language.[14] It may also be a critique of the Milesian attempts to explain nature: Who are we to explain generation and becoming? Can humans reliably discuss Being? In the *Poem*, discussing Being is a divine prerogative, and mortals are always, to use Gadamer's expression, "on this side of Being"—that is, far beneath the level of divine discourse.

The hero's ascent is meant to underline how the poem's reader is raised to a level of wisdom incomprehensible to mortals. Although the goddess states simple truths, namely, that what is "is" and what is not "is not," with a smile worthy of the Mona Lisa, she seems to suggest that mortals cannot understand even this simple message.

We learn in the first verse that the hero is led to "the resounding way of the goddess."[15] He is carried away by mares and escorted by young girls said to be "daughters of the sun," who having "left behind the realms of the night to pass into the light had flung back with their hands the covering from their heads."[16] The passage from night to light is the *Poem*'s essential movement. The hero is himself invited to turn away from mere opinion and raise himself to the level of a higher form of wisdom despite its disconcerting simplicity. During his ascent, the hero remains completely passive and does not say a word. We are only told the he has *thumos*, or "a good heart." It would not be inappropriate to speak here of him having courage because courage is required when turning away from opinions. This spiritual ascension is akin to the rites of the oldest religious traditions (of which we know so little). It reappears in Plato's famous allegory of the cave in the *Republic*. The theme of a revelation by a goddess also appears in Plato's *Symposium*, where it describes the ascension leading to the contemplation of the idea of Beauty.

The hero's chariot is then led to a threshold guarded by the goddess of justice:

> There stand the gates of night and day. A lintel and a threshold of stone hold them above and below, while the gates themselves, all aetherial, are filled by great doors. Of these two doors, Justice, who metes out many penalties, holds the keys that fit them. With gentle words the young girls pleaded with her, and cleverly persuaded her to fling back for them from the gates without delay the bolts fitted with its pin. The gates swung back to reveal the yawning gap of the open doors, turning round in their sockets one after the other the hinge-shafts, heavy with bronze, fitted with pegs and rivets. Then there, through the gates, the young girls were holding chariot and mares on their way, straight along the high-road.[17]

The human thus never speaks to the first goddess, *Dike*. Rather, it is the nymphs of the sun who employ their charms and their caresses to beseech her to open the door leading to the roads of day and night. The doors open onto an open space, and the girls must once again push the mares and the chariot "straight along the high-road." Then, a new unnamed goddess welcomes the hero. She takes the hero's right hand (a sign of rightness), like a child, and reveals the way to truth to him:

> Young man, companion to the immortal charioteers, reaching our home with the mares who carry you, welcome, since it is not at all an evil fate that sent you to travel on this way—for far indeed is it from men, away from the paths they tread,—but right and justice.[18]

The goddess reassures the anxious hero by telling him that it is not a *moira kake*, a "terrible fate" that awaits him. Destiny can indeed be both benevolent and terribly cruel. In both cases, mortal humans are passively subject to the pronouncements of the immortal gods.[19] Here, our hero is fortunate; the goddesses that have led him are friendly deities: Themis, goddess of the law, and *Dike*, goddess of justice, the same that guarded the doors of night and day.

Although an exceptional individual, our hero still has much to learn from the goddess:

> You must hear about all things [*panta*],
> [1] both the still heart of persuasive truth and
> [2] the opinions of mortals, in which there is no true conviction.
> [3] But even so, these things you shall learn: how opinions can have real existence, passing the whole way through all things.[20]

In accordance with what his posterity has retained, it is often said that Parmenides' goddess distinguishes two important ways: the way of truth and the way of opinion. Yet, the text that we have just examined, fragment 1 (which is confirmed by fragment 6), identifies three separate ways.[21] If we are then to learn "all things," we must know what the *Poem* calls:

1. The "unshaken heart of well-rounded truth" (according to the variant used by Tarán),[22] the "unshaken heart" connotes assurance and "well-rounded" connotes the perfect figure of truth, which has neither beginning nor end. This form of wisdom, which can be called divine and, in a sense, superhuman, forms the doctrinal and best-preserved part of the *Poem*.

2. The opinions (*doxas*) of mortals, "in which there is no true belief" (trans. Tarán). This is the domain of opinion (although Parmenides always uses the plural, *opinions*), which lacks credibility according to the goddess. From this is it often argued that, according to Parmenides, there are only two types of knowledge: truth and opinion.

3. This may not be case, however, since the goddess announces that some opinions (*dokounta*) may be partially true. These truthful opinions were most probably presented in the second part of the *Poem*, which has been only partially preserved. The reason why this part was not preserved is easily understood. Simplicius, in his commentary on Aristotle's *On the Heavens*, only cited the passages in which generation and corruption were rebutted. Unfortunately, this limits our understanding of the *Poem*. We must simply keep in mind that it is improper, despite being quite common, to turn Parmenides—or rather, the goddess—into an intractable opponent of the truth of becoming and opinion. The goddess does recognize the legitimacy of this type of knowledge, *that it is plausible*, and that it corresponds to what is thought by mortals. But she says little of it, and even then, condescendingly, because she has seen, and offers the sight of, something even more fundamentally important, namely, "Being."

The Enigma of Being

After two millennia of metaphysics, which have turned Being into a familiar and perhaps even an inoffensive term, Being may connote more than it did in Antiquity. The term was probably overly abstract for the period. For the *Poem*'s author it most probably meant "that which is" in the most concrete sense of the term, and probably designated the universe, which was represented in the rest of the text as a sphere. But Parmenides' expressions are already much too disconcerting and almost unheard of.

The goddess begins her speech by saying that the only path of which one may speak is the one of "that is" or of "it is" (ὡς ἔστιν / *hôs estin*). Obviously, this does not mean much in English, nor does it in Greek either since there is no real precedent to Parmenides' discourse. Although impersonal verbs, or verbs that do not have a true subject ("it snowed"), do exist in Greek as they do in English, this impersonal form appears odd in the case of the verb "to be" (if one has never read the later writings of Martin Heidegger). As Hermann Fränkel has noted, in Greek there are no known impersonal uses of the verb "to be."[23] Interpreters have therefore searched for the "subject" of the clause "it is," which could plausibly be in a later sentence.[24] In poetic discourse, postposition, as it is called, is used to focus attention by delaying the appearance of the expected and decisive element. The best candidate appears in verses 19 and 32 of the lengthy fragment 8, thus in a rather distant position: τὲόν, τὸ ἐόν / *t'eon*, the being (*l'étant*), which we can simply call, out of respect for tradition and the English language, "Being." If this postposition is grammatically possible, we are allowed to think that this subject was presupposed in the "that it is" (*hôs estin*) of the first verses. It is doubtless "that it is" is the subject matter of the discourse on truth, on the evidence of Being, of the "it is." The goddess does nothing other than reaffirm the evidence of Being, which Pierre Aubenque calls the thesis of Being itself.[25]

Everything that can be said about Being—or about the "it is"—follows from this evidence. But it would be inappropriate to speak of a logical deduction, however, since at the time logic did not yet exist. What we may say, though, is that logic as well as metaphysics are being invented here in Parmenides' poem. The thought of Being (or of the "it is") reveals that thought has its own intrinsic rigor even if it may sometimes differ from the opinions of mortals. But this rigor does exist and it is bound to the thought of Being, the evidence of which the goddess ceaselessly repeats in almost tautological fashion.

The foremost consequence that the goddess draws from this is that "on this road there are many signs showing that Being is ungenerated and imperishable."[26] This "consequence," namely, that Being eludes generation and destruction, would later trouble Parmenides' posterity. Yet it follows naturally from the goddess's perspective and from the positing of Being. If Being is, it cannot "not have been," because this would mean that it would have been its opposite, Nonbeing. And it cannot cease to be because Being would then become its opposite, again, Nonbeing. An unsophisticated argument, one might say, but it is nevertheless irrefutable. The goddess calls upon a series of arguments to show how generation and corruption are unthinkable. We will examine two of them here.

1. "What origin [*pothen*] could one search out for the 'it is,' asks the goddess?"[27] Indeed, if Being emerges out of something else, it must either emerge from something other than Being, thus something that it is not, or it must emerge from nothing whose existence would thereby be acknowledged.
2. Despite implying the paradoxical existence of Nonbeing, this unthinkable thought leads to another problem.
3. "What necessity would have impelled it sooner or later to appear out of nothing?"[28] Or, to put it otherwise, why would "Being" have suddenly decided, at some particular time, to be? And how could it have been "impelled" if it had not yet come to be?

If Nonbeing, from which Being emerged and to which it would return when it ceased to be, is unthinkable, then Being must always have been and will always be. Being is therefore characterized by permanence, understood as either timelessness or eternity.[29] This is an important point because the history of metaphysics will maintain this link between Being, in the full sense of the word, and permanence. One may even speak of the importance given to permanence from the outset of Western "'metaphysics." Heidegger later forcefully underscored the way that Being had always been thought within an implicitly temporal horizon.[30]

Obviously, one can attempt to rebut this claim by saying that generation and corruption do in fact exist, as we can all easily observe. But the goddess is already a step ahead of us and is well aware of this objection. It is but a conviction held by mortals, says she, and "this I tell you is a way of which we can learn nothing."[31] We must therefore turn our minds away from it because it implies the existence of Nonbeing and goes against the evidence of Being. Fragment 2, which seems to follow the prologue, stresses this point by insisting on the dichotomy of the two ways so important for Parmenides' posterity:

> Come then, I shall tell you, and do preserve the account as you heard it,
> What are the only ways of inquiry that can be conceived:
> The one says "is" and "it is not possible not to be,"
> This is the way of persuasion, for persuasion follows upon truth;
> The other says 'is not' and 'it is necessary not to be,'
> This I tell you is a way of which we can learn nothing
> For you could not know what is not
> Nor could you express it.[32]

It is indeed impossible to express Being with Nonbeing without being nonsensical. But, one might ask, what of the testimony of the senses that seems to contradict the idea of Being as calm permanence? The goddess also explains where that impression comes from: It is merely the product of word play and the importance garrulous mortals give to words:

> They will therefore be mere name [and word play, *onomasthai*]—all things
> that mortals, convinced they were true, laid down as coming into being
> and perishing, as Being and not Being, as change of place and altering of
> bright color.[33]

The realm of opinions, says Parmenides, is ruled by "aimless eye, ringing ear and tongue (*glossa*)."[34] What mortals see as birth and death are really appearances produced by the power of language and words. The *Poem* here distinguishes two types of discourse. The first speaks (*legein*) of "that which is." It is called true discourse and is related to thought (*noein*). The second is called empty discourse; it remains on the level of nominal entities (frag. 8, v. 38; *onomastai*) and stems from idle talk and meaningless words (see the use of *glossa* in frag. 7, v. 6–8). Ernst Hoffman was one of the first to insist on the importance of this distinction between language and thought (*noein*) or true discourse (that of *legein* and of *logos*) in the vocabulary of the *Poem*.[35] According to Hoffman, the *Poem* establishes "the threefold unity" between Being, thought, and discourse. This unity is evoked in fragment 6, where it is said: "it is necessary to say (*legein*) and to think (*noein*) that there is Being (*t'eon emmenai*),"[36] which summarizes the *Poem*'s thesis about Being.

True discourse (*logos* and *legein*) and thought (*noein*):	Being ("it is"):
To speak (*onomastai*) using mere names (*onomata*) drawn from language (*glossa*) and stories (*epea*).	Becoming, generation, and corruption, which imply Nonbeing.

The unity between Being, thought, and true discourse helps us understand the famous, but enigmatic, fragment 3 according to which "thinking and Being are the same thing." One should not, however, understand it as resembling Hegel's idealism or Berkeley's *esse est percipi* for whom "To be is to be perceived or thought by consciousness." Rather, the fragment should be understood as the reciprocal relation between Being and thought. Once one begins to think, one enters the realm of *noein*, and one can then only think Being; and inversely, once one considers Being, one is thinking, and one then enters the realm of *logos* and truth.

But the idea expressed in fragment 3 may also be an *answer* to a possible objection to the discourse on Being. Indeed, the goddess simply states that only Being can be thought because everything else is not. But this could be countered by saying there is, on the one hand, Being, and, on the other, the *thought* of Being. How must we then account for this duality or difference in thought's relation to Being? The goddess seems to answer this objection in fragment 3 in which we can almost hear her say in an exasperated tone: "No, thinking and Being are the same thing." All thought can only think Being, and Being is all that can be thought. However, because of the condition of the source documents this must be considered only a fragile hypothesis, like almost everything else that can be said of the goddess's remarkable discourse.

One thing is certain: Parmenides' text initiated the thought of Being in the Western world. But can we then say, as Pierre Aubenque has, that it is "the birth certificate of Western metaphysics"?[37] Many interpreters are reticent to say so, and not only because the term "metaphysics" is absent from Parmenides' text (an argument that is not very useful since it also applies to Plato and Aristotle). Unlike Plato, Parmenides does not clearly distinguish between two types of reality and separate the visible world from the intelligible world. But is the idea of a metaphysical separation of reality completely foreign to Parmenides' *Poem*? Leaving aside the distinction between the realms of the gods and that of mortals, which provides its backdrop, the *Poem* also carefully disassociates true thought and discourse, which pertains to Being, from all discourse that stubbornly attributes reality meaninglessly to becoming. The first type of discourse, the only coherent one, is raised to a superior level of knowledge, which can only be reached by transcending all too human discourse. But can we speak here of metaphysical transcendence? It is hard to say.

Metaphysical thought, it is often said, is foreign to Parmenides because Being is not for him an abstract entity. Indeed, he seems to have a fairly concrete view of it, most notably when he associates its shape to a sphere. The poem may in fact be referring here to what we call the physical universe. For this reason, some interpreters[38] think it appropriate to disassociate Parmenides' physical reflection from all "metaphysical speculation" on Being. Although there is little doubt the poem, when speaking of Being, refers to the obvious reality of the surrounding world, it also was the first to speak of it as "Being" (*to eon*) or as "it is" (*hôs estin*) instead of speaking of a world, of earth, or of nature, as the physiologists did (and whose premises Parmenides calls into question as he deconstructs the notion of becoming). His expressions are already major abstractions and usher us into the realm of metaphysics. The question of what these terms mean will dominate the thought of his intellectual heirs. The important thing is that Parmenides taught us to ask this question—that is, to think about the inextricable relation of (permanent) Being, thought, and true discourse, which is the basis of Western metaphysics.

The Legacy of Parmenides' Onto-Theology

Although using the term "metaphysics" here may be premature, we may perhaps allow the use of the term "ontology" to characterize the inextricable relation the *Poem* urges us to think, despite the fact that it would be extremely anachronistic since the term *ontologia* did not appear before the seventeenth century. Here, the word ontology simply means that the true, or rational, discourse—that is, the *logos*, is dedicated to Being in its most basic sense—that is, imperishable and incorruptible. And it would be accordingly an overestimation of the mortals' linguistic capacities to believe there actually are such things as birth and death, change and becoming. Since then, philosophy or Western science has been enraptured by a stable and permanent Being, and enthralled to the rigors of "thought," which did not really exist prior to Parmenides.

Parmenides' *Poem*'s most important point lies in its proposed break from the forms of explanation favored by mortals. As the Milesian school demonstrates, mortal discourse had previously sought the principles of generation for what does not have an origin, namely, Being, that which has always been and always will be. And in doing so, Parmenides' *Poem* passed on a twofold legacy to metaphysics.

1. The disassociation of two types of knowledge: that of truth (*aletheia*)—the true discourse, and that of opinion. In the *Republic*, Plato will distinguish science (*episteme*), which belongs to the wise, from opinion (*doxa*), which belongs to everyone else. Although Parmenides, unlike Plato, held that opinion (*doxa*) may not always be mistaken, the most truthful form of discourse is nevertheless science *because* it pertains to an unchanging reality (Being), and *because* it is a product of reason and thought alone. Obviously, thinking is, in this way, often opposed to the senses, but the senses merely express a pseudo-reality, or shadows, and to a certain extent pertain to Nonbeing. The goddess's warning to her disciple is unequivocal:

> Hold back your thought from this way of inquiry, and let not habit force you upon this road and ply an aimless eye and ringing ear and tongue; but judge with reason the much contested argument which has been given by me.[39]

2. The object of thought: Being in its fullest sense—that is, exempt from becoming, which is akin to Nonbeing. In their own way, both Plato and

Aristotle would later claim that Being is thought's favored object, belonging to what they would respectively call philosophy and first philosophy. But their task was to be the reconciliation of Being in its fullest sense with the experience of becoming. So what is this Being that cannot be understood as permanence? Can it be thought?

For Parmenides' school it obviously cannot be thought. Parmenides' disciples even went so far as to use eristic arguments to refute the existence of becoming and movement. But this was not what the goddess had argued since she *never contested the existence of becoming as it pertains to mortals*; she simply described it as an abusive use of language. Parmenides' successor at the head of the Eleatic school, Zeno, developed a rhetorical arsenal to demonstrate how the very notion of movement was fraught with paradoxes. The philosophical tradition has turned him into the inventor of "dialectics" (from *dialegestahai*, to dialogue), the art of confounding one's adversary with arguments. In Book VI of his *Physics*, Aristotle relates four paradoxes Zeno had developed relating to movement.[40] These paradoxes are not free of sophistry, but they are famous and quite humorous.

The first is called the "dichotomy" paradox. If one moves from point A to point B, one must first cover half the distance between the points. But before reaching the halfway mark, one must first cover half the distance of that half, and so on until infinity. Thus one can never actually reach point B. The second argument is the paradox of the race between Achilles and the turtle. Being a good sport, Achilles lets the turtle have a head start. Both start running at the same time. According to Zeno, Achilles can never catch up to the turtle because when he will have reached the point from which the turtle started running, the turtle will have already moved forward by a few strides and so on every time Achilles reaches the turtle's previous location.

These paradoxical arguments seek to demonstrate how becoming and movement are unthinkable, whereas Being, as it is immobile and unchanging, can be thought. But these eristic arguments are probably not in the same class as Parmenides' thought of Being since the *Poem* never denied the existence of movement where mortals are concerned, it revealed a more essential thought, namely, the stability of Being, which escapes the vicissitudes of mere language.[41] Thus Zeno's dialectic, since it negates more than it affirms, does not really belong to the same intellectual category as Parmenides' *Poem*.

It is common to see in Leucippus and Democritus's atomism a consequence of Eleatism. According to a doxographical tradition, Leucippus was educated at the Eleatic school.[42] Their atomism is also based on the idea that Being is an unchanging, eternal, and in-divisible (which is the etymological sense of "a-tom") reality. Only Being, or atoms, would then exist, the *plurality* of which would be the great heresy that distinguishes the atomists from the Eleatics for whom Being is one. However, "there is" also Nonbeing, but only as the emptiness between atoms. For it is in this void, this Nonbeing, that atoms exist. Some atoms deviate from their course and join with other atoms to form bodies, which can then decompose to form other composite objects. These bodies would be held together by the atoms' hooks, which allow them to link themselves to one another. The world as we know it would thus be born of the haphazard linking of atoms. Although this attempt to account for the diversity of the physical world may seem rather modern, it does so on the basis of Eleatism. If we wish to speak of nature or of "that which is," we must start from an indivisible, unalterable, and eternal reality. Thus what is, and what can be studied by science, is permanent and unchanging Being.

The Sophistic Crisis: Human Discourse Left to Its Own Devices

The Eleatics also left their mark on the Sophists, the most illustrious of whom were Protagoras (c. 486–410 BCE) and Gorgias (c. 483–374 BCE). Their names are familiar as they are the titles of important Platonic dialogues. It was Plato who gave them their devastating reputation even though their name (*sophistès*) identifies them as masters of wisdom (*sophia*). And yet it was also a *sophia* the goddess had shared with Parmenides. In principle, the term *sophistès* is far from being pejorative. Plato, in the *Symposium*, even used it in a positive sense to speak of the wisdom of priestess Diotima who initiated Socrates to the idea of Beauty.[43]

According to Philostratus's testimony,[44] Protagoras of Abdera, generally considered to be the first Sophist, was a student of Democritus (460–370 BCE) who came from the same city. The story is unlikely because Protagoras was 26 years older than Democritus, but it is not completely impossible. According to Porphyry, he was the author of a treatise entitled *On Being*,[45] of which we know unfortunately nothing. He was especially known in Antiquity for his treatise *On Truth* that Plato cites in several places (*Theaetetus* 152 a, 161 c; *Protagoras* 338 c). In this work, Protagoras argued a famous and profoundly ontological thesis: "man is the measure (*metron*) of all things—alike of the Being of things that are and of the Nonbeing of things that are not."[46] The Sophists, of whom Protagoras was the first, is thus also defined by a conception of Being. In the *Theaetetus*, Plato summarizes it in the following terms: "any given thing 'is to me such as it appears to me, and is to you such as it appears to you.'"[47]

Thus Protagoras the Sophist's wisdom is obviously anthropocentric and imbued with a form of "relativism," as it is often called. It is also the diametrical opposite of the truth expressed by Parmenides' goddess. As we have seen, she argued that human opinions are unreliable and truth is to be found in the divine perspective on Being (an idea that Plato will adopt in his *Laws*, 716 c, where he says that "God is the measure of all things"). However, it is important to notice the hidden *continuity* between the goddess's discourse and Protagoras's truth. By arguing that the true discourse, the *logos*, pertains only to unchanging Being, the goddess implied that the "divine" discourse was impossible for mortals. Humans cannot transcend the level of sensual appearances, illusions, and Nonbeing. There is therefore a chasm between the divine *logos*, oriented by Being and truth, and the elements of human discourse (*epea, onomasthai, glossa*), which cannot overcome appearances.

Yet, the Sophists rigorously *maintained* the link between human discourse and the realm of appearances. Since we can only participate in human discourse, we can never overcome appearances. As humble humans, we cannot pretend to speak in the name of the gods whose very existence we cannot know. "Too many things prevent us from knowing it," says Protagoras, such as "their invisibility and the brevity of human existence."[48] One can only speak of "perceptible" things—that is, things as they appear. But in this all too human realm, things undeniably appear differently to each of us. Humans are therefore always the measure of all things. In fact, Parmenides' goddess did not say anything different from this when she spoke of the idiosyncrasy of human discourse. She simply enjoined us, however, to avoid it the better to follow the divine discourse on the veritable Being. And yet, Being—unchanging and permanent—is not very "phenomenal" according to the Sophists. In its absence, the only teachable wisdom is limited to the realm of appearances and words,[49] which can be mastered with varying levels of success. Because such a realm is solely governed by language, *epea* as the goddess knew, true wisdom is essentially rhetorical.

The majority of Sophists were masters of rhetoric. They excelled at the form of discourse which, despite not pertaining to Being and having no claim to "truth," can sway an audience and aspire to verisimilitude. This emphasis on eloquence is a direct consequence of the Eleatics whose ideas still remain pertinent. Since the discourse on Being, as it is in itself or as it is divinely understood, is inaccessible to us, the only possible form of wisdom available to mortals is the art of persuasion. Such is the position that Callicles defends in Plato's *Gorgias* (although we do not know whether he actually existed). While truth and Being are inaccessible, verisimilitude, appearance, and oratorical success are well within our grasp.

The value placed on rhetoric by the Sophists, which accompanied their rejection of the discourse on Being, can be clearly seen in the ontology of the master rhetorician Gorgias (c. 485–374 BCE; he would therefore have lived for more than one hundred years).[50] His ontology was in fact an "anti-ontology." Gorgias authored a work called "On Nonbeing or on Nature," which Diels included in his compilation of Presocratic fragments.[51] Using eristic arguments that are similar to Zeno's, Gorgias argued three things: (1) nothing is; (2) even if something is, it is unknowable; and (3) if it is unknowable, it is impossible to explain to someone.

The first demonstrates that Being is not. If Being exists, it is either eternal or begotten, or both. (1) If it is eternal, it does not have a beginning (as it was for the goddess in Parmenides' *Poem*). But if it does not have a beginning, it would be unlimited. Yet, if Being were unlimited, it would not exist in one place. Thus since everything that is exists somewhere and since Being is nowhere, it is absurd to think that it is. (2) Being cannot be begotten either. If it came to be, it came to be either through Being or Nonbeing. It cannot have come to be through Being because that would mean Being preceded Being and it would therefore not have been begotten. Being cannot have been begotten through Nonbeing because Nonbeing cannot beget anything. Being is therefore neither eternal nor begotten.

Gorgias concludes that if neither Being nor Nonbeing exist, then nothing exists. Gorgias acknowledges that his discourse may only be sophistic (but then again, so are all discourses!) and since he argues that even if Being did exist (which he has already rejected) it would remain "unknowable and incomprehensible to man."[52] The fact is, argues Gorgias, that there is a gap that separates Being from thought. One cannot derive the actual existence of flying humans or of a chariot capable of being driven over water from the thought of such men or chariots. Similarly, one may also think of imaginary creatures such as chimera. Hence, it is impossible to claim that Being is the sole object of all thought. Thinking only pertains to thoughts (or words). Therefore, Being cannot be apprehended.[53]

But that is not all: Being, if it could be apprehended, would not be communicable. Only discourse is communicable, and never Being, "for that by which we reveal is discourse, but discourse is not substances and beings. Therefore, we do not reveal Being to our neighbors, but discourse, which is something other than substances."[54] Powerless as we to overcome the limitations of discourse, Being remains forever elusive.

Although Gorgias's arguments may appear, as do Zeno's, specious and as mere sophistry in the pejorative sense of the term, their intent is to show that a coherent discourse on Being is impossible. All human discourse is limited by rhetoric and opinion.[55] Can *sophia* transcend opinions and appearances? How is a discourse on Being even possible?

CHAPTER 2

PLATO

The Hypothesis of the Idea

The Indirect Character of Plato's Writings

Having found our way through the Presocratic fragments and deconstructed the imperceptible layers of doxography under which they are buried, we are tempted to sigh with relief as we turn to Plato's writings and say: finally real texts! And, moreover, what magnificent texts! Plato's dialogues are indeed among the crowning achievements of philosophical thought and world literature.

In fact, Plato is the first, and only, major philosopher of antiquity whose texts have been transmitted to us in their virtual entirety. We have all his most important texts, the *Republic*, the *Phaedrus*, the *Phaedo*, the *Symposium*, the *Sophist*, the *Timaeus*, to name a few. The only remaining philological or critical problems associated with Plato's works relate to the authenticity of some dialogues, to their chronological order, and identifying the original text. Fortunately, these problems have been resolved insofar as there is a general consensus as to their status in Platonic studies.

So if we compare the Platonic corpus with that of *all* the other Greek philosophers, its philological status seems to be the most assured. Unfortunately, this is not the whole truth. The first difficulty, which has been raised so many times it may now appear to be banal, is that Plato never speaks in his own name. He uses imaginary or real interlocutors such as his teacher Socrates, thinkers such as Parmenides, Sophists such as Protagoras or Gorgias, politicians, and others. In some cases, the dialogues will even refer to other dialogues the participants have memorized and quote from memory! One may circumvent this difficulty by saying that Plato speaks his "doctrine" through the mouths of his participants (but this always depends on what the interpreter believes is Plato's doctrine). The most formidable difficulty is quite different however. Plato often says that the essence of his thought *is not found* in his writings. Both the *Phaedrus* and the *Seventh Letter* give excellent reasons for Plato's distrust of philosophical writing. Since he lived with the great tradition of dialogue that he inherited from Socrates, Plato knew all too well that if the author is not there to explain his writings what is written down can easily fall into the wrong hands and be subjected to bizarre interpretations. But there is a more important reason why philosophy cannot be written down. If philosophical wisdom aspires to a transformation of the soul (*metanoia tes psychès*), it cannot be reduced to the mere teaching of doctrinal conventions. Hence the much-debated question in Platonic studies: How can a philosophy so reluctant to accept the written word be expressed in writing? Plato solves this apparent contradiction in an admirable fashion by writing "dialogues," which inscribe living dialogue into the very structure of the written text.

Moreover, we should not regard Plato's dialogues as the straightforward presentation of a "doctrine," something they are only rarely. Even when they appear to be lectures, the dialogues are almost always marked by irony and reference to things the interlocutors supposedly already know. In the *Republic* for instance, where Plato speaks for all intents and purposes for the first and last time about the idea of the Good as the main principle of the realm of ideas, he says that since his interlocutors have already heard him speak of this many times (504 a, 506 e, 532 d) he will discuss an "offshoot" of the idea of the Good by speaking of the sun! Nobody can therefore really claim to know the "core" of Plato's position on this very important topic.

Did Plato give a more authoritative or a more systematic version of his philosophy in the lectures he gave at the Academy, which he founded in 387 BCE and where he worked for 40 years? To answer this question, one would have had to attend those classes, which nobody can claim to have done. We only have secondhand testimony of his teaching, which must be read cautiously.[1] Some accounts, such as Aristotle's, have more weight than others. Aristotle, in his *Physics* (209 b 11–16), mentions the existence of ἄγραφα δόγματα (*agrapha dogmata*), or "unwritten doctrines," that he attributes to Plato and most probably existed. This is not the only telltale expression he uses. When speaking of his teacher's thought in the brief history of philosophy in the first book of the *Metaphysics* (chap. 6), he alludes to the "theory of principles" contained in the oral teachings. Again, this reference must have meant something to his contemporaries. It is not hard to imagine that the teaching given at the Academy would have been more doctrinal than the indirect exposition of the dialogues.

That said, it is important to remember that the dialogues' primary function was probably not to teach a doctrine. They were rather meant to incite brilliant minds—those that had a real "philosophical nature"—to join the Academy and perfect their education. Thus the dialogues had an exhortative or "protreptical" function limited to giving a general, yet catchy, idea of the type of philosophy practiced in the Academy.[2] In fact, all the philosophical schools in Athens employed protreptical writings as a way of advertising themselves. Like Plato's dialogues, Aristotle's *Protreptic* and Isocrates' *Antidosis*, which promoted his own school of rhetoric, may be described in the same manner. Nevertheless, despite clearly referring to a philosophical exposition that goes beyond their specific setting and the written word, Plato's dialogues remain philosophical and literary masterpieces. And, in a way, Plato's writings and their insistence on the written word's transcendence square with the account tradition gives despite the unfortunate lack of adequate testimony to support such claims.

All the same, the situation is quite paradoxical. The only philosopher of antiquity whose writings have been completely preserved ceaselessly reminds us that the essence of his thought is not contained in his writings! As for his oral teachings, which must have existed in some form or another, we only know of them indirectly through the rather schematic testimonials that are a stark contrast to the vivacious dialogues that have been preserved. Nevertheless, priority must be given to the dialogues. Even the school of Tübingen, represented by the likes of Krämer, Gaiser, and Szlezak, seems to acknowledge this point, despite what is often said. After all, one must always *read Plato*,[3] and thus read his dialogues. One must accordingly take into account their *intended meaning* since their discourse is already indirect. It refers to a "doctrine," or better, a form of wisdom that does not rely on the written word. Because of this, Plato must always be quoted using doubled quotation marks. The first pair indicates that we cannot know whether what is said is "authentically Platonic" (because Plato himself never speaks, but this is not a serious problem), while the second pair reminds the reader the quote probably does not exhaust all that might be said.

Although Socrates imparted the importance of dialogue to Plato, his understanding of Being came from Parmenides. Indeed, Plato treats Parmenides with great deference, which he does not always do with Presocrates. When the Stranger (is he Plato's mouthpiece? we have no way of knowing) in the *Sophist* (241 d) tries to demonstrate the existence of Nonbeing, the Stranger says he fears committing "parricide." The affectionate superiority Plato bestows on the wise man of Elea in the *Parmenides*, in which the latter lectures a young Socrates and someone called Aristotle, illustrates how Parmenides was a kind of father-figure for Plato.

Parmenides' Legacy

In the *Sophist* (246 a), Plato speaks of a struggle of giants over the problem of Being (*gigantomachia peri tes ousias*). In fact, Parmenides was the only pre-Socratic author really interested in Being. As we have seen, the Sophists only discussed Being to disqualify it as a possible subject of human discourse. Human discourse, according to the Sophists, is characterized by the fact that it *has no* access to Being, but only to appearance, and its essential elements are rhetoric and opinion rather than science and truth.

This debate was important for Plato and he takes Parmenides' side by arguing that:

1. True, or full, Being, is the most important object of philosophical research.
2. This Being, always equal to itself, is neither subjected to becoming nor to movement. It is characterized by constancy, permanence, and timelessness.
3. True Being can only be approached through the intellect, by thought or by the mind (*nous*) because it is not immediately perceptible by the senses, which are clouded by the appearance of becoming and human discourse (which the Sophists were unable to transcend).
4. It is therefore important to distinguish two levels of knowledge: opinion (*doxa*), which is limited to objects of the senses, and science (*episteme*), which is concerned with genuine Being. The first belongs to the multitude. The second is the exclusive domain of the wise—that is, of philosophers, who seek to attain divine wisdom by thought and by freeing themselves from the tyranny of the senses (an approach Parmenides had prefigured in the motif of the ascension and revelation, which Plato would adopt[4] when he attempted to describe the ultimate philosophical elevation).

Plato conserves the essential parts of Parmenides' legacy. The "struggle of giants" is therefore exclusively over Being itself. As with Parmenides, Plato's Being is defined by constancy, timelessness, immutability, and unity. All that becomes, all that "happens," has but a fleeting reality, or is unreal, if not Nonbeing. According to Parmenides' goddess, only "Being" (*t'eon, hôs esti*) is distinguished by its permanence. Being is what always is, and all that is not Being "is not." For Plato, Being, which always is and remains identical to itself, is identified with the *idea*. Plato's major metaphysical thesis is the assertion that Being is idea (*eidos*).

Being Attentive to the *Eidos*

To us Moderns, the term *idea* refers to some mental representation: It is only an idea (meaning that it is only a representation). Although the idea as a mental representation is distantly related to Platonism, Plato used it to mean something different. An idea is not necessarily mental for Plato. It is something real, which, for reasons we shall soon see, can be said to exist autonomously. It is in this sense that the idea of Beauty, or of the Good, exists on its own. We think, and even perceive, these ideas when we see good or beautiful things. These things are said good or beautiful because they participate in the idea of Beauty or of the Good, which can be thought, and seen, for itself.

This idea may seem strange, but without it, we could never speak of ideas today. The concept of the idea has become so familiar that we forget its creation was quite a feat for its creator, Plato. The "abstract" use of the term idea, which even a six year old can understand now, did not exist before Plato. He was the first to give a general and vaguely "intellectual" meaning (intellectual is another adjective that Plato made possible) to the Greek word *eidos*. In common Greek, the term εἶδος only designates a thing's exterior shape or aspect. The shape of an urn, for example, is its εἶδος, its configuration, or its figure. The word εἶδος is etymologically related to the Greek verb "to see" (*eido*, I see; *oida*, I saw, but also "I know," meaning, as in English, "I see," that is, "I understand"). Something's εἶδος is its general form that allows us to recognize it as such and such. Before Plato, and even to some extent for him as well, the term εἶδος had a tangible and very visual sense. For this reason, some commentators prefer translating it as "form" or "intelligible form" to avoid all mental, abstract, or subjective connotations. Although these are rather infrequent misunderstandings, the translation does have its merits, the most notable of which is that it leads to a better understanding of the origin of the Aristotelian theory of "form."[5] However, it is preferable to speak

of ideas, in part because it is the traditionally used term, but also because
of the rather formalist character that the term "form" has in English. More
importantly, though, Plato's use of εἶδος does not stray far from the realm of
ideal objects. To better understand how and why this happened, let us examine certain characteristics of the term εἶδος already present, or latent, in the
Greek, which Plato's genius was able to exploit.

Form, the εἶδος, designates what is *common* to several things and what per-
sists in all things having the "same form." The form, or shape, of an urn, of a
dog, are common to all urns or dogs. There may never be two identical dogs,
but all dogs have the same general form. One may say, as Plato does, that the
"form" is what allows one to say that a dog is a dog and an urn is an urn. This
will lead Plato to ascribe a "principial" status to the idea. The idea or "form"
is what makes something what it is. But let us not get carried away. Let us keep
to simple vaguely visual examples for now, even though their visualization is
increasingly related to the realm of thought, which Plato is in the process of
discovering.

To understand what is meant by an idea, we must not only consider physical forms or the external appearance of things. We may also speak of a certain
"sameness" in the forms of relatively abstract objects that are no less perceptible by the senses (it is always by these that one must start if one wishes to
reach the idea in its fullest sense). Such is the case for beauty. Indeed, many
different things can be said to be beautiful, even those most readily appreci-
ated by the senses like the sight of a beautiful child, a beautiful sculpture, an
enchanting countryside, a beautiful oration or melody. Although these things
are heterogeneous (a countryside, a melody, a living being, an oration are
ontologically distinct things), they all have a common "form": beauty.[6] So
what is this beauty that is *common* to all these things, just as the form of a dog
is common to all dogs? Although it may differ from one thing to another, it is a
form, an idea that is "the same" in all of them. This could also be shown to be
the case for the idea of the just, the good, the same, of unity and so on.

Although these ideas are perhaps only grasped by the mind (in the case of
beauty though, it is possible to see what beauty is), they are no less real for
Plato. And, they may be more real than all that simply "participates" in them.
Beautiful things come and go, but beauty remains the same: beauty in itself,
which Plato calls the idea of Beauty.

This is particularly obvious when one pays attention to one of the meanings of the term εἶδος that Aristotle, on Platonic grounds, used to important effect. In Greek, the term εἶδος also means what we now call a "species"
(the Latin *species* is in fact the most common translation of εἶδος). Thanks

to Aristotle's analyses of the workings of the Greek language, species has become a classificatory term used to group together beings of the same genus that share similar characteristics; literally a speci-fic difference—that is, one that "defines the species." The human εἶδος is the animal species that has rationality as a specific difference, which *defines*, according to Aristotle, what we are. The definition is derived from the difference that characterizes a particular εἶδος. An εἶδος therefore defines the "Being" of things. Thus when one wants to know "what something is" (what is this or that?), one answers by giving its εἶδος: it is an urn, a dog, modern art or so on. An εἶδος amounts, quite literally, to the thing's Being, or what it is. One can even say, using an abstraction both Plato and Aristotle employ, that εἶδος is the "what it is" (the *ti esti*) of a thing, what "it is." It also has an interrogative sense in Greek and the question *ti esti* can be translated as "what is it?" The Romans later translated this expression as *essentia* (*essence*). One knows what something is when one knows and can identify its εἶδος, which expresses "what it is" (*ti esti*).

Clearly, the species has more reality, more Being, than its individual members. An individual grows and dies, but the species remains the *same* in all its members. The εἶδος is thus permanent and endures throughout all its diverse manifestations without ever being reducible to any one of them.[7] Although the εἶδος's sameness can only be grasped by the mind (which is Plato's argument and his discovery), it is nevertheless stable and permanent, and much more so than the individuals that belong to it.

The Separation of the Ideas

Socrates, he said, your eagerness for discussion is admirable. And now tell me. Have you yourself drawn the distinction you speak of and separated apart on the one side ideas themselves and on the other the things that share in them?

RHETORICAL QUESTION ATTRIBUTED TO PARMENIDES

IN PLATO'S *PARMENIDES* (130 A-B)

Today we would probably describe Plato's use of the term εἶδος as an abstraction. The ideas of Beauty, or Human, are for us general notions, albeit ones we still call ideas (thanks to Plato). We judge them to be abstractions of particular observable cases. Because of our "nominalism" we believe only individuals exist and "names" are general abstract terms that designate a group of things that share a common characteristic.

Plato would have readily admitted the use of the term abstraction to designate the process by which *we* raise ourselves to ideas. He himself describes the thought of an idea as a movement that starts from the sensible—that is, what can be perceived by the senses—and draws out a common characteristic by which one can raise oneself to the "contemplation" of the idea. A good example of this can be found in the *Symposium*, which discusses the ascension that leads to the idea of Beauty. The repeated exposure to Beauty in amorous relationships, for example, leads one to the recognition of numerous other forms of Beauty. Starting with beautiful bodies, one then comes to recognize beautiful acts, beautiful souls, beautiful maxims, beautiful sciences, and eventually the science of beauty, and then finally one comes upon the idea of Beauty itself (*Symposium*, 210 e). In the *Symposium*, a priestess named Diotima reveals to Socrates the ascension to Beauty, even though she knows, as did Parmenides' goddess, that her mortal audience has great difficulty understanding her:

> And here, she [Diotima] said, you must follow me as closely as you can. Whoever has been initiated so far in the mysteries of Eros and has viewed all these aspects of the beautiful in due succession, is at last drawing near the revelation. And now, Socrates, there burst upon him that wondrous vision which is the very nature of the beauty he has toiled so long for. It is an everlasting loveliness which neither comes nor goes, which neither flowers nor fades, for such beauty is the same on every hand, the same then as now, here as there, this way as that way, the same to every worshiper as it is to every other. ...And this is the way, the only way, he must approach, or be led toward, the sanctuary of Eros. Starting from individual beauties, the quest for the universal beauty must find him ever mounting the heavenly ladder, stepping from rung to rung—that is, from one to two, and two to *every* lovely body, from bodily beauty to the beauty of institutions, from institutions to learning, and from learning in general to the special lore that pertains to nothing but the beautiful itself—until at last he comes to know what beauty is. And if, my dear Socrates, Diotima went on, man's life is ever worth living, it is when he has attained this vision of beauty itself.[8]

Although a heavenly text, in all the senses of the word, it is also one that starts from the sensible. Plato knows quite well that if one is to ascend to thought, one must start with the visible. The observation is so self-evident to us today that we forget its mystery: We "know" our thoughts refer to "objects" that are not physical objects, but we forget that Plato was the first to express this now-obvious fact. But Plato not only knows one must start with the "sensible" (a word that has meaning only since Plato), he also knows it is difficult to separate oneself from it when comes time to think in general terms. What Plato is urging us to do, here in the *Symposium* but elsewhere as well, is to think and perceive Beauty itself: Beauty as it is regardless of any particular occurrences. But this is difficult since Beauty always appears to us, as it did to Plato's contemporaries, as this or that beauty. He therefore enjoins us to set aside the tangible manifestation of beauty, and to think it "in-itself"— that is, not the beauty of a particular object, action or figure, but beauty itself, or the idea of Beauty that always remains the same. What is then revealed is the "noetic" (*noèton*) space belonging to thought and which Plato was the first to describe. Since Plato gave so much importance to showing that this "noetic space" was evident, the question of its actual existence, whether it is separate from ours or not, *sometimes* appears to be of secondary importance. In fact, it was his disciples and adversaries, including Aristotle, who saw a problem in this separation of the idea from the sensible, which has famously been called the *chorismos*.

They may have thus contributed to hardening the separation that remained flexible for Plato. According to Plato, one must conceive the relation between the idea and the sensible as *both* a separation *and* a nonseparation. Knowledge, and vision, may indeed call for a *separation* of the idea from the sensible, but only to underline how Beauty, as it can be thought, must be distinguished from its concrete occurrence. Mortals have a habit of confounding the thought of the idea with its physical manifestation. Thus in order to signal that it is a methodologically distinct order, we may *distinguish* the idea from the sensible, the "intelligible world" from the "visible world." Although these terms, and their numerous equivalents, are found in Plato's works, it would be hasty to infer an ontological separation from this, as the wise Parmenides warned the young Socrates (*Parmenides*, 130 a). The ideas are not really separate from our world because they are responsible for its harmony, its order, its symmetry, and its beauty. Thus, if we look closely, we realize that the ideas are already at work everywhere in the visible world.

That said, the sensible's mysterious "participation" in the ideas is quite difficult to understand. Unfortunately, Plato never really explained it, and Aristotle later criticized him for his use of simple metaphors (such as imitation). Nevertheless, the *Parmenides* (131 b) evokes two ways that participation can be illustrated: as the light of day, and as a veil. (1) In answering Parmenides' question about how the idea can come to form a *unity* when it is found in multiple things, Socrates suggests the idea can be portrayed as the light of day that is one but shines in different places. (2) Parmenides then answers that this is a nice idea and makes him think of a veil draped over several men that is the same but covers several individuals. The problem with this image is that only a part of the veil covers one individual while another part covers another. But this is not the case for the idea since it would be absurd to claim Beauty resides partly in one object, and partly in another. Rather, what Plato seeks to underline is the difficulty of having a sensible representation of this participation even though, for him, ideas are obviously present in the sensible. In fact, Plato says that the world itself seethes with ideas (all things "are full of gods" says *Laws* 899 b) and our discourse ceaselessly broods over them.[9]

Paul Natorp, in *Plato's Theory of Ideas*,[10] attempted to express this basic idea by comparing Plato's ideas with the physicist's laws of nature. The comparison was largely dismissed as a naive and anachronistic reading (as if Natorp was just anybody) inspired by Kant's transcendental philosophy and modern science, which indeed it probably was. Natorp's interpretation is unfortunately more often derided than read or understood. He was not foolish, however, to remind us how Plato, in speaking of the *eidos*, wished to bring attention to the regularity, or the order, that pervades the sensible world without being necessarily reducible to it. Assuredly, Plato was not thinking of Newtonian laws, but neither was he thinking of entities simply floating in a world completely severed from ours as Aristotle's caricature of them would have it, where they are portrayed as a useless duplications of our universe that—we must agree— have never been seen. And yet, Plato's *Parmenides* had already forcefully criticized this caricature of the ideas. What Plato really sought to express was something different, namely, that *ideas completely pervade reality.* But as soon as one speaks of ideas, humans stubbornly persist in seeing "another" world. Indeed, their thickheadedness is such that we readily understand why Plato sometimes did prefer to insist on the idea of a separation.

An Effort at Reminiscence

Although the world is indeed full of ideas, and we may in fact catch sight of them and "rediscover" them everywhere, it never displays a purely noetic order completely distinct from its sensible elements. Nevertheless, we must be attentive and recognize how the world does participate in such an order. Such a recognition is already an important accomplishment. Plato not only emphasizes the gap between the sensible and the idea (and thus avoids the confusion prevalent among obtuse minds who might, for example, identify the idea of the Just with justice as it is realized in this or that state: there will always be a *difference* between the sensible and the idea), he also emphasizes the idea's *immanence* to the sensible world. The best terms to describe the interlacing of the sensible and the intelligible are participation (*methexis*) or imitation (*mimesis*). The sensible "imitates" the intelligible: It moves toward it, it aspires to it, it is part of it without completely corresponding to it. But does it mean there is a *chorismos*, a fatal separation of the intelligible and the sensible? Although Plato never dismisses this possibility, he does so only to signal their *difference* rather than their separation, a difference that Plato was the first to describe as belonging to thought.

Plato sometimes uses the very lovely image of reminiscence to describe this difference, most notably in the *Meno*, the *Phaedo*, and the *Phaedrus* (it also appears in the *Symposium*). Drawing his inspiration from the mythical peregrination of souls, Plato suggests our souls may have once contemplated the ideas in their "pure state" before they entered our bodies, which prevents us from recognizing the original splendor of ideas. Nevertheless, according to Plato, from time to time we do "recall" the marvelous ideas we once glimpsed when we "recognize" their imperfect occurrences in the sensible world. The ideas are rendered almost unrecognizable by their intermingling in the sensible, but reminiscence can put us on the road to thought. Obviously, this theory of anamnesis or reminiscence should not be taken literally since it simply seeks to underline the difficulty of thinking from within the confines of a body. To think, as Parmenides had already taught, is to unburden ourselves of the corporeal, which makes us blind to the ideas we were able to perceive in another world. The point is therefore not to exalt the perfect vision we once had (and which nobody remembers), but rather to underline the extent to which thought requires an incredible effort. Like Parmenides, Plato says that, if we are to focus on what is essential and only accessible through thought, we must liberate ourselves from the grips of popular opinion. Nonetheless, according to Plato, reminiscence always begins *with* the sensible. The sensible itself leads us to acknowledge the presence of an *eidos*, a regularity, harmony, or symmetry, much too beautiful to be merely sensible.

Platonism's and metaphysics' fundamental hypothesis is thus the plausible, and defendable, possibility that our world is founded upon some intelligible order, which belongs to the *eidos* because unlike the sensible word, it displays permanence, constancy, and light. In the *Phaedo* (100 a), Plato speaks of the *hypothesis* of the *eidos*. How are we to understand this use of hypothesis? Some Plato specialists insist one must not understand it in the modern sense of a "conjecture,"[11] which a (scientific) mind articulates and then tests experimentally. Although Plato certainly never read Karl Popper, it would be a mistake to exclude the notions of supposition or "hypothesis" when the time comes to speak of *eidos* since the idea is never visible and can only be thought (*noeton*, as one reads in the *Republic*).

Plato must have been inspired by the mathematical usage of the term hypothesis when thinking of the *hypothesis* of the idea. In mathematics, a hypothesis is a presupposition used in the beginning of a demonstration. Thus a geometer, for example, *assumes* the existence of a circle or triangle the properties of which he wishes to analyze. The ideas may be similarly posited, or placed (*thesis*, from *thithèmi*), as the basis that lies beneath (*hypo*) what we perceive. The term hypothesis thus has two meanings here: On the one hand, it is a foundation or a starting point, and, on the other hand, it is a starting point one must necessarily acknowledge, or suppose, when one thinks.

Just as sight pertains to sensible objects, Plato "posits" that thought also has its own objects—that is, objects susceptible to be thought or seen (as when we say "I see" to indicate we have understood something abstract). The hypothesis of the *eidos*, which is only accessible through thought, explains the glints of stability and permanence we find in the sensible world. The idea can therefore be understood as the model or archetype for the breathtaking constancy we sometimes see in our universe.

But how are we to understand the sensible world's "imitation" of the intelligible? Plato, as we have seen, says little about it. Although he does acknowledge the difficulties of representing its modalities, he nevertheless believes that it is the most credible hypothesis for the "objects" we can think of but do not belong to the sensible world.

> It seems to be that whatever else is beautiful apart from absolute beauty is beautiful because it partakes of the absolute beauty, and for no other reason. Do you accept this kind of causality [*aitia*]?.... the one thing that makes that object beautiful is the presence in it or association with it, *in whatever way the relation comes about*, of absolute beauty. I do not go so far as to insist upon the precise details—only upon the fact that it is by beauty that beautiful things are beautiful. This, I feel, is the safest answer for me or for anyone else to give.[12]

The safest (100 d) and strongest (100 a) answer is therefore only a hypothesis or an admission. But it is the most reliable starting-point since our thoughts do in fact bear on objects that differ from simple opinions and human discourse because of their august permanence. Plato's answer is therefore also an answer to the Sophists who had contested the idea that human discourse could relate to a perceptible and communicable Being in itself. Such a Being does "exist" according to Plato inasmuch as it is the best hypothesis one can present if one is to explain the fact that our thoughts do pertain to something real that transcends discourse and opinion.[13] Conversely, it is easy to see that if Plato's hypothesis does not stand, the Sophists are correct: Being remains unknowable and there are only opinions and some arguments are simply more persuasive than others. Plato's wager, which inaugurates metaphysics, is that thought can always aim higher. And it is to philosophy, which Plato characterizes as "dialectical," that we must raise ourselves.

Dialectics, or Minding Being Itself

For Plato, the term dialectics has a Socratic meaning: It embodies the art of dialogue (διαλέγεσθαι / *dialegesthai*) practiced by his master and used to great effect in the dialogues. It is through the exchange of ideas and the confrontation of opinions that one can hope to near the truth. Dialectics, or the art of discussion, is thus used to challenge belief and uncontested evidence by demonstrating the absurd consequences that may follow from their acceptance. Occasionally used to eristic ends, Platonic dialectics preserve certain characteristics of Zeno of Elea's dialectics.

But one must also distinguish the formal, or methodical, sense Plato gives to dialectics from the more substantial one. In the formal sense, the art of dialogue (*dialegesthai*) can be taught as the rigorous division of concepts and ideas. Dialectics thus become the art of *analyzing* (*dia-legein*) concepts by attentively differentiating their main articulations, genera and species (an analytical method Aristotle would later refine in his logical writings). Plato's later dialogues, the *Sophist* and the *Statesman*, give many examples of such divisions and attempts to produce definitions. But they also clearly suggest there is more to dialectics that the art of producing formal divisions. Simply knowing how to subdivide notions and concepts is insufficient. Otherwise, we are led to preposterous assertions like defining humans as "featherless bipeds".... One must also *see* what is being discussed—that is, one must have a sense of the idea. Thus in a more substantial sense, for Plato, especially in the *Republic* and the *Sophist*, dialectics also designates the knowledge and grasp of the idea—that is, of Being itself.

Plato is aware that this kind of "sight" is neither natural nor common, but it can nevertheless be developed through dialectics. In the *Republic*, he argues this sight can only be acquired by patient instruction. According to the ambitious pedagogical program given in book VII, this education entails lengthy military and mathematical training. Urged on by Glaucon (*Republic*, 540 a), with whom he is speaking, Socrates goes so far as to give the precise number of years that must be devoted to it (15 years of military service to put in before having a chance to contemplate the idea!). As if all depended on the number of years, and pedagogy was simply a function of programs!

But what is more important though is developing what Socrates calls the dialectical spirit or faculty, which should not be confused with a technique that one can simply learn. The principal requirement is a dialectical (537 d) or philosophical nature (*phusis*) marked by the ability to see things from above and grasp them in a comprehensive view (*sunoptikos*). A person having this dialectical nature "is able to disregard the eyes and other senses and go on to Being itself in company with truth" (*ep'auto to on met'aletheias* / ἐπ' αὐτο το ὄν μετ'ἀληθείας [537 d]). The terms used are precisely those of Parmenides' goddess. Plato will even go so far as to say the Being to which we then gain access is the *ontôs on* / ὄντως ὄν (490 b),[14] literally the "beingly being" (*l'étamment étant*), Being in its fullest sense, which in Latin was later translated as true Being, the *vere ens*.[15]

So what does this mean? Is it an authoritarian, or elitist, program, in the worst sense of the term? Are the Sophists not justified in mocking it? And yet, it is precisely the Sophists Plato seeks to keep at bay when speaking of *Being itself*, which the mind can "contemplate." And doubly so when he reminds us that one *must posit* such a Being (without which our discourse speaks only of fleeting shadows) and when he suggests this vision cannot be taught. Dialectical wisdom is not a technique even though it must be cultivated and allowed to ripen.

This wisdom is expressed negatively by the distinction that must always be made between appearances or spectacles where opinions reign, and Being itself, which thought can seek to attain. "I set apart and distinguish those of whom you were just speaking, the lovers of spectacles ... and separate [!] from them again those with whom our argument is concerned and who alone deserve the appellation of philosophers or lovers of wisdom."[16] The philosopher is the one who attempts to think "Being itself" (478 c; 484 b–c; 486 d; 508 e; 523 a), beyond conventions and appearances. The essential point is therefore to distinguish the level of opinions, which overwhelm us, from another, which we can catch a glimpse of, albeit only through extraordinary effort. It is, after all, quite difficult to separate ourselves from the sensible. But once we think, or try to, we succeed, at least in part. And again, what is important is not the ontological separation, but the methodological difference of thought. When thinking about this difference, Plato used the recently discovered evidence from mathematics.

The Exemplary Ideality of Mathematics

Although he always gave dialectics greater importance, Plato was also fascinated by mathematics. Several credible accounts relate that he inscribed above his academy a warning saying: "Let no man ignorant of geometry enter." The reason is that mathematics, more than any other discipline, teaches us that true knowledge pertains to ideal shapes and sizes rather than sensible ones. When a geometer discusses the properties of the triangle or the circle, he does not speak of the figures he can draw on the board (although he does refer to them), but only of the triangle or the circle as it can be apprehended by the mind and which one can "see" when one follows the progression of his thought. In the so-called real world, there are no really parallel lines, nor any triangles whose angles actually add up to 180 degrees. In mathematics, one must *posit* "intelligible" entities; the likeness of which can only be achieved through thought. This means that the philosopher is not alone in saying that such entities can be thought. Mathematics has the pedagogical merit that it "directs the soul upwards"[17] and compels it to think of intelligible sizes that cannot be perceived through the senses.

The importance Plato ascribes to mathematics is not limited to the existence of intelligible entities. Not only does mathematics attest to the existence of distinct intelligible entities—or at the very least thinkable ones—but the type of knowledge that it leads to is also infinitely more certain than the type derived from the sensible world in which opinions fluctuate as much as its objects. Mathematical knowledge is apodictic: The sum of a triangle's angle is always and necessarily equal to 180 degrees. It is to this type of knowledge that belongs truth and science (*episteme*) in the narrowest sense of the term.

It is as if there were some correlation between Being and knowledge: Whereas sensible Being leads to opinion, ideal Being, which, at the very least, can be thought, seems to lead to an absolutely certain, almost superhuman, form of knowledge. The association of knowledge with Being will now be explained by a line drawn in book VI of the *Republic*.

The "Metaphysical" Separation of the Line: *Republic* VI

Platonic philosophy's main concern is the distinction between the sensible world and another more fundamental one. We have seen it was important to think both the separation *and* the non-separation of the sensible world from what Plato calls, for a lack of a better term, the noetic or "intelligible world." But for pedagogical reasons, the distinction may also be made to illustrate how there is a class of things that we can strive to attain through thought that does not belong to the sensible world and cannot be reduced to the level of discourse (if it could, the Sophists would then be justified and truth would be an illusion). This didactic goal is quite apparent in book VI of the *Republic* in which Plato divides a line into two parts representing the two regions of Being, the visible and the intelligible, to which correspond two types of knowledge: opinion (*doxa*) and science (*episteme*). One can easily imagine "professor" Plato drawing the line on the equivalent of a blackboard in order to explain what he is trying to get us to understand. This illustration, which does not reappear in any systematic way in his other dialogues, perhaps represents the birth of metaphysics insofar as it implies a level of reality distinct from the physical world and which explains the latter's regularity.

In fact, Plato's dualist ontology (sensible-intelligible)—as well as its corresponding epistemology (opinion, science)—is even more complex: It is, in fact, quadruple. Each of the two sections, the sensible and the intelligible, can be divided into two other sections since in the sensible world one may distinguish living things from their related reflections and shadows. Obviously shadows are less real than the objects of which they are the reflections and images. The metaphor of reflection is important for at least two reasons. Not only is each level to be understood as the reflection or mirror of some superior level,[18] but the idea of such a reflection also presupposes a light source that does not belong to the objects themselves. Just as shadows are dim outlines of natural objects, which are more real than them, these real objects are themselves but the reflection of a more original reality itself illuminated by a light stronger than ours.

Plato lays the groundwork for this idea by distinguishing two classes within the sensible world: first, the images, shadows, or reflections, and second, the objects themselves. He then assigns to them two types of opinions (*doxa*). He uses *eikasia* (often translated as "imagination," but we will here speak of opinions associated to images) to designate our grasp of reflections and shadows, and *pistis* ("sensible credence") to designate a strong conviction in the reality of sensible things. The word *Pistis* has had a singular history in the New Testament where it was translated as faith (*fides*). Although some translators have not always shied away from doing so, it would be a misinterpretation, and an anachronism, to speak of faith in the context of Plato's dialogues. Here, *pistis* corresponds to the credence given to the sensible world by most people who hold sensible objects to be the be all and end all of things.[19] For Plato, however, this credence is nothing more than a conviction (the verbs *peitho* and *peithomai*, which have the same origin as *pistis*, respectively mean "to convince" and "to be persuaded") that belongs to an inferior level of knowledge.

Just as visible space (*topos horatos*) is segmented into two parts, the intelligible world (*topos noétos*) can also be divided in two. Mathematical hypotheses belong to the first level of the noetic realm, and the ideas belong to the second. A distinct capacity for knowledge is attributed to each level: discursive knowledge (*dianoia*) for mathematical hypotheses and pure intelligence (*nous*) for the direct grasp of ideas.

We will return to this division of the intelligible world shortly, but in the mean time, we may already distribute the divisions in Being and knowledge on a line. The line is vertical[20] and divided into unequal segments (*anisa*, 509 d 6) because there are, obviously, an infinite number of images, copies and simulacra of living objects just as there are numerous sensible copies of ideas.

VISIBLE REGION *TOPOS HORATOS* τόπος ὁρατός		INTELLIGIBLE REGION *TOPOS NOÈTOS* τόπος νοητός	
Images: shadows, reflections, simulacra *eikasia* εἰκασία imagination, opinions linked to images	Sensible objects, animals, plants, etc. *pistis* πίστις sensible credence	Mathematical hypotheses *dianoia* διανοία discursive knowledge	Ideas *nous* νοῦς intelligence
Opinion *doxa* δόξα		**Science** *episteme* ἐπιστήμη	

Although the relation of reflections to sensible objects is easily understandable, as the latter are more real than the former, the one between mathematical hypotheses and ideas is more difficult to grasp. We have seen that Plato used the ideality of mathematics to give credence to his hypothesis of an ideal Being, which is attained only by thought and leads to an incomparably exact form of knowledge. We now discover that the Being of mathematics is only the first rung of the intelligible hierarchy. Philosophical, or dialectical, knowledge is therefore even more rigorous and fundamental. Mathematicians, according to Plato, always remain on the level of simple hypotheses when developing their demonstrations and posit their objects as hypotheses without proving their existence or necessity. Moreover, mathematicians deal with entities that are always partially sensible (insofar as they use lines, circles, and triangles), even though they do lead to an intelligible reality. The term *dianoia* that Plato uses to characterize this type of knowledge illustrates well the way in which it leads one to think (*noein*) the intelligibles through (*dia*) a reality that preserves a visible configuration.[21]

Philosophical knowledge does away with mathematical knowledge's conjecture. It not only pertains exclusively to ideas and their interrelations, it also *justifies the hypotheses themselves*. Plato unfortunately does not tell us, or at least not here, how this is possible, and we are as confused as Glaucon who thinks these relations are mysterious (510 b 10). But Plato does say something important when he claims that this superior knowledge, which exceeds the level of hypotheses, leads us necessarily to an *anhypotheton* / ἀνυποθέτον, or the "non-hypothetical."[22] This is probably the first appearance of an unconditioned principle in the history of metaphysics.

The Idea of the Good's Supereminence

It is rather difficult to understand what this principle means, all the more so since the term *anhypothenon* never reappears in his other writings![23] Moreover, we can only speak of it negatively and say *it is not* a hypothetical principle, like those used in mathematics. Mathematical knowledge has a limit; it starts from hypotheses it never fully justifies. Plato's idea seems to be that "hypothetical" knowledge does not lead to a genuine science (533 c). Therefore, higher and more assured principles must exist. These would be the ideas (*eidè*).

We recall, however, that Plato used the term *hypothesis* to introduce the ideas in the *Phaedo*. Do the ideas now lose their "hypothetical" status? Maybe, maybe not. The difference between these two texts, which are relatively close chronologically, is perhaps explained by their context. The *Phaedo* is the account of Socrates' last hours. Plato summarizes his life by saying it was given over to the hypothesis that there are ideas residing beyond the sensible. The purpose of the *Phaedo*'s drama was to show it was a life-orienting hypothesis. But in the *Republic*, the ideas are characterized by the fact *they are not hypothetical* (unlike mathematics). The emphasis is put on the difference between mathematics and dialectics, which is supposedly more rigorous as it seeks to make sense (*logon didonai*) of the hypotheses (510 c 6–7; 511 b 3–c 1).

But does Plato in the *Republic* really account for his non-hypothetical principle? The question is important because he unceasingly states how this form of knowledge can only be gained through an unmediated vision or insight. Hence the following paradox, or irony: Can intuitive knowledge be "demonstrative" knowledge and account for hypotheses? Can we explain or demonstrate what can only be gained through insight? If the dialectician's knowledge is more rigorous than that of mathematics, one may then suppose it is *another form* of knowledge, which is no longer tied to discourse (as was the case with sophistic knowledge).

The nonhypothetical principle appears to receive another name in the *Republic* since it is said to be identical to the idea of the Good. "The commentators of our passage unanimously identify the nonhypothetical principle with the idea of the Good in the image of the Sun (506 b–509 c)."[24] But is this correct? Would it not be in keeping with the text to see *each idea* as an occurrence of the *anhypotheton*? The unqualified identification of the *anhypotheton* with the idea of the Good seems imprudent to me. (1) Plato never directly identifies the one with the other. (2) In the *Republic*, the "*hypotheton*" defines and limits the realm of mathematics.[25] The ideas, as nonhypothetical principles, are said to be beyond the level occupied by hypotheses. (3) Finally, and most importantly, when he speaks of the idea of the Good, Plato says it is a "principle" or a "king" that reigns over all the intelligible realm, which, as we have seen, contains both mathematical hypotheses (hypothetical) *and* the ideas (nonhypothetical). Thus everything beyond the level of hypotheses is already nonhypothetical (*anhypotheton*).

Without a doubt, however, the idea of the Good is a particularly important principle because it is the principle (*archè*), or cause (*aitia*), that governs the intelligible world. But what kind of cause is it? The text of the *Republic* is vague on this point and claims to have already discussed it many times elsewhere (504 a, 506 e, 532 d)! Plato may be referring here to his oral teachings.[26]

The *Republic*, in fact, never discusses the idea of the Good directly, but only its offshoot (506 e): the sun. We must therefore begin by the sun's causality if we are to understand, by analogy, the Good's (for this reason Plato can be considered to be one of the fathers of analogical thought in metaphysics). So in what way can the sun be a principle? According to Plato, the sun allows sensible objects to be seen and our eyes to see them. The cause of seeing thus resides neither in the eye nor in the visible things, but in a third term: the sun's light. We may therefore say that the sun is the principle or "king" of the visible world. Now, the idea of the Good, says Plato, has a similar role in the intelligible world. It is the intermediary between intelligence and the intelligible. The principle of the idea of the Good would therefore be the cause (*aitia* / αἰτία) that makes the sight of what is intelligible possible (because they do not apparently need a principle to exist) and bestows on our mind the ability (δύναμις) to grasp them:

This reality, then, that gives their truth [*aletheian*] to the objects of knowledge and the power of knowing to the knower, you must say is the idea of the Good [*idea tou agathou*], and must conceive it as being the cause of science and truth [*aitian epistemes kai alètheias*], in supposing it to be something fairer still that these you will think rightly of it.[27]

This passage seems to imply that the idea of the Good is but a middle term between the intelligible and our intelligence, as though it was the intelligible light that allows us to grasp the ideas. A couple of lines later, Plato bestows on it a considerably greater importance when he says that the idea of the Good can be considered as the principle of Being:

In like manner, then, you are to say that the objects of knowledge not only receive from the presence of the Good their being known, but their very Being [τὸ εἶναι / *to einai*] and essence [*ousia* / οὐσία] is derived to them from it, though the Good itself is not essence but still transcends essence [ἐπέκεινα τῆς οὐσίας / *epekaina tes ousias*] in dignity and power.[28]

This passage is the high point of Platonism. It asserts without any explanation that all the other ideas derive their *Being* and their *essence* from the idea of the Good. Assuming that the term Being (τὸ εἶναι / *to einai*) is relatively straightforward, the most difficult one is assuredly essence (*ousia* / οὐσία). The English term essence is really a makeshift solution, but the meaning of the Greek term *ousia* is itself not easy to understand. Plato uses it sparingly, and it is only after Aristotle that it takes on a precise meaning (that is, "substance" as it was to be translated by the Latin tradition). As Heidegger, among others, has shown, in common Greek οὐσία designated somebody's holdings, possessions and goods—that is, his estate, property and wealth. Applied to Plato's text, this would mean that all the other ideas draw their dignity or *distinction* from the idea of the Good.

This is not, however, the only possible meaning of the term *ousia*. Plato sometimes uses it as an emphatic synonym for Being (*einai*, like in the passage from the *Republic* we just saw). The term is itself derived from a participial form of the verb "to be." As we have seen, the *Sophist* (246 a) spoke of a struggle of giants over *ousia* to evoke the most important conceptions of Being. In the *Republic* (525 b), Plato also uses the term *ousia* as a synonym for Being to say that when the soul turns away from becoming, it "lays hold of truth and Being" (*ep'aletheian te kai ousian*). Thus *ousia*, along with its distinctive meaning denoting excellence, is also used in a more strictly ontological sense to mean Being.

But if this were the case, Plato's reference to "Being and essence" that emerges from the idea of the Good would employ two words to say the same thing. Perhaps. The expression would then correspond to what is called in rhetoric a *hendiadys* (*Oxford English Dictionary*: "a figure of speech in which a single complex idea is expressed by two words connected by a conjunction"). Such is the case when we use a series of synonyms to mark and emphasize a point when speaking of something important.

So we may reconcile the two possible meanings of the term *ousia* (distinction and Being) by speaking of the "true Being" of things or of ideas that stems from the idea of the Good. Indeed, where does the ideas' unique excellence come from if not from an idea that makes them stand out?

And yet, since it is the apex of the hierarchy of intelligibles, Plato says the idea of the Good is *epekaina tes ousias*, "beyond essence." One might spontaneously think this refers to the idea of the Good's *ontological transcendence* in relation to the other beings, or to Being itself. According to this reading, which will later be that of Plotinus, the cause of Being (the Good, or the One) is separate from beings. If this were the case, the metaphysical principle of Being must be in some way "meta-ontological." This super-elevation (*epekeina*) of the idea of the Good is undoubtedly the first apparition of a *transcendent* principle in the history of western thought, which will later reappear as Aristotle's Prime mover and as the Christian God.

But for Plato, the *epekaina* may designate something other than an ontological transcendence. The text, in fact, says the idea of the Good surpasses "Being" in "dignity and power." The Good's *epekeina* thus connotes less an ontologically transcendent being than some qualitative excellence or superiority:[29] The idea of the Good surpasses the level of *ousia* by its dignity and power.

The idea of the Good is a principle that Plato never completely explains however. He dispenses with its explanation because it is supposed to account for all that is. It is the ultimate principle or, to put it differently, the first principle by which all is "clarified." But Plato does not give a reason why this idea is called that of the "Good."[30] We must remember here what Socrates says in the *Phaedo* (97 b ff. where Plato also writes that Socrates is repeating what has already been said, 100 b) on the subject of the Good or reason acting in the world: All exists for some reason, pure chance does not rule the universe. Aristotle will later take up this universal teleology of beings.

Plato does not specify how this super-eminent idea must be understood because it can only be intuited. Nor does he say how to produce such a vision, although he does express its ideal: The world, as we might say in a more contemporary way, makes more sense, and is more vivid, if we presuppose such an idea that exceeds all the others in dignity and power.

Therefore, despite its apparent transcendence, the idea of the Good is not entirely separate from the world. We can find splendid instances of the Good—the idea—in the world whenever we see outstanding "sameness." One need only open one's eyes with the help of dialectics. It is true though that in our cavernous world it is sometimes difficult to see. And, in our world, there is not only "sameness" but also "otherness."

The Demiurge's Cosmos: The Same and the Different

While the idea of the Good may be the first glimmer of a transcendent principle in the history of philosophy, it is not a creative principle like the one found in the Judeo-Christian tradition. For the Greeks, the world was eternal and the idea of its creation *ex nihilo* was incomprehensible. How could something emerge out of nothing? But some formative process may nonetheless have shaped the world's form. In his *Timaeus*, Plato puts forward the idea that the world may have been structured by what he calls a "demiurge" or artisan. As with all artisans, the demiurge had a model from which he drew inspirations as he fashioned our world: the ideas. Although he claims that in such matters one must settle for "only verisimilar stories" (*eikôs logos*), Plato says the demiurge's essential work consisted in mixing two ideas: the same and the different.[31] The same is what is forever and always remains identical to itself (*Timaeus* 28 a). The different is what has a body and is subject to becoming. The demiurge would therefore have given an order to our cosmos by bringing together these two ideas. Thus our world contains both the "same" and the "different." We may also assume the "same" is just another name for the ideas, if not the Good itself—that is, the principle of constancy and order that counterbalances the contrary tendencies of the "different."

Thus there are two important models for what we may call a transcendent principle in Plato's writings:[32] the super-eminent idea of the Good and the demiurge's work. The Judeo-Christian conception of transcendence, through the mediation of Neoplatonism, would later bring them together and even merge them by identifying the *summum bonum* with the creator of the world. In Plato though, they remain separate. Being mythical, the demiurge simply contemplates the eternal ideas when shaping the world. The real principle lies in the idea, the idea of the Good or of the "same," which may be different names for the very same idea.

The Principle of the One in Plato's Academy

As we already emphasized, Plato, in the *Republic*, alludes to other discussions of the nature of the Good, which he says is "the greatest thing to learn" (*Republic*, 505 a: *hè tou agatou idea megiston mathèma* / ἡ τοῦ ἀγαθοῦ ἰδέα μέγιστον μάθημα). He also suggests in other writings (*Phaedrus* and the *Seventh Letter*, for example) that he never wrote down everything he had to say on the subject. Truly, the *Republic* remains allusive on the question of the principle of principles.

So did the oral teachings give a more adequate presentation of this subject? Unfortunately, there is no reliable or direct information on what Plato taught at the Academy. But Aristotle, who studied at the Academy, seems to use these oral teachings to depict Plato as a theorist of principles (see *Metaphysics*, A, 6). According to his testimony, Plato would have ascribed two important principles to reality: the One (*hen* / ἕν) and the indeterminate dyad (*aoristos duas* / ἀόριστος δυάς). The One was thought as a formative principle that imprinted a unitary form and order on reality. Its order and unity bring to mind the workings of the ideas. Indeed, in his dialogues, Plato often said that the ideas should be understood as a principle of unity:

— We predicate "to be" of many beautiful things and many good things saying of them severally that the *are*, and so define them in our speech.

— We do.

— And again, we speak of a self-beautiful and of a good that is only and merely good, and so, in the case of all the things that we then posited as many, we turn about and posit each as *a single idea* or aspect, assuming it *to be a unity* and calling it that which each really is [*ho estin*].[33]

It is more than reasonable to understand the idea as a principle unifying reality. And if the ideas are principles of unity, their own principle may then be ascribed to the principle of the One that Aristotle mentions, but which also exists in some of Plato's writings.[34] The idea of the Good can then be seen as a principle of unity, which would be the cause of the ideas because it encapsulates their activity. After all, is unity not the common denominator shared by all ideas? According to Krämer's reading, unity is what enables an object to be what it is and allows our intelligence to know it. The ultimate principle of reality—the idea of the Good according to the *Republic*—can therefore be called the One.

But this is not the only principle however. In addition to the principle of unity, there is also the principle of the "indeterminate dyad" that brings to mind the idea of a "duality," which Plato would have opposed to the unity of the first principle. This duality would therefore be a factor of multiplicity and dispersion, as the adjective "indeterminate" implies. This multiplicity and dispersion, unified by the idea, requires, or awaits, a determination (according to Aristotle, this Platonic principle could also have been called the principle of the "great and small"[35]). For Aristotle, the dyad is without a doubt a reference to what one may call "matter," or "un-formed" matter. Although Plato does not speak of matter in the same sense as Aristotle, the indeterminate dyad is surely its precursor. Despite the fact that the principle of the dyad is not found in Plato's writings, there are equivalents, most notably in the *Philebus* (16 c ff.) where the important principle of unlimitedness (*apeira*) is discussed. There is also the enigmatic *chôra* of the *Timaeus*, which can be read to mean matter, place in space, and even matrix. Thus the idea that the matter of our world receives its essential determination from an ideal principle, represented by the One, would have been the heart of the Platonic doctrine of principles. This agrees with the doctrine expounded in the dialogues according to which ideas govern the world.

It is important to understand that for Plato, the One, or the idea, is not the only principle governing the world. Order, regularity, and unity are not to be found everywhere, which explains why a second principle of division, of diversity, and indeterminacy is required. The didactic dualism of Platonic ontology, which divides the world into sensible and intelligible realms, thus coincides with a dualism of principles. But to speak of a dualism of principles implies that the two divisions of reality are not completely disassociated, but are somehow intertwined, even interdependent.

This is exactly what we encounter in our world. Although it may be sensible, we often encounter occurrences of unity that can always be brought back to some "idea" or unity.[36] But in the very heart of the intelligible realm, we also encounter the work of the dyad as the plurality of ideas.[37] Whereas the dyad is seemingly predominant in the sensible world, which is not devoid of unity, the One reigns over the diversity of the intelligible world. According to indirect testimony, Plato would have given great importance to the interaction between these two antinomical, but complementary, principles in his philosophical explanation of the world. We can find traces of this in his later dialogues (especially the *Timaeus* and the *Philebus*) where he ascribes an increasingly important place to mathematics in the explanation of reality. And Speusippus, Plato's successor at the head of the Academy, would have supposedly argued that all ideas are numbers, a rather Pythagorean notion, but one that was probably adumbrated by his master's speculations.

So is Plato the founder of metaphysics? It depends on what is meant by metaphysics. If it is taken as a name for a distinct philosophical discipline that seeks the principles of Being as a whole, one will have to wait until Aristotle (and even then!). But, if metaphysics is associated with some transcendence, which, following Parmenides, seeks to overcome the shackles of opinion and discover a stable, permanent, invisible yet conceivable Being, a Being both transcendent and immanently present in the sensible realm, whose supereminence is that of the illuminating *eidos*, then metaphysical thought has its first and most inspiring poet in Plato.

CHAPTER 3

ARISTOTLE

The Horizons of First Philosophy

The Text and Object of Metaphysics

It is well known that Aristotle never used the word "metaphysics" as a title or a philosophical term. In fact, the term *metaphysikè* (and its derivatives) never appears in Greek literature, with Simplicius's use of the term in the sixth century CE being the notable exception.[1] But as we have already seen, during the first century BCE, Andronicus of Rhodes used the expression *meta ta phusika* as a title for a collection of fourteen small works, which he inserted "after the writings on physics." This has led some to say that the term "metaphysics," or rather *meta ta phusika*, came about by accident. But such accidents are not always as fortuitous as they sometimes appear. There are, in fact, at least two reasons unrelated to any bibliographic considerations for thinking that the term may have had another meaning.[2] Indeed, *meta ta phusika* could have connoted, on the one hand, the *dignity* of a science pertaining to a supersensible object (as was the status of Plato's ideas); and, on the other hand, the chronological order of a science that would have followed *Physics* in *the progression of knowledge.*[3] The study of nature would then lead to a "meta-physical" science studying higher principles. This consecutive sequence of types of knowledge is not foreign to Aristotle's texts as he closed the eighth and final book of his

Physics with the hypothesis of a prime immobile mover. Aristotle's earliest commentators probably, in fact, favored this chronological reading.[4] But the question was of little interest for Aristotle himself since there is no reference to *metaphysikè* or to any order of realities, or of types of knowledge, that he would have qualified as *meta ta phusika*.

The question of identifying the object of Aristotle's metaphysics is not devoid of interest however. There is no doubt that for Aristotle there is a fundamental and universal science, which he called *protè philosophia*, first philosophy. His later commentators would then have given it another name and called it metaphysics. The writings called *Metaphysics* do definitely discuss a first philosophy, but it is characterized in several more or less compatible ways:

1. *Metaphysics* book IV or Gamma (Γ) speaks of first philosophy as a science of "Being as Being" that would consider Being through its universality: metaphysics is a *universal ontology*.
2. Book I or Alpha (A) argues for a science of first causes and first principles, which we may call an *etiology* or a *theory of causes*.
3. Book VI or Epsilon (E) (the essential of which is taken up again in book XI or Kappa (K) whose authenticity is contested) describes the first science as an investigation into the causes of Being and of Beings as Beings (*des êtres en tant qu'êtres*)—that is, the first causes, immobile and separate from matter [a science that is further developed in book XII or Lambda (Λ)]. Metaphysics is *theology*.
4. Finally, book VII or Zeta (Z) elaborates on the idea of a general science of substance including those substances belonging to the sensible world: metaphysics is *ousiology*.

Thus for Aristotle first philosophy or "metaphysics" can be any of these four things: an *etiology* (a theory of first causes or principles), a *universal ontology* (introduced as a science of Being as Being, but which must also deal with the major principles of thought), an *ousiology* (a universal theory of Being in its fullest sense—that is, as substance) or a *theology*. It is easy to understand how etiology can be coupled to theology (a term that Aristotle, in fact, uses rather infrequently), but it remains to be seen how first philosophy can also be a universal ontology that gives pride of place to the notion of substance. The various interpretations of Aristotle's *Metaphysics* differ on the important question of its object.[5]

Even if they are our one and only source, Aristotle's texts must be treated with caution. First, it is uncertain whether they were all written by Aristotle (it is rather certain the compiling of the texts that make up the *Metaphysics* was not done by him). Second, it is even more improbable that they all date from the same period or are all part of the same inquiry. It is therefore tempting to explain the "contradictions" between the texts using a genetic explanation. Werner Jaeger employed such an approach and tried to show that Aristotle's more theological writings belong to an early, more Platonic, period, whereas the texts dealing with the notion of substance came later. Although this genetic explanation need not be discarded, it may not be appropriate in Aristotle's case since we know very little about his writing's chronological order (which is easier to establish in Plato's case). But what is most important here is not to give a thoroughly coherent interpretation of Aristotle's metaphysics but to describe the problems that these texts were first to raise and which have since become the main problems of Western metaphysics.

A Science of First Principles

We begin with the first book (A) of the *Metaphysics* because it gives a general description of philosophical wisdom (*sophia*) and has an introductive or didactic character. This explains why Andronicus placed it at the beginning of the *Metaphysics*. It must have been one of Aristotle's many *protreptic* writings, which can be found throughout his corpus. The book opens with famous statement: "All men by nature desire to know." From this "nature," Aristotle draws out the idea of a universal wisdom dealing with first principles in a maieutic manner. So what does knowing mean? One speaks of knowing, says Aristotle, when one knows the "why" of things. If every science is a science of a "why," then the highest form of wisdom is obviously the one that pertains to "the first causes and principles" (*peri ta prôta aitia kai tas archas*, A, 1, 981 b 28–29). This claim is rather unsurprising coming from one of Plato's disciples: Plato had also defended the idea that philosophy was a science of principles (*archai*, which are manifestly the ideas, no matter how we understand the doctrine of principles that was supposedly taught at the Academy). Without a doubt, for Plato the most important principle was the Good, which was clearly singled out as the object of the highest form of knowledge (*magiston mathema*, *Republic*, 505 a 2). As an echo to this, Aristotle asserts in the first book of the *Metaphysics* that the most important science pertains to what "is the most knowable" (982 b 1, *hè tou malista epistetou*)— that is, "the first principles and causes" (*ta prôta kai ta aitia*, 982 b 2). It is, in fact, by virtue of these first principles that all the rest may be known. Although he does refer to Plato here, Aristotle adds that the principal or "archical" (*archikè*) science is the one that knows to what end each thing exists. Or, to put it differently, this science knows the Good (*t'agathon*, 982 b 10) of all things, or even the "supremely Good" (*to ariston*) of nature. Quite obviously, Aristotle does not stray very far from Plato here.

Aristotle can therefore be said to construe his first philosophy as a historical and thematic extension of the Platonic science of principles. This may also be the reason why with almost uncompromising criticism he so carefully distinguishes his fundamental science from Plato's. One must understand that a philosopher, especially a disciple, criticizes a precursor's thought primarily because he, or she, hopes to better determine what had been sought but not completely attained.

As to the "theory of first principles," which is how in an almost tautological way he presents first philosophy, Aristotle criticizes Plato for not having distinguished two things: (1) the varied meanings of Being, the principles of which he claims to have found; and (2) the meanings of the notion of cause, an important and essential distinction for any philosophy of first causes. Indeed, "if we search for the elements of beings without distinguishing the many senses in which things are said to be, we cannot find them, especially if the search for the elements of which things are made is conducted in this manner."[6] If a science of Being, which Parmenides and Plato had sought, is really possible, first philosophy must then discern the senses of Being. Not only must it do so in order to see whether or not Being is an unequivocal concept, but it must also do so to determine of what kind of Being it is seeking the principles. But here in the protreptical context of the first book of the *Metaphysics*, the many meanings of the concept "cause" will be front and center, in contrast to Plato who did not tackle this question when describing the ideas as principles or causes.

The Theory of Causes

If [motion] were unknown, the meaning of "nature" too would be unknown.
ARISTOTLE, *PHYSICS*, III, 1, 200 B 14–15

Aristotle was particularly proud of his theory of the four causes, which he often presents as his most important contribution to the development of first philosophy.[7] It allowed him not only to present a rigorous conceptual analysis—in analytic continuity with the Platonic dialectical method—of the notion of cause, but it also allowed him to enter into debate with his predecessors, especially Plato. By summarizing his precursors' arguments, Aristotle thought he was exhaustively outlining all possible conceptions, and then showed how his own synthesis was the most satisfactory.

It is important to understand that the distinction between the four causes attempts to explain nature in general and justify the existence of a science called physics, which Aristotle, and others, ardently promoted. The essential fact about the physical world is its movement. According to Aristotle's famous definition given in *Physics* II, 1, "nature" is what contains the principle of its own movement and rest. How to explain such movement, which implies not only a dynamic and almost living universe, but also one that is not devoid of constancy, purpose, and finality insofar as all moving things susceptible of change seem to strive "naturally" to some goal? This teleology is obviously that of purposeful human endeavors. But for Aristotle it is first that of nature itself since it is natural for air and fire to be directed upward and for humans naturally (*phusei!*) to aspire to knowledge and happiness.

It is this secret but powerful teleology that Aristotle wants to explain. In a rather stylized way, in his *Physics* Aristotle distinguishes three important philosophical positions that might be held about movement: one held by those that deny its existence (the Eleatics); another held by those that argue, on the contrary, that all is movement (Heraclitus); and Plato's that acknowledged a certain permanence, that of the *eidos*, behind change, without recognizing the actual existence of movement itself. We can see that in the first two cases a science of movement as such is impossible.

Plato is thus the author to whom Aristotle is closest. But the disciple severely judges his master's "theory of principles" because it does not really account for *change* itself. Plato's ideas, argues Aristotle, "cause neither movement nor any change" (*Metaphysics*, A, 9, 991 a 11). In fact, Plato would have probably agreed with Aristotle on this point. Plato had not sought to explain movement but the occurrences of permanence and constancy that persist in change itself. In Plato's perspective, movement (or change) does not require explanation: It is undeniable. But for science, which seeks what is ideal and permanent, it is a factor of dispersion that conceals what is essential—that is, essence itself, or the *eidos*. However, according to Aristotle, this perspective is as fatal to physics as Parmenides' immobilism since what must be explained is precisely *physis*. But since nature is so complex, one can only do so by first identifying the different meanings of the notion of cause.

1. Cause denotes first and foremost the "matter" (ὕλη / *hulè*, sometimes ὑποκείμενον / *to hypokeimenon*, the subject or substrate) of which things are made. This may seem trivial, but the invention of the term "matter" was an exceptional achievement. Before Aristotle, the term ὕλη only meant lumber. All the Greek terms derived from ὕλη relate to forestry (the adjective *hyldeis*

means "wooded" and *hylèkoitès* "somebody who lives in the forest"). The term ὕλη only appears once in Plato's writings: In the *Timaeus* (69 a), it is used to mean lumber, but it appears in a context that in a way announces the Aristotelian conception of matter. As he discusses the elements—and the causes!—that the demiurge must assemble, Plato writes:

> Seeing, then, that we have now prepared for our use the various classes of causes [*ta tôn aitiôn genè*] which are the material out which the remainder of our discourse must be woven, just as wood [*hylè*] is the material of the carpenter [*dialasmena*], let us revert in a few words to our beginning, and hasten back to the point from which we set out on our road hither.[8]

Plato thus compares the elements available to the demiurge, which are also the elements of his discourse, to the lumber available to carpenters. The context of this passage from the *Timaeus* is quite revelatory since in it Plato *also* discusses the *khôra*, which is the material or the receptacle with which and in which the demiurge assembles things.[9] According to the *Timaeus* (48 e ff.), there are, in fact, three major genera of Being: (1) the intelligible type, the ideas; (2) their copies; (3) the *khôra*, which is presented as a receptacle but also as womb from which all bodies "spring." In itself, the *khôra* is invisible because we are only aware of already fashioned things, or copies (2) of the intelligible world (1). We can therefore only apprehend this *khôra* by means of "spurious reason" (52 b). Although Plato may never call *khôra hylè*, it is nevertheless tempting to see in it an ancestor of Aristotelian matter.

But Aristotle's matter is never found in a raw state since all matter is already formed. Nevertheless, it embodies a principle that exists in all physical things. Aristotle, in fact, frequently calls it the "substrate" or the "subject" (*to hypokeimenon*, the ancestor of our notion of "subject," in the sense of that which "lies beneath": The later Latin term *subjectum* will be its literal translation).

Aristotle refers to matter first not only because is it the most elementary, but also because it was this type of cause—the material cause—which the first physiologists had sought. For Thales this principle was water, for Anaximander it was air, and Heraclitus, fire. Although their search for the material causes was essential, according to Aristotle, the first thinkers of *physis* made one common mistake in believing there was only one cause (*Metaphysics*, A, 3, 984 a 17). Aristotle supports his argument with the evidence of movement: if everything were caused by a single (material) principle, how are we to explain *change*? Wood did not cause this table nor did it cause this sheet of paper. Or, as he put it himself: "the substrate itself does not make itself change" (*Metaphysics*, A, 3, 984 a 22). Thus there is some other cause, different from the material cause, that explains *from whence comes* change.

2. This second principle is the efficient cause, which literally designates the principle or *beginning of movement* (ἡ ἀρχὴ τῆς κινήσεως / *hè archè tès kinèseôs*). This form of causality is probably the most familiar to us moderns, but Aristotle's examples are not always those that we would use.[10] It is as an efficient cause that the seed is cause of the plant, or the medical doctor the cause of a patient's health (the medical art can also be considered an efficient cause, albeit a more remote one). Another notable difference is whereas the Judeo-Christian tradition will describe divine causality as an efficient cause, Aristotle understood divine causality as a final cause. The reason being that the celestial bodies' movement is eternal and therefore does not have a beginning (*archè*). The cause of the eternal movement of heavenly bodies can therefore only be explained in terms of some finality or purpose.

3. The third cause is the formal cause. It was probably the most familiar to Plato's students since Aristotle often calls it *eidos* (but also οὐσια / *ousia*, τὸ τὶ ἦν εἶναι, / *to ti èn einai*, μορφή / *morphè*).[11] According to Aristotle, its first adherents were the proponents of the ideas (*Metaphysics*, A, 7, 988 a 35). It is important to understand this similarity in terms, which translations often conceal when they call Plato the philosopher of ideas or intelligible forms, and Aristotle the thinker of form or substance. In both cases, it is always the term *eidos* that is used. Although it is true that Aristotle understands it differently from Plato, as we will see when discussing his theory of substance, he does agree with his master that it is an essential form of "causality." Plato's mistake would then have been to limit himself to only two types of causes—matter and the *eidos*. For Aristotle, it is impossible to account for how wood took on the form of a table without any reference to an "efficient cause," namely, the artisan or the art of carpentry, which gave a form to the wood. But there is a fourth way of saying "why" things are that is very important for Aristotle.

4. A cause quite often says "for what" (οὗ ἕνεκα / *hou heneka*) something happens—that is, it gives the action's goal. As Aristotle likes to point out, this can be seen in our use of language: "Again [we also speak of cause] in the sense of end or 'that for the sake of which' a thing is done, e.g., health is the cause of walking about ('Why is he walking about?' we say, 'To be healthy,' and having said that, we think we have assigned the cause)."[12] Aristotle sees this teleological bent of human activity throughout nature: leaves are there to protect fruit (199 a 25) and plants grow roots downwards to find nourishment (199 a 33). This teleological outlook is essential to all of Aristotle's thought, including his ethics. One can say that it is in virtue of this same teleology that

solid bodies are naturally inclined to move downward and humans aspire to happiness.

According to Aristotle, the only thinker prior to him to have considered this type of cause was Anaxagoras when he spoke of the spirit (*nous*) that governs the world. But Anaxagoras would not have showed *how* reason was the final cause of things.[13] Although the idea of a final cause belongs to Aristotle, one can also say that it was at least prefigured by Plato's idea of the Good, which was said to be the universal principle of beings, in both the *Pheado* and the *Republic*. The first book of the *Metaphysics* had, as we have seen, named the Good (*t'agathon* and *to ariston*) as the supreme knowable for any science seeking principles and first causes. But Plato had also imagined a form of causality resembling Aristotle's efficient cause when, in the *Timaeus*, he spoke of the demiurge using the ideas as models when shaping the "matter" of the *khôra*. For these reasons, some commentators have judged Aristotle to be overly critical of Plato when he claimed that his master had no knowledge of efficient or final causes.[14]

Aristotle's greatest achievement was to have identified the different ways language has for "saying why."[15] Although it is difficult to contest its analytic merit, Aristotle's theory of causes is not really a theory of first causes but a theory of the ways of using the term cause. Aristotle's explanation is thus semantic rather than the one about "first causes and principles" (*peri ta prôta aitia kai tas archas*, A, 1, 981 b 28–29) that first philosophy had promised. In fact, when Aristotle distinguishes the primary meanings of the notion of cause with as much pride as finesse, he never specifies *which* causes are first.

Even after reviewing the theory of causes, the problem of the object of first philosophy remains unresolved. And now, with a brief comment that opens book Γ of the *Metaphysics* the whole issue will be raised once again.

It Is a Science of Being as Being

Aristotle's intention of differentiating various specialized sciences from a general science of Being is unequivocal:

> There is a science [ἐπιστήμη / *episteme*] that investigates Being as Being [*on hè on*] and the attributes which belong to this in virtue of its own nature. Now this is not the same as any of the so-called special sciences; for none of the others treats universally of Being as Being. They cut off a part of Being and investigate the attribute of this part. (*Metaphysics*, Γ, 1, 1003 a 20)

Here the most important question is one of knowing the object of this universal science, especially since Aristotle's expression "Being as Being" is unprecedented (one should say "beings as beings" (*l'étant en tant qu'étant*) as is more and more common following translations of Heidegger's works. But we will respect the classic English usage, which is more natural and supple). As we saw, Parmenides had identified the *éon* (the being that is) as the only object worthy of thought, and Plato had given to dialectics the task of thinking true Being (the *ontôs on* and *ousia*). Prior to Aristotle, however, nobody had spoken of Being "as Being." The particle "*hè*" (ἤ, *ut* or *qua* in Latin) is used here as a dative relative pronoun. Aristotle's expression thus means "beings inasmuch as they are beings" (*l'étant et en lui, ou de lui, le fait qu'il soit étant*), Aristotle differentiates this point from what characterizes the other sciences, which consider Being as such and such (mathematical, physical, and so on). Whereas these sciences are special, the one Aristotle imagines here aspires to universality. It is in fact ontology before its time since it is interested in Being inasmuch as it is only Being. But this type of science is obviously not without its difficulties.

One may ask whether such a science is even possible. Aristotle claims that a science (*episteme*) can only deal with one particular genus—that is, a part of Being having the same common attributes. According to the position Aristotle argues in the *Posterior Analytics* (I, 19, 76 b 12–23), the goal of a science is to analyze one genus by identifying its species, its essential properties and divisions.[16] Yet Aristotle claims with comparable conviction and rigor that Being *is not* a genus. Otherwise, it would have generic attributes that would distinguish it from an other genus, which is quite impossible as everything is "Being."

Another difficulty, which Aristotle did try to resolve, is that Being is not an unequivocal concept. As Aristotle often emphasizes (as we have seen in his anti-Platonic polemic, for example) and repeats it in the second chapter of book Γ: "there are many senses in which a thing may be said to 'be.'" Obviously, a science can only deal with one genus having an unequivocal meaning.[17] So as Pierre Aubenque has remarked: "It is as if Aristotle when presenting himself as the founder of the science of Being as Being offered countless arguments demonstrating its impossibility."[18]

But must the expression "Being as Being" only be understood in an ontological sense? Instead of designating Being's universality, it could designate the "principle" of Being—that is, the principle having the greatest distinction attributable to Being. Being as Being would then be equal to the *ontos on*, or Plato's beingly being (*Republic*, 490 b), the most exemplary of beings (*l'étant par excellence*). This principial sense of "Being as Being," which commentators have often called "theological," seems to be implied by the rest of *Metaphysics* Γ. Having distinguished the object of this science from the special sciences, Aristotle states: "since we are seeking the first principles and highest causes, clearly there must be some thing to which these belong in virtue of its own nature" (1003 a 26–30). Thus Aristotle seemingly associates the projected science of Being as Being to the idea of a first philosophy pertaining to first causes and principles.

This "theological" interpretation of "Being as Being" prevailed throughout Antiquity and the Middle Ages until the twelfth century.[19] Even though it was long dominant, it has its own problems. One may wonder, first, whether this science of the principle of Being would not thereby become like any other science. Although it may be called first, it seems to deal with a region of Being—the "divine," for a lack of a better word—the properties of which it studies. Furthermore, some of Aristotle's texts also suggest that the first causes are not identical to "Being as Being," because what must be studied are the "causes" of Being as Being.[20] The problem remains unsolved: does the expression "Being as Being" designate first causes in the theological sense or Being in a universal and ontological sense?

The Onto-Theological Perspective of *Metaphysics* E, 1

Metaphysics Book E (Epsilon, or VI) offers an elegant solution to this classic dilemma. Unfortunately, as we will see shortly, it entails its own problems. Aristotle begins by repeating as if this were only a small matter, that "we are seeking the principles and the causes of the things that are, and obviously of Beings as Beings." The plural form of "Being as Being" is in stark contrast to the singular used in *Metaphysics* Γ, 1. But if the theological interpretation is correct, the plural form could be an echo of the plurality of first and immobile causes like Plato's ideas or the causes of the regular and eternal movement of heavenly bodies that Aristotle discusses elsewhere. This is all the more probable since Aristotle does state in *Metaphysics* E, 1 that first philosophy must inquire into immobile substances separate from matter.

In this context, Aristotle distinguishes three theoretical sciences—that is, sciences pursued for the love of knowledge unlike the practical or technical sciences that aim at some other end. These sciences are physics, mathematics, and the theological science (*theologikè*).

1. Physics, writes Aristotle, pertains to mobile beings that are not separate—that is, inseparable from matter:[21] physical substances. Physical substances are indeed moving and are not separate from matter.

2. Mathematics pertains to immobile and probably inseparable beings, meaning that mathematical entities are not as such subject to movement, but do not have a separate autonomous existence.

3. The first science then pertains to immobile beings separate from matter. Aristotle calls this science "theological" (*theologikè*). According to him, "if the divine is present anywhere, it is present in things of this sort [separate and immobile]. And the highest science must deal with the highest genus" (1026 a 19–22). This text confirms the principial, or theological, orientation of first philosophy, but one might wonder, as does Aristotle, whether the science of the principial therefore pertains to a particular genus. His answer is famous:

> One might indeed raise the question whether first philosophy is universal, or deals with one genus.... We answer that if there is no substance other than those which are formed by nature, natural science will be first science; but if there is an immovable substance, the science of this must be prior and must be first philosophy, and universal in this way, because it is first. And it will belong to this to consider Being as Being—both what it is and the attributes which belong to it as Being.[22]

"Universal...because it is first" (καί καθόλου οὕτως ὅτι πρώτη / *kai katholou houtôs hoti prôtè*) is a famous expression that identifies the requirements for any first philosophy. First philosophy, here identified as theology, pertains to one particular object said to be the "first" of all objects. Thus it is first because of its object's primacy, or its principial status. But such a science is more than just another particular science. It is also universal since the study of the first being entails the study of *all* other beings that follow from this principle.[23] The inquiry into first beings is therefore an inquiry into all that is from the unique standpoint of Being. Thus theology includes ontology.

The relation, or complicity, between ontology and theology clearly exemplifies what Heidegger calls the "onto-theological constitution" of metaphysics.[24] The expression means that when metaphysics treats Being as a whole it always does so to assure its divine or theological principle. And, on the other hand, any discussion of the divine implies some kind of universal ontological pretension. Philosophy is therefore both a science of all that is—it is a universal ontology—and a science with a theological vocation—that is, a science of the principle of all that is. Thus it is only since Aristotle that a theological principle explains Being in its totality, and Being is said to be intelligible solely when it is bought back to a first principle. This relation between ontology and theology is the framework of Western metaphysics, and even of science itself. But this principle of intelligibility need not be God. As will be the case later in the history of metaphysics, this principle can also be ascribed to the human subject, either individual or collective, to history and even to language. As soon as one seeks a common denominator to one's experience, one thinks in an onto-theological manner.

Thus according to the harmonious solution that *Metaphysics* E proposes, the science of Being as Being would be a principial science and *therefore* a science of all that is. Yet this overly elegant solution has it problems. For one, it only appears in this one text. Nowhere else does Aristotle put forth the idea of a science that would be "universal...because it is first."[25] Somebody else, in an attempt to reconcile Aristotle's texts, may have penned its solution to the problem of first philosophy's object. Moreover, the term *theologikè*, which has now become familiar, is not to be found anywhere else in Aristotle's work. It is rather curious that the term does not appear in any of the texts that mention first philosophy's principial or "theological" orientation (*Metaphysics*, A, Z, Λ; *Physics*, VIII; *On the Heavens*). This led Paul Natorp, one of the first authors to draw attention to the dilemma of the unity of Aristotle's metaphysics,[26] to question the authenticity of book E. Ingemar Düring, however, interpreted the use of the term as the product of sudden inspiration.[27] Werner Jaeger preferred to read it as an early text written when Aristotle was perhaps still under the influence of Plato's theory of ideas. Aristotle would then have slowly distanced himself from the Platonic idea of first philosophy as a science of first and transcendent principles and eventually conceived first philosophy as a systematic theory of substance.[28] One must therefore read the text, and its solution, with utmost caution, but one must also give it credit for expressing the onto-theological constitution that the history of metaphysics will ceaselessly reassert.

Whether it is conceived as a (theological) science of first principles or as a universal and purely ontological science of Being as Being, first philosophy must always confront the problem of the many meanings of the verb "to be."

The Many Meanings of Being

Throughout his writings, Aristotle reasserts this important philosophical problem. As we have seen, it sometimes appears in the context of an anti-Platonic polemic (*Metaphysics*, A, 9): How may one claim to seek the principles of beings if one has not already determined the meanings of Being? But since he is himself seeking an ontological or principial science of Being, Aristotle cannot ignore that the verb "to be" has many meanings. Indeed, he identifies four major ones:[29]

1. Being can first be said of something accidental (κατὰ συμβεβηκός / *kata sumbebèkos*): literally, a kind of Being that "happens" or befalls something. Being, in this sense, does not exist autonomously, as substance does, but is predicated of a substance. We may think of it as a qualitative-Being (for example, the whiteness of a piece of paper), which does not have a separate existence, but expresses something nonetheless: an accidental way of being ascribed to something that exists autonomously.

2. Being can also be expressed according to the categories (*kata ta schemata tes categorias*). Aristotle's categories are the major rubrics by which Being is articulated and thought. Aristotle generally lists ten such categories: substance (οὐσία / *ousia*), quality (*posón*), quantity (*potón*), relation (*prós ti*), place (*poú*), time (*poté*), position (*keîstai*), possession (*échein*), action (*poieîn*), passion (*páschein*).

Everything that exists autonomously can be called substance. It is therefore the substrate of the other qualities. The most surprising thing about these categories is that Aristotle had already spoken of this qualitative Being when discussing accidental Being. The only really "new" category is that of substance. Aristotle obviously saw in it Being in its fullest sense since all the other categories only express the properties of substance. So what is substance?

In the small treatise called the *Categories*, which Andronicus inserted at the beginning of the logical writings of the *Organon* despite its undeniable "metaphysical" import, Aristotle claims that two things can be called substance: first, individual things and second, ideas or species (εἴδη / *eidè*). Substances of the first type are "substance strictly, primarily, and most of all," and those of the second type are called "secondary substances":

A substance—that which is called substance most strictly, primarily, and most of all [κυριώτατα τε καὶ πρώτως καὶ μάλιστα / *kuriôtata te kai prôtôs kai malista*]—is that which is neither said of a subject nor in a subject; for instance, the individual man or horse. The species [εἴδη] in which the things primarily called substances are, are called *secondary substances*, as also are the genera of these species. For example, the individual man belongs in a species, man, animal is the genus of the species; so these— both man and animal—are called secondary substances.[30]

Even though the first meaning of substance is individual things existing by themselves, obviously the Aristotle of the *Categories* seems to have willingly ascribed substance to the ideas of species and genera, which brings him close to Platonism. We may, for this reason, doubt the authenticity of the *Categories*. But it may be more reasonable to read it, like Jaeger did, as an earlier work, especially since the *Metaphysics* never mentions secondary substance.

3. Being can also be used to designate something as potentiality or as actuality. This thesis (of Being as potentiality and actuality) is generally seen as a response to the immobilism of Parmenides which denied the existence of movement or change as implying a passage from Nonbeing to Being and therefore the existence of Nonbeing: an immobilism that would be fatal to physics, the whole purpose of which is to provide an account of movement. By distinguishing actuality from potentiality, Aristotle underlines the fact that movement need not necessarily imply a passage of Nonbeing to Being since it can also be understood as actualizing what had only been potentiality. Just as the artist can give a form to a statue that had been part of the marble's potentiality, a seed can become a tree and a human can become wise.

Aristotle devoted lengthy and carefully thought-out explanations to the idea of act and potentiality (particularly in *Metaphysics*, Θ) because it is important for thinking *physis*. All things in the world accomplish an act (*energeia*) that is also their purpose, which Aristotle calls their *entelechy*, their "realized Being." Everything in nature fulfills an end. Things that are not actualized and only exist as potentiality strive to achieve their purpose. Such is the case, for example, when a seed becomes, or "actualizes," a tree, when a human becomes wise or happy (according to the double purpose of theoretical philosophy and practical philosophy).

4. Finally, Being can also mean "being true." This sense is perhaps less obvious to us and owes much to the Greek language. When one says in Ancient Greek "it is," it often means that it "is true."[31] This can also be found in some modern languages. Thus in English we can say "is it not (isn't it)?" to mean "is it not true?" In French, one can say "*n'est-ce pas*," which means roughly the same. In Spanish, we can say, for example, *eso es* to signify that what has been asserted is "true" (the same goes for the German: *so ist es*). It is essentially a Greek use of the verb "to be" that Aristotle had the analytical skill to recognize and distinguish from the other uses.

It is difficult, however, to determine the exact status Aristotle gives to these different uses of the verb "to be." It is hard to tell whether it is a purely semantic distinction (which pertains solely the meaning of the term "is") or a more ontological distinction, which would distinguish different kinds of Being. For Aristotle, Being as potentiality certainly seems to be more than a linguistic devise since it expresses some ontological reality belonging to Being itself.

Obviously, there are other meanings of the verb "to be" of which Aristotle was aware but does not mention in this nomenclature. Indeed, he does not mention the difference between being (εἶναι ἁπλῶς / *einai haplôs*) and being something (εἶναι τε τι / *einai te ti*). He does, however, mention it in *On Sophistical Refutations* and the distinction will become in the Middle Ages the famous distinction between existence and essence.[32] Today we also distinguish between the predicative sense of the term (S is P: snow is white) and its use to connote something's existence (God "is").

Moreover, in the passages in which he distinguishes the different meanings of Being, Aristotle does not seem concerned with dispelling the polysemous expressions of the verb "to be." But in the books in which he expressly deals with substance, he does manifest a desire to establish its unequivocal meaning. He argues that Being has a unique or common sense (πρός ἕν / *pros hen*) that belongs to substance. All the other senses of Being relate to it as their ultimate ground in such a way that a universal theory of Being is nothing other than a theory of substance. The beginning of book Θ confirms this: "we have treated of that which *is* primarily and to which all the other categories of Being are referred—i.e., of substance. For it is in virtue of the concept of substance that the others also are said to be" (1045 b 27–30).

First Philosophy as Ousiology: *Metaphysics* Z

Aristotle's texts on the notion of substance (especially *Metaphysics*, Z, H, Θ, but also Λ) are among the hardest of the *Metaphysics*, but if first philosophy is to be a universal science of Being, they are also among its most essential. At the beginning of book Z, Aristotle "recalls" that Being's fundamental meaning is to be found in the notion of substance:

> There are several senses in which a thing may be said to "be," as we pointed out previously in our book on the various sense of words [*Metaphysics*, Δ, 7]; for in one sense it means what a thing is or a "this," and in another sense it means that a thing is of a certain quality or quantity or has some such predicate asserted of it. While 'Being' has all these senses, obviously that which is primary is the "what" [πρῶτον ὄν τι ἐστιν / *prôton on ti estin*], which indicates the substance of a thing [τὴν οὐσίαν / *tèn ousian*].[33]

If substance (*ousia*) expresses the primary meaning of Being, then first philosophy must be an ousiology: "and indeed the question which, both now and of old, has always been raised, and is always the subject of doubt, viz. what Being is, is just the question, what is substance?"[34]

So what is substance? In accordance with his laudable habit, Aristotle identifies several uses of the term in addition to the major conceptions of substance proposed by his predecessors (*Metaphysics*, Z, 2), even though many of his distinctions employ Aristotelian terms.

1. Substance first means "quiddity" (τὸ τί ἦν εἶναι / *to ti èn einai*). The term is even more extraordinary in Greek than it is in English or Latin. Quiddity, in Greek, or rather in Aristotle's Greek, literally means "what it is for it to be." The expression must have been incredible for his contemporaries. By it, Aristotle seeks to identify what is sought in a definition. When one wishes to know what a thing is, one enquires as to its "what" (*ti*), which in Latin is its *quid* and from which we get the notion of *quidditas*. And when one asks, "what is it?" the answer is always "what" the thing "is"—that is, by indicating the *to ti en einai*, the quiddity, or its "whatness" (here, more than elsewhere, a little inelegant playing with words is permitted). Aristotle's idea is that a thing's substance first means what its definition indicates. It is easy to hear an echo of Plato's ideas (*eidos*), which were said to express the essence (*ti esti*) of things.

2. Substance can also designate the universal (τὸ καθόλου / the *katholou*). Although this expression is much more familiar to us than *to ti en einai*, we must not forget, however, that Aristotle was the first to use it.[35] It must therefore have seemed quite bold when it was first used. It literally signifies "what is grasped in general"—that is, what applies to "all" beings of a given type or species. For example, all humans have in common the same "universal substance" and its associated properties. This meaning of substance or "that what it is really" is, once again, quite close to Platonism.

3. Substance can also be the genus (γένος / *genos*), according to Aristotle. This use can be seen as analogous to the "secondary substances" of the *Categories*, which ascribed the status of substance to genera and species.

4. Finally, substance can also designate the subject or substrate (τὸ ὑποκείμενον / *to hypokeimenon*). This expression, which is again Aristotle's own, literally designates what underlies ("what lies under") or is the foundation of...(an idea the Latin preserves in the terms *substantia* and *subjectum*, subject).

Aristotle obviously favors this last meaning since it fulfills the conditions required of any notion of substance-Being better than the three others. A substance cannot be a predicate of something else because it is "of which all else is predicated" (Z, 3, 1029 a 7). It is important to remember that the substrate (*to hypokeimenon*) also designates in Greek (as in English) the grammatical subject of a clause—that is, the subject of which things are predicated. This criterion for substantiality is insufficient, however, because all predicates can also be employed as subjects. Aristotle's objection (which is only intelligible on Aristotelian grounds) is that even matter could then be a substance (1029 a 10)! This would be absurd for Aristotle because matter is never a determinate something. The reason is that the decisive criteria of substantiality, of *ousia*, are "separability and individuality" (*khôriston kai tode ti*). "Separability" means that substance must exist for itself or independently. "Individuality," or being a this or a that (*tode ti*), specifies that the being in question must be a particular, or, as translators often say, an individual. But Aristotle's term need not be so abstract, he literally says a "this" and we can easily imagine professor Aristotle holding out a stylus, an apple, or some other object that exists autonomously.

For this reason, neither universals nor genera can be substances for Aristotle, or at least for the Aristotle of the *Metaphysics*. They may be grammatical subjects, but they cannot exist separately or as an easily indicated "this." Aristotle then moves on to consider three other possible candidates for the title substance (Z, 3, 1029 a 2): matter (ὕλη), form (μορφή, εἶδος / *morphè*) and the compound of matter and form (τὸ σύνολον / *to sunolon*).

Matter is immediately excluded because it does not exist autonomously— that is, without having been given some form: A pile of wood is always a pile of *wood* and not of straw. And for this reason, Aristotle says matter is "posterior" to the form that it receives and always presupposes.

Could form then be the ultimate meaning of substance, as the Platonists claimed? As we will see, *Metaphysics* Z, which evokes such a possibility without taking sides, will eventually settle on a modified version of this solution. Posterity will especially remember the third possibility, which consists in identifying substance as the compound of form and matter. It will frequently use Aristotle's most important argument for it: Substance must be a "this," which the *eidos* cannot be since it is a universal or genus.

Yet this third solution that favors the compound of form and matter has its own difficulties, which are rigorously emphasized by Aristotle himself. If substance is a compound of matter and form, its elements must then precede the compound and would be "more substance" than it.[36] And since matter is already excluded, then all that is left is form, as per Plato's claim.

So how did Aristotle then manage to distance himself from Plato? His polemic against the separate and independent existence of ideas (which Plato had rejected in the *Parmenides*) is well known. In arguing against Plato, Aristotle claims all that really exists is always a determinate "this." But what is "this," and how are we to define it? One can certainly not define it, say "what it is" or identify its quiddity, unless it is a form or an *eidos*. And Aristotle insists that an *eidos* does not exist autonomously, but only within matter. His solution consists in saying that substance is the form that already inhabits matter. "Substance is the immanent form, from which along with the matter the so-called compound substance is derived" (ἡ γὰρ οὐσία ἐστι τὸ εἶδος τὸ ἐνόν, ἐξ οὗ καὶ τῆς ὕλης ἡ σύνολος λέγεται / *hè gar ousia esti to eidos to enon, ex hou kai tes hulès hè sunolos legetai, Metaphysics*, Z, 11, 1037 a 29). Although his later commentators only remembered the emphasis on the compound, Aristotle's text states clearly that substance is not so much the compound as the "indwelling form" (*to eidos enon*), the *eidos*, even if it exists only in relation to matter. The privilege of the *eidos* is thus maintained.

Aristotle knows quite well that the compound cannot be defined. A definition, and its reference to some quiddity, always pertains to some *quid*, and thus to an *eidos*. When one wishes to define a "this," one must always refer to some *eidos*: this is an orange, a table or a piece of paper. From this follows a paradox, the consequences of which Aristotle fully accepts (see *Metaphysics*, Z, 15). If all that can be known is the *eidos*, what really exists is the *eidos* embodied by matter in accordance with such and such singular existence. Thus there is a kind of divorce between the requirements of thought and those of Being: the universal is stripped of any ontological autonomy, but it alone can be known. Only the *tode ti* or the individual exists, but it remains unknowable, or even ineffable.

Aristotle does not only speak of forms immanent to sensible matter however. There are also immaterial substances, which, in its most theological version, are supposedly the favored objects of first philosophy.

The Theology of *Metaphysics* Λ

As we already noted, although *Metaphysics*, E does give it some importance, *theologikè* is an extremely rare, even suspect, term in Aristotle's corpus. The same applies to the term *theologia*. Richard Bodéüs has argued that it may even have a pejorative sense like all the terms finishing in –*logia*.[37] Aristotle would have used the term to designate the implausible stories told about the gods. Aristotle's "theology" is not a story about the gods, however. It is a discourse on the Prime Mover (*prôton kinoûn*) that draws its essential inspiration from his physics and explains the heavenly bodies' continuous and eternal movement. Although it can be found in the *Physics* and *On the Heavens*, the most classical version of this physical explanation of celestial movement, which is the core of Aristotle's "theology," is in book XII (Lambda) of the *Metaphysics*.

Metaphysics Λ is one of the founding texts of Western theology for two very important reasons. (1) When he speaks of the Prime Mover as the cause of the heavenly bodies' movement, Aristotle is, in fact, articulating the first causal and rational explanation for the physical universe that is derived from a divine first principle (although he was only concerned with explaining celestial movement). (2) Aristotle is also the ancestor of Western theology insofar as he argues that this Prime Mover is an act that only performs the highest activity: thought. For the first time in the history of metaphysics, "God" is conceived as both the principle explaining the world and as the supreme intelligence. It will keep both characteristics in all subsequent metaphysics that speak of the divine.

The beginning of book Λ's theology (chap. 6–10) is physical: how to explain the movement of the heavenly bodies? Unlike sensible substances, the heavenly bodies' movement is circular, continuous, and eternal. This movement cannot have been caused by some prior principle—that is, by an efficient cause since it does not have any beginning (in Aristotle's Greek, the efficient cause is the *archè tès kinèseôs*: "the principle or beginning of movement"). However, all movement has some purpose; it has a goal. This final cause is the Prime Mover, which produces movement "by being loved" (*hôs erômenon*, *Metaphysics*, Λ, 7, 1072 b 3). But this mover is not itself moved since it would then require another principle to explain its movement. According to one of Aristotle's favorite arguments, "the series must stop somewhere."[38] The Prime Mover is such an ending. It is also unique, argues Aristotle in the *Physics*, because one unique mover is better than many. Quoting the *Iliad* (II, 204), he writes at the end of book Λ that "beings do not want to be governed badly: 'the rule of many is not good; let there be one ruler'" (*Metaphysics*, Λ, 1076 a 3).

Things get complicated, however, in chapter 8, which may have been inserted into book Lambda at some later time (the authenticity of this chapter is contested). Aristotle argues that if we are to explain the heavenly bodies' movement, we must posit the existence of several movers. The continuous translatory movement of the fixed stars' sphere is not the only type of movement (1073 a 26). Some bodies have a more irregular movement. Such is the case for the planets, which sometime seem to wobble or stray (from which they get their name, *planesthai*). Must we then conclude that eternal and immobile substances do not move these bodies? Certainly not, since the movement of these bodies is eternal. We must therefore posit both the existence of a plurality of "spheres," each having a regular and continuous movement, as well as their associated movers. And, since some planets seem to retrace their steps (this is the case for Mars, Jupiter, and Saturn), regressive spheres must also be posited. Ultimately, the course of each planet becomes the product of the movement of the equivalent of seven spheres. Depending on the tally, which is not all that important here, there would be forty-seven or fifty-five spheres in Aristotle's sky, all moved by an immobile and eternal mover.

How are we to reconcile the plurality of immobile and eternal movers with the unicity of the Prime Mover presented in the *Physics* and the rest of *Metaphysics* Λ? This is a problem Theophrastus,[39] Aristotle's successor at the head of the Lyceum, had to contend with. But in Platonism's wake, the idea of a hierarchy of immobile and separate substances was not exceptional. For Plato, there was a plurality of ideas all "under" the authority of a supreme principle (the idea of the Good, or the One). For Plato's disciples, Speusippus and Xenocrates, who were Aristotle's main interlocutors in book Lambda, there was a similar stratification delimiting the One from the "number-ideas" that belonged to a lower level of the intelligible realm.[40]

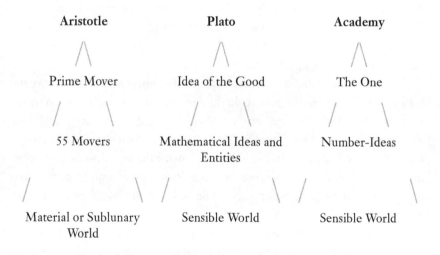

Aristotle	Plato	Academy
Prime Mover	Idea of the Good	The One
55 Movers	Mathematical Ideas and Entities	Number-Ideas
Material or Sublunary World	Sensible World	Sensible World

This stratification of transcendence was to have an important legacy in the history of metaphysics. Neoplatonism later elaborated an even more diversified hierarchy stretching from the intelligible to the sensible, derived from the idea of an *emanation* of layers or "hypostases" of reality beginning from the One. In Christian theology, which was marked by Neoplatonism, angels naturally came to occupy the lower level of the intelligible world.

In chapters 7 and 9 of book Lambda, Aristotle describes the activity of the Prime Mover, which he speaks of only in the singular. The *Physics* (256 b 25) already had already spoken, and lauded, Anaxagoras' account of the imperturbability of the Spirit that acts as the supreme cause (and final cause, for Aristotle). For Aristotle, this imperturbability means that the first principle is not moved, nor agitated, by anything. Otherwise, it would need a principle to explain its movement. But imperturbability does preclude any activity. Since immaterial beings do not have any potentiality—the potential to be something, the first mover must then be pure actuality. What would be its actuality, asks Aristotle? The only activity befitting it must be the highest. It can therefore only be thought. Its thought is one that never ceases, and would thus always be an actuality. Aristotle adds that this activity of thought corresponds to a pleasurable state or one of supreme "joy" (τὸ ἥδιστόν / *to hèdiston*) particular to the divine. Only God is capable of always thinking and of always being happy. This only happens to us in rare fleeting moments (ὡς ὑμεῖς ποτέ / *hôs humeis pote*).[41]

What would be the object of these thoughts, Aristotle also asks? Assuredly, it can only be the most dignified and most noble. It is hard to imagine the Prime Mover lowering itself to the thought of something less noble than itself. It can therefore only think itself. The activity of God can only be described as the thought of thought (νοήσις νοήσεως / *noesis noèseôs*). And we must then conclude that Aristotle's God knows nothing about our world just as he knows nothing about what he is not.

Aristotle's God, who is the final cause of the movement of the heavenly bodies and whose activity consists in thinking himself, is characterized by its supreme transcendence from our world, which he does not seem to know. Things were less neatly ordered for Plato. Although Plato was the first to separate the sensible and the intelligible and to place the principle of principles in a kind of "beyond" (*epekeina*) of the *ousia*, Plato also claimed that the idea of the Good, and the ideas that depend on it, invest our world and assure its order, symmetry, and beauty.

This brings us to a startling conclusion: although he never ceased stigmatizing Plato's ideas for their *chorismos* or being-separate, Aristotle turns out to be the real philosopher of separation. Unlike Plato who had seen the presence of the ideas and the divine everywhere, Aristotle now appears as the thinker of the great chasm separating the divine from the sensible.[42] Thus Plato and Aristotle offer two distinct ways of thinking about the metaphysics of divinity. Whereas Aristotle incites us to meditate on the radical transcendence of the divine, Plato (for whom the *epekeina tes ousias* of the idea of the Good can be thought as the supereminence of beauty and dignity) brings us to think about the immanence, the omnipresence of the divine: "all things are full of gods" (*Laws*, 899 b).

CHAPTER 4

THE LAST SUMMIT OF CLASSICAL METAPHYSICS

The Neoplatonic Eruption

Although they never practiced metaphysics in the modern sense of the term, Plato and Aristotle do nevertheless embody the summits of metaphysical thought. They were obviously oblivious to the term itself—it did not appear until the twelfth century—and when they spoke of the Ideas, of the Good, of Being as Being, and of the Prime Mover, their intention was not to inaugurate a new discipline. The idea that human thought must seek its ultimate principles and the foremost of all beings was simply a function of the natural way to wisdom. Nevertheless, Plato and Aristotle did invent the vocabulary of metaphysics. They defined its object (the *archè*, the *prôton*, the *eidos*, the Supreme Good, Being as Being), determined its universal scope (*katholou*), pursued its fundamental impulse (the *epekeina*, the *hypothesis*, the *meta*), and discovered the realm of thought (reason, the pure act, the thought of thought). All subsequent "metaphysics" has been the work of epigones—a fact recognized more often than not. The division between *platonici* and *aristotelici* separating thinkers who identify with the idealism of Plato's dialogues from those that identify with Aristotle's analytic realism, lasted through the Middle Ages, and continues even up to the present day.

One could say that School metaphysics is to the Platonic-Aristotelian inauguration of metaphysics what a literature department is to poetry. That is, a didactic attempt to understand, and even systematize, the creative impulse that precedes it but which it can never equal. Following Plato and Aristotle, the academic divisions of philosophy proliferated, Xenocrates probably being its primary instigator.[1] Philosophy was broken up into hermetically segregated, and less creative "schools" (Skepticism, Stoicism, Epicureanism) in which metaphysical thought was absent. The eclipse of metaphysics stems partially from the paucity of extant texts: Almost all of these schools' manuscripts have been lost. But the fragments we do have from the Hellenistic, or post-Aristotelian, period reveal that metaphysics was not highly regarded. In the Stoic division of philosophy into logic, physics, and ethics, physics serves as ontology since for the Stoics only bodies are real. Although Stoicism did acknowledge a Being (a something, *ti*) belonging to what can be reached by thought or language (Being as it is signified by significations or *lekta* / λεκτά), Stoic physics is anti-metaphysical, which is also the case for Skepticism and Epicureanism. Some have appropriately spoken of a "philosophy of immanence" to qualify Hellenistic thought:[2] the immanence of the universal *logos* for the Stoics, which commands moral stoicism in the face of what exists, the immanence of happiness for the Epicureans, and a doubt in transcendence, and in all truth, for the Skeptics. That said, the most important and most original revival of metaphysical thought in Antiquity appears in the thought of Plotinus.

Plotinus's Metaphysics of the One

Whoever thinks that reality is governed by chance and accident and held together by bodily causes is far removed from God and the idea of the One, and our discourse is not directed to these people, but to those who posit another nature besides bodies and have gone up as far as soul.[3]

Plotinus (c. 205–270 CE) probably considered himself quite modestly as an epigone—that is, an exegete giving new life to Plato's philosophy.[4] He is often said to be the founder of Neoplatonism, but one should not forget that this term dates from the eighteenth century. All we know of his life we owe to his biography written by his student Porphyry (c. 234–310) to whom Plotinus had entrusted the editing of his manuscripts. Porphyry tells us that Plotinus, who was born in Egypt, studied in Alexandria under the Platonist Ammonius Saccas (of whom we know nothing) before moving to Rome in 247 to teach philosophy. Plotinus's philosophy owes much to his reading of Plato, which was influenced by his reading of Aristotle, but also to religious sources that are harder to identify. His reading of Plato has continued to influence our understanding of Platonism. Even today, those who contest the testimony on Plato's unwritten doctrine—the supreme principle of which would be the One—see it as a Neoplatonic-inspired reading. But Neoplatonism, by way of Saint Augustine and Boethius, also left a mark on Christian dogmatics and thereby influenced all medieval and modern philosophy.

Plotinus read Plato as a thinker of the One from which all things proceed and to which all things aspire to return—a procession and return (even a conversion) to the One that beats the rhythm of the universe's cosmic drama. Although the One is the principle of all things, it lies beyond Being. Plotinus thus takes the radical transcendence of Plato's first principle, the *epekaina tes ousias*, quite literally. For a lack of a better word, he calls this principle the One, but he also calls it the Good, the First, or the Divine. Indeed he uses the term for lack of a better word since the One can be neither expressed nor apprehended. All that can be said of it is what it is not. Plotinus is thus the founder of what will be called, much later, negative theology. Plotinus's metaphysics is both rigorous and mystical. It is rigorous because it endeavors to show how everything, including Being itself, proceeds from the One, but it is also mystical since it appeals to a vision of the One to which the soul can be united in an ecstatic experience.

We owe Plotinus's biography to Porphyry who attended Plotinus's courses in Rome. It is often regarded with suspicion since it seems to present an idealized image of Plotinus skewed because it is presented largely from Porphyry's perspective (as if he could have written one from any other!). But his portrayal corresponds to the Plotinus we encounter in Plotinus's own writings. The first line of the *Vita Plotini*[5] sets the tone: "Plotinus seemed ashamed of being in a body." Since the body is a dispersion factor that immerses us in the multiple, it separates us from the One.

Porphyry also edited the *Enneads* (Plotinus himself never published anything). He assembled his master's small treatises together in six volumes, each having nine (*ennea*, hence the name) sections. He classified them according to a thematic ascension starting with ethics (*Enneads*, I) then moving on to physics (II), to cosmology (III), to the soul (IV), the intellect (V), and finally to Being and the One (VI).[6] Although its doctrinal relevance is obvious, one need not adopt this classification since Porphyry also gives the different chronological order of the *Enneads's* writing. It is not known whether this order is reliable, nor whether there actually were fifty-four distinct treatises to begin with, but there is no other thinker of Antiquity about whom we have such precise and precious information.

There are several ways of speaking of the One. Each of the *Enneads* is a way that leads to it or follows from it. The simplest way is found in *Treatise 9* (*Enneads*, VI, 9).[7] It recalls that nothing can be if it is not *one*.[8] There is no army if it is not *one*, nor any chorus if it is not one. Plotinus here refers to the last hypothesis of Plato's *Parmenides* (166 c): "if there is no one, there is nothing." This hypothesis is the foundation of Neoplatonism.

Now, the way just evoked—that is, the way in which all things participate in the One by virtue of their unity (an army, a chorus), may seem somewhat sophistic. If it is, this is because it seemingly implies that the One is a predicate—that is, a quality of an army or chorus. And yet, Plotinus's One is not a predicate. It is One so to speak—and this "so to speak" is applicable to all discourse on the One—because it has no other predicate than of being one. It is simply the One, the One itself. All that is not the One is multiple and is derived from it since even what is many is made up of unities. The One is therefore at the root of all things. To paraphrase Plotinus, the One is prior to all things *and* all things flow from it inasmuch as they are one. Plotinus ceaselessly tackles the questions that arise as a consequence of this: How do things emerge from the One? Does the One become multiple when it gives birth to things? The *Enneads* are fundamentally nothing more than a long and patient discussion of these questions. Although the reader must be patient, his patience is rewarded with an overflowing fountain of poetry, the source of metaphysics.

Plotinus's metaphysics takes some of Plato's most daring metaphors literally, notably the one that places the principle beyond Being (*epekeina tes ousias*). According to Plotinus, the *principle* of Being cannot belong to the domain of Being itself. Being is therefore derived from the One, a derivation akin to a "procession," which Plotinus explains with his famous three "hypostases."[9] As it is first, the One is necessarily perfect. As it is perfect, it "superabounds" and begets a thing—an "existence"—different from it:[10] Being is thus born out of the One's extreme abundance. But since it proceeds from it, this newly begotten thing, which still bears a trace of its origin, returns (*epistrophè*) or flows back to the One. Plotinus calls this vision directed at the One, intelligence or *nous*. Intelligence and Being thus constitute the One's second "hypostasis." Plotinus thus differs from Aristotle here: Intelligence is not the principle of reality since it presupposes vision and something seen, and therefore a duality. Unity is always first. The One thus suffuses Being and intelligence since what is seen, or made intelligible, is always the One and Being as its emanation. Then, continuing the work of the One, the second hypostasis, or existence, flows outward and gives birth to another unity, the third hypostasis, namely, the soul. Thus the layering of this generative process produces the world, hypostasis after hypostasis.

Let us pause here a moment because Plotinus seems to speak of the One as though he was present at the moment of the first emanation! What does he mean? One could indeed begin to suspect that Plotinus is speculating about that which precedes the soul and the intellect as their forgotten cause. However, he states that when he speaks of the One, he is in fact speaking of *us*, of our long lost origin. Pierre Hadot was right to have insisted on the following beautiful passage from *Treatise 9*:

> For to say that it is the cause is not to predicate something incidental
> of it, but of us, because we have something from it while that One is in
> itself; but one who speaks precisely should not say "that" or "is"; but we
> run round it outside, in a way, and want to explain our own experiences
> of it, sometimes near it and sometimes falling away in our perplexities
> about it.[11]

The self-sufficient One has no need of us to be what it is. All discourse about the One is a discourse of the soul about itself longing to return to the One. Plotinus often compares the One and its outpouring to the sun's rays. "The only reasonable explanation of the act flowing from the One lies in the analogy of light from the sun."[12] The metaphor is obviously of Platonic origin, but it nevertheless allows Plotinus to suggest how everything exists in the One's light without being the One itself. Moreover, something thus lit up cannot glimpse the One itself which is both transcendent and immanent in relation to it. Prior to all things, the One is rigorously ineffable (*arrheton*, V, 3, 13) to use an expression similar to Plato's in the *Seventh Letter* (341 c 5). No matter what we say, sighs Plotinus, we always say *something*. Strictly speaking, the One does not have a name (Ibid.). To say that it is one is really a makeshift solution, a manner of speaking. But despite the impossibility of expressing or understanding it with words, we may still grasp it, says Plotinus. Since we proceed from it, we are always bathed in its light. We can feel its presence and be reunited with it.[13] For Plotinus, love best expresses this union insofar as love is to desire a union with the one that makes us whole. But unlike the lovers' external embrace, the love Plotinus evokes is one in which we are reunited through an inner embrace that leaves no part of us bereft of the One.[14]

How are we to carry out this union? Plotinus answers with a famous imperative: "take away everything!" (ἄφελε πάντα / *aphele panta*).[15] Obviously, it is easier said than done. And, once again, it is a negative act of the soul on itself, which is urged to focus solely on what is essential, or even, what is beyond essence!

Now, quite obviously, this is the soul exhorting itself. The soul, which proceeds from the One, seeks in vain to exist by itself and to be, like the One, a self-sufficient principle. Such is the vanity of all souls carried far from the One as if by some centrifugal force. Plotinus's discourse thus tries to draw the soul back from its estrangement, from its separation (διάστασις) in time,[16] and return it to its essential Center. He calls on it to convert and to return by following in reverse order the procession of things back to the One. A long solitary road, but one that expresses the essential, perhaps even tragic, tendency of the human soul. This may be the reason for the last line of the treatise, which Porphyry placed at the end of all the *Enneads* and which must have appeared to him as Plotinus's final words: "the passing of solitary to solitary" (μόνος πρὸς μόνος / *monos pros monos* [VI, 9]).

Plotinus's metaphysics is both simple and demanding. Indeed, it is easy to understand that all things are a unity, that a "principle" is required to understand them, and that this principle is so unique that it can only be called the One. Metaphysics, insofar as it seeks "first" principles, is necessarily Plotinian or it is not metaphysics. By this same rigor, "so to speak," the One remains inexpressible. All discourse belongs to a soul attempting to understand from whence it comes and where it is headed. How else are we to accomplish this reflection, and become conscious of our centrifugal separation, than by ridding ourselves of the inessential things that distract our attention in this life?

Plotinus's very human metaphysics has had a profound impact on western spirituality. All persons that question the meaning of their existence, or feel it is multifariously dispersed, all those who feel their life is an odyssey or an adventure needing direction will recognize their plight in Plotinus's meditation. On that count, we are all Neoplatonists.

It is easy to see how the Church Fathers spontaneously recognized themselves in the Neoplatonic vocabulary and silently arrogated it. Not only did they borrow its terms when developing the doctrine of the three hypostases of the Trinity, but the Plotinian procession from the One was also easily reconciled with a *creatio ex nihilo*, which did not have any real equivalent in Plato or Aristotle's metaphysics. Moreover, since for Plotinus this generation of Being was the result of the superabundance or generosity of the first principle, it was then easy to recast it as love and light. Christian authors would also understand the soul's descent into sin as a flight from its Center, towards which it can always return (by *con-version*, thought as a return to its origin). It is Neoplatonism that never did and never would recognize itself in the idea of a god made flesh. One must wonder if Christian doctrine itself was ever able to think this incarnation as anything other than a debasement—that is, in any way other than Neoplatonically.

But even if it was above all the Christian world that appropriated Plotinus's thought—an appropriation that was not devoid of polemics given that orthodox Neoplatonism was often considered one of the principal heresies that had to be stamped out—Plotinus gained considerable following in Greek antiquity from Porphyry to Proclus (412–485). A commentary on Plato's *Parmenides* by Porphyry contains the first occurrence in Western thought of the "ontological difference" between Being and *beings* (αὐτὸ τὸ εἶναι τὸ πρὸ τοῦ ὄντος / *auto to einai to pro tou ontos*).[17] Boethius (480–524), a Christian author who had studied in Athens, then took up this ontological distinction in the *Hebdomades* (*De hebdomadibus*). He was also the author of a classical work in the Latin tradition, *Consolation of Philosophy*, written during his captivity after an arrest on charges of conspiracy and magic for which he was executed in 524. Nevertheless, Boethius's influence on the Middle Ages was very important. Not only did he import Neoplatonism from the Eastern to the Western Roman Empire.[18] He also translated and wrote a commentary to Aristotle's logical writings (*Categories, On Interpretation, Prior Analytics, Topics, Sophistical Refutations*). These translations were the basis of scientific education throughout most of the Latin Middle Ages. But before Boethius, Saint Augustine of Hippo (354–430) had already incorporated large parts of Neoplatonic metaphysics into Christian thought, which was to dominate all of the history of Western metaphysics up to and including Descartes, Kant, Hegel, and Heidegger.

Augustine's Christianization of Metaphysics

Of all the ancient authors whose texts have survived, Augustine is the most prolific: He left us no less that five million words![19] His most important work is a stirring autobiography, the *Confessions* (written between 397 and 401), which is one of the few books in the history of Western metaphysics that is also a masterpiece of world literature. We may speak of "metaphysics" here since Augustine, in his *Confessions*, gives an account of his intellectual development that was influenced by Greek metaphysics, especially Neoplatonism.[20] However, he was first schooled in literature and rhetoric under the influence of

Cicero's writings, which left a profound impression on his style and thought. Augustine was a talented orator and a brilliant professor of rhetoric. In 384, when he was only thirty years old, he was granted the prestigious post of official rhetor in Milan, which James J. O'Donnell describes as the most important "chair" of the entire Latin world.[21]

But in his later writings, starting with his *Confessions*, Augustine tends to deprecate this strictly literary art at which he excelled. Instead, he lauds a more philosophical, more "Platonic," wisdom, one that he rather ingenuously linked to Christian revelation, an identification that subsequent metaphysics would never call into question. The sources of his conversion are indeed surprisingly philosophical. In his *Confessions*, Augustine makes much of the philosophical turn that he ascribes to reading Cicero's *Hortensius* when he was nineteen. Although the work itself is lost, we can nevertheless get an idea of it from its surviving fragments and from Cicero's philosophical works. Cicero's *Hortensius* was inspired by Aristotle's *Protrepticus* and was written as an incitation to wisdom—Augustine understood it as an *exhortatio ad philosophiam* (*Confessions*, Book III, chapter 4, section 7)—to a philosophical life that renounces temporal affairs to devote itself to a spiritual life dedicated to the intelligible world. This (Neo)platonic ideal of wisdom and transcendence imbued Augustine's first dialogues, which are often called the Cassiciacum writings after the name of the small village near Milan where they were written shortly after his religious conversion in 387 (*Against the Academics, The Good Life, On Order, Soliloquies, On the Immortality of the Soul, The Teacher,* and others).[22] Written a decade after these dialogues, the *Confessions* further maintained the view that his *conversion to philosophy* in 373 was the first step to his religious conversion in 387. It may be read as a sign that Augustine did not wish to insist on what separated Christian revelation from Platonic metaphysics but on what united them. If one may speak of Augustine's Christianization of Greek metaphysics, one may also speak of a metaphysical rendering of Christianity itself.

Augustine begins his *Confessions* with the human heart's inquietude, the *inquietum cor nostrum* (*Confessions*, I, 1). Our existence's perpetual restlessness—an existence that is a question for itself—stems, as Augustine explains in a Plotinian way, from its multifarious dispersion (*in multa defluximus*),[23] which he associates with corporeal, or sensual, temptations. His *Confessions* are the tale of the heart's conversion and flight from bodily temptations, curiosity, and ambition, toward the One in which the soul can finally find solace. God is thus "rest" itself, as he says in the last lines of the *Confessions*.

Augustine's metaphysics is novel insofar as it is written in the first person (Descartes can be considered Augustinian in this respect). It relates his conversion's odyssey and is a confession in all the senses of the term. It is both a laudatory confession (*confessio laudis*) addressed directly to God, and an admission of guilt (*confessio peccatorum*) recognizing that our finitude, when it seeks in vain to be its own principle, turns away from the divine *stabilitas* (II, 10, 28) and enters a state of extreme poverty (*regio egestatis*).

But where is this divine stability and rest to be found? Although Cicero may have introduced him to philosophy, Augustine was first seduced by the Manichean doctrine professed by the Babylonian prophet Mani (216–277). Today Manichaeism is often understood to be a sect offering cheap esotericism, and Augustine is certainly partially responsible for this caricature. But at the time it was, in fact, a widespread doctrine that offered a rational explanation of our universe's genesis and could therefore claim to be a form of wisdom. Its main ideas are well known: there is in God a duality of two great principles, Good and Evil, engaged in a fierce struggle. In a first, primeval war, the principle of Evil revolted against the principle of Light. This struggle had implications for human nature: Whereas the human body is cloaked in darkness, the soul is a parcel of light waiting to be saved through the intercession of Christ the promised mediator. His final victory will be that of the principle of the Light over Darkness.

Mani's wisdom had the obvious virtue of explaining the existence of evil. Augustine admits to being close to the Manichean sect for at least nine years. But he started to doubt its credibility because its followers had an overly material conception of divinity. How, asks Augustine, could there be in God, the seat of the highest Good, an original duality of good and evil? If, as Greek metaphysics teaches, God were incorruptible, it would then be blasphemous to see him as a principle of corruption. But, as James O'Donnell has pointed out, it is uncertain whether the great metaphysical principle of divine immutability is really in keeping with the Holy Scriptures.[24]

For Augustine, the solution to this aporia lies in a new approach to the Scriptures and divine nature, which he surprisingly discovered in "Platonism." He describes this decisive reading in a dramatic and enigmatic passage from his *Confessions* (VII, 9, 13): "Therefore You brought in my way by means of a certain man—an incredibly conceited man—some books by the Platonists (*quosdam platonicorum libros*) translated from Greek into Latin." Although nobody has yet accurately identified what books he is speaking of,[25] it must surely have been texts by Plotinus or Porphyry translated by Marius Victorius, a Latin writer who, before Augustine, had converted to Christianity. Although he does not identify the book, he does say what he read:

In them I found, though not the very words, yet the thing itself and proved by all sorts of reasons: that *in the beginning was the Word and the Word was with God and the Word was God: He was in the beginning with God; all things were made by Him and without Him was made nothing that was made; in Him was life and the life was the light of men, and the light shines in darkness and the darkness did not comprehend it.* I found in those same writings that the soul of man, though it gives *testimony of the light,* yet is not itself the light; but the Word, God Himself, *is the true light which enlightens every man that comes into this world;* and that He was in the world and *the world was made by him, and the world knew Him not.*[26]

How astonishing! Augustine claims to have found in the books written by Platonists a passage quite obviously drawn from the fourth Gospel! What is all the more astonishing is that this passage from the New Testament asserts something no Neoplatonist would ever accept: the Word made flesh. Indeed, they had always considered incarnation to be contrary to the idea of the divine. Augustine does make a point of saying he never found the idea of incarnation in these texts,[27] it was an idea he only found in Holy Scriptures. So why does Augustine say he found in the Platonic books a passage echoing the fourth Gospel? Even though the practice goes against our philological scruples, Augustine here employs a rhetorical device[28] that was not unusual for the period and which allowed him to emphasize the *fundamental agreement* between Christian revelation and the most powerful philosophy of his time: (Neo)platonism. Whereas we would be tempted to emphasize the difference between the two, Augustine underlines their convergence without glossing over their differences. Basically, what Augustine says is that in the books written by the Platonists one can find all of Christianity's main ideas, except the doctrine of the incarnation of the Word. At a time when Christianity was not yet dominant and still competed with the pagan cults, Augustine needed to show how it agreed perfectly with the metaphysics of his time. But for Augustine, this was not Plotinus or Porphyry's metaphysics, it was the metaphysics of the principle itself that had to be thought.

Nevertheless, Augustine uses (Neo)platonic imagery to describe this divine principle. He claims that the *libri platonicorum* introduced him first to an exhortation to return inward into his most intimate Being.[29] It is there, says Augustine, in a text that all agree is drawn directly from Plotinus, that

... with the eye of my soul, such as it was, I saw Your unchangeable Light, shining far above my spiritual ken, transcending my mind [*supra eundem*

oculum animæ meæ, supra mentem meam, lucem incommutabilem]. It was not the
light of everyday that the eye of flesh can see, nor some light of the same
order, such as might be if the brightness of our daily light should be seen
shining with a more intense brightness and filling all things with its greatness. Your light was not that, but other, altogether other, than all such
lights.[30]

Augustine clearly uses Platonic rather than scriptural terminology to
describe his ecstatic experience. But he also refers to biblical texts when he
says this ecstasy led him to understand what God had said to Moses when
he had proclaimed: "I am I who am," *ego sum qui sum* (Exodus 3: 14, quoted in
VII, 10, 16). It is easier to doubt one's own existence, explains Augustine, than
Truth's. God's Being should be understood as the fullest Being, the permanent Being, the source of all Being. All things inferior to him "neither absolutely are nor yet totally are not: they are, in as much as they are from You:
they are not, in as much as they are not what you are. For that truly is, which
abides unchangeably."[31] Augustine seems here to unknowingly develop an
ontology that affirms the Platonic identity between Being, real Being (*id enim
vere est*), and permanent Being (*quod incommutabiliter manet*), a tripartite identity which alone can be the object of a spiritual vision.

Augustine consistently calls God's Being the *Idipsum*,[32] meaning "the very
thing itself." One could say, following Exodus 3: 14, "Being itself," in the permanent sense of the verb "to be." But the *idipsum* also refers to Being in itself,
to the *kath'auto* of the Platonic idea that exists by itself and is "the very thing
that is." Augustine also says that this being, which has the highest degree of
existence, is supremely good ("*qui summe Bonus est, quia summe est*"; XII, 15,
19). Thus there is an identity between the supreme being and the supreme
goodness, or the supreme good. But this good is of so high a rank that it is
even greater and better than anything we can imagine ("*neque enim ulla anima
umquam potuit poteritve cogitare aliquid quod sit te melius, qui summum et optimum
bonum es*": VII, 4, 6), says Augustine in striking anticipation of an expression
Saint Anselm will later make famous. Thus this intelligible reality can only
be perceived through an illuminating experience that exceeds our comprehension. As with Plato, Aristotle, and Plotinus, we can only draw near it in
very brief ecstatic moments such as those described in books VII and IX of
the *Confessions* because we are always subject to time, a difficult condition that
prevents us from adequately grasping the eternal reality.

Augustine's reflections are also of foundational importance for metaphysics since they are also a meditation on our temporal condition. Unlike what

Aristotle had argued in his *Physics*, for Augustine time is more than a measure of movement. It is primarily the expression of our Being's agitation and multifarious dispersion. The reflections on time, found in book XI of the *Confessions*, follow Plotinus (*Enneads*, III, 7), who had been the first to speak of a *diastasis* of the soul. Augustine expresses this as a *distentio animi*, a distension of the soul—literally, a "diversion" (*dis*) of the tension (*tentio*) essential to the soul, which seeks a return to its Center. The diverted soul lives in a state of dispersion represented by the "ecstasies" of time: the past, present, and future, which are, for Augustine, real only insofar as the soul has a memory (of the past), pays attention (to the present) and anticipates (the future). How is one to escape from this distention, from this "diverted tension," other than by redirecting the *intentio* towards the eternal, like the way the One draws us away from our multifarious distractions?

This is why Augustine borrows the important Neoplatonic theme of conversion (ἐπιστροφή / *epistrophè*) that runs throughout the *Confessions*. For the Neoplatonists, it was a return to the One. The theme also comes from the New Testament: *metanoiete*, "convert!" said John the Baptist (Matthew 3: 2). But it was Plato, once again, who first called for a μετανοία / *metanoia*, or for a complete transformation of the soul.

But what is specific to Augustine, and the Christian message, is the insistence that Christ is the mediator. An intercession that nevertheless employs the language of (Neo)platonic metaphysics:

> behold my life is no more than anxious distraction [*ecce distentio est vita mea*]. Thy right hand has help me up in my Lord, the Son of Man who is the Mediator between you, the one God, and us, the many, who are pulled many ways by multifarious distractions [*te unum et nos multos in multis per multa*]—that through Him I may apprehend in whom I am apprehended and may be set free from what I once was, to pursue the One: forgetting the things that are behind and drawn on, undistracted, [*non distentus, sed extensus*] not to future things doomed to pass away, but to my eternal goal. With no distracted mind but with focused attention [*non secundum distentionem sed secundum intentionem*] I follow on to the prize of our heavenly calling, to that place where I may hear the sound of Thy praise and contemplate Thy delight, which neither comes nor passes away.[33]

Although the Word was made flesh, the most important idea for Augustine is its call to transcend the sensible. The soul is distracted in this sensible world. It is agitated, rest-less, it pines for the "intelligible world,"[34] which is its real home. In the masterpiece of his later period, Augustine calls the soul's intelligible home, *The City of God*, an idea also inspired by Neoplatonism. Augustine was fond of quoting a passage form the *Enneads* (*Enneads*, I, 6, 8): "We must fly, therefore, to our beloved fatherland, where dwells both our Father and all else. Where is the ship, then and how are we to fly? We must become like God."[35]

Augustine, more than any author, thus contributed to the Christian appropriation of Platonic thought's horizon and its idea of an intelligible world, more essential than our own. By this, Augustine erected the foundations of "medieval metaphysics" that rested on the identity of the supreme wisdom sought by the Greeks, the science of the first principles of Being as Being, and the revealed wisdom of Holy Scripture.

CHAPTER 5

METAPHYSICS AND THEOLOGY

IN THE MIDDLE AGES

A "Metaphysical" Era?

According to common belief, the Middles Ages were the golden age of metaphysics. Medieval philosophers were united by a common and uncontested "theology" that posited God as the first principle from which all beings are derived. The entire medieval period would thus have been an incessant scholastic reiteration of the onto-theology of *Metaphysics* E, 1, which Augustine had supposedly consolidated. But this view overlooks the fact that Augustine owed much more to Neoplatonism, which was less readily accessible during the medieval period. Moreover, it also holds that Modernity overturned this metaphysics by showing that human reason can know nothing outside of the realm of experience. Modernity, which is founded on a human subject's capacity to know, would therefore be thought to *define itself* by its rejection of metaphysics, which the "middling" Middle Ages supposedly practiced ad nauseam. However, as recent medieval scholarship shows, this stubbornly held view is unfounded.

Unlike what is commonly believed, medieval thought did not identify itself as "metaphysical" thought. Even philosophers such as Albert the Great and Thomas Aquinas, who are often made into the illustrious representatives of medieval metaphysics, never presented their work as metaphysics. To my knowledge, no thinker of the Latin Middle Ages (the case is different in the Arab world) presented *his* own philosophy as "metaphysics" and said: Here is "my" metaphysics or my "conception of the world." Doing so will become quite frequent during Modernity, however, when metaphysical visions of the world became dominant.[1] But no such attitude can be found in the Middle Ages. The term metaphysics is most often used during this period to designate Aristotle's text, which thinkers strove to *comment.* And in these commentaries on the *Metaphysics,* the first concern was in fact to seek its "subject," which was universally recognized to be ambiguous and in need of clarification. This has led Jean-Luc Marion to say: "Paradoxically, the historical period generally recognized to be the golden age of "metaphysics" was characterized by an extreme reticence to use a term which, more than any other, was thought to be eminently problematic."[2]

In fact, medieval Latin thought always considered metaphysics to be a science inherited and *received from the Greeks* by way of the Arab world. Although it always tried to assimilate this inheritance through commentaries that de facto extended that of the older Greek commentators, medieval thought perceived it as the product of circumstances very different from its own, marked as it was by Revelation. For this reason, it is perhaps inappropriate to speak of "Jewish," "Christian," or "Islamic" metaphysics. For most medieval thinkers (the situation was different for Augustine, as we have seen), metaphysics was always the *other* way of thinking developed by the great, albeit pagan, thinkers of the Greek world. Medieval Latin thought was well aware that Aristotle's classical metaphysics contained elements contrary to Revelation, foremost of which was the idea that the world was eternal.

Thus in a way, metaphysical thought was foreign to the Middle Ages. Medieval thinkers reacted in one of two ways when confronted with this different way of thinking. They either reinforced its heterogeneity by discrediting metaphysical (or rational) thought because it was judged heretical or vain, or they attempted to appropriate its strangeness by showing how Revelation fulfilled the explanatory impulse of natural reason's metaphysics.

It is important to remember that metaphysics, which was then essentially Aristotelian, entered the Latin West in the *latter* part of the Middle Ages. Until the thirteenth century, the only known and sanctioned Aristotelian writings in Western Europe were the texts on logic translated by Boethius. The Neoplatonists, starting with Porphyry, considered Aristotle's *logical* writings as the most important (they were the only ones Augustine knew). They were seen as the rigorous, and definitive, analysis of the working of the human mind and served as a propaedeutic to Plato's more advanced writings. For example, the *Isagoge*, Porphyry's introduction to the *Categories*, was undoubtedly the most elementary treatise of medieval philosophy since all doctrinal education began with its study.[3] Thus Aristotle's, or Porphyry's, logical writings were important for the early "pre-metaphysical" Middle Ages, which was completely ignorant of Aristotle's metaphysical texts.

Aristotle's *Metaphysics* arrived in Western Europe after a complex sojourn beginning in the Byzantine world, which passed it on to the Syrian and the Arab world.[4] Arab philosophers were the first to honor metaphysics once again at a time when it was still denounced in the West for its defense of the eternity of the world. The most important figures in the revival of metaphysics were al-Farabi (870–950), Avicenna (980–1037), and Averroes (1126–1198), along with the theologian al-Gazhali (1058–1111). The latter criticized Avicenna, opposed the "incoherence of the philosophers," and called for a return to Qur'anic orthodoxy. But despite their doctrinal differences, al-Farabi, Avicenna, and Averroes all spontaneously recognized that metaphysics, or the "divine science" as they called it, was the highest science since it offered a principial and universal explanation of Being as a whole. More importantly, however, they also understood that despite its pagan origin this science could be reconciled with Qur'anic teaching, which *also* taught that the world had been "caused" by a supreme principle.[5] Thus through these Arab thinkers the "divine science" was once again honored and eventually drew the attention of the most ambitious thinkers of the Latin West.

The Latin translation of Aristotle's metaphysical works, then largely unknown in the West, was made possible by the contact between the Latin and the Arab worlds in what is now Spain.[6] There was then an important school of translation in Toledo where the masterpieces of the Arab world, along with Aristotle's *Metaphysics*, were translated into Latin.[7] The most important figures in the introduction of metaphysics into the West were Albert the Great (c. 1193–1280, the author of an important commentary on Aristotle's *Metaphysics*) and Thomas Aquinas (c. 1224–1274). It is to them that we owe the conciliation of Aristotle's metaphysical thought, transmitted by the Arabs, with Latin Christianity. It led to what has been called "rebirth of metaphysics in the twelfth and thirteenth centuries."[8] Following Thomas Aquinas's example, the late Middle Ages often referred to Aristotle as the *philosophicus* (the philosopher), and all medieval philosophy is often called Aristotelian. In fact, Aristotle did not become important until late, around the thirteenth century, and Thomas Aquinas was perhaps an isolated, or less important, figure than has previously been thought. On this, Alain de Libera, one of the great proponents of a reading of the Middle Ages less centered on Thomas Aquinas, wrote:

> For most historians of philosophy, the Middle Ages in general and the thirteenth century in particular, are the dark years of Aristotle's intellectual dictatorship. Nothing is farther from the truth. Aristotelian philosophy is not all of medieval thought. One could even say that anti-Aristotelian philosophy was the predominant tendency in the Middle Ages.[9]

His assessment may be a tad extreme. The reader should note that his primary goal was to oppose the previously canonical description given by Etienne Gilson, notably in *L'Être et l'essence* (1948; partially translated into English as *Being and Some Philosophers*, 1949) for whom Thomism represented the summit of "medieval metaphysics" (although, as we have seen, there was no such thing and we will see later why speaking of "Thomistic metaphysics" is inaccurate). As De Libera recalls, the Church banned the reading of Aristotle in the thirteenth century because his metaphysical writings were contrary to official doctrine. Although it may be hard to believe today, in his time, Thomas Aquinas was heretical. The universities of Paris and Oxford even censured some of his ideas in 1280, six years after his death.

Thus it is perhaps inappropriate to associate the Middle Ages with the high-point of Aristotelian, and more importantly, Thomistic metaphysics.[10] The Middle Ages produced a more varied and more audacious philosophical landscape than the one Modernity's monochromatic vision of the time would credit. But these conceptions are difficult to identify. The Middle Ages did not value originality and innovation as much as we do since truth and novelty were not believed to be coextensive concepts. Nor did the Middle Ages see any metaphysics written in the first person like Augustine's *Confessions*. We will have to wait until the beginning of Modernity and the works of Descartes before metaphysics reappears in a rather hyperbolic form that will set-off the modern metaphysics of the *ego*.

The Importance of *Pistis*

The principal difference between medieval "metaphysics" and that of the Ancients from which the former was derived is the obvious importance of faith. To varying degrees, faith has since become a largely unnoticed part of our philosophical heritage (the idea that philosophy stems from a personal commitment or conviction is one of the many almost invisible traces it has left). The Middle Ages was well aware of the opposition between faith and reason, a point it ceaselessly discussed. Faith (πίστις / *pistis*) acknowledges that it draws its essential truths from a revelation inscribed in a holy text (the Bible, the New Testament, or the Qur'an). Although Greek metaphysics, as we have seen, did sometimes allude to something like a "revelation," especially in the works of Parmenides and Plato, reason (*nous*, *noesis*) always justified its reflections. It is important to remember here that Plato, in *Republic* VI, contrasted reason with πίστις. His use of the term should not be translated as "faith," however, since, for Plato, it represented a lower, and imperfect, level of knowledge that he associated with opinions or "sensible certitude," which are produced in us by the visible world. For Plato, πίστις, rendered in Latin as *fides*,[11] is naturally inferior to rational knowledge, which pertains to the eternal truths of the ideas. The Middle Ages, however, inverted this hierarchy and contrasted the "credence" of faith, founded upon Revelation, with the pretensions of human reason. Thus the Middle Ages were marked by a decisive confrontation between faith and reason.

The conflict between faith and reason may go back as far as the first century of the Christian era. Saint Paul, who was one of the first to spread the Christian faith, and probably the author of the oldest texts of the New Testament, gave a speech to philosophers gathered together in the Areopagus in Athens. He had wanted to hold forth on the resurrection of the dead, but the philosophers were not very receptive and said: "we will hear you on this subject some other time" (Acts 17: 32). This antipathy was mutual. According to Paul, God has "shown that this world's wisdom is foolishness" (I Corinthians 1: 20) and stigmatized the vanity of the *sapienta mundi*, which Augustine would further assail by denouncing the voyeurism of the *curiositas*.[12] True wisdom comes from *divine* revelation and can only be attained through faith, which is a gift of God (Ephesians 2: 8).

The Christian faith's anti-intellectual response to rational wisdom led the Christian apologist Tertullian (c. 155–220) to his emblematic expression *credo quia absurdum*, "I believe because it is absurd."[13] Emperor Constantine's conversion in 312 gradually imposed Christianity on the Roman world and its successors. From then on, theology dominated philosophy in the Latin West. The most important thinkers of the early Christian era were the Church fathers (such as Origen and Jerome) who drew inspiration, as Augustine did, from the Neoplatonic doctrines of the time. But their efforts were directed towards the consolidation of Christian doctrine and its defense against pagan heresies. Christianity and pagan philosophy appeared to be irreconcilable in many ways, especially on questions pertaining to the creation and eternity of the world. Two contrary paths to truth could not coexist. Some fathers, such as Clement of Alexandria (150–215) in the *Stromata*, attempted (unlike Tertullian) to reassert the value of philosophy by arguing reason had been created and therefore willed by God. Although this irenic position was most probably shared by many philosophers, during a part of the Middle Ages, the intransigence with which Saint Paul and Augustine had criticized the vanity of human *curiositas* justified and encouraged a rather intolerant attitude toward the now-pagan philosophies. In 529, the emperor Justinian closed the last Greek school of philosophy, the Neoplatonic school in Athens.[14]

So for many centuries the cultural legacy of Western metaphysics was interrupted. The classic works of Greek philosophy, those of Plato, Aristotle, and Plotinus were only preserved in the Byzantine and Arab world. In 529, when the Platonic school was closed, Simplicius, who gave us Parmenides' *Poem* and who was the last pagan philosopher, fled to Persia. The transfer of knowledge called the *translatio studiorum* then began and would continue until the end of the Middle Ages.[15]

Marked as it was by the importance of faith, it is easy to understand how "metaphysics" was mainly theological during the Middle Ages. The Greeks had themselves defined wisdom and philosophy as the search for truth[16] and for *first principles*. But for Christianity, truth had been revealed once and for all in the Holy Scriptures and the apostolic tradition carried on by the Church and councils, and all possible wisdom a human could hope for was contained therein. Hence the temptation, or necessity, of condemning as heresy everything that appeared to stray from this divine authority, naturally superior to human reason. But this essentially theological outlook sometimes took on a more philosophical character especially when came time to elaborate rational arguments proving the existence of God. One of the first great medieval philosopher-theologians to have developed such an argument was Anselm of Canterbury.

Anselm and the Ontological Argument

For several reasons, Saint Anselm of Canterbury (1033–1109) is one of the most important figures in history of metaphysics. Bishop and theologian, his writings give us an idea of the state of medieval thought *before* the reintroduction of Aristotle's *metaphysical* works into the West. Furthermore, Anselm developed an argument for the existence of God, which was much later called the ontological argument. This argument is a red-thread that runs through the history of metaphysics. It was criticized by Thomas Aquinas, taken up by

Descartes (in his fifth *Meditation*) and Spinoza, and then dismissed by Kant,[17] before being rehabilitated by Schelling and Hegel. One can say that Anselm practiced metaphysics—or ontology, if we are to speak like Kant—unaware, or despite himself. In addition to its great legacy, Anselm's proof is simple and classic, but often misunderstood.

His argument appears in 1077 in the *Proslogion* (address, allocution), which is part of a work originally tellingly entitled *Fides quærens intellectum*, or faith seeking reason (a expression attributed to Augustine). Although faith is posited first, it seeks to understand what it believes. Faith is the condition that makes intelligence possible, rather than the contrary: I do not seek to understand in order to believe; I believe in order to understand.[18]

How does faith understand God? We believe, answers Anselm, You are—it is first a prayer addressed to God—"something than which nothing greater can be thought" (*aliquid quo nihil majus cogitari possit*), or, according to the expression used in chapter XIV "nothing better (*melius*) can be thought." The existence of God is not a problem for faith as it is its absolute *prius*. Only the fool (the *insipiens*), the senseless, says: "There is no God" (Psalm 14: 1). Anselm writes his *Proslogion* to show the fool that if he, the fool, thinks God, the fool can only acknowledge that He is, or if the fool thinks that He is not, He is not God.

Anselm asks the fool to begin with what he means when he says that God is something so great that nothing greater can be thought. If the fool understands what he means when he speaks of God in this way, even if it is to foolishly deny God's existence, he cannot then deny God's existence. Indeed, and this is the crux of Anselm's argument, if God only exists as a thought, and not as a reality, he is not the *greatest* thing that can thought—and he is consequently not God—because what really exists is greater that what exists only in thought:

> But when this same fool hears me say "something than which nothing greater can be thought," he surely understands what he hears; and what he understands exists in his mind, even if he does not understand that it exists [in reality]. For it is one thing for an object to exist in the mind, and another thing to understand that an object exists [in reality]. When a painter, for example, plans beforehand what he is going to paint, he has [the picture] in his mind, but he does not yet think that it actually exists because he has not yet painted it. But once he has painted it, then he both has it in his mind and understands that it exists because he has now painted it.[19]

The analogy of the painter, which is sometimes ignored by interpreters, is crucial for understanding Anselm's argument. We may distinguish two things: (1) the painting that does not yet exist and only exists as a project in the painter's mind; (2) the painting that exists in reality. The distinction can be made again once the painting has been painted. One can always distinguish the painting as it is thought from the real painting. Since this distinction can always be made, Anselm then asks a purely quantitative question: Which of the two is the "most" (*majus*), the greatest, of the two? Anselm answers the real painting is the greatest, since it comprises both the painting existing in the mind *and* the one that exists in reality. Together these things are greater than the one that is only thought. Anselm then transposes this argument to that than which nothing greater can be thought, namely, God:

> So even the fool must admit that something than which nothing greater can be thought exists at least in the mind, since he understands this when he hears it, and whatever is understood exists in the mind. And surely that than which a greater cannot be thought cannot exist in the mind alone. For if it exists only in the mind, *it can be thought to exist in reality also, which is greater* [*quod majus est*]. So if that than which a greater cannot be thought exists only in the mind, then the very thing that than which a greater *cannot* be thought is something that than which a greater *can* be thought. But this is obviously impossible. Therefore there is no doubt that something than which a greater cannot be thought exists both in the mind and in reality.[20]

Anselm's argument applies the distinction between the two paintings—the real and the thought—to God. If that which is greatest than any thought only exists in thought, then *it is not that which is greatest* since one can always think of something even greater. That is, something that exists also in reality, which is "more" (*quod majus est*), or greater than anything that can only be thought.

A God who only exists in our mind is not the greatest thing that can be thought since a God who *also* exists in reality is even greater. Gilson says the argument "works by comparing Being that is thought to real Being, which obliges the mind to posit the second as superior to the first."[21] But it is not only ontologically superior, it also something "more"—that is, more than something that is only thought.

After Anselm, the same argument will reappear elsewhere and will come to be expressed in different ways, sometimes in ways that go well beyond what Anselm says in this text. One of its customary forms uses the concept of *perfection*, such as in Descartes's version. If God did not exist, God would lack a perfection, namely, existence. It could therefore not be the most perfect being.[22] But Anselm's argument never uses the idea of perfection or the idea of a God that must contain all perfections.

Another common misinterpretation of Anselm's argument—and probably the most tenacious—is the claim Anselm starts from a prior *concept* of God or a certain idea of God.[23] This is again to read Anselm from the perspective of Descartes. For what does Anselm himself say? He says that *God is greater than everything that can be thought*. It is a way of saying that I *have no* prior idea, or any adequate idea, of God, and if I were to have one, God would be greater still. God is such that he exceeds all concepts. Anselm thus starts with what Jean-Luc Marion has called a "non-concept" of God:

> What is here a non-concept is stated in a first formula: *id quod majus cogitari nequit* or *aliquid quo nihil majus cogitari possit*, 'that than which a greater cannot be thought.' The only thing that God admits as a quasi-concept is his own transcendence with regard to any thinkable concept.[24]

I may develop as many concepts of God as I want, but he will always be greater than any of them; he exceeds them all. So since the God who transcends all my concepts is always more or better (*majus, melius*) if he exists, then God exists even though I cannot have an adequate concept of him.

Why has this argument been called ontological? It was Kant who first used the term some six hundred years after Anselm. According to Kant, "ontological" means here that the argument only stems from the *Being* or idea of God as it may be analyzed by reason. The ontological (or *a priori*) argument is thus distinguished from an argument from the effects, or an *a posteriori* argument. To argue God's existence *a posteriori* is to show that a first and necessary being must exist because of its effects, which can be observed in the world. But to argue God's existence *a priori* is to only consider God's "Being," such as reason thinks it. It is therefore starting from a concept of God's Being (or "essence") that his existence can be deduced, an inference whose legitimacy Kant will contest.[25] Yet Anselm never mentions anything like God's essence, and even less his "Being," which we cannot even think. The crux of Anselm's argument is the fact that God is *a really existing God who exceeds any possible thought* of his Being.

Anselm knew nothing of Aristotle's *Metaphysics* and his reflection on Being as Being. Nor did he know of Avicenna and the Arab tradition that had, well before him, renewed metaphysical thinking.

Avicenna: The Metaphysics of the Shifa

Avicenna is, in fact, the first author to have developed a real system of metaphysics.[26]

Avicenna (980–1037), a Persian author whose works were written in Arabic, is an authentic giant in the history of metaphysics. In a recent article published in *Le Monde* on the most important people of the year 1000 CE, he is called the greatest genius of his time.[27] Avicenna was probably neither a philosopher nor a metaphysician, but a physician. His important and monumental work, *The Canon of Medicine*, which was translated into Latin during the twelfth century, was the most important medical reference book during the medieval period and beyond (he was, for example, the first to describe meningitis). Even in his "metaphysics"—his term, the Arabic word *Ilâhiyyât*,[28] was translated in Latin as *scientia divina*, the Latin term *metaphysica* was coined only in the twelfth century by Jacques de Venise[29]—Avicenna remained a physician. He held that the "divine science" was also therapeutic: Just as medicine seeks to heal the body, the *Ilâhiyyât* was medicine for the spirit. Moreover, Avicenna's metaphysics are found at the end of a monumental work called *Kitâb al-shifâ* (1027), or "The Book of Healing." It is a five-thousand-page encyclopedia, which probably makes it the most colossal work in the history of philosophy. The book has four main sections each subdivided into several books:[30]

1. Logic (nine books)
2. Physics (eight books)
3. Mathematics (geometry, arithmetic, music, and astronomy)
4. Metaphysics (ten books)

There are two other versions of Avicenna's metaphysics, one in the *Kitâb al-najât*, or "The Book of Salvation" that dates to the same period. It is a condensed version of the *Kitâb al-shifâ*. The other is *The Book of Science* or *Dânisch-nâma* written in Persian.[31] Avicenna's metaphysics became known in the West because of the *Kitâb al-shifâ'*, which was translated into Latin in Toledo by Domingo Gundisalvo (Dominicus Gundissalinus) during the twelfth century. Gundisalvo was archdeacon of Segovia and worked in Toledo between 1130 and 1180.[32] Avicenna's work was known in the West *before* Aristotle's *Metaphysics* because "the translators in Toledo were more interested in the Arab-Muslim and Jewish philosophy than the *corpus aristotelicum*," to such an extent that "Aristotle's entry was [...] prepared and accompanied by the Arab peripatetics,"[33] namely, by Avicenna and Averroes.

In an autobiography that his disciple Zawajani included in the biography he wrote of his master,[34] Avicenna recounts how he read and reread Aristotle's *Metaphysics* some forty times and came to know it by heart despite never fully understanding it.[35] Only after he chanced upon al-Farabi's (870–950) commentary, *The Intentions of Aristotle's Metaphysics*—and which he acquired only because the vendor insisted he buy it at a bargain price!—did the meaning of Aristotle's *Metaphysics* suddenly become clear to him. Unfortunately, the anecdote does not tell what new light the work shed on the *Metaphysics* thereby making it clear. It only says that Avicenna began to make generous donations to charity (as if metaphysics was a model of charity!). Zawajani does tell us, however, how Avicenna came to write his *Metaphysics of the Shifa*. Pressured by his disciple to write a commentary on Aristotle's newly deciphered *Metaphysics*, Avicenna answered he was too occupied for such a task, but was ready to give a personal account in which he would include what he thought were the most important elements of Aristotle's doctrine.[36] Luckily for us, this led to a profoundly original metaphysics, which was surely inspired by Aristotle's and al-Farabi's writings and, unsurprisingly, by Neoplatonism, then the prism through which Aristotle's work was read.[37]

Although he draws his inspiration mainly from Aristotle, Avicenna also argues for the idea of our world's eternal emanation from a necessary being, as well as the idea that the first emanation from the first principle is an Intelligence existing separately. These ideas are obviously neither very Aristotelian, nor Qur'anic, as his Arabic critics, staring with al-Ghazali, never failed to point out. Averroes would later dispute Avicenna's reading of Aristotle.

Avicenna understood metaphysics as a rational explanation of reality. Although it was his daring reflections on the emanation of all things from necessary Being, on the eternity of the world and the negation of God's knowledge of individual things that led to the greatest polemics, his importance in the history of the reception of Aristotle's metaphysics stems from his reflections on the *subject* of metaphysics.[38]

Obviously, argues Avicenna, every science has its own object. Either this object arises from our action, or it exists independently from us. In the first case, it is a *practical* science, and in the second case, it is a *theoretical* or speculative science. For Avicenna, there are three practical sciences (the science of civil administration, economics, and ethics) and three speculative sciences: physics, or the inferior science, mathematics, or the intermediary science, and finally the science of what is beyond nature: the "superior" science (one easily recognizes the three theoretical sciences of *Metaphysics* book E). This last one is the divine science. So what is its object?

One could naturally think it is God since the very idea of a "divine science" seems to imply it. But Avicenna, who follows the Aristotelian doctrine of science quite closely, answers that this cannot be the case "because the subject matter of every science is something whose existence is admitted in that science."[39] Can metaphysics presuppose the existence of God? Obviously not, as this science must, among other things, *demonstrate* his existence. Perhaps another science demonstrates his existence, which the divine science then studies. There are two reasons why this is impossible. First, all the other sciences are either practical, or they are like physics or mathematics and do not therefore demonstrate the existence of God. Second, if this existence is not to be sought by metaphysics, then it cannot be sought any other science. Even though the divine science discusses God, it cannot claim God as its subject.

But Avicenna mentions another possibility: Its object could be the first causes as is the case in Aristotle's conception of first philosophy (*Metaphysics*, A). Obviously, the divine science will deal with causes, but, for similar reasons, these causes are not its object since it must *also* demonstrate the existence of supreme causes. Thus no other science than divine science will discuss the supreme causes, and yet these causes are not its *subject*.

Avicenna solves the problem by stating that the object of metaphysics is Being as Being—that is, Being common to all things that are.[40] Avicenna is the first thinker in the history of metaphysics to have adopted this solution.[41] He comes to it by comparing the subject of metaphysics to that of the other speculative sciences (Book I, chapter 2). He argues that physics does not study objects as beings (or substances), but as objects *subject to movement and rest*. Similarly, mathematics studies measure and number: Being whose accident is "mathematical." Thus, in both these sciences, Being is studied in relation to a particular limitation: *insofar* as it is contingent upon matter (*materia*), number (*numerus*) or measure (*mensura*). In both physics and mathematics, Being (*ens*) is presupposed rather than studied for itself. Metaphysics therefore studies Being.[42] It thus studies all that is related to Being without any limitation or condition.[43] According to Avicenna, it studies all the categories that are the species of Being,[44] namely, substance, quantity, and quality, which all pertain to Being in general. Obviously, the most universal of these categories is Being, which encompasses them all.

The question of the preeminent subject of metaphysics is thus solved or, to use the Latin, "settled" (*stabilire*). It is Being as Being, understood as what is *common* to all things that are (Book I, chapter 2, section 12). In another famous passage—Thomas Aquinas, Duns Scotus, and Heidegger will take up the idea—Avicenna says Being is "impressed in the soul in a primary way."[45]

Here, Being designates an intention or a disposition of our mind that asserts the *existence* of something.[46] It does not consider the thing as such and such, but only insofar as it exists. Thus Avicenna explicitly distinguishes something's Being or existence (Avicenna also speaks of the intention that aims for the "thing," *res*, to use al-Farabi's terminology) from a thing's quiddity or nature. This is far from trivial because Avicenna is thereby responsible for the important distinction between essence and existence, or Being, that will have a profound impact on the Latin West during the thirteenth century.

Avicenna famously expresses this distinction by saying existence can be considered to be an accident of essence—that is, something that occurs to essence when it is said to exist (or be). This Being will become the foremost object of metaphysics.[47]

What can be said about existence understood in such general terms? First off, and for reasons that will soon become clear, Avicenna favors *necessity*. According to him, necessity is a clear affirmation of existence.[48] Avicenna once again follows Aristotle's *Second Analytics* closely: What is necessary is most worthy of being thought. This privileged position given to necessary existence leads him to describe God as the *ens necessarium*, which will be the crux of his first argument for God's existence.

According to Avicenna, one may distinguish necessary Being from possible Being. Whereas possible Being has a cause, necessary Being does not. The distinction between essence and existence has a determining role here: Where necessary Being is the principle of its own existence (it is "in itself," *a se*), possible Being is not. The existence of possible Being is an accident "added" to its essence. Possible Being needs something to make it exist as an act, and this can only be necessary Being.[49] All possible things require an agent—that is, a cause that imparts Being to it and maintains its existence. What causes its existence can then be either necessary or possible. If it is a possible being, it must also have been made possible by a necessary being. Thus a necessary being must necessarily exist, from which all things draw Being. In necessary Being, adds Avicenna, Being and essence are identical: its essence is its necessary existence.[50]

Avicenna's argument necessarily implies the *eternity* of the world. In a temporal succession, each thing is caused by a possible cause that can be traced back to another cause, and then to another, and so on ad infinitum. For Avicenna, if one seeks a strictly necessary form of causality, one must posit a cause that exists *at the same time* as what it causes and for which it is the necessary cause. The idea of "creation," Avicenna explains, does not mean existence follows from a decision that is temporally prior to it (a divine "decision" that would ascribe multiplicity to God),[51] but that a thing exists because of a necessary being. Creation thus signifies an ontological dependence rather than a temporal succession (a doctrine ostensibly contrary to Islamic orthodoxy,[52] but which does not appear to have offended Avicenna). Avicenna gives two arguments to show why it would be a mistake to think that the First Principle could have preceded the world temporally. (1) If God had the power to create before the creation of nature, there would then be a time "before" the creation of the world, and this would attribute determined moments to God prior to creation, which would be unthinkable. (2) If God only began creation at the moment it began, it would then imply that the creator passed from impotency to potency at a given moment.[53] What necessity would have impelled the beginning of creation?

Avicenna concludes from these arguments that God could not have temporally preceded the world. Creation must therefore be understood as an emanation (*sudûr*) of beings from God understood as pure intelligence. This intelligence thinks itself and in so doing, in a single act, it also thinks the *essence* of all existing things. Avicenna insists that God only knows things *in a universal way* through their essences. He does not know particular or individual things since it would imply that God could be affected by things existing outside himself, which would attribute passivity to him.[54] As he is the principle of Being, God can only think essences. He is the principle of these essences, which he only knows in a universal manner. This is an important idea that will be the object of fierce debates throughout the Middle Ages.

Avicenna insists on eliminating any reference to the multiple from the First necessary principle, which is One. His knowledge of essences is a single act: "He intellectually apprehends things all at once, without being rendered multiple by them in His substance, or their becoming conceived in their forms in the reality of His essence. Rather, their forms emanate from Him as intelligibles."[55] Essences exist because they are thought. The world thus emerges from the First necessary principle understood as an intelligence of itself. In order to imagine this complex procession of beings from the One, Avicenna employs the Neoplatonic doctrine of hypostasis. As it is one, the First necessary principle, in accordance with the Plotinian principle (*ex uno nihil fit nisi unum*), can only beget something that is also one. The First Intelligence is, according to Avicenna, also the One's first emanation (or hypostasis), which then begets another intelligence, and another. He then associates a celestial sphere to each intelligence (Avicenna supposes some ten intelligences all existing separately).[56] Thus in an extraordinarily complex stratification, Avicenna adopts the Neoplatonic thesis of a world engendering itself by an auto-emanation of the divine Intelligence.

Avicenna's contributions to metaphysics are numerous and important. They stem from: (1) his "settling" of the question pertaining to the subject of metaphysics (Being as Being—an idea that will remain canonical despite being contested by Averroes); (2) his thesis, which will be later taken up by Aquinas and Heidegger, that Being is the first thing to enter the mind; (3) his distinction between essence and existence (or Being) unknown to the Greeks, but which will be important for medieval and modern metaphysics; (4) his positing of God as necessary Being in whom Being and essence are necessarily linked; finally (5) his idea that the world (of essences) follows from God who thinks himself without knowing particular beings.

Averroes's Critique of Avicenna

Whereas Avicenna was a physician, Averroes or Ibn Rushd (1126–1198), born in Cordoba, was a jurist. He is the author of *The Decisive Treatise*[57] on the conflicts and possible accord between religion and philosophy (in which Averroes almost always sides with philosophy). Averroes contested Avicenna on several points. He contested the latter's conception of the object of metaphysics, which favored for the first time an ontological reading of "Being as Being." Instead, Averroes returned to Aristotle's Greek commentators[58] and argued that the object of metaphysics, or the *scientia divina*, was God or substances separate from matter. As we have seen, Avicenna used Aristotle's *Posterior Analytics* to argue that a science cannot demonstrate the existence of its object.[59] Although Averroes also refers to this text, according to him, it is *physics*, rather than metaphysics, that must demonstrate the existence of the Prime Mover. Moreover, only through the movement found in nature can God's existence be proven.[60] This led Averroes to criticize Avicenna's proof of a First necessary principle. All of metaphysics would thus presuppose the physical proof of the Prime Mover (or the proof by movement, which will become Thomas Aquinas's *first way*). After all, the argument could already be found in Aristotle's *Physics*, which closed its last book with a proof of God's existence. The proof *also* appears in the *Metaphysics* because Aristotle the metaphysician borrowed it from Aristotle the physicist. Only in nature, and in its eternal translatory movement, are traces of the supreme being found, but the discussion of which belongs to a more noble science: *metaphysics*.[61] As with Avicenna, the creation of the world is eternal. If this were not the case, there would have been a time when God was not a creator and there would be a cause that would have provoked his creation.[62]

The physical proof of God—understood as the only possible proof—was strengthened by Averroes's use of Aristotle's texts. In fact, he came to known as their best *commentator*, and was nicknamed, in the Latin West, "The Commentator." Avicenna's thought, however, is not only the more original, but, metaphysically, it is also more systematic. Avicenna continued to fascinate medieval philosophy because his thought is founded on a universal consideration of Being and thereby leads to the essence of the first principle, understood as pure Being in which Being and essence are identical. Thomas Aquinas's discussion of the object of metaphysics testifies to Avicenna's importance.

The Object of Metaphysics According to Thomas Aquinas

Despite his intimidating reputation, Thomas Aquinas was fond of neither metaphysics nor philosophy.[63] He most probably considered himself a theologian. His masterwork was a *Summa theologiæ* (1274, or, to be more precise, *Summa de theologia*[64]) that presented the essential truths of faith and has since become one of Christianity's main doctrinal works. These truths are what he called in the *Summa*, the *sacra doctrina* (always identified to the *theologia*[65]). Thomas always expressly distinguished this sacred doctrine from the "philosophical sciences," which are, as they were for Avicenna, either speculative or practical. According to Thomas, the *sacra doctrina* is both speculative and practical. Its principles are derived from no other science however: they are revealed directly by God. The other sciences are, in a way, its handmaidens, *ancillæ*, which lead the intellect "by what is known through natural reason (from which proceed the other sciences) to that which is beyond reason."[66]

Saint Thomas's other doctrinal masterpiece is his *Summa Contra Gentiles*.[67] Obviously, it is another theological work, even an apology. But Thomas also kept abreast of the changes that were transforming knowledge during this period. He was drawn to the superiority of Arab and Aristotelian philosophy and worked carefully to show how the truths of faith could concord with what can be known by natural reason alone in its reflection on Being and its principles. This spirit of harmony animated Thomas's interest for the works of Aristotle, and, like his teacher Albert Magnus, he was also known for his commentary on the "*philosophus*," as Aristotle was then called. Of Thomas's few works on metaphysics, it is perhaps appropriate to begin with the very short *prologue* that opens his commentary on Aristotle's *Metaphysics*. Although it has been much commented in the last decades, the text is perhaps not the best known of the Doctor Angelicus, but it is significant since it offers a good introduction to his reading of Aristotle.[68] It is of particular importance because it distinguishes the different ways that the subject matter of the *Metaphysics* can be understood.

According to Thomas, only the one science that is master of all the other sciences deserves to be called wisdom (*sapientia*). But which science is it? If all sciences stem from an intellectual activity, then it would be *the most intellectual science*. As it is said in chapter II of Aristotle's *Metaphysics* (982 b 1), the highest science is the one that inquires into the most intelligible objects (*maxime intelligibilia*). What are these *maxime intelligibilia*? Thomas, always the good Aristotelian, identifies three possible meanings of *maxime intelligibilia*, which correspond to three different regulative sciences:

1. From the perspective of our knowledge:

> those things from which the intellect derives certitude seem to be more intelligible. Therefore, since the certitude of science is acquired by the intellect knowing causes, a knowledge of causes seems to be intellectual in the highest degree. Hence that science which considers first causes also seems to be the ruler of the others in the highest degree.[69]

For us, causal knowledge is what assures the intelligibility of things. Therefore, the first meaning we can give to the supreme intelligible, and candidate for the title of wisdom, is knowledge of the *first* causes (*quæ primas causas considerat*), as was the case in the first book of the *Metaphysics*.

2. But we may also conceive the intelligible by comparing the intellect with the senses. Whereas the senses are always limited to the particular, the intellect can apprehend the universal (*quod universalia comprehendit*). The most intelligible science would then be the one that inquires into the most universal principles (*principia maxime universalia*). What are the most universal principles? Thomas answers, following Avicenna but without naming him: Being and what accompanies it, namely, unity and plurality, potentiality and act (*quæ quidem sunt ens et ea quæ consequuntur ens, ut unum et multa, potentia et actus*). It is interesting how Being founds the universality of Thomas's inquiry. These universal principles, he points out, cannot be grasped by any particular science because they always study a determined genus (as Avicenna had already argued). Only a science of Being can account for the universal principles *common* and prior to all the other sciences. Thus there is a science of universal principles that is the master of all the other sciences.

3. The third way of conceiving the most intelligible is to separate it from matter. The most intelligible things would therefore be the most distinct from sensible matter (as were Plato's ideas or Aristotle's Prime Mover). The intelligible object of this science is therefore God and intelligences separate from matter.

Thomas then gives names to each of these three sciences of the most intelligible:

1. He calls the science studying first causes first philosophy (*prima philosophia*).
2. He calls the science studying Being and its accompanying attributes metaphysics (*metaphysica*). Thomas here follows Avicenna's lead.
3. Finally, he calls the science studying substances separate from matter the divine science or theology (*scientia divina sive theologia*), which matches Averroes's reading of the Metaphysics.

Is wisdom thereby split into three distinct objects? No, answers Thomas diplomatically. Wearing the vestments of a commentator of Aristotle (that is, he is not interested here in imposing his conception of the holy science), Thomas claims that it is really a tripartite division of considerations relating to one unique science. Clearly, immaterial substances are also the first and the most elevated causes of Being. There is a fundamental accord between first philosophy (1) and theology (3).

In a denser passage, Thomas tries to link theology to *metaphysica* and its object, Being as Being. The study of the causes of a genus and the genus itself belongs to one and the same science, recalls Thomas. As we have seen, theology and first philosophy both study causes, but only metaphysics includes the cause and what is caused, all of Being. The only and unique object of metaphysics is Being as Being, which itself refers to its divine cause. Since it is more encompassing, metaphysics is thus the directive science. This is rather surprising however, as one would expect Thomas to give this title to theology. But it is as a commentator of Aristotle that Thomas is speaking here, and he knows quite well that Aristotle had no knowledge of revealed theology, which is the true foundation of the *sacra doctrina* the principles of which are presented in the *Summae*.

Moreover, Thomas never calls this sacred doctrine metaphysics. There is a good reason for this. Although considering Being as a whole does lead us to the original source of Being, Thomas insists that we are unable to grasp this source because it exceeds our intellectual capacities. There is no *metaphysical* knowledge of God's essence for Thomas—that is, knowledge drawn from the consideration of Being. All knowledge of God can only be drawn from Revelation.[70] Revelation founds *theologia* or the *sacra doctrina*. Thus, as Olivier Boulnois shows quite well, the (metaphysical) consideration of Being stops where the consideration of God begins, which belongs to the *sacra doctrina*. For this reason, Boulnois argues there is no onto-theology, but rather a "juxtaposing" of ontology (= *metaphysica*) and theology in the works of Saint Thomas.

For this reason, Thomas is very critical of Anselm's "ontological" argument for God's existence. He criticizes it severely before presenting his own five ways to God, object of the *sacra doctrina*. According to Anselm, or according to Anselm as Thomas presents him, the existence of God would be self-evident because it would follow from the notion of a being than which one cannot think anything greater (*significatur enim hoc nomine id quo majus cogitari non potest*)[71]. Thomas objects to Anselm's argument on two points. First, it is possible to distinguish something that is self-evident in itself, though not for us, from something self-evident not only in itself but for us as well. (1) Something can be said self-evident, explains Thomas, when the predicate is included in the subject, such as when one says "man is an animal." (2) But there are also cases where one does not know the nature of the subject or predicate. In this case, the proposition may be self-evident (Thomas's example: "incorporeal things are not in space"[72]), but not readily understood by all. Who indeed can claim to *know* the subject God? Thus although the proposition "God is" may be self-evident in these terms, it is not necessarily evident for us, nor, quite obviously, for those who contest the existence of God.

Second, Thomas argues (*Summa Theologica*, I, q 2, art. 1), following Gaunilo of Marmoutiers, that Anselm may have employed a notion that can only be found in *our* mind. Even if one grants Anselm that God is such that nothing greater can be conceived, this could be no more than a mental notion. After all, who are we to know God's Being? Would the existence of God follow from our concept? One can admit God's existence only if God actually exists in reality. But this is precisely what nonbelievers deny. Therefore, concludes Thomas, the existence of God cannot be evident in itself, it can only be demonstrated by God's *effects* (much as Averroes had argued).

Whether God Exists? The Five Ways

Having first addressed the necessary question of the object of the *sacra doctrina*, which he distinguishes from the philosophical sciences and metaphysics, Thomas begins the *Summa Theologica* with the question of the existence of God. Thomas Aquinas identifies five possible ways of demonstrating the existence of God that are now generally associated with the Thomist tradition although they are really condensed versions of older arguments predating Thomas. They are found in article 3 of question 2: "Whether God exists?" As is his habit, Thomas follows the didactic style of the *disputatio*: having stated the "difficulties" raised by the question, against which (*sed contra*) he invokes expert testimony, he offers in the *conclusio* his own doctrine, after which he answers, point by point, the objections raised in the beginning of the discussion. Often derided, this method of discussion, which is in keeping with Plato's dialectics, is perhaps not the silliest way of developing critical thinking.

So what are the difficulties raised by the existence of God? Thomas underlines two difficulties, which are still pertinent today. First, the existence of evil: Since God is generally understood as infinite goodness, if God existed there would be no evil in the world. Second, is this hypothesis of the existence of God even required, asks Thomas? Can we not explain phenomena using principles that are independent from God? "For all natural things can be reduced to one principle which is nature; and all voluntary things can be reduced to one principle which is human reason, or will. Therefore, there is no need to suppose God's existence."[73]

Sed contra, Thomas refers to a passage drawn from Exodus 3: 14: "I am I who am." He could have chosen many other passages to assert the existence of God, but his choice is far from innocent. Indeed, the expression drawn from the book of Exodus (a *hapax legomenon* in the biblical text) not only states that God is, which would be rather trivial for a biblical text, but also that *he is the one that is*! The fact is that, while expounding the *sacra doctrina* he keeps a deferential distance from metaphysical knowledge, which is ignorant of Revelation, Thomas has willingly spoken of God as pure Being (*esse tantum*) or as *esse ipsum*, "Being itself."[74] What Thomas in trying to express is that "any being other than God . . . is necessarily composed of 'what it is' *and* the act of existing (*esse*)."[75] But, in God, both are merged (an idea Avicenna had already espoused): in God, and only in God, Being and essence are identical.[76] The term *existence* has often been used to describe the act of being (*actus essendi*), but Gilson is right to recall that the term *existentia* does not belong to Saint Thomas's language. In the case of God, it would even lead to misinterpretation because *existere* means in Latin: "being (*sistere*) outside (*ex*) of," in the sense of "to exit."[77] What "is," in this way, "springs" (*ex*) from a cause. One may represent the Being of all essences, or of all the beings (*étants*) that exist in this way, as something that "ex-ists" from God, who is the being that subsists on its own (*ipsum esse subsistens*). One would certainly not say that God "exists" in this way—that is, we would not say that God is derived from a cause! God does not "exist" according to Thomas, God "sub-sists." God is only Being, pure Being, nothing but Being, pure Being *subsisting* by itself, the *ipsum esse per se subsistens*.[78] Five ways leads to it in the *Summa de Theologiae*.

1. The argument by movement, which is a simplified version of the argument for the Prime Mover found in Aristotle's *Physics* that Averroes had revived (Thomas gives a more complex version of it in *Summa Contra Gentiles*). Movement is for Thomas, as for Aristotle, more than what we normally designate as movement—that is, spatial movement or movement from point A to point B. A plant's growth, qualitative alteration, generation, and corruption are also forms of "movement" according to Aristotle and Thomas. But all that moves is always moved by something, says Thomas. In Aristotle's terminology, what is moved is always potential movement compared to what actually moves insofar as something moving receives its movement from a being in act (the example Thomas gives is the following: "Fire actually heats the wood that was once only potentially hot"). Yet, something cannot be both moving and moved, its movement cannot be both potential and actual. If something moves, then some other thing has imparted movement to it (*oportet ergo omne quod movetur ab alio moveri*). Since one cannot trace this movement back to infinity (*non est procedere in infinitum*), thus there is a Prime Mover that is not moved by anything.

2. The argument by efficient cause (it is the *third* in *Summa Contra Gentiles*), which Thomas claims to have taken from book II of Aristotle's *Metaphysics* (994 a 1–19). This argument is similar to the previous one, but the accent is put on the effect. In a sequence of causes, says Thomas, there is an order such that A causes B that causes C and so on. In this sequence, two things are impossible. (1) Something cannot be cause of itself (this will change with Descartes for whom God is *causa sui*); (2) it is impossible to trace back the sequence of efficient causes to infinity. Thomas's argument consists in saying if there were no first cause, there would be no intermediary or last cause. The sequence B, C, D, etc. makes sense only if there is a first cause that begins the sequence: if there were no beginning there would be no intermediary cause. Indeed, if one removes the cause, one also removes the effect. Thus if one follows the series of causes back to infinity, one abolishes the series itself because without any *first* cause, there would be no *intermediary* or *last* causes. One must therefore suppose a necessary first efficient cause.

3. The third way is that of the *possible* and the *necessary* and takes up the main points of Avicenna's argument. This argument is not included among the five ways in *Summa Contra Gentiles* (see I, chap. 15 where it is used as a proof of the eternity of God). There are things that are simply possible—that is, things that can or cannot be. But, for Thomas, it is impossible for all things to have this nature. Avicenna's argument was the following: possible or contingent Being requires a cause to exist. And this cause can be either possible or necessary. If it is only possible, it must have been made possible by some necessary cause without which it could not be.

The third way is slightly different for Thomas. What can not-be, once was not (*quia quod possibile est non esse, quandoque non est*). Therefore, if all could not have been, then there would once have been nothing, *nihil*! However, if such had been the case, argues Thomas, there would now be nothing because no thing can emerge out of nothing. And yet, this is obviously false since Being must come from somewhere. It emerges either from something possible or from something necessary. If it comes from something simply possible, the aporia remains: there would have been nothing. Being must therefore have emerged out of a necessary unique being. There must therefore be a necessary being whose necessity has no cause (*aliquid quod est per se necessarium, non habet causam necessitatis aliunde, sed quod est causa necessitatis aliis*).

4. The fourth way is the argument by the "degrees" of things. The things we observe are more or less good, more or less true, or more or less noble. If one can say things are more or less, there must be a maximum. Thomas concluded from this that: "there is thus something supremely true, supremely good, supremely noble, and consequently [!] supremely Being" (*est igitur aliquid quod est verissimum, et optimum, et nobilissimum, et per consequens maxime ens*). It is sometimes said that this is Thomas' most vague argument since it is difficult to see in it a "proof" of something (if there is degrees of greed, does it then mean there is some maximal greed?). It is also difficult to identify the author of this argument.[79] Thomas, for his part, attributes it to Aristotle (*Metaphysics*, 2 where he claims to have found the idea that the *maxime intelligibilia* were the object of metaphysics). In fact, the argument can be traced back to Plato and the idea developed in the *Symposium* and the *Phaedo* according to which all things are what they are because they relate to some maximum, which must be posited if one is to speak, which one can, of things as more or less something. The argument is slightly embarrassing for Christian apologetics since it is not so much a proof of God's existence as it is one of a certain maximum, of a certain excellence, which is perfectly compatible with Platonic ideas. One could even argue that it is a proof of the existence of Beauty in itself! More importantly, it is also evidence of the influence Platonism had on Thomas's thought.

5. The firth argument is a classic. It is the proof by the governance of things, *ex gubernatione rerum*. One can easily observe that things, despite being deprived of intelligence, seem to have some purpose. Could this be by chance? No, answers Thomas. "What is deprived of knowledge cannot have a purpose unless it is directed by some intelligent being, as is the case with Sagittarius's arrow." "Therefore, there is an intelligent being that orients all things toward their end, and this being, we call God." This is the teleological argument, which, when we contemplate nature, is still believable today, even for atheists.

The Idea of a *Scientia Transcendens* in Scholastic Thought from Duns Scotus to Suarez: The Origin of Ontology

The tradition of which Étienne Gilson is the most illustrious representative has often argued that Thomas Aquinas's thought is the summit of medieval "metaphysics." Although Thomas does assert (following Exodus 3: 14) that God is a pure act of being, he also acknowledges that one can only speak *analogically* of God's Being. We can only speak of God from the perspective of the Being we know: a creature's Being, which is not *ipsum esse subsistens*, but exists through God. God's Being would be totally unknown to us were it not for Revelation. Therefore, one cannot really speak of metaphysics—or metaphysical knowledge of God's Being—in the works of the doctor Angelicus.

Things changed in the following generation with Duns Scotus[80] (c. 1265–1308), who the Middle Ages called the *Doctor Subtilis*. In the prologue to his *Quaestiones super libros Metaphysicorum Aristotelis,* Duns Scotus takes up the well-known problem of metaphysics' subject as developed by Avicenna and Averroes. Like Thomas, Duns Scotus refers to chapter II of the *Metaphysics* (982 b 1) in which Aristotle supposedly argued that the first science studied the prime knowables (*maxime scibilia*). The expression "prime knowables" can be understood in two ways, says Scotus. (1) It can designate either the first knowables insofar as "without them, or prior to them, nothing can be known."[81] These are what he calls the *communissima*, the most common notions: Being as such and all that follows from it (*ens intanquam ens, et quæcumque sequuntur ens inquantum ens*). (2) The expression can also designate the *certissima cognoscibilia*, the most certain *principles*—that is, (as with Thomas) principles and causes.

Although he is in continuity with Avicenna, Scotus's originality lies in his understanding of the *communissima* and the universal science that follows from them. Jean-François Courtine's commentary explains why:

> Since they are common to all things, the prime knowables are presupposed by all knowledge of "special" objects. The *communissima* must be known beforehand, or known *a priori*. They are the theme of a universal science that pertains to what is 'most common' to all the particular sciences insofar as what is thereby shared *exceeds* the determination of each of these sciences, but is nevertheless necessarily implied by them. This universal science studies the transcendentals and is what we call metaphysics.[82]

Duns Scotus himself speaks of a transcendent science (*transcendens*), but others will later speak more readily of a transcendental science (*transcendentalis*).

This science pertains to the "transcendentals—that is, the most general (*communissima*) notions, which "transcend" all genera and are therefore common to all sciences. The most universal of all notions is obviously Being, as it is presupposed by every science (this undoubtedly the reason Heidegger was so interested in Duns Scotus). This notion, in the absence of any determination and because of its universal value, is studied by the first science, the *scientia transcendens*.

This leads Duns Scotus to argue for four, rather than three, speculative sciences.[83] Other than physics, mathematics and theology, which are all special sciences (*speciales*), there is also a science that precedes them as their foundation. This is the *alia metaphysica*, the "other metaphysics," which is a *scientia transcendens*, a science of the "*transcendens*"—that is, of Being. One could think that Duns Scotus is here taking Avicenna's side against Averroes, but things are more complicated than they appear. Scotus's intention is to reconcile the two opponents by asserting that if God is neither the principal object nor the principal subject of metaphysics, it is nevertheless its ultimate design, or its end, in such a way that the theme of the "transcendent" science is the transcendent and infinite being that is God.[84]

But for there to be a universal science of Being, it must have an unequivocal concept of Being. But is Being, or beings (*ens*), an unequivocal concept? Yes, answers Scotus vigorously. Unlike Thomas,[85] Scotus says that even when speaking of God, one cannot but have a concept of Being that is common to God and to creatures:

> Every intellect that is certain about one concept, but dubious about others has, in addition to the concepts about which it is in doubt, another concept of which it is certain. . . . A man can be certain in his mind that God is a being and still be in doubt whether He is a finite or an infinite being, a created or uncreated being. Consequently, the concept of 'Being' as affirmed of God is different from the other two concepts but is included in both of them and therefore is unequivocal.[86]

Thus in virtue of its primacy of "commonness and virtuality,"[87] the concept of Being is prior in two ways. Not only is the concept of Being common to all that is, but, according to Scotus, this concept also contains *virtually* all others as its determinations (he also says *passiones*). But unmistakably what Duns Scotus means by "Being" is essence or quiddity, the seat of the *ens*. The reason is that Scotus, unlike Thomas, refuses to make the distinction between *esse* and essence. For him, "it is simply false that Being is other than essence" (*simpliciter falsum est quod esse sit aliud ab essentia*).[88] Scotus thus contests the idea of a *real* distinction between essence and Being (or existence). Whereas a logical (or nominal) distinction is one of thought, a real distinction is a distinction between two different "things." For Duns Scotus, Being is nothing other than essence, conceived as a "common nature." Yet, an existing common nature is no more than an actually realized essence,[89] which exists as a mode of effective existence that is in itself indifferent to any common nature. The distinction between essence and existence is therefore not a real difference, but a "mode" (*modus*). Existence is simply "a modality of essence" (from which we get the expression "modes of being").[90] Thus in a way, Duns Scotus reinstates the (Aristotelian) primacy of essence (or *eidos*) over existence, which will be preserved by the great metaphysicians of the later Middle Ages such as William of Ockham and Suarez. Nevertheless, Duns Scotus is one of the first thinkers of the Latin West to have argued for a first, universal and unequivocal science of Being or beingness.

The Scotist idea of a transcendent science (*scientia transcendens*) of Being as Being defines the universal topic of metaphysics by differentiating it from the *metaphysicæ speciales* and more especially from theology, the object of which is *particular*. This led to a distinction between *metaphysica generalis*, pertaining to Being, and the special metaphysics that pertain to metaphysical objects understood as objects separated from the sensible. Prepared by Duns Scotus, this "division of labor" in metaphysics gradually gained importance in School metaphysics.[91] This division culminates in the work of the Spanish Jesuit Francisco Suarez (1548–1617). Although the soon-to-be-canonical terms *metaphysica generalis* and *specialis* are not found in his works, it is nevertheless striking that Suarez, the *Doctor eximius* ("eminent"), organized his "system" of metaphysics, presented in his *Disputationes metaphysicæ* (1597), in two tomes.[92] The first tome deals with Being in all its extension (and Being conceived as essence), but the second tome deals with particular metaphysical objects that can be conceived by reason, the first of which is God. *Theologia* is thus the first part of the special metaphysics. But there are others, such as psychology, which also studies a distinct metaphysical object, the soul. From Suarez to the eighteenth century, the divisions of special metaphysics by what has since been called late Scholastics or School metaphysics (*Schulmetaphysik*), varied from author to author. For Goclenius, the three parts of special metaphysics were theology, angelology, and psychology.[93] For some, such as Pererius, mathematics was also to be considered as part of special metaphysics.[94] At the end of the evolution begun by Suarez, there appears in the work of Christian Wolff (1679–1754) the following division of metaphysical disciplines (an important division since Kant will judge it to belong naturally to human reason):[95]

METAPHYSICA GENERALIS	METAPHYSICA SPECIALIS
= *ontologia* or	*Psychologia*
philosophia transcendentalis	*Cosmologia*
	Theologia

In this tradition that goes from Duns Scotus to the Wolffian school, the object of general metaphysics is Being (or beings, *ens*) as Being (sometimes *res*). From then on, general metaphysics would be always understood as a "transcendental" science, which is a very important notion if one is to understand the passage from the Middle Ages to Modernity. Although the idea of a science of Being and its "essential attributes" had been evoked as early as book IV of Aristotle's *Metaphysics*, it was the Middle Ages, well before Suarez, that determined the precise content of the doctrine of the essential predicates of Being. These predicates of Being are what the Medievals called, using a term that will have a fertile future, "transcendentals" (often called the "universals") because they transcend all particular genera, following the example of Being.[96] A quarrel over these transcendentals even shook the later Middle Ages. The quarrel stemmed from the question of whether the existence of these transcendentals was real or intellectual (also called nominal).

The Nominalists, often associated with William of Ockham (end of the thirteenth cent.–1350) and Jean Buridan (1300–c. 1358), argued that the transcendentals were simply abstractions or names, and that only individual objects really existed. This importance given to individual existence, rather than to essences, may appear rather modern. And yet, for Ockham, the argument is made in the name of God's omnipotence. God's absolute power is incompatible with a constraining cosmological order: God can, at any moment, change the order of Being and of the "common natures" (Duns Scotus). *That is the reason why* there are only individual and always contingent things, which we can know with the help of our uncertain experience.[97] One can therefore speak of the nominalists' *theological absolutism*, which Modernity opposed with its own absolutism, as Hans Blumenberg has argued.[98]

The Essentialists (or "Realists" more or less associated with Duns Scotus) argued that these predicates stem from Being itself, and surpass a simply nominal existence. Scotus spoke here of "common natures." Since they asserted that the universals were more than words, it is easy to see why the "Realists" were often called Platonists, whereas the Nominalists, for whom only individual beings existed, were called Aristotelians.[99] This is perhaps an oversimplification. Alain De Libera has identified no less than eight important positions in the conflict between the Nominalists and the Realists (whether reality is a mental Being, is to be found in God's mind, or is only the Being intelligence aims at, etc.).[100]

It is more important, however, to understand that by the end of the Middle Ages, and under the influence of Duns Scotus and Suarez, metaphysics as transcendental philosophy was gradually separated from theology even though its onto-theological horizon was never questioned. Modernity would then radicalize the marginalization of theology begun during the late Middle Ages.[101] It is also important to note that it was in the Scholastic context that the neologism *ontologia* appeared, sometime during the seventeenth century. It appears for the first time in 1613, in the works of Goclenius,[102] where it is used synonymously with *philosophia transcendentalis*—that is, the first part of philosophy, the part that studies Being and its universal properties.

Today the term "transcendental philosophy" has been enriched with new connotations, especially following Kant. Since Kant, it is used to designate a reflection on the "conditions of the possibility of things." These conditions are usually found in the constitution of the knowing subject (and, more recently, in its use of language, which is the domain of "transcendental pragmatics"). Insofar as the knowing, and speaking, subject contains the condition of possibility of things, all philosophy dealing with the subject as the condition or foundation of the intelligibility of things can claim the status of transcendental philosophy. But the medieval meaning of transcendental philosophy still lurks in the background: Modern transcendental philosophy still deals with the universal predicates of all that is. The only difference is that these predicates stem less from Being, or from God, than from the subject that knows and thinks Being. A mutation of transcendental philosophy or metaphysics made possible by René Descartes.

CHAPTER 6

DESCARTES

First Philosophy According to the *Cogito*

Is there a Cartesian Metaphysics?

Did René Descartes (1596–1650) ever address the classical problems of metaphysics? Did he ever inquire into metaphysics' *subjectum* or ponder the Aristotelian, Avicennian, Scotistic question of Being as Being? The short answer is no. There are no systematic reflections from him on the object of metaphysics or on the problem of Being that had preoccupied Antiquity and the Aristotelian Middle Ages. Nor does Descartes use the term "ontology" even though it had appeared in Goclenius's *Lexicon philosophicum* in 1613,[1] and was used by some of his students—notably by Clauberg in 1647—thus during Descartes lifetime.[2] Neither metaphysics nor ontology seem to have been among Descartes major preoccupations. One may even say there is a latent but powerful anti-metaphysical tendency in his writings. Jean-Luc Marion, who is among the most attentive Cartesians on this question, has spoken of Descartes's "nothing ontological" or "non-ontology."[3] Obviously Descartes's new foundation for philosophy sought to oppose Scholasticism and its project of a science of Being as Being. More importantly however, Descartes turned his attention, and with it that of modern philosophy, to the activity and persistence of the "I think" or the *cogito*, which is the source and the site of the intelligibility of Being as a whole. It is thus as if metaphysics were implicitly replaced by something like an "egology." For these reasons, no metaphysics is to be found in Descartes. Metaphysics, or ontology, is what Descartes wished to avoid.

Sed contra, obviously Descartes opposed traditional metaphysics in the name of a more rigorous method—a method that promised to achieve what metaphysics had hoped to be: a universal and principial science of what is. A couple of clues reveal metaphysics' latent presence in Descartes writings. First, one cannot avoid noticing that Descartes lays claim to the title "first philosophy." His 1641 masterpiece is called *Meditationes de Prima Philosophia* (Meditations on First Philosophy), later translated during his lifetime into French as *Meditations métaphysiques* (Metaphysical Meditations). One can therefore legitimately assume that his *Meditations* offered answers to metaphysics' classic questions: "What is Being?" "What is its principle?" in accordance with metaphysics' onto-theological orientation. Descartes thus could not have produced his meditations on first philosophy without adopting the heritage of this thousand-year-old tradition as his own, albeit by modifying its terms.

Second, this change in terms revived the question of metaphysics. In the passage from Being to the *ego*, which affirms the *cogito*'s precedence over the *cogito* became Being's common denominator by which it is given meaning and becomes intelligible. True Being—what is, foremost and preeminently—will from then on reside in the *ego cogito*. Being is thereby considered in the first-person singular, as *sum*,[4] which is also the first determination of the *cogito* in Descartes's *Meditations*: *sum*, *existo*, I am, I exist. Moreover, the evidence of the *sum* will even precede the *cogito*, as we will soon see.

Descartes is thus a very important figure in the history of *metaphysics*. But as he takes up the heritage of first philosophy and transforms its essential elements, he is also an ambiguous figure. One should therefore speak of Descartes's reconfiguration of first philosophy in accordance with the *cogito*. This transformation takes place for the most part in the *Meditations on First Philosophy*, the essential steps of which we will now follow in order to bring to light the way it inaugurated the metaphysical decisions of Modernity.[5]

The title *Meditationes de Prima Philosophia* was slightly modified when the Duke of Luynes first translated it into French in 1647. In this translation, which Descartes revised, the meditations became "*metaphysical*" meditations. Are the terms "first philosophy" and "metaphysics" synonymous? Descartes sometimes referred to his masterpiece as "his metaphysics," but he nevertheless refused to call it "metaphysical" meditations. He explicitly preferred the expression "first philosophy" as he explains in a letter to Mersenne written November 11, 1640:

> Yesterday I sent my *Metaphysics* to M. Zuytlichem [Huygens] to post to you ... I have not put any title on it, but it seems to me that the most suitable would be *Renati Descartes Meditationes de Prima Philosophia* [René Descartes' Meditations on First Philosophy] because I do not confine my discussion to God and the soul, but deal in general with all the first things known by philosophizing.

A few days later, he writes again to the same person:

> I am finally sending to you my work on metaphysics, which I have not yet put a title on, so that I can make you its godfather and leave the baptism to you. I think, as I wrote to you in a my previous letter, that it could be called *Meditationes de Prima Philosophia* [Meditations on First Philosophy]; for in the book I deal not just with God and the soul, but in general with the first things that can be known by philosophizing in an orderly way.[6]

Descartes thus acknowledges that his work is metaphysics. But he also says he had decided to speak of first philosophy rather than metaphysics because he deals *not only* with the question of God and the soul, but *all first things* that can be known philosophically. First philosophy's problem is thus greater than metaphysics' problem, which appears to be limited to God and the soul. It is as if Descartes equates metaphysics (which deals with the soul and God) with what had been known as special metaphysics. Since it is interested in special objects, it would not be a "universal science" like Aristotle's science of Being as Being or Suarez's general metaphysics. This universal science is precisely what Descartes prefers to call "first philosophy." It would be first, explains Descartes, because it deals with "the first things that can known by philosophizing in an orderly way." Its primacy thus stems clearly from the order of knowledge. The emphasis on the order of knowledge is not as original as it may seem: Duns Scotus had already said metaphysics pertained to the first *scibilia*, first of which were the *communissima*, to which belonged Being. What is new here is the idea the first things known (the first *scibilia*) can be known according to a certain order or method, which Descartes does not define in the *Meditations* of 1641, but which he had presented in his *Discourse on Method* written in French in 1637. In his more learned work of 1641, written in Latin and addressed "To those Most Wise and Distinguished Men, the Dean and

Doctors of the Faculty of Sacred Theology of Paris," Descartes proposes to address:

> ... the starting points of the whole of first philosophy, but not in a way that causes me to have any expectation of widespread approval or a large readership. On the contrary, I do not advise anyone to read these things except those who have both the ability and the desire to meditate seriously with me, and to withdraw from the minds from the senses as well as from all prejudices. I know all too well that such people are few and far between.[7]

The text helpfully explains what is meant by "meditation." To meditate is to withdraw one's mind from the workings of the senses and liberate it from prejudice. The term comes from Christian spirituality in which *meditatio* designates the period of reflection between the *lectio*, the reading of the biblical text, and the *contemplatio*, the contemplation of divinity.[8] Meditation marks a period of rest and reflection that allows the mind to be alone with itself.

First Meditation: What Can Be Called Into Doubt, or Classical Metaphysics Brought Into Question

The first *Meditation* is that of doubt, as its title announces: "Concerning those Things that can be called into Doubt." It also implies that *all things cannot* be doubted. If one doubts, then one is seeking some certitude. Descartes thus sets off looking for something certain in order to make it the new foundation of first philosophy. But as a means to this end, he promises to employ systematic doubtfulness, which can be read, and has been read, as a suspension of all metaphysics:

> Several years have now passed since I first realized how numerous were the false opinions that in my youth I had taken to be true, and thus how doubtful were all those that I had subsequently built upon them. And thus I realized that once in my life I had to raze everything to the ground and begin again from the original foundations, if I wanted to establish [*stabilire*] anything firm and lasting in the sciences.[9]

Although Descartes promises to "begin again from original foundations," his terminology is very traditional. Parmenides and Plato had, indeed, already spoken of *opinions*, or of *doxa*, to characterize (sensible) knowledge that is not science, understood as a form of knowledge resting not on hearsay but on "principles" that are legitimate foundations (*archai* that are Plato's ideas). All metaphysics exists through this hope of overcoming *doxa*, an effort that Plato had begun by speaking of the hypothesis of the idea. Descartes is thus preoccupied by the fact that knowledge rests on "false opinions." To put it differently, it is less a matter of seeking the principles of what is, than of ensuring once and for all the nature of these principles here posited as the principles of knowledge. So how are we to ensure these principles which are supposedly the source all assurance and certitude? The *Meditations'* task is to carry out this principial reflection.

Looking for such a principial assurance, Descartes exhorts his reader to adopt a *radical* doubt. Radical here means that the doubt must reach the very root of one's convictions. In order to proceed "to this general demolition of my opinions" says Descartes, it is unnecessary to "show that all my opinions are false." There is no need to examine each individual opinion, a task that would require an infinite period of time (Suarez excelled at discussing his predecessor's opinions in his *Disputationes Metaphysicae* of 1597, a work Descartes most probably knew). Attacking the *roots* suffices since "undermining the foundations will cause whatever has been built upon them to crumble of its own accord."[10] Descartes therefore proceeds by attacking "those *principles* which supported everything I once believed," and by rejecting "these opinions, if I find in each of them some reason for doubt."[11]

Descartes observes that everything he once believed to be true had been learned through his senses. Yet the senses may deceive us, such as when they show us a sun a mere two feet wide,[12] or a tree in the distance that appears to be a person. Therefore, concludes Descartes, taking advantage of the ambiguity of the dative of the Latin demonstrative adjective *illis* that can designate both things and persons, "it is a mark of prudence never to place our complete trust in those (*illis*) who have deceived us even once."[13] Since we have had reason to doubt what our senses show us, we may reject any truth that stems from them.

But, one may say, even though the senses may deceive us, there are many things that one cannot doubt and are known for certain through them. Notably, "that I am sitting here next to the fire, wearing my winter dressing gown, that I am holding this sheet of paper in my hand, and the like."[14] Descartes then invokes two reasons to doubt this evidence: insanity and dreams. Do not the insane think they are dressed in gold when they are naked? Who is to say we are completely sane? What if we were all mad? The argument is the same in the case of dreams. I am not completely assured of the reality of things I see when dreaming. Who is to say we are not always living as if in a dream? One thing is certain, observes Descartes speaking of the principles of our convictions, "there are no definitive signs by which to distinguish being awake from being asleep."[15] What is important is that one may here find *reasons* for doubt.

It is therefore possible to doubt all knowledge that claims to present something matching external reality like "pictures" do and claim to speak of "physical nature in general." Descartes here names physics, astronomy and medicine. But there is another *type of knowledge* that one cannot doubt as easily. Such is the case for mathematics, arithmetic and geometry, which do not present pictures of reality, but simple and evident relations. Whether we are sleeping or awake, sane or insane, it is necessarily true that two and two equal four and the sum of a triangle's angles is equal to 180 degrees. Can one seriously doubt *this* knowledge, the most certain of all?

Descartes then introduces the hypothesis of a deceiving God to show one may also doubt this *type* of knowledge. "There is in my mind a certain opinion of long standing," namely, the idea that God can do *everything* (*Deum esse qui potest omnia*), a God whom he does not yet call an evil genius as he will later. If he can do everything, "may I not . . . be deceived every time I add two and three or count the sides of a square. . . ?"[16] Perhaps this God wished that I simply have the "impression of all these things." In other words, even mathematical knowledge can be doubted if one supposes by a hyperbolic hypothesis that an "evil genius . . . has directed his entire effort at deceiving me."[17]

Descartes thus underscores the *lack of assurance* of all the principles on which rested his prior knowledge. No form of knowledge seems capable of resisting such a radical form of doubt. So how are we to find something certain? The second *Meditation* will tackle this problem by tying the indubitable experience of being to thought itself. The certitude of Being will be that of the *sum* which will emerge from self-aware thinking—in a way, the thought of thought.

Second Meditation: I Think, I Am—the Metaphysics of the *Cogito*

The second *Meditation* takes place the next day and with a firm confidence in doubt. Is this doubt not the sign of a desire for certitude that must be satisfiable?[18]

Yesterday's meditation has thrown me into such doubts that I can no longer ignore them, yet I fail to see how they are to be resolved. It is as if I had suddenly fallen into a deep whirlpool; I am so tossed about that I can neither touch bottom with my foot, nor swim up to the top. Nevertheless I will work my way up and will once again attempt the same path I entered upon yesterday. I will accomplish this by putting aside everything that admits of the least doubt, as if I had discovered it to be completely false. I will stay on this course until I know something certain, or, if nothing else, until I at least know for certain that nothing is certain.[19]

Descartes here evokes the possibility of radical skepticism, according to which there is nothing certain in the world. It was a well-known philosophical position in Antiquity revived by Michel de Montaigne (1533–1592) even though it implies a famous paradox (nothing is certain except that nothing is certain, so at least one thing is certain). But if the only certitude is skepticism's then no knowledge is possible. What will be Descartes's solution? All he requires, almost quantitatively, is *one* certitude much as the one Archimedes had sought and to whom Descartes refers:

Archimedes sought but *one* firm and unmovable *point* in order to move the entire earth from one place to another. Just so, great things are also to be hoped for if I succeed in finding just *one thing*, however slight, that is certain and unshaken [*quod certum sit & inconcussum*].[20]

This is not the first time metaphysics has drawn its inspiration from geometry. The discipline was precisely the model that had incited Plato to posit the hypothesis of an intelligible world having apodictic and indubitable certitude unattainable by the *doxa*. But Descartes is not only seeking something certain (since mathematical knowledge is certain), he also seeks knowledge that is *inconcussum*. That is, knowledge that cannot be undone by a single hypothesis, even one as hyperbolic as positing God as an evil genius. This requires something certain and unshakable (*quod certum sit & inconcussum*), sure and "unassailable."[21] Descartes will then link this certitude, which is also self-ensured, to the act of doubting itself, or to be more precise, to the *Being* of that which doubts and thinks. The Being of the one who thinks—Being understood as existence—will then have a pivotal role in Descartes's decisive argument:

Am I not at least something? But I have already denied that I have any senses and any body. Still I hesitate; for what follows from this? *Am I* so tied to a body and to the senses that I cannot exist without them? But I have persuaded myself that *there is absolutely nothing* in the world: no sky, no earth, no minds, no bodies. Is it then the case that *I too do not exist*? [This is the tipping point of the first, ontological, certitude, that of the Being of thought] But *I assuredly was existing* [*eram*]; if I persuaded myself of something.[22]

Descartes's first certitude appears in Latin as the verb "to be" used in the imperfect (past continuous) tense, which denotes duration and even an underlying permanence to the act of thinking or doubting "I assuredly was existing; if I persuaded myself of something." If I doubted, I am. But could an evil genius not have deceived me on this point? No, answers Descartes, the affirmation of thought and of its implied Being, resists the assault of a deceiving God:

> But there is some deceiver or other who is supremely powerful and su-premely sly and who is always deliberately deceiving me. Then too there is no doubt that I exist, if he is deceiving me. And let him do his best at deception, he will never bring it about that I am nothing so long as I shall think that I am something. Thus after everything has been most carefully weighed, it must finally be established that this pronouncement "*I am, I exist*" [*ego sum, ego existo*]" is necessarily true every time I utter it or conceive it in my mind.[23]

Ego sum, ego existo. This is the *first* certitude of the thought that can doubt everything, except itself. Or, to be more precise, if it can doubt and be deceived, it can doubt everything except that it doubts and that it *is*. Descartes's first cer-titude—the *sum* reinforced by the *existo* using a *hendiadys*—is thus ontologi-cal.[24] As Marion has shown, this certitude of my existence presupposes, in fact, an *other* who can deceive me, but one who must *also* exist if it is to deceive me. Indeed, Descartes says: "*haud dubie igitur ego* etiam *sum, si me fallit; & fallat quan-tum potest, nunquam tamen efficiet, ut nihil sim quandiu me aliquid esse cogitabo*" (Then *too* [*etiam*, often forgotten in translation] there is no doubt that I am, if he is deceiving me. And let him do the best at deceiving me, he will never bring it about that I am nothing so long as I think that I am something).[25]

The certitude that I exist thus presupposes the intervention, if only the existence, of an other that can deceive me. But this is not its only condition. The certitude of one's existence exists only as long (*quamdiu*) as I think of something (*quamdiu me aliquid esse cogitabo*). Indeed, as Descartes argues, the proposition "'*I am, I exist*' is necessarily true every time I utter it (*quoties a me profertur*) or conceive it in my mind (*vel mente concipitur*)." It is this link between the statement of the *sum*'s existence and the act of thinking that Des-cartes will now explicate.

The first certitude is the *existence* of the *sum*, its *existentia*. And having acquired this certitude, the next question Descartes will then ask in proper Scholastic fashion pertains to the essence, the *essentia* of the *sum*. I know *that*

I am and *that* I think, but what am I exactly? What does "is" mean when I say that I am? "But now what am I?"[26] Descartes will now show, again using the hypothesis of an evil genius "who is always deliberately deceiving me," how I can set aside, or doubt, all that can be ascribed to "the nature of the body," and even some activities of the soul, such as sensibility. But there is one activity that cannot be separated from the "I," namely, the act of thinking:

> What about thinking? Here I make my discovery: thought exists; it alone cannot be separated from me. I am; I exist—this is certain. But for how long? For as long as I am thinking; for perhaps it could also come to pass that if I were to cease all thinking I would then utterly cease to exist. At this time I admit nothing that is not necessarily true. I am therefore precisely nothing but a thinking thing [*res cogitans*]; that is, a mind, or intellect, or understanding, or reason—words of whose meanings I was previously ignorant. Yet I am a true thing and am truly existing; but what kind of thing? I have said it already: a thinking thing.[27]

From this it is now possible to lay the foundations of what can be called the Cartesian metaphysics of the *cogito*. For Descartes, what is foremost—what he will call "the first principle" in the preface-letter to his *Principe de la Philosophie* (Principle of Philosophy)—is therefore the existence of thought.[28] What is the essence of this first principle? It is that of being a thinking thing, a *res cogitans*. And what of the Being of all that is, of all that I am not? According to Descartes, all of this Being can be brought back to the Being of thought, to the *cogitata* or the *cogitationes* of the *cogito*, which thinks them. These determinations clearly show that Descartes is definitely a figure of metaphysics, a figure corresponding on all points to the "onto-theological" constitution of metaphysics, but with this difference, that this is a metaphysics according to the *cogito*. This metaphysics starts with a first principle and a determination of its essence that allow an understanding of the mode of being of all that is. Schematically:[29]

> First Principle: The Being of the *cogito* or of the "I think"
> Its Essence: *Res cogitans*, a thinking thing
> Being as Being: *Cogitatum*, the thought-Being

Being is thus accessed by thought, or by knowledge. We can therefore say, following Marion, that Descartes's metaphysics is gray—that is, it stems completely from thought (gray matter).[30] This is quite an appropriate term because it can also be said gray in the sense of an *eminence grise* or something that operates behind the scenes, unseen.

Third Meditation: Concerning God, That He Exists—the Return to the Metaphysics of Divinity

Having defined the metaphysics of the *cogito*, the third *Meditation* finally addresses the question of God. Perhaps this step is a little tardy, since making the *cogito* the principle of "first" philosophy jostles the ontological hierarchy of classical theology, which was inclined to ascribe to God (or to the Being that emanates from him) the status of first principle. Nevertheless, in the *Meditations*, Descartes still attributes this status to God, but only to solve an epistemological problem related to thought, namely, ensuring the truth of what I perceived clearly and distinctly.

There is no doubt the nature of our thought, the *cogito*, is perfectly evident. I am certain that I am (*sum, existo*) and that I am a thinking thing (*res cogitans*). Descartes never calls into question this obvious fact—or "first instance of knowledge"—and it does not need to be specifically ensured.[31] However, Descartes does seek to know if he can justify *other* forms of knowledge, since he must "begin again from original foundations" if he is to "establish anything firm and lasting in the sciences."[32] For this reason, he announces programmatically in *Meditation* III: "Now I will ponder more carefully to see whether perhaps there may be *other* things belonging to me (*apud me alia sint*) that up until now I have failed to notice. I am certain that I am a thinking thing. But do I not therefore also know what is required for me to be certain of anything?"

This program is perhaps more complex than it appears. Descartes recalls the evidence of my Being and of my essence (*res cogitans*). Yet, Descartes asks, what is required (*requiratur*) "to be certain" of something? He answers right away: "Surely in this first instance of knowledge (an important expression), there is nothing but a certain clear and distinct perception of what I know." Since it is immediately present to itself, the thought of the self is clear and distinct. Descartes then draws from the fact that thought is an evidence for itself what he calls a "general rule."[33] This rule stated at the beginning of *Mediation* III stipulates "that everything I very clearly and distinctly perceive is true." This *regula generalis*, later becomes in *Mediation* V a *regula veritatis*.[34] what is perfectly obvious, subjective certitude, also corresponds to the objective truth of things[35]—that is, the inference from certitude to truth is correct.

But this general rule is itself less than obvious. This feeling of certitude could always deceive me: "Be it as it may, I have previously admitted many things as wholly certain and evident that nevertheless I later discovered to be doubtful."[36] Descartes recalls two such certainties that he later came to doubt:

1. That of the earth, the stars and all things he perceived through the senses. What did I clearly and distinctly conceive in this case? "Surely the fact that the ideas or thoughts of these things were hovering before my mind." But I was mistaken, observes Descartes, in thinking "that certain things existed outside me, things from which those ideas proceeded and which those ideas completely resembled."

2. Descartes recalls he was also mistaken—or could have been deceived—regarding "something very simple and easy in the areas of arithmetic and geometry, for example that two plus three make five."[37] Why could he doubt such facts? Because, says Descartes, "it occurred to me that some God could perhaps have given me a nature that I might be deceived (*deciperer*) even about matters that seemed most evident." And yet, this idea of a God that can deceive can also be used against the general rule (of truth), which has just been established because "were he to wish it, it would be easy for him to cause me to err even in those matters that I think I intuit as clearly as possible." It is through this perspective—putting into question the general rule of truth—that God enters into the Meditations:

> And certainly, because I have no reason for thinking that here is a God who is a deceiver [*deceptor*] [and of course I do not yet sufficiently know whether there even is a God], the basis for doubting, depending as it does merely on the above hypothesis, is very tenuous and, so to speak, metaphysical [a very pejorative use of the term!]. But in order to remove even this basis for doubt, I should at the first opportunity inquire whether there is a God, and if there is, whether or not he can be a deceiver. For if I am ignorant of this, it appears I am never capable of being completely certain about anything else.[38]

This passage, although decisive, seems to be astonishingly casual (I will get to this vague "metaphysics" when I have the time...), but it is at the same time very serious as well (since without it, I will never be certain of anything!). Nevertheless, Descartes calls upon God in his "Metaphysics" to resolve the epistemological problem of the stability of his general rule. God is only needed for this: He is there to answer the *cogito*'s need to *ensure* the certainty of his rule of evidence (or of truth). What must be shown about God is simply that he exists. Hence the title of the third *Meditation: De Deo, quod existat*. All I want to know about God, is whether he exists, as though it was the *cogito* asking God to exist simply to ensure its general rule of truth.

In order to establish the existence of God, Descartes starts from the idea of God that he has in his mind. He thus remains within the bounds of the metaphysics of the *cogito*. According to this idea, he understands God as "a supreme deity, eternal, infinite, omniscient, omnipotent, and creator of all things other than himself." The most important notion here is God represented as an infinite reality.[39] Descartes's argument consists in showing that a finite being could not have been the author of the idea of infinity. If I have the idea of infinity, then it can only be because God placed it in me, much as an artisan leaves a trace on his work.

Descartes introduces the argument using a seemingly self-evident principle: "Now it is indeed evident by the light of nature that there must be at least as much (reality) in the efficient and total cause as there is in the effect of that same cause. For whence, I ask, could an effect get its reality, if not from its cause?"[40] Descartes never justifies the authority or the evidence of this "light of nature." But it is with it that Descartes will escape, or posit a possible exit, from the metaphysics of the *cogito* established in the second *Meditation* where the *cogito* acted as the one and only principle of Being, universally conceived as *cogitatum* ("thought-Being"). Yet, now Descartes argues, if I am a thinking being and principle of my thoughts, I cannot be the cause of this idea of infinity because I am a finite being (who doubts, hesitates, and can err, and so on). It follows from the light of nature that "what is more perfect (that is, what contains in itself more reality) cannot come into being from what is less perfect."[41] As I am finite, I cannot have produced the idea of infinity. But nor could it have emerged out of nothing, it must therefore stem from God. God is thus "the cause of his idea in me"[42] (this is generally called Descartes's *a posteriori* argument, but the "effect" is, quite strikingly, the idea I have of God!). It follows from this that I am no longer alone in the world; God "too" exists:

> If the objective reality of any of my ideas is found to be so great that I am certain that the same reality was not in me, either formally or eminently, and that therefore I myself cannot be the cause of the idea, then it necessarily follows that I am not alone in the world, but that something else, which is the cause of this idea, also [*etiam*, omitted in many translations!] exists. But if no such idea is found in me, I will have no argument whatsoever to make me certain of the existence of anything other than myself.[43]

It is now possible to solve the problem of ensuring the *regula generalis*. The God that exists and is infinite can only be perfect. He cannot be *deceptor*, assures once again the *lumen naturale*: "it is quite obvious that he cannot be a deceiver, for it is manifest by the light of nature that all fraud and deception depend on some defect."[44] God, or what commentators have called "divine veracity,"[45] therefore guarantees the truth of my clear and distinct perceptions. And accordingly, God also guarantees truth and science, to such an extent that Descartes will argue in the *Sixth Reply* that an atheistic science is unthinkable.[46]

Descartes seems here to relinquish the immanence of the metaphysics of the *cogito*, which he had so firmly established in the first two meditations. In speaking of light, Descartes refers tacitly to another metaphysics, governed by the idea of a divine causality posited as the principle of Being as a whole, and God now conceived as *causa sui*. Marion insightfully describes how Descartes here employs an onto-theology different from the one he had defined in the second *Meditation*. He speaks of a "second take on Being as Being," which interprets Being not as *cogitatum*, but as *causatum* (caused). This surreptitious, older and more fundamental metaphysics also employs a unitary conception of onto-theology, federated by a first principle, which implies a universal intelligence of its dependents' mode of being. Being as Being is thus understood as caused-Being. Marion lists these two metaphysics in the following table:[47]

	METAPHYSICS OF THE *COGITATIO*	METAPHYSICS OF THE *CAUSA*
Being as Being understood as	thought-Being *ens ut cogitatum*	caused-Being *ens ut causatum*
The principle of Being	*ego cogito*	*Deus* (as *causa sui*)
In accordance with the logic of	*cogitare* (thought)	*causare* (cause)

Thus we find two "metaphysics" in Descartes, which are not so much in competition as subordinated insofar as the ontology of the caused-Being (*ens ut causatum*) founds, supports and upholds the metaphysics of the thought-Being (*ens ut cogitatum*). At the beginning of the chapter, we had wondered whether there was any metaphysics in Descartes. Now we are faced with a veritable excess of metaphysics: We can identify not one, but two distinct ontologies in the *Meditations on First Philosophy*.

The Legacy of Descartes's Double Metaphysics

For this reason, one can ask which is the most fundamental metaphysics for Descartes, that of the *cogito* or that of divinity? It is certainly by the *cogito* that one arrives at God, but it is God that ensures the truth of the general rule. Which is the first principle? Is the argumentation not circular? Arnauld, one of Descartes's contemporaries, was the first to notice this in his objections to the *Meditations*.[48] It is through the *cogito* that one arrives at God, but it is God who founds, after the fact, the rule of truth. What then founds what? We seem to be confronted with a dualism of principles (the *ego* and God), which corresponds to the cohabitation of the two metaphysics in Descartes (according to whether the *ens* is understood as *cogitatum* or as *causatum*). Descartes must have wanted to subordinate the metaphysics of the *cogito* to that of the created-Being, but God is only arrived at by way of the reasons deployed by the "subject" itself (although the term *subjectum* did not yet have a anthropological sense, as is often thought). Indeed, it is the *cogito*, and only the *cogito*, that "requires" (*requiratur, Meditations,* III) God as a means to ensure the objectivity of its representations. One could say that God is only an "idea" of the *cogito*, which would then confirm its "grey" primacy. The step toward turning God into a subjective "fiction" (Kant, Feuerbach, Nietzsche) has now become metaphysically possible.

But, it is perhaps more appropriate to refer to a *tension* between the two faces of first philosophy. In one, God is the first principle, following the oldest tradition of metaphysics; the other establishes the absolute priority of the *cogito* and of what will soon be called subjectivity. This tension between these two forms of metaphysics allows one to appreciate the avenues that Descartes's successors will take. Descartes's heirs, rather than maintaining the balance of the two, will more often that not chose one metaphysics over the other. Some will choose God as the first principle, and others will choose the second way and make human "subjectivity" the principle of the intelligibility of things. God thus becomes a simple product of subjectivity, and even a fiction that one can avoid by accounting for Being through the human *ego*, which is now seen as being on its own.[49]

Among those who opposed Descartes—sometimes explicitly—and reaffirmed the primacy of God over the simply human *cogito*, we can count Malebranche,[50] Spinoza, maybe Leibniz, certainly Schelling, Hegel, and Whitehead. But we may also include all the thinkers who construed human reality as dependent on "structures" they judged more fundamental be they socioeconomic (Marx, Althusser), linguistic (Structuralism), or historical (Historicism). Among the more numerous thinkers who radicalized the primacy of the human subject we may name Locke, Berkeley, Hume, Kant, Fichte, Nietzsche, Husserl, Heidegger, Sartre, and Merleau-Ponty (to name a few). In Descartes, both metaphysics still cohabit: Whereas the metaphysics of divine causality stems from a more classical tradition, the metaphysics of the *cogito* carries with it the seed of modern ontology.

CHAPTER 7

SPINOZA AND LEIBNIZ

The Metaphysics of Simplicity and Integral Rationality

Ethical Metaphysics: Spinoza

Cartesian metaphysics spread with unprecedented speed throughout Europe. Although it did contribute to the extraordinary growth of metaphysical thought, "modern rationalism," as it is often albeit somewhat imprecisely called, is today justly considered an affront to School metaphysics. One of its first and most brilliant commentators was the philosophical outsider *par excellence*, Baruch de Spinoza (1632–1677), who wrote some ten years after Descartes's death. A Jew of Portuguese descent living in Amsterdam, Spinoza was excommunicated by his synagogue in 1656 for criticizing the superstition he discerned in his religion. As is testified to by his iconoclast *Tractatus Theologico-Politicus*, he extended his criticism to all so-called revealed religions as well—that is, to all religions not founded solely on human reason, which Spinoza defended in everything he wrote. In Descartes, he welcomed the free reign given to reason and the desire to cast aside the prejudices of tradition. In fact, the only text published during Spinoza's lifetime under his name was *Principles of Cartesian Philosophy* (1663), to which he annexed his own "metaphysical reflections," his *Cogitata Metaphysica*, which were inspired by textbooks of school metaphysics, including Suarez's. The juxtaposition says much about

Spinoza: Although he was imbued quite early on with the spirit of Descartes's philosophy, he also saw that he could revive "metaphysical" thought, which had largely come to be the preoccupation of those who were called, slightly pejoratively, the "Peripatetics" or Scholastics, whom Descartes had vigorously opposed.

Spinoza, who was well-known during his lifetime, was offered a chair at the University of Heidelberg (one of the oldest in Europe), which he declined because he feared his freedom of thought would not be respected in religious matters, which were then also political. For this reason, he lived his life as a simple lens grinder and taught his friends and disciples privately. They hastened to publish his *Works* (*Opera Posthuma*), which included his very famous *Ethica*, six months after his death in 1677. Beholden to neither Church nor School, Spinoza was the quintessential freethinker, the likes of which are rare in the history of metaphysics. All Spinoza wished for from philosophy was genuine liberation and the greatest good in which man could participate. Just as Descartes had begun his *Meditationes* by deciding to "raze everything to the ground" in order to "begin again from original foundations," Spinoza also opens his *Treatise on the Emendation of the Intellect*, which was never completed, by promising to turn away from what is unessential and turn towards the only real truth:

> After experience had taught me that all the things which regularly occur in ordinary life are empty and futile . . . I resolved at last to try to find out whether there was anything which would be the true good, capable of communicating itself, and which alone would affect the mind, all others being rejected—whether there was something which, once found and acquired, would continuously give me the greatest joy, to eternity.[1]

On this, his remarks are resolutely existential and oriented toward the liberation of Humankind. It is for good reason that his masterpiece was an *Ethic*, which also presented itself as "metaphysics." His metaphysics is one of the "highest good": If all good is relative to another good, then the absolute good is one sought for itself. In order to enjoy it, one must develop man's "superior nature." I will show, says Spinoza, that this superior nature "is the knowledge of the union that the mind has with the whole of Nature."[2]

But this is just another way of saying that the greatest happiness, ethical as well as metaphysical, resides in the union with the supreme being. That is why,

> to unite and order all our perceptions, it is required, and reason demands, that we ask, as soon as possible, whether there is a certain being, and at

the same time, what sort of being it is, which is the cause of all things, so that its objective essence may also be the cause of all our ideas, and then our mind will . . . reproduce Nature as much as possible. For it will have Nature's essence, order, and unity objectively.[3] [. . .] For it is a unique and infinite being, beyond which there is no Being.[4]

The thought of the infinite being, understood as "beyond which there is no Being," is the core of what can be called Spinoza's ethical metaphysics. Around 1660, he wrote a "Short Treatise on God, Man, and his Well-Being." In it, he took up Descartes's *a priori* argument ("Whatever we clearly and distinctly understand to belong to the nature of a thing, we can truly affirm of that thing: But we can understand clearly and distinctly that existence belongs to God's nature."),[5] along with his quite particular *a posteriori* argument ("If man has an idea of God, then God must exist formally. But man has an idea of God", and since a "finite intellect cannot comprehend the infinite,"[6] God must be the cause of this idea). It is the former, the *a priori* argument that opens the *Ethics* "demonstrated in geometric order." Spinoza therein presents the idea of God as *causa sui* as a self-evident definition: "By cause of itself I understand that whose essence involves existence, *or* that whose nature cannot be conceived except as existing."

The human mind's most essential and most liberating thought is therefore that of God, who is the cause of all that is, to such an extent that all that is cannot be distinguished from him. Hence Spinoza's well known expression: *Deus sive natura*, "God or Nature," which earned him the reputation as a hardened atheist. His reputation was not redeemed until the advent of German Idealism at the turn of the nineteenth century, which took his "pantheism" (all is God, God is in everything) as the only possible starting point for any metaphysics. But in the seventeenth and eighteenth centuries, his atheism was thought to be the grievous consequence of the rational interpretation of the Bible proposed in his daring *Tractatus* of 1670.

Although famous, "*Deus sive natura*" is not the canonical expression of Spinoza's philosophy. It is absent from the first book of the *Ethics*, which is devoted to God.[7] It only appears in book IV (on human bondage!) as an aside linking the infinite being (*étant*), nature, God, and the *ratio* together. "That eternal and infinite being we call God, *or* Nature acts from the same necessity from which he exists . . . . The reason therefore, *or* cause, why God, *or* Nature (*sive natura*), acts, and the reason why he exists, are one and the same."[8] Indeed how can one think of an act of nature without thinking of it as an act of God, and vice versa? And more fundamentally: How is one not to think that all things are "in God" (*omnia in Deo sint*) since all things "so depend on him that without him they can neither be nor be conceived."[9]

To achieve this thought of the "immanence of all things in God," the human mind must liberate itself from the bondage of its affects and passions, which divert its attention away from this essential knowledge, the only one offering sovereign felicity. Thus Spinoza's "metaphysics" is marked by transcendence—human auto-transcendence—and is radically ethical.

In his *Ethics*, Spinoza hardly ever speaks of metaphysics. But he did so frequently in his early writings, notably in his *Cogitata metaphysica* (Metaphysical Reflections), in which he presupposed, unlike Descartes, that the academic, and recent, distinction between general and special metaphysics was self-evident.[10] In the first section of his *Cogitata*, Spinoza deals with the main questions "that commonly occur in the general part of Metaphysics, concerning Being and its Affections." And in the second section, he addresses the questions "which commonly occur in the special part of Metaphysics about God, his Attributes, and the human Mind." In his *Cogitata*, as in the rest of his work, Spinoza seeks to reconcile Descartes's "metaphysics," which Spinoza understood as a call for integral rationality aligned with the fundamental idea of an infinite substance cause of itself, with the legacy of School metaphysics, which Descartes had rejected. Spinoza thus sought to synthesize classical, or School, metaphysics with the new Cartesian metaphysics, in the name of the metaphysics of absolute divinity, posited as the unique substance without which things "can neither be nor be conceived."

Like Avicenna, the *Cogitata metaphysica* identify two types of Being. (1) Being that necessarily exists in virtue of its nature—that is, its essence involves existence; and (2) Being whose essence only implies a merely possible existence.[11] Necessary Being, in which all things "are," is nevertheless conceived, in accordance with Scholastics, as a perfectly *simple* reality. If it were a composite, its parts would exist prior to God, which would be absurd.[12] The divine substance's simplicity stems from the fact its essence involves its existence.[13]

Although conscious of his debt, Spinoza frequently speaks impatiently of school metaphysics. His impatience can be felt at the beginning of this *Cogitata*: "I shall say nothing," announces Spinoza, "concerning either the definition of this Science [metaphysics] or the things it is concerned with; my intention here is only to explain the more obscure things which are commonly treated by Writers on Metaphysics." Having reminded the reader that God is "a perfectly simple being," he sighs: "We pay no attention to the hodge-podge of Peripatetic distinctions."[14] Spinoza is wary of metaphysical treatises that since Descartes have become outdated and obscure. Following Descartes's lead, Spinoza values clarity, simplicity, and the sort of "metaphysical thinking" all can comprehend as long as one wishes to use his or her mind, in order to rise to the level of the contemplation of the spirit from which all things proceed. This is the reason for the singular importance of simplicity for Spinoza, simplicity of the fundamental ideas, simplicity of the idea of God, and their exposition. Instead of the Scholastics' metaphysical disputations, Spinoza prefers an exposition "in geometric order" that arrives at conclusions by deriving them from clear and simple definitions. This mode of explanation, which may appear slightly artificial, stems from an emphasis on clarity that is characteristic of the classical age of metaphysics: If God is defined by his simplicity and order, the same must apply to metaphysics' method as well.

Leibniz and the Search for the Metaphysics of Substantial Forms

A metaphysics of simplicity and integral rationality also characterizes the thought of Gottfried Wilhelm Leibniz (1646–1716). Although Leibniz was a universal genius—he was a diplomat, a historian, a theologian, and a mathematician who (along with Newton) gave us calculus—what we shall focus on here is Leibniz the "metaphysician." He was well versed in the classical authors and was fond of recalling how Aristotle considered metaphysics a desired or "sought-after" science: "That is the sort of metaphysics which Aristotle asked for—it is the science which he called *zetouménè* meaning 'the desired' or what he was looking for. It was to relate to the other theoretical sciences as the science of happiness does to the (practical) arts upon which it relies, and as the architect does to the builders."[15] The science that the ancients had "sought" may have been the highest science in the Peripatetic's manuals, but, as we have seen, thinkers such Descartes and Spinoza distrusted these manuals and gave more importance to mathematics, geometry, physics, and medicine. Traditional metaphysics was thus in crisis. The idea of a universal science of Being as Being, or of substance, had been supplanted by a first philosophy inflected in the first person of the present tense of the indicative mood (*ego sum, ego cogito*). Little room was left for talk of essence, substantial forms, and final causes that the Peripatetics, who were ignorant of the evidence of mathematics and experimental natural science, still attributed to beings. And Leibniz, who tried throughout his life to reconcile the Christian denominations and the great European nations following the Thirty Years' War, was very much aware of this crisis. A crisis of credibility in modern metaphysics, torn as it was between the Ancients' dream of a universal science of substance and the Moderns' project of a universal mathematics.

Although he did read the works of the Moderns, such as Descartes and Spinoza, Leibniz, as he states in his *Discourse on Metaphysics* (1686), did not share their harsh opinion of the Scholastics:

> I know that I am advancing a great paradox by attempting to rehabilitate the old philosophy in some fashion and to restore the almost banished substantial forms to their former place. But perhaps I will not be condemned so easily when it is known that I have long meditated upon the modern philosophy, that I have given much time to experiments in physics and demonstrations in geometry, and that I had long been persuaded about the futility of these beings, which I finally was required to embrace in spite of myself and, as it were, by force, after having myself carried out certain studies. These studies made me recognize that our moderns do not give enough credit to Saint Thomas and to the other great men of his time and that there is much more solidity than one imagines in the opinions of the Scholastic philosophers and theologians, provided that they are used appropriately and in their proper place. I am even convinced that, if some exact and thoughtful mind took the trouble to clarify and summarize their thoughts after the manner of the analytic geometers, he would find there a great treasure of extremely important and wholly demonstrative truths.[16]

This "exact and thoughtful mind," who is called to discover just how solid scholastic philosophy is, is perhaps Leibniz himself. His metaphysical ambition is to reconcile the solidity of the Ancients, their understanding of substance, and the Moderns' demonstrative and analytic rigor. Leibniz worked toward this reconciliation in all his writings without ever publishing a definitive version of his "desired" metaphysics. His metaphysics gradually emerged in countless letters and texts that are now well known but were for the most part published posthumously. For example, the *New Essays on Human Understanding*, which is a dialogue between Leibniz and Locke, was written in 1703 but left unpublished until 1765, and his *Discourse on Metaphysics*, written in 1686, and the *Monadology* (1714), a mature synthesis of his ideas, were not published until the nineteenth century. And other manuscripts were not published until the twentieth century as part of his complete works by the Academy of Berlin.[17] As with most great metaphysicians, Leibniz never presented a definitive version of his system. The philosopher Fichte even claimed that nobody has ever been so convinced of his own philosophy as Leibniz was of his. According to Fichte, Leibniz was so suffused by the spirit of his philosophy that he would have overlooked its word.[18]

Despite his thirst for simplicity, Leibniz's metaphysical journey is extraordinarily complex. The idea of "substantial forms" was undoubtedly for Leibniz the Ancients' most interesting idea. Plato spoke of the *eidos*, as did Aristotle, albeit using the idea of *ousia*, which he thought to be an autonomous entity that fulfilled a goal, a *telos* (*entelecheia*), or energy (*energeia*). The vitality of the substantial form, *source of its own movement*, was important for Leibniz who saw it as a correction of the Cartesian *res extensa*, which was moved solely by external mechanical force. According to Leibniz, all bodies are animated by a tension, an appetite, or a certain force:

> Now, this force is something different *from size,* shape, and motion, and one can therefore judge that not everything conceived in body consists *solely in extension* and in its modifications, as our moderns have persuaded themselves. Thus we are once again obliged to reestablish some beings or forms they have banished.

From this, Leibniz argues that: "The general principles of corporeal nature and of mechanics itself are more metaphysical than geometrical, and *belong* to some indivisible forms or natures as the *causes of appearances*, rather than to corporeal mass or extension."[19]

To express this vitality, Spinoza had sometimes used the term *conatus*—that is, a force inherent to all things, which, as Hobbes also held, was a will to persevere in its Being.[20] But Leibniz, hoping to reform the notion of substance along with first philosophy itself, came to conceive of this drive inherent to all substantial forms as force and as appetite (*appetitus*).[21] Appetite is not a prerogative of souls, he argues, it also animates all of nature's elementary substances inasmuch as one conceives them as "*primitive forces,* which contain not only *act* or the completion of possibility, but also an original *activity*."[22] Fond of Greek terms, Leibniz would later use the term *monas*, or "simple substance," to express the original activity of all beings. These monads are "the true atoms of nature and, in brief, the elements of things."[23] And if it is to live up to its name, "first philosophy" must be a *monadology*, a science of the original simplicity of all that is. But since the monads are many, there must be certain intrinsic qualities that distinguish them. Hence the important Leibnizian principle of the indiscernibles: "There are never two beings in nature that are perfectly alike, two beings in which it is not possible to discover an internal difference, that is, one founded on an intrinsic denomination."[24] This inner principle of each monad stems from their appetition, or a desire particular to each monad. Leibniz is thus not only one of the first metaphysicians of individualism, but he is also the theorist of modern pluralism: Each being seeks to realize itself in a universe constituted of the infinite diversity of monads in which it is impossible to confuse one monad with another. But are not these monads almost human? It is common to have this impression when reading Leibniz, as his comments do seem anthropological. However, the principles of force and appetite characterize, according to him, all beings insofar as they are the actualization (*entelechy*) of a substantial form.

Regulated by an inner principle, each monad is endowed with "perception." Leibniz uses this expression to designate the capacity shared by all monads to represent a multiplicity in a unity. It is only in humans that this capacity for perception is raised to its highest level such that the capacity for perception is "more distinct and accompanied by memory."[25] And in the case of human monads, this capacity, which accounts for the origin of our rationality, allows one to speak of souls. Now, these monads are founded on two important principles, which recapitulate classical metaphysics' will to integral explanation. On the one hand, the principle of non-contradiction, already formulated by Aristotle, and, on the other, the principle of sufficient reason first formulated by Leibniz: "by virtue of which we consider that we can find no true or existent fact, no true assertion, without there being a sufficient reason why it is thus and not otherwise, although most of the time these reasons cannot be known to us."[26]

Leibniz thereby expresses the principle of reality's integral rationality that is at the root of modern science's will for explanation: Nothing is without reason (*nihil est sine ratione*). But the principle is also the keystone of metaphysics since the reason for all things can be found in a necessary substance "and this is what we call God," writes Leibniz perhaps referring to the expression used in Aristotle's *Metaphysics* (*Metaphysics*, XII).[27]

As with Spinoza, God is the only necessary substance because he is the only one whose essence includes existence: to be possible is sufficient for him to be actual.[28] All the other beings are contingent insofar as their possibility does not entail their actuality. The passage from possibility to existence depends on God considered as the primitive monad. It is in God, the primitive unity, in which all the other monads are like "fulgurations," that one finds "*power,* which is the source of everything, *knowledge,* which contains the diversity of ideas, and finally *will,* which brings about changes or products in accordance with the principle of the best."[29] This sequence of power, knowledge, and will, is not unimportant. God is first the principle of power, the power that is the origin of every monad's power. But this power is also the intelligence that thinks all the determinations of all possible beings prior to their existence. Therefore, things pass from potentiality to actuality in accordance with this divine will. But the divine will is not arbitrary since it is necessarily regulated by the "principle of the best." If there is an infinity of possible worlds in God's mind, there obviously must be "a sufficient reason for God's choice, a reason which determines him towards one thing rather than another."[30] This is the principle of Leibnizian optimism. It does not claim that we live in a perfect world, but only that we live in the best of all *possible* worlds. Why? Because only this principle of sufficient reason can have guided God when he chose this world, or this set of actualized possibilities, rather than another.

Thus Leibniz's metaphysics leads to a "theodicy," a justification of God's choice, which stems from the principle that God himself can only have been governed by sufficient reason. God certainly wished to realize the most perfection possible when he compared the suitability of each monad. We therefore live in the best of all possible worlds because it would be impious to think otherwise.

But this impiety soon became possible and led metaphysics—and Western rationality—to a new crisis. In 1755, an earthquake destroyed Lisbon killing some thirty-thousand people and destroyed the Enlightenment's optimism. In 1756, Voltaire (1694–1778), who had written a *Traité de métaphysique* as a young man,[31] wrote his famous poem "The Lisbon Earthquake": "Oh wretched Man," "Come ye philosophers, who cry 'all's well,' / And contemplate this ruin of a world." Four years later, his *Candide, or the Optimist* appeared anonymously. It tells the satirical story of the misfortunes and calamities of a naïve young man from Westphalia (where Leibniz was from), who had been taught by his teacher Pangloss, professor of "metaphysico-theologo-cosmolonigology," that we live in the best of all possible worlds. It was more than a critique of Leibniz and his metaphysics, however. The idea of reality's integral rationality was also pilloried. And it then fell to Kant, and all modern metaphysics, to respond to this humiliation of metaphysics and human reason.

CHAPTER 8

KANT

Metaphysics Turned Critical

Metaphysics is without a doubt the most difficult of all things into which man has insight.
But so far no metaphysics has ever been written.[1]

The question whether metaphysics is possible looms over the philosophy of Immanuel Kant (1724–1804). Although he is reputed to be the gravedigger of metaphysics—and he did certainly bury traditional metaphysics, which he identified with Wolff and Baumgarten's School metaphysics in which he was trained—nobody spoke so much about metaphysics nor pondered its failings, its promise, and its future as did Kant. In fact, from the beginning to the end of his career, Kant is probably the author who used the term "metaphysics" the most in the titles of his works. Beginning with his habilitation thesis of 1755, which offered *A New Explanation of the First Principles of Metaphysical Knowledge*, to his satirical work of 1766 on the *Dreams of a Spirit Seer Elucidated by Dreams of Metaphysics*, to his *Prolegomena to any Future Metaphysics* (1783), his *Groundwork of the Metaphysics of Morals* (1786), and on to his last works on *The Metaphysical Foundations of Natural Science* (1791) and the *Metaphysics of Morals* (1797), Kant never ceased to inquire into the fate of metaphysics. Two important, apparently contradictory, tendencies characterize his work on metaphysics. On the one hand, he ceaselessly attacks and berates it because it has yet to become a science; but on the other hand, he seeks to make such a science possible at last.

He treats metaphysics harshly because it is dear to him. He actually admits at the end of his *Critique of Pure Reason* that "we shall always return to metaphysics as to a beloved one with whom we have quarreled."[2]

Natural Metaphysics

Kant begins with what he believes is an indisputable fact: Up until now, metaphysics has been riven with strife. For some time now, sighs Kant, metaphysics has fallen into a state of "complete anarchy."[3] This state of anarchy, or lack of principles (*an-archè*), is almost ironic for a discipline that has understood itself ever since Aristotle as a science of *first principles*.

But there may be worse than this anarchy: total *indifference* toward metaphysics' unfortunate condition. The failure to turn metaphysics (or philosophy) into a science has not been seen as a scandal. During the Enlightenment, and in the wake of Locke and Hume's empiricism, metaphysics was often derided, as we saw with Voltaire's "metaphysico-theologo-cosmolonigology." True, or scientific, knowledge can only be found in the experimental sciences. This is a modest form of knowledge, perhaps, but one that is certainly more reliable and more useful than anything metaphysics has ever produced: Kant never disputes the fact that metaphysics had been unable to become as rigorous as physics or mathematics. But he is far from heaping scorn on metaphysics, which he believes to be essential to human reason. As Ferdinand Alquié has recalled in his book *La critique kantienne de la métaphysique* (1968), Kant did not seek to destroy metaphysics, but rather wanted to fight his contemporaries' indifference to it. Although metaphysics may never have fully justified its scientific pretensions, the "metaphysical need" is nevertheless quite real. One may laugh at the scholarly controversies over metaphysics, but one cannot be indifferent toward the question of the existence of God or of the soul's immortality. "For it is pointless to feign *indifference* to such inquiries, the object of which can *never* be *indifferent* to our human nature."[4] Metaphysics may well inquire into problems that may seem insoluble, abstruse, or contradictory, but one cannot deny that metaphysics is a natural human disposition:

> Yet, in a certain sense, this *kind of knowledge* is to be looked upon as given; that is to say, metaphysics actually exists, if not as a science, yet still as natural disposition (*metaphysica naturalis*). For human reason, without being moved merely by the idle desire for extent and variety of knowledge, proceeds impetuously, driven on by an inward need, to question such as

cannot be answered by any empirical employment of reason, or by principles thence derived. Thus in all men, as soon as their reason has become ripe for speculation, there has always existed and will always continue to exist some kind of metaphysics [*irgendeine Metaphysik*].[5]

Irgendeine Metaphysik. There will always be some sort of metaphysics. His text explains why: Driven by its nature, human reason is irresistibly led beyond the limits of the sensible world and asks metaphysical questions. Why is reason driven to these questions? Because it seeks to know the reason for things: In seeking the condition for all things, reason cannot help asking itself about the condition of this condition. Only something unconditioned can satisfy this quest for the condition of the condition. Never satisfied with what is conditioned, because it does not fulfill its search for explanation, reason seeks out what it unconditioned, or absolute. Reason is thus inherently metaphysical, and humans are condemned to ponder metaphysical questions. But are these aspirations legitimate? Are there any metaphysical forms of knowledge? This is Kant's most important question.

Is Metaphysics Possible as Science?

The metaphysical disposition, or *metaphysica naturalis* as Kant calls it, is thus a part of human reason. Kant will take great pains to show how reason, because of its inner structure, seeks particular forms of the unconditioned. Naturally inclined to metaphysics, pure reason necessarily develops ideas such as the *soul, freedom*, or *God*. In the first case, the soul is the ultimate substrate of thought, in the second, freedom is the unconditioned principle of action, and finally, God is the ultimate principle of reality. The ultimate aim of reason pertains exclusively to these three objects insists Kant: the freedom of the will, the immortality of the soul, and the existence of God.[6] Ultimately, metaphysics is limited to these three considerations. But can metaphysics, as a real natural disposition, produce a reflection rigorous enough to live up to *metaphysica naturalis*'s legitimate questions? Kant writes his *Critique of Pure Reason* (1781) to answer this very question. As a propaedeutic to metaphysics, the *Critique of Pure Reason*'s intention is to answer one specific question, which Kant claims to be the first to ask: How is metaphysics possible? Or rather, since metaphysics is a real disposition: is metaphysics possible as *science*?[7]

But what does he mean by "science"? Unfortunately, Kant never states it clearly when discussing the possibility of metaphysics being a science. The idea of a science is today commonly associated with an experimental and verifiable form of knowledge. But this cannot be the case here, as metaphysics exceeds the confines of experience. So what is a science according to Kant? In the *Critique of Pure Reason*, he states that a science is not an aggregate of knowledge, but a system,[8] or the "unity of manifold modes of knowledge under one idea."

This conception of science obviously stems from the rationalist idea that the most rigorous form of knowledge is the one that follows from principles (*cognitio ex principiis*). Experimental knowledge, however, rests solely on experience (*ex datis*).[9] For example, one finds this kind of principled rational knowledge in pure mathematics or physics the principles of which Newton had demonstrated in the *Philosophiæ naturalis principia mathematica* (1686). The rigor of these pure sciences is uncontested. But what of metaphysics, which also claims to be a rational science? Is it possible *as science*?

The question conveys Kant's exasperation, which is palpable in the first lines of the work of 1781. Metaphysics is compared to a "battle ground" (*Kampfplatz*) where human reason, confronted with questions exceeding its power and which it cannot answer, interminably and vainly struggles with itself. After two millennia of metaphysical reflection what does metaphysics have to show for itself? In a text from 1766, Kant already had spoken sardonically of the "dreams of metaphysics." Perhaps metaphysics bites off more than it can chew. If metaphysics seems impossible, is it not precisely because it is "metaphysics"—that is, a form of knowledge beyond our grasp?

However, before engaging in metaphysics, says Kant, we must first ask ourselves whether metaphysical knowledge is even possible—that is, determine what are its principles. And if, having carried out such an examination, metaphysics is shown to be impossible, we must then redefine the whole philosophical project along with a new set of principles. This is the orientation Kant gives to his inquiry into the possibility of metaphysics carried out in the *Critique of Pure Reason*.

But what does he mean by "pure reason"? It is reason seeking knowledge without any recourse to experience. Ever since Parmenides and Plato, "metaphysics" has had the pretension of being a purely rational science, which exceeds empirical observations not only on account of its rigor but also because of the dignity of its object. But what is the *foundation* of such a form of knowledge, asks Kant? Is pure reason capable of knowing something outside of experience?

Kant answers this question in a complex and nuanced manner that makes his position on the possibility of metaphysics all the more difficult to understand. His answer is clear though: He thinks pure reason can indeed justify its pretensions to *a priori knowledge* (universal and necessary knowledge), but only as it pertains to mathematics (which is based on axioms and demonstrations derived from an *a priori* intuition) and pure Newtonian physics since it contains the principles that account for the general laws of nature (universal and necessary, and must therefore be of rational origin). In both cases, however, pure reason is shackled to *possible experience*. Mathematics depends on the possibility of intuition and physics on the possibility of laws of nature. But can pure reason justify forms of knowledge that are more *metaphysical* than mathematics and pure physics? Kant's attitude is at first skeptical, even sarcastic. If such forms of knowledge are indeed possible, then one must show *why* they are possible. And as long as this question remains unanswered, one must, as a matter of principle, suspend all metaphysical inquiry.

Pure reason is thus asked to justify its pretensions in a "tribunal" that is "no other than the *critique of pure reason* [itself]."[10] This tribunal has a twofold task: justification and critique. The legitimate pretensions of pure reason, in the realm of mathematics and physics, will be justified, and its illegitimate pretensions will be censured. But most of the censured pretensions will belong to metaphysics. So must we then conclude that metaphysics is impossible? Yes, for some metaphysics, but Kant does not give up on all forms of metaphysics since he does speak positively of a metaphysics of nature and morals that is yet to come.

Kant first drags "metaphysical reason" to court and tries it harshly for its mistaken claims to knowledge, which he attributes to its nature. Hence the need to cross-examine pure reason itself in order to identify—once and for all—the source of its misbegotten claims about itself. This cross-examination does not bring up the historical accomplishments of metaphysics. It pertains exclusively to pure reason's capacities themselves. Thus by a critique of reason, one should not imagine

> a critique of books and systems, but of the faculty of reason in general, in respect of all knowledge after which it may strive *independently of all experience*. It will therefore decide as to the possibility or impossibility of metaphysics in general, and determine its sources, its extent, and its limit—all in accordance with principles.[11]

By asking this question in such a solemn manner, Kant reveals his twofold intellectual origin. Although initially schooled in German rationalism, in which metaphysics was a very respectable science, Kant was also marked by Anglo-Saxon empiricism, that of Hume in particular,[12] which argued that all metaphysics was chimerical. Who is right? Either metaphysics is a mirage, or it is a legitimate science, in which case its principles must be demonstrated in order to found its knowledge. Which position will Kant choose? Unfortunately, it is never quite clear since Kant quite evidently struggled with this difficult question. In many texts, he seems to endorse empiricism and argues metaphysics is an impossible science because it claims to know something that exceeds its ability to know. This is the Kantian critique of metaphysics as it is generally remembered. In this case, Kant is quite obviously the destroyer of any metaphysics that cannot justify its pretensions and gingerly transgresses its limits. This is a point the *Critique* makes over and over.

Nevertheless the *Critique of Pure Reason* was evidently written *to make* metaphysics possible. Kant in fact promised many times to deliver such a metaphysics, the ground for which was prepared in the *Critique* of 1781. The avowed aim of this work was to define the "prolegomena to any future metaphysics will be able to come forward as science" as announced in the title of a work written in 1783 that partly summarizes the work of 1781. If Kant had really wished to show how metaphysics was futile, he could have avoided writing this eight-hundred-page-long *Critique*!

So what does he mean by metaphysics? Kant offers many definitions and we may begin with the one given in the preface to the first edition of the *Critique of Pure Reason*. Metaphysics is there defined as "nothing but the *inventory* of all we possess through *pure* reason, systematically arranged."[13] An obvious definition since all metaphysics does indeed exclusively pertain to the productions of pure reason. But how can these productions claim any objective value, asks Kant? That is the real Kantian question.

What are these elementary productions, and how do they lead to metaphysics? Kant has less difficulty answering this question. As a son of the rationalist tradition, Kant never doubts that an exhaustive inventory of all productions originating from pure reason is possible. That is, everything that stems from our mind's *a priori* activity. Broadly conceived, our mind has a capacity for synthesis that allows it to organize and unify sensory data. "Metaphysics," Kant says, is essentially the inventory of reason's *a priori* capacities for synthesis. And such an inventory may be called a system, says Kant, because everything belonging to reason, regulated as it is by the idea of a synthesis and unity, obeys a certain order, a certain architectonic. He also calls this "system of metaphysics" by the name "transcendental philosophy"—an expression obviously heavily laden with meaning for both Kant, and for School metaphysics as well since, as we have seen, "transcendental philosophy" had already been a name for general metaphysics. In the works of Duns

Scott, Suarez, and Wolff, this metaphysics, or transcendental philosophy, had inquired into the predicates of Being.

Kant and the Ancients' Transcendental Philosophy: Phenomena and the Things in Themselves

Kant was well aware the term "transcendental" belonged to an ancient tradition. He even briefly evokes this point in a passage from the 1781 *Critique* (in which historical references are rare, since its exclusive topic is pure reason itself) when speaking of "the transcendental philosophy of the ancients" (*die Transzendentalphilosophie der Alten*).[14] Kant never refers to any author in particular, but he does evoke the well-known scholastic adage about the transcendental concepts of Being: "*quodlibet ens est unum, verum, bonum*" ("all Being is one, true, good"). He does not give precise references and simply underlines that the use of this principle leads to "very meager consequences" (*sehr kümmerlich ausfiel*), which illustrates the contempt he liked to affect for this tradition. But being a charitable soul, Kant assumes that if such a principle has existed for so long it must have some useful principle at its base. The mistake, he explains, lies perhaps in understanding the transcendentals as the "transcendental predicates of things" rather than "logical requirements and criteria of all knowledge of things in general."[15] This is an important point since Kant thereby differentiates himself from the traditional metaphysics of the Ancients. For Kant, the universal concepts of things that stem from our reason *are not* the universal predicates of "things themselves." The things-in-themselves are unknowable since we know of them only insofar as "they are known"—that is, conceptualized with the aid of *our* mind's categories. Hence the important Kantian distinction between phenomena and the things-in-themselves: we cannot know (or speak of) the "things-in-themselves," we only know things as they appear to us by applying our mind's ("*a priori*") categories to them. These *a priori* concepts are only objectively valid in the realm of phenomena, the only realm in which we may legislate, or determine its laws. The reason for this limit is particular to Kant's epistemology: In the act of knowing, our sensory apparatus only gives us access to a completely disorganized "manifold" of sensible impressions. These impressions become orderly, thinks Kant, only through our concepts' active synthesis of them. As they stem from our mind, these concepts are necessarily *a priori* and impose their laws (order, unity, coherence and causality) to phenomena. "Thus the order and regularity in the appearances, which we entitle 'nature', we ourselves introduce. We could never find them in appearances, had not we ourselves, or the nature of our mind, originally set them there."[16] Kant, in a way, both exalts and belittles human reason. He exalts it because pure reason thereby appears as the source of the laws of nature. But he also belittles it by showing how it can know nothing of the laws (or the "predicates") governing the things themselves, nor any principle that exceeds the horizon of possible experience.

According to Kant, since the mind participates in the elaboration of what is given to us, *ontology*—the science of Being as it is in itself—is impossible. Nevertheless, Kant does agree with traditional ontology in saying it is the *a priori* determinations—now attributed to our mind—that constitute the system of metaphysics or transcendental philosophy. One need only replace the "proud name" of ontology with that of "transcendental analytic," which inventories all the original productions of our pure understanding[17] (the analytic is the first major section of Kant's *Critique*). These determinations (or categories) can be known *a priori* because they are immanent to reason itself. And, says Kant, since objects are known only through the categories, these categories are the "*a priori* principles of possible experience," meaning it is through them that objects can be known. Therefore, what can be known *a priori*, concludes Kant, are not the *a priori* principles of things or Being, but only the "conditions of possibility of objects of experience."

The major difference between the Kantian project and classical ontology is the accent Kant puts on the notion of *object* in general, which replaces the thing-in-itself: the only possible *a priori* knowledge is that of the *object in general*, rather than of Being. But is this nuance really important and is it really a revolution compared to traditional ontology? Kant certainly believed these *a priori* determinations to be "conditions of the possibility of the object as such," but did transcendental philosophy, from Duns Scot to Suarez and Wolff, seek anything different? In his own classes on metaphysics, Kant spoke of Baumgarten's definition of ontology by saying that it was "the science of the universal predicates of all things,"[18] and its universality justified its primacy in metaphysics' architectonic. "Ontology is the first part that actually belongs to metaphysics. The word itself . . . just means the *science of beings*, or properly according to the sense of the words, the *general doctrine of Being*. Ontology is the doctrine of elements of all my concepts my understanding can have only *a priori*."[19]

This characterization of ontology agrees on all points with the Kantian project of a transcendental philosophy identified with metaphysics. Indeed, Kant proposes to inventory our understanding's *a priori* determinations that preside (when used legitimately) over the ordering of experiences. Such a metaphysics of our reason's "legislative" faculty is therefore possible for Kant.

But in 1781, it must be first preceded by a critical reflection that defines the conditions and limits of metaphysical knowledge.

Critique and Metaphysics

In the preface to his 1781 *Critique*, Kant proclaims without any hesitation and rather nonchalantly that he will complete the science of metaphysics rather quickly and promises to publish it as soon as is his *Critique* is finished:

> Metaphysics, on the view which we are adopting, is the only one of all the sciences which dare promise that through a small but concentrated effort it will attain, and this in a short time, such a completion as will leave no task to our successors save that of adapting it in a *didactic* manner according to their own preferences, without their being able to add anything whatsoever to its content. For it is nothing but the *inventory* of all our possessions through *pure* reason, systematically arranged. . . . Such a system of pure (speculative) reason I hope myself to produce under the title *Metaphysics of Nature*. It will be not half as large, yet incomparably richer in content than this present *Critique*, which has as its first task to discover the sources and conditions of the possibility of such criticism, clearing, as it were, and leveling what has hitherto been a waste-ground.[20]

Thus before deploying this metaphysical system, understood as an inventory of our mind's *a priori* determinations, which contain the conditions of the possibility of objects, one must first inquire into the possibility of metaphysics itself: How is such a form of knowledge possible? Before building this metaphysics, its "prolegomena" or conditions of possibility must be first clarified. Now, when elaborating his critical philosophy, Kant uses the very important concept of "conditions of possibility" in two ways. (1) Obviously, the first *Critique* pertains to the "conditions of possibility" of metaphysics itself, the credibility of which has been called into question. (2) But transcendental philosophy is an inquiry into the "conditions of possibility" of *all objects*, and accordingly inquires into our mind's *a priori* determinations (our categories), which are the same for all phenomena. The two projects will ultimately merge into one since the critical reflection (1) into metaphysics' conditions of possibility leads Kant to claim that metaphysics (2) has no other task than to clarify the conditions of possibility of experience (or of objects in general).

However, before carrying out the increasingly apparent "merger" of critique with metaphysics, Kant begins by clearly distinguishing the two. Critical

reflection, assures Kant as he defines his project, has no other task than to prepare a metaphysics whose system must be presented *after* the *Critique*.

> A system of such concepts might be entitled transcendental philosophy.
> But that is still, at this stage, too large an undertaking . . . it is, so far as
> our present purpose is concerned, much too comprehensive. We have to
> carry the analysis so far only as is indispensably necessary in order to
> comprehend, in their whole extent, the principles of *a priori* synthesis,
> with which alone we are called upon to deal. It is upon this enquiry,
> which should be entitled not a doctrine, but only a transcendental cri-
> tique, that we are now engaged. Its purpose is not to extend knowledge,
> but only to correct it, and to supply a touchstone of the value, or lack of
> value, of all *a priori* knowledge. Such a critique is therefore a preparation,
> so far as may be possible, for an *organon*; and should this turn out not to
> be possible, then at least for a *canon*, according to which, in due course,
> the complete system of the philosophy of pure reason . . . may some day
> be carried into execution.[21]

The way forward thus seems to be already well marked: a critical reflection on the "touchstone" of metaphysical knowledge must come *before*
deploying the systematic doctrine of transcendental philosophy. But this
project of a future metaphysics appears already under a different and problematic light since the "touchstone" (which is a matter for the critique) must
allow one to decide the value or the "lack of value" (*Unwert*) of metaphysical knowledge. If the promise of metaphysics is maintained, why then evoke
the possibility of it being invalid? But even the promise of a new metaphysics seems less assured. Indeed, Kant appears to be rather hesitant about
what needs to be prepared ("as may be possible", he says!): is it an *organon* or
"only" a *canon* of the *a priori* forms of knowledge? The difference between
the two is not clearly explained, but an organon does seem to be more constricting that a simple canon ("at least for a canon," says Kant), in accordance with which "a complete system of the philosophy of pure reason" can
"some day" (!) be presented "be it in extension or merely in limitation if its
knowledge" (again!).

Kant seems to suddenly multiply the warnings about this ambitious twofold project (critique and metaphysics). Is it to be an *organon* or a simple
canon? Is it to extend or limit the scope of metaphysics? Why be so vague in
the introduction to a work that hinges on the idea that the critique is to prepare the way for scientific metaphysics?

When one considers the historical development of his thought, the *critical project* obviously captivated Kant more than he let on, or even than he thought it would. Instead of the metaphysics he repeatedly promised, he ended up first writing two more *Critiques* even though in 1781 he had planned only one. After the *Critique of Pure Reason,* he wrote the *Critique of Practical Reason* (1788) and the *Critique of the Faculty of Judgment* (1790). Did the critical project eventually replace the projected doctrinal metaphysics? Should metaphysics therefore be considered to be only a "science of the limits of human understanding" as he had presciently claimed in *Dreams of a Spirit Seer*?[22]

Actually, the Kantian project of a purely limitative metaphysics or critique, as well as the projected metaphysics of the irreducible products of pure reason (under the name transcendental philosophy) eventually came together. For Kant, along with the whole metaphysical tradition, philosophy must remain on the level of pure reason. How else is it to differentiate itself from experimental knowledge if not as a science of the *a priori* legislation that stems from our reason? But in order to produce such a science one must first determine the *limits* of human understanding and realize that the *a priori* is limited to the conditions making experience possible. Since it is so easy to limit and circumscribe these conditions, according to Kant, "metaphysics" represents "the only one [!] of all the sciences which dare promise that through a small but concentrated effort it will attain, and this in a short time, such a completion as will leave no task to our successors save that of adapting it in a *didactic* manner."[23]

And yet Kant never produced the metaphysics that had seemed so easy in 1781. It is as though the founding pair, critique and metaphysics, gave way to a project of a critical reflection on the limits *within which* legislation worthy of pure reason can be deployed. To mark the limits of pure reason is not only to censure metaphysical reason as it tries to exceed its bounds, those of possible experience, it is also, and more importantly, to circumscribe the legitimate domain of pure reason and its *a priori* legislation. Kant limits this legitimate and legislative power to the metaphysics of nature and the metaphysics of morals. What Kant thus made possible was a "critical metaphysics." Convinced his critical reflection was a turning point in the history of metaphysics, Kant proclaims on the last page of his *Critique*: "the *critical* path alone is still open." This means several things:

1. Historically, Kant implies that all prior metaphysics, which aspired to a supersensible form of knowledge that exceeds all possible experience, was stillborn because it never inquired into its conditions of possibility, or its limits.

2. Starting with Kant and his "critical path," metaphysics must be a *science of the limits of pure reason*. Our pure reason can know nothing more *a priori* than the conditions of possible experience.

3. For this reason, in its more positive vein, metaphysics can only become the doctrine of *a priori* legislation of pure reason in the two areas it can act in a legitimate way, or in a way that can be legitimated: nature and morality.

Indeed, it was the critical metaphysics of nature and morality that monopolized all of Kant's attention following his first *Critique*. In its first part, the 1781 *Critique* already produced, for all intents and purposes, the "metaphysics of nature." It showed that our universal and necessary, thus *a priori*, laws stemmed from our pure understanding. It also showed that these laws preside over our knowledge of phenomena and even constitute nature itself insofar as we know nothing of nature independently from our faculty of knowing. This "theoretical" metaphysics justified the Newtonian project of an *a priori* knowledge of the laws of nature, but also refuted Humes's empiricism that claimed all *a priori* knowledge of nature was impossible. Kant later produced a new exposition of this metaphysic of nature in *The Metaphysical Foundations of Nature* (1786). Nonetheless, because it was also the most able to respond to the questions of natural metaphysics, the metaphysics that most absorbed Kant was the metaphysics of morals.

The Metaphysics of Freedom

Whereas the task of theoretical philosophy, or the "metaphysics of nature,"[24] is to discover the categories and principles governing phenomena, the task of the metaphysics of morals is to shed light on the rational, and therefore universal, principles that regulate human activity. Metaphysics is possible in both cases since their task pertains to our reason's *a priori* legislation. Pure reason's legislation not only covers the realm of Being and nature as theoretical or speculative reason, but as *practical* reason it also legislates in the realm of "what ought to be done" (*Sollen*).

Kant is aware that almost all motives governing human action are empirical and contingent. Although our practical reason is certainly influenced by experience, if there were something like *pure practical reason* it would be reason as it ascribes maxims to our actions independently of experience. But what can be commanded *a priori* or in a strictly rational manner? It cannot be a particular determined action because it would then be related to experience. The only thing that can be commanded *a priori* is a universal requirement, which can only have an effect on the form of our maxims: act only according to that maxim which you can also will that it become a universal law. Such is the general form of the categorical imperative that can be derived from pure practical reason. Thus the task of the *Metaphysics of Morals*, as well as its *Groundwork* (*Grundlegung*) written in 1785, is to bring to light this major principle of pure practical reason and set it apart from all empirical motives.

The metaphysics of morals is obviously an ethic—a morality of rational action the norms of which are susceptible of universality. But as its title clearly indicates, it is also "metaphysics." It is said to be "metaphysics" because it inquires into the *a priori* principles of moral action (Kant often uses "metaphysics" as a synonym of *a priori*). Furthermore, it also offers answers to the major questions of classical metaphysics.

For Kant, as we have seen, our reason's ultimate aim is concerned with three objects:[25] freedom of the will, immortality of the soul, and the existence of God. These are for Kant reason's three essential metaphysical ideas. Now the metaphysics of morals is intrinsically related to freedom: action, moral action, only makes sense if we are free—that is, if we are only partially determined by natural necessity. Yet as we have seen, natural necessity is universally valid since our understanding imposes it *a priori* on all nature. But this *a priori* legislation, Kant now claims, only pertains to the phenomenal world, or the world of things as they appear to us and which can be known. Thus insofar as we are part of the phenomenal world, we are governed by natural necessity, but as free beings, we may escape its necessity. We are free only because we also belong to the non-phenomenal realm. As a part of this realm, we are "things-in-themselves." But since things-in-themselves cannot be known, we cannot know our freedom nor verify it empirically. For this reason, according to Kant, freedom is only an idea of our reason.

But the idea is nonetheless useful. In the *Groundwork of the Metaphysics of Morals* (1785), Kant asserts that there are two ways of considering oneself. Insofar as I am part of the sensible world, the necessary laws of nature govern me, but insofar as I consider myself to be free or independent of nature, I am also part of the intelligible world, the *mundus intelligibilis*.[26] Here Kant adapts the Platonic and metaphysical distinction *par excellence* between the sensible world and the intelligible world, and gives the latter practical importance. By my practical reason, and only by my practical reason, I may consider myself to be part of the intelligible world. Why? Because I can act in accordance with laws that are not determined by any natural necessity, laws that reason gives to itself autonomously. Freedom is therefore to be understood in two ways according to Kant: negatively as independence from natural necessity, and positively as the capacity to legislate for oneself (which is the essential meaning of auto-nomy). Kant thus differentiates nature's heteronomy from freedom's autonomy.

Thus it is freedom, and only freedom, that "makes me a member of the intelligible world."[27] But since I am also part of the sensible world, the laws of the intelligible world, which pertain to moral action, are somewhat constricting. For this reason, these laws take the form of an imperative, and a categorical one because the actions they impose on me are subject to no conditions other than those prescribed by reason when it establishes its own law. This autonomy allows me to participate in a realm other than nature. Any reasonable being can therefore "act as if he were through his maxim always a lawgiving member of the universal kingdom of ends."[28] "As if," says Kant: freedom must always remain an assumption in practical philosophy. Kant insists freedom "is no concept of experience."[29] "The concept of an intelligible world is thus only a standpoint that reason sees itself constrained to take outside of appearances in order to think of itself as practical."[30]

But this "standpoint" makes possible what we may call, for a lack of a better word, the metaphysics of freedom. Now this metaphysics, although it rests on an assumption, a *hypothesis* to use Plato's expression, might offer a way of answering the metaphysical preoccupations of the human heart related to the two other major objects of reason: the existence of God and the immortality of the soul. How? By asserting that free action, or action determined by the idea of freedom, is autonomous. An important point for Kant is that free action must be disinterested: when acting morally, I cannot consider my interests or my own happiness, otherwise my moral actions would no longer be autonomous but would become "heteronomous"—that is, influenced by motives other that those of pure practical reason, which requires complete compliance with the categorical imperative and gives no consideration to any possible reward. But if I do act morally, I can nevertheless, says Kant, hope to be "worthy of happiness." This hope is the cornerstone of the metaphysics of the Highest Good that Kant presents in the Canon of Pure Reason at the end of his first *Critique*.

The "Metaphysics" of the Highest Good

The idea of a "canon" of pure reason is important in the organization of the *Critique of Pure Reason*. Kant had already evoked it when he defined the project of his *Critique*: if it could not lead to an *organon* of metaphysical knowledge, it may at least lead to something like a "canon."[31] In fact, Kant never developed the *organon* of metaphysical knowledge, but he did propose a canon of the legitimate use of pure reason in the conclusion of his *Critique*.[32] So what is a canon? "I understand by canon," says Kant, "the sum total of the *a priori* principles of the correct employment of certain faculties of knowledge."[33] But does this definition of the canon of pure reason not correspond exactly to the most rigorous task of the critique of pure reason, which is to inquire into the legitimate use of reason's *a priori* principles? Yes, but here the reference to its legitimate use is not theoretical, says Kant, it only pertains to the *practical* use of reason,[34] which the metaphysics of freedom has allowed us to glimpse.

Kant underscores the urgency of this subject by calling the first section of the Canon, "On the *Ultimate End* (*letzten Zwecke*) of the Pure Employment of our Reason," and the second, "On the Ideal of the Highest Good, as a Determining Ground of the *Ultimate End of Pure Reason*." In this second section, Kant presents three questions, which summarize the aims of reason:

What can I know? *Was kann ich wissen?*
What ought I do? *Was soll ich tun?*
What may I hope for? *Was darf ich hoffen?*

These questions are not only famous; they also remind us that metaphysical reason asks *questions*. These questions not only pertain to knowledge, action, and hope, but the modal verbs Kant uses also have important roles to play. *Kann, soll, darf* respectively refer to our capability, our duty, and what we may reasonably hope for. The first question thus refers to a real capacity, that of our intelligence's ability to dominate nature. The second, however, has nothing to do with our capabilities. In fact, it even admits of a certain incapacity, or even a degree of impotency, since it refers to a duty (*sollen*) categorically ascribed to me. The third question uses the verb *dürfen*, which refers less to some capacity (*können*) that an "authorization" that has neither the certitude, nor the assurance of the first two, which are both imposed as capacity (*kann*) and duty (*soll*).

Kant congratulates himself for having exhausted all possible answers to the first question in his *Critique*: All we can know is limited to possible experience. We can only know phenomena and the *a priori* conditions of the possibility of nature because they stem from our pure understanding. Knowledge of the supersensible is accordingly out of our reach. The answer to the question: "what must I do?" which pertains to practical philosophy, is also obvious. I must act in accordance with the principles of pure practical reason, which belong to the metaphysics of freedom. Although happiness cannot be the motive for moral action, I can at least do "what makes me worthy of happiness."[35]

These answers are obvious for Kant, as they are to any reasonable individual. In fact, Kant's attention in his Canon is monopolized by the third question: what may I hope for? All hope, observes Kant, aspires to happiness.[36] Now, the happiness we hope for in the most profound way is a sovereign happiness, the happiness of felicity (*Glückseligkeit*). What allows us to hope for this type of happiness? We know that acting morally makes one worthy of being happy. The main question is therefore if—Kant's use of the negative form is important here—"I behave so as not to be unworthy of happiness, may I hope thereby to obtain happiness?" To answer this decisive question "we have to consider whether the principles of pure reason, which prescribe the [moral] law *a priori*, likewise connect this hope necessarily with it."[37]

Kant's hope, along with pure reason's, is to show that it is correct, or "permissible," to connect a moral action to an associated happiness proportional to the morality of our maxims. The hoped for link between morality and happiness would then connect the philosophy of freedom with the major question of natural metaphysics: God and the immortality of the soul, both of which theoretical philosophy has been unable to answer:

> I maintain that just as the moral principles are necessary according to reason in its *practical* employment, it is in the view of reason, in the field of its *theoretical* employment, no less necessary to assume that everyone has ground to hope for happiness in the measure in which he has rendered himself by his conduct worthy of it, and that the system of morality is therefore inseparably—though only in the idea of pure reason—bound up with that of happiness.[38]

The system of morality is tied to what Kant calls the ideal of the Highest Good, which he introduces in a section heading as the "determining ground of the *ultimate end of pure reason*." This is important. By recognizing the Highest Good as the ultimate principles of rationality, Kant is strikingly close to Plato, the father of metaphysics and the first to say that the idea of the Good (*agathon*) embodies the supreme principle, and was consequently the most elevated object of study (*megiston mathema*). Now, it is this Highest Good (*das Höchste Gut*) that became the *summum bonum*, which the metaphysical tradition, both Medieval and Modern, identified with God who was endowed (as we have seen with Leibniz) with power, intelligence, and an infinite will.

It is this God endowed with an infinite intelligence that Kant presupposes when he speaks of the Highest Good, but a God thought exclusively from the standpoint of practical reason:

> The idea of such an intelligence in which the most perfect moral will, united with supreme blessedness, is the cause of all happiness in the world—so far as happiness stands in exact relation with morality, that is, with worthiness to be happy—I entitle the *ideal of the Highest Good*.[39]

According to Kant, I may only hope to be happy if I act in accordance with the moral law of practical reason. But such happiness is only possible on two conditions. One must admit: (1) the existence of an omniscient being such as God capable of evaluating the moral value of our actions and dispense happiness of matching value; and, (2) a future existence in which this happiness is dispensed. Therefore, the metaphysics of freedom grounds reason's two articles of faith, "there is a God, and a future life." These two "postulates," as Kant calls them in the *Critique of Practical Reason* (1788), are the *conditions* or the presuppositions of the supreme happiness that we hope for, or at the very least, may hope for.

Thus Kant rediscovers traditional metaphysics' most important objects: the existence of God and the immortality of the soul. But he only reaches them through a practical use of reason. Only practical reason allows me to detach myself from the sensible world and consider myself as part of a *mundus intelligibilis*.[40] By acting in a way worthy of being happy, I may then hope to participate in the felicity of the Highest Good. If God embodies the original Highest Good, then the happiness proportional to the morality of my actions corresponds to the highest good that we may call derived:

> It is therefore only in the ideal of the highest *original* good [i.e., God] that pure reason can find the ground of this connection, which is necessary from the practical point of view, between the two elements of the highest derivative good—the ground, namely, of an intelligible—that is, *moral* world. Now since we are necessarily constrained by reason to represent ourselves as belonging to such a world, while the senses present to us nothing but a world of appearances, we must assume [*annehmen müssen*] that moral world to be a consequence of our conduct in the world of sense (in which no such connection between worthiness and happiness is exhibited), and therefore to be for us a future world. Thus God and a future life [*Gott also und ein künftiges Leben*] are two postulates [*Voraussetzungen*]

which, according to the principles of pure reason, are inseparable from the obligation which that same reason imposes upon us.[41]

It is now easy to understand why Kant claimed that the ideal of the Highest Good was nothing less than the determining principle of our reason's ultimate end (*Endzweck*). It is also perhaps Kant's frankest answer to the question of the possibility of metaphysics. His critical metaphysics made possible by the *Critique of Pure Reason* would thus be the metaphysics of practical reason, or "metaphysics according to ethics" to use Bernard Carnois's expression.[42]

Thus Kant's metaphysics does not produce the grand system of pure reason that would have inquired into the reason for all things. No: it culminates in two articles of faith; "there is a God—there is a future life." These two articles of faith, says Kant, are not to be reached through abstract and academic metaphysical inquiry. No, they simply express and justify the natural metaphysics of common understanding. Leaving a purely theoretical and academic metaphysics behind, philosophy takes the form of the metaphysics of practical reason's interests:

> But, it will be said, is this all that pure reason achieves in opening up prospects beyond the limits of experience? Nothing more than two articles of belief [there is a God, there is a future life]? Surely, the common understanding could have achieved as much, without appealing to philosophers for counsel in the matter. . . . But I may at once reply: Do you really require that a mode of knowledge which concerns all men should transcend the common understanding, and should only be revealed to you by philosophers? Precisely what you find fault with is the best confirmation of the correctness of the above assertions. For we have thereby revealed to us, what could not at the start have been foreseen, namely, that in matters which concern all men without distinction nature is not guilty of any partial distribution of her gifts, and that in regard to the essential ends of human nature the highest philosophy cannot advance further than is possible under the guidance which nature has bestowed even upon the most ordinary understanding.[43]

Can the Existence of God Be Demonstrated?

The metaphysics of freedom thus strengthens the common understanding's faith or belief in the existence of God. But is God's existence thereby demonstrated? Kant did say that practical reason's two presuppositions—there is a God and a future existence—were "as necessary" as moral law itself. But their necessity is part of the logic of practical reason's metaphysics in which freedom is only an idea or a supposition. The existence of God, outside of its necessity for pure practical reason, cannot be theoretically demonstrated, thinks Kant. All demonstrations of existence must be based on real experience: this book exists because I can see it. But God remains an idea, an ideal, of pure reason. A necessary idea, perhaps, but whose existence is not thereby demonstrated.

According to Kant, metaphysics' greatest dream was pure reason's demonstration of God's existence. But how can one demonstrate something that is, after all, but an idea of reason? A sublime idea it may be, and Kant says as much, but one that does not actually exist:

> It is evident, from what been said, that the concept of an absolutely necessary being is a concept of pure reason, that is, a mere idea the objective reality of which is very far from being proved by the fact that reason requires it. For the idea instructs us only in regard to a certain unattainable completeness, and so serves rather to limit the understanding than to extend to new objects.[44]

The concept of God is a given for pure reason and perhaps its most intimate idea. But can one demonstrate the reality of this concept by reasoning from the idea our understanding has of it in accordance with the "ontological" argument (which Kant was the first to call by this name)? The question Kant raises is that of knowing if something's actual existence can belong to its *concept*. Kant thinks not. An actual existence cannot be part of a concept because existence only signifies that an objective reality (which only experience can attest to) corresponds to the concept. Existence thus designates something's "position" in Being, but positing it in Being cannot stem from the concept. It can only be attested to by experience. Trees exist and unicorns do not because they have—or do not have—a corresponding objective reality—that is, a position in Being. Thus a position is not an intrinsic part of the "concept" tree, or unicorn: only experience can authorize their position, or not.

Kant's whole point is summed up in the simple, yet important, affirmation: "Being is obviously not a real predicate" (*Sein ist offenbar kein reales Prädikat*).[45] A real predicate is one that positively determines what is part of a concept's essence. One could here replace "real" by essential. If I say, for example, God is "omnipotent" or "infinitely good" I explicitly indicate what is contained in the concept or essence of God. All these determinations of God are real predicates—that is, notions that are part of the concept God without which there is no concept "God."

But to say God "is," is to say something completely different. I do not add anything to the *concept* God, argues Kant, when I say that he exists. I only assert an objective reality corresponding to the concept God:

> Being is obviously not a real predicate; that is, it is not a concept of something which could be added to the concept of a thing. It is merely the positing of a thing, or of certain determinations, as existing themselves. . . . The proposition, "God is omnipotent," contains two concepts, each of which has its object—God and omnipotence. The small word "is" adds no new predicate, but only serves to posit the predicate *in its relation* to the subject. If, now, we take the subject (God) with all its predicates (among which is omnipotence), and say "God is," or "there is a God," we attach no new predicate to the concept of God, but only posit the subject in itself with all its predicates, and indeed posit it as being an *object* that stands in relation to my *concept.*[46]

Actual existence is therefore foreign to the concept, it stems only from it being *posited* in Being, to use Kant's expression. To explain his point, Kant uses the famous example of the one hundred thalers. I am richer with one hundred real thalers than with one hundred imaginary thalers. But on the *conceptual* level, what is designated by the thought of one hundred real thalers is the same as one hundred imaginary thalers. The reality has the same properties, the same value or ideal content as the one hundred thalers that are only thought.[47]

According to Kant, I add nothing to something's concept when I say it exists. Applied to God, this means existence does not belong *a priori* to the concept God. It is not a real determination. It simply means this concept has been posited in existence, which the concept cannot establish on its own, since the realm of Being is distinct from that of thought. To put it negatively, to deny the existence of God does not remove anything from its concept. Therefore, God's existence cannot be theoretically demonstrated.

But the idea of God is justifiable, even necessary, on the practical level because it is an indispensable presupposition for the ideal of the Highest Good, which determines the ultimate end of reason. But is this metaphysics of freedom really *science?*

The Future of Metaphysics After Kant

Kant had initially set out to know whether metaphysics was possible as science. Contested as it was by empiricism, Kant understood that metaphysics was at a crossroads. It had to either justify its pretensions or stop claiming it was science. According to him, metaphysics' pretensions of having theoretical knowledge of the supersensible are illegitimate. Legitimate knowledge is limited to possible experience. All that can be known *a priori*, or metaphysically, are the *conditions* of possible experience. Yet the "possibility" of experience operates on two levels: knowledge and action. Therefore for Kant there is a metaphysics of nature's *a priori* principles and a metaphysics of practical action's *a priori* principles. Thus schematically:

Metaphysics of Nature (theoretical philosophy)	*a priori* principles of knowledge	Principles of "Being"	Highest principle: the conditions of my knowledge are also those of nature and therefore of any *object* of experience.
Metaphysics of Morals (practical philosophy)	*a priori* principles of moral action	Principles of "what ought to be done"	Categorical imperative: act only according to that maxim whereby you can at the same time will that it should become a universal law of nature.

Although Kant contested the possibility that metaphysics can produce knowledge outside the realm of possible experience, he established a new metaphysics inquiring into the rational, or *a priori*, principle of experience. By forsaking all "transcendent" metaphysics, which vainly sought knowledge of the supersensible, Kant opened the door to a "transcendental" metaphysics inquiring into the condition, and conditions, of cognitive and moral experience. He thus opened the way for the philosophy of the last two centuries and its reflections on the principles—by which it is considered metaphysics—of science and action. These two philosophical domains are today what contemporary philosophy calls epistemology and ethics. Obviously, Kant sought to maintain the preferred objects of classical and natural metaphysics, namely, the existence of God and the immortality of the soul. He did so, however, only in his moral philosophy, which understood these objects as the necessary consequences of a rational system of morality. But do these admissions—or "postulates"—of pure practical reason constitute a science? Is the metaphysics (of freedom) a science? Actually, the Kantian metaphysics of freedom only leads to two "articles of faith." Freedom is just a reasonable supposition allowing one to construe the efficacy of pure practical reason. It does not, however, stem from the spatiotemporal phenomenal world, which is the only one we can know in an objective and verifiable way. Nevertheless, freedom seems much more essential to human reason than all that can be known. Thus Kant's initial question—the possibility of metaphysics as science—was perhaps not asked correctly. It was less a question of assuring the scientific value of metaphysical knowledge than a defense of pure reason's hopes, which Kant knew quite well no longer related to any science. The discussion of the Highest Good, in fact, only answers the question of hope ("what may I hope for?") and not the question "what can I know?" Indeed, does not speaking of metaphysics, freedom, the existence of God, the immortality of the soul, necessarily overstep the very limited boundaries of science as they relate to the ends of human reason?

Although one may think that Kant brought into question its status as a science, in fact, and quite ironically, German Idealism will now argue, and show, that philosophy (or metaphysics) is a science and a system.

CHAPTER 9

METAPHYSICS AFTER KANT?

Was There Any Metaphysics After Kant?

Kant began by asking whether metaphysics was possible as science. By lowering reason to the level of experience, Kant's contemporaries saw him as the annihilator of metaphysics. Moses Mendelssohn exemplifies the period's sentiment when he spoke in 1785 of the *alleszermalmenden* Kant, the philosopher who destroys everything. Heinrich Heine later said that Kant was metaphysics' Robespierre! In fact, the *Critique of Pure Reason* was published the same year as Beaumarchais's *The Marriage of Figaro* and eight years before the French Revolution. His iconoclast attitude towards the metaphysical tradition was obviously in keeping with the spirit of the times. Indeed, Kant called for "a revolution in the way of thinking," and said his critique was an "attempt to alter the procedure which has hitherto prevailed in metaphysics by completely revolutionizing it [*gänzliche Revolution*]."[1] The Kantian metaphysics of freedom, which strongly influenced the staunch Jacobin Fichte, rendered the old metaphysics as obsolete as it increasingly appeared. Even though Kant had been trained in the old metaphysics and still borrowed his conceptual tools from it, it had lost much of its former importance. So metaphysics was dead and the future belonged to . . .

Indeed, what, or to whom, did the future belong? Throughout the last two centuries, all philosophy, or metaphysics, has tried to answer this Kantian question *par excellence*. One thing is certain: Traditional metaphysics seemed unable to answer Kant's challenge. Until a satisfactory answer was given explaining how metaphysical knowledge was again possible, "all metaphysicians are solemnly and legally suspended from their occupations,"[2] proclaimed Kant in a fatal blow from which metaphysics has yet to fully recover.

Metaphysical thought did not end with him, however—far from it. Kant, in fact, profoundly revitalized metaphysical (or philosophical) thought by calling for its redefinition. Conscious as they were of living in revolutionary times, Kant's immediate successors sought to develop the "metaphysics" that Kantianism seemed to require or make possible. This was the spark that set off what has since been called German Idealism, which is identified with the works of Johann Gottlieb Fichte (1762–1814), Friedrich Wilhelm Schelling (1775–1854), and Georg Wilhelm Friedrich Hegel (1770–1831).

But was Idealism "metaphysical"? This important question was the theme of a colloquium of the *Hegel Society* held in 1987: "*Metaphysik nach Kant?*" (Metaphysics since Kant?).[3] The question perhaps says more in German than it does in English:

1. The question "*Metaphysik nach Kant?*" is first a question of the possibility of metaphysics according to ("*nach*") Kant himself. Was metaphysics possible according to him, and if so, how? Had Kant wished to destroy or rebuild metaphysics? If his successors never unanimously answered this question, it may be because Kant himself never gave a clear and distinct answer.

2. But "*Metaphysik nach Kant?*" also asks a question on the nature of philosophy after Kant: German Idealism. Was it metaphysics? In what way? The question may at first seem mean-spirited. Indeed, it is rather common to see this school of thought as a "return" to the metaphysics Kant had criticized (in fact, toward the end of his life he did condemn some Idealists who claimed to be his heirs for this very reason).[4] This verdict was certainly that of the neo-Kantians in the second half of the nineteenth century, who rallied around Otto Liebmann's 1865 call for a "return to Kant"[5] and sought to differentiate themselves from the "metaphysical delirium" of German Idealism. This was also true of analytical philosophy born, as we all know, in England in opposition to Hegelianism.

But the question can be asked in another more benevolent way: Could post-Kantian "metaphysics" be the consequence and indeed the very systematic culmination of the metaphysical tradition? Although the great thinkers of German Idealism were indebted to Kant, their ambitious systems were also inspired by elements drawn from authors belonging to classical metaphysics, namely, Spinoza and Leibniz. Hegel, for example, undoubtedly saw his system as the culmination and synthesis of all metaphysical thought.

Nevertheless, the authors of German Idealism were rather reticent (Schelling being perhaps the exception) to call their systems "metaphysics," for two reasons. On the one hand, Kant had sounded metaphysics' death knell. And on the other, the term "metaphysics" was still marked by a dualism of the physical and meta-physical, which Idealism preferred to replace with their monist, totalizing, and systematic way of thinking. Neither Fichte, nor Hegel, nor even Schelling for that matter, presented their philosophies as "metaphysics." Fichte preferred to speak of "science of knowledge" (*Wissenschaftslehre*), Schelling spoke of a philosophy of nature, of a philosophy of identity or of a system of transcendental idealism, and Hegel published books with such titles as *Phenomenology of Spirit*, *The Science of Logic*, and *The Encyclopedia of Philosophical Sciences*.

The situation is therefore quite striking and even upside-down. Whereas Kant argued a resolutely anti-metaphysical philosophy, but recurrently used the term metaphysics, German Idealism elaborated powerfully metaphysical philosophies without ever using, *expressis verbis*, the title metaphysics.

Metaphysics thus remained identified with pre-Kantian, or "pre-critical" philosophy. If Kant had destroyed metaphysics, then the new post-Kantian philosophy could not be "metaphysics." So what should we call it? One of the names that acted a rallying cry was *transcendental idealism*, which Kant had already used and which post-Kantian idealism radicalized. For Kant who still thought it through the Leibnizian tradition, the expression meant that the conditions of possibility of our intuition—space and time—did not belong to the things-in-themselves, but were *only forms belonging to our mind*, which it used to make sense of phenomena. It was a modest form of idealism since it only attributed to our mind the synthesis of phenomena. It was so modest in fact that Kant took pains to argue it had a concomitant "empirical rationalism" that stressed the fact that what our mind organized came from "outside" or from the world of things. For the Idealists, this position was much too mild and even inconsistent with the Kantian revolution the magnitude of which, they argued, Kant had not fully realized. What inspired the Idealists was the idea of an original activity of the "transcendental subject," which had first appeared in the *Critique of Pure Reason*. But the Idealists claimed Kant's presentation of it was incomplete because he was still ensnared by traditional "dogmatic" metaphysics for which objects must always enter consciousness from the outside.

Fichte held that one must chose between idealism and dogmatism. Either one adopts a consistent form of idealism that understands all that is through a spiritual principle or as a position of the I, or one adopts realism, which begins with things-in-themselves and for which the mind is purely passive. It was a choice between two possible "metaphysics," which the first Idealists construed as an opposition between dogmatism and criticism (or Idealism). These were also argued to be as the only possible philosophies: one starting from Being itself, the other from the original activity of the subject, the virtues of which were spontaneity and freedom. The philosophy one chooses, proclaimed Fichte, depends on the type of person one is.[6]

When working out their philosophy of the I and freedom, the first thinkers of German Idealism—Fichte and Schelling—preferred the term "transcendental philosophy" to "metaphysics" (Kant used the terms synonymously). Transcendental philosophy was for them a systematic and deductive philosophy founded upon the activity of the knowing and acting subject, which they erected into an "absolute subject" in which all otherness was either to be integrated to itself or overcome. If reality is not yet fully suffused with the I, then *so it must become*. This is the great imperative of practical philosophy: the world must be made to conform to the requirements of the I. Practical philosophy, in the spirit of the Revolution, hoped to transform reality and the so-called things-in-themselves that seemed to limit the I. Accordingly, Fichte sometimes associated metaphysics with practical philosophy (which Kant had also done, but in a rather different way). "Thus if the Science of Knowledge were after all to possess a metaphysic, as a supposed science of things-in-themselves, and such a metaphysic were demanded of it, it would have to refer to the practical part of the system."[7] But his preferred term was assuredly *Wissenschaftslehre* or "Science of Knowledge."

Science and System in Kant

Fichte's expression is rather redundant since the terms "science" and "knowledge" can sometimes be used as synonyms. Yet these are terms Kant had used when he had spoken of his project for a "doctrine" (*Lehre*) or a "system of transcendental philosophy."[8] It was project that must be preceded, said Kant, by an inquiry into the touchstone or the "principle" of the science, the responsibility for which lay with his "critique." And it was this inquiry that Fichte's *Science of Knowledge* attempted to renew in order to present the system's principle in a new light.

Kant's metaphysical or systematic ambition is therefore incontestable. The Idealists however felt he was overly ambivalent toward metaphysical speculation. Kant had, after all, attacked metaphysics precisely for being "speculative":

> Theoretical knowledge is *speculative* if it concerns an object, or those concepts of object, which cannot be reached in any experience. It is so named to distinguish it from *the knowledge of nature*, which concerns only those objects or predicates of objects which can be given in a possible experience.[9]

Speculation thus had a pejorative connotation. But was Kant not thereby hiding his own speculative interests or even the highly speculative character of his own search for the "conditions of possibility" of experience derived from the *a priori* and original activity of the understanding?

Kant certainly denounced traditional metaphysics *because* it was quite obviously "speculative." But was not the Kantian revolution itself a way of *thinking* that transcended experience? In fact, Kant sometimes used the term "speculative" in a positive sense, as in the preface to his 1781 *Critique*:

> Such a system of pure (speculative) reason I hope myself to produce under the title *Metaphysics of Nature*. It will be not half as large, yet incomparably richer in content that this present *Critique*, which has as its first task to discover the sources and conditions of the possibility of such criticism, clearing, as it were, and leveling what hitherto has been wasteland.[10]

Kant presented the idea of a system of pure reason in the penultimate chapter of his *Critique*, the Architectonic. An architectonic is "the doctrine of the scientific in our knowledge" (*die Lehre des Scientifischen*) says Kant, singularly anticipating Fichte's "science of knowledge." But what makes knowledge scientific? Knowledge is science, says Kant, when is does not form an aggregate of knowledge, but a system. "By system I understand the unity of the manifold modes of knowledge under one idea." An idea is "the concept provided by reason—of the form of a whole—in so far as the concept determines *a priori* not only the scope of its manifold content, but also the positions which the parts occupy relatively to one another."[11]

An unorganized manifold resists becoming knowledge. For knowledge to be possible, it must therefore possess a certain, albeit necessarily rational, order that forms a *system*. The idea of such a system will run through all of Idealism. Although Kant did define the idea of a system "as the unity of the manifold modes of knowledge under one idea," one may ask whether he ever defined the "idea" that gives systematic unity to knowledge. According to the Idealists, Kant did not so much define the idea as give an example of it by describing how the transcendental subject determines the *a priori* conditions of cognitive and practical experience. It is the subject's unifying, original, and synthetic act that the system of philosophy must present.

For Kant, as for the Idealists, knowledge must be understood as a whole determined by an idea (or a principle), which can only be understood systematically. As a rational system, philosophy has no other task than of deploying such a system of the unity of knowledge under an idea.

Did Kant ever present such a system? According to Kant, it was in philosophy that a system of rational knowledge could be *found*.[12] But he did not think such a philosophy actually existed. It is simply philosophy's guiding principle. "Thus regarded, philosophy is a mere idea of a possible science which nowhere exists *in concreto*."[13] This led Kant to state, in a famous passage, that one cannot learn philosophy, but only how to "philosophize."

This is an important insight that is still important today: Metaphysics is only the idea of a science that will never be realized once and for all. And yet, the Idealists will try to realize this idea, in all the multiple meanings of the verb "to realize": They will try to produce it, actualize it, and make it aware of itself. The Idealists were certainly much more ambitious than Kant.

But were they overly pretentious—as almost all critics of Idealism have claimed—in trying to accomplish what had simply been an idea for Kant? The Idealists certainly believed they were more consistent than Kant. For them, the idea of a system of philosophy governed by an Idea was already being realized. After all, was Kant's criticism anything other than the first expression of this systematic transcendental philosophy? The post-Kantians thus paid little attention to Kant's claim philosophy was only an idea of a possible science that did not exist *in concreto*. Or rather, the Idealists believed it was Kant who had been unable to present such a system and thus gave themselves the task of completely rebuilding transcendentalism. It was then as a response to this metaphysical challenge that Fichte wrote his *Science of Knowledge*, Schelling wrote his *System of Transcendental Idealism*, and Hegel wrote his *System of Science*, works marked by the repeated occurrence of the terms science and system.

But why had Kant not grasped the magnitude of his metaphysical revolution? According to the Idealists, it was because he had been unable to liberate himself from the shackles of metaphysics. And so, in the spirit of Kantianism they strove to liberate Kant's thought from all residual metaphysics. They worked to purge transcendental philosophy of all its dogmatic blemishes and to understand Kant better than Kant himself had. In fact, Fichte will often say that if he did not always follow Kant to the letter, he did so in order to better conform to his spirit.[14]

The essence of the Idealists' critique of Kant is the following: Although Kant identified the activity of the transcendental subject, he did not fully systematize the new principle. It makes no difference whether the subject is called pure reason, transcendental apperception, or practical subject. It is much more important to understand that the subject is the unconditioned principle of systematized science and knowledge. Dogmatic philosophy's gravest mistake, which the Idealists believed was Kant's as well, was to construe reality as a given prior to any subjectivity and to take it as its point of departure. Hence the importance Idealists gave to showing how the thing-initself was nonsensical for any rigorously transcendental philosophy.

The Idealist Dismissal of the Metaphysics of the Thing-in-Itself

For Kant, the distinction between phenomena and things-in-themselves acted as a *limit* to human knowledge: we cannot know reality itself, or its ultimate essence, but only phenomena as they appear already schematized by thought. The German author Friedrich Heinrich Jacobi (1743–1819) made his contemporaries see how Kant had thus proposed a radical form of idealism, which could not be reconciled with the empirical realism he also professed.[15]

Kant was an idealist, claimed Jacobi, because he argued that objects only exist in and for our understanding in which all determinations of phenomena are conceived. But Kant also asserted that the things-in-themselves were the causes of phenomena and produce an impression on our senses. Kant would therefore have favored a form of realism. But, asks Jacobi, how do we become conscious of the influence of the things-in-themselves if we cannot escape our representation of them? The realism of the things-in-themselves thus seems irreconcilable with Kant's idealism. According to Jacobi, Kant, in order not to be self-contradictory, should therefore have rejected the notion of things-in-themselves:

I ask: How is it possible to reconcile the presupposition of objects that produce impressions on our senses, and in this way arouse representations, with an hypothesis intent on abolishing all the grounds by which the presupposition could be supported? . . . The transcendental idealist must have the courage, therefore, to assert the strongest idealism that was ever professed, and not be afraid of the objection of speculative egoism, for it is impossible for him to pretend to stay within his system if he tries to repel from himself even just this last objection.[16]

Kant's "empirical realism" seemed to describe the thing-in-itself as a cause acting on our faculty of representation. But, says Jacobi, Kant would have then contradicted himself by seemingly attributing the category of causality to the thing-in-itself when his doctrine restricted it to phenomena. The thing-in-itself is thus paradoxical. As Jacobi famously stated: "without the presupposition [of the thing-in-itself,] I was unable to enter into [Kant's] system, but with it I was unable to stay within it."[17] Kant needed this notion not only to explain the fact we are "affected" by things exterior to ourselves, but also to secure the idea of freedom. However, all reasons for admitting this notion are undermined by his radical phenomenalism. Confronted with this absurdity, Jacobi believed a more realist position was required, albeit one that relied on sentiment rather than knowledge to access reality and its ground.

Although the Idealists did not agree with Jacobi on this last point, they did accept Jacobi's verdict on the thing-in-itself and rejected it as the *persistence of dogmatic metaphysics*. But they did not back down in the face of the complete idealism Jacobi had dreaded: All experience is the product of subjectivity positing itself. For the Idealists, these products are more than mere "phenomena," they are very real beings, since their reality stems from the subject, the principle of all that is. Thus the Kantian position obviously underwent a major metamorphosis, but the Idealists believed they were being more consistent than Kant himself. After all, did not his revolution assert the primacy of the transcendental I or subject over the world?

Fichte often wrote that Kant was too "gentle" with the thing-in-itself, which may be the reason he was so often misunderstood: How could anybody have a representation of what can never be represented (the thing-in-itself)? The whole notion is contradictory:[18] "the thing-in-itself is a pure invention (*Erdichtung*) and has no reality whatever."[19] Unless, of course, it has a purely practical meaning: "and if the *Science of Knowledge* should be asked, how then, indeed, are the things-in-themselves constituted, it could offer no answer, save, as we are to make them."[20] The passage is not without irony since things "as we are to make them" would obviously no longer be "in-themselves," but completely suffused with the requirements of the I. But the passage is not completely ironic since the things-in-themselves—"the things themselves"—are, for Fichte, the things such as they are subjected to the "I," which is the first reality.

For this reason, Fichte could say that it was in a practical philosophy that one can hope to find metaphysics, or the science of the "so-called things-in-themselves."[21] But since the in-itself stems here solely from our action, this metaphysics would be the metaphysics of the subject determining itself through action. It is therefore from it that first philosophy must take its start.

Reinhold's First Philosophy

Our use of the term "first philosophy" might seem to imply that Fichte speaks of first philosophy in the same way as Aristotle, Descartes, or Leibniz. In fact, it is a translation of Karl Leonard Reinhold's expression *Elementarphilosophie* or "Elementary Philosophy." Reinhold (1758–1823) rarely makes it into history of philosophy. He was a minor author, but one that all the Idealists read and commented upon. The works of Fichte, Schelling, and Hegel (who devoted the last chapter of his 1801 *Differenzschrift* to him) were all deeply inspired by him.

Reinhold is important because he was the first to popularize Kantian philosophy. Between August 1786 and September 1787, he wrote the widely read "Letters on the Kantian Philosophy"[22] in the journal *Teutscher Merkur*, which were published as a book in 1787. His *Letters* were much easier to read than Kant's *Critique of Pure Reason*, and many thinkers in the 1780s and 1790s used them as the basis of their understanding of Kant's philosophy. Reinhold's intention was first apologetic. He sought to present the project of critical philosophy and defend it using simple terms. In so doing, he wanted to show how it did not undermine the foundations of morality and law, as was often feared in this period when Kant was often seen as a "destroyer." Reinhold's *Letters* made him famous. In June 1787, he was named professor at the prestigious University of Jena where his courses were very popular.[23] In 1794, he accepted a position in Kiel, apparently for financial reasons and remained there until his death in 1823. Fichte replaced him at Jena in 1794 and remained there until 1799 when he was forced to resign following accusations of atheism. Schelling then quickly replaced him (Hegel also taught there at the beginning of his career). It is as though the chair of philosophy of the University of Jena reflected the evolution of German Idealism and its metaphysics. Jena also had an important role in European history. In 1806, Napoleon won an important victory at Jena at the same time as Hegel was there, writing his *Phenomenology of Spirit*.

Reinhold's contribution to idealist metaphysics is minor, but it is never-theless important. As we have seen, Kant's *Critique* had a devastating effect on the philosophical scene. In one fell swoop, traditional metaphysics was sud-denly passé. But according to Reinhold, Kant's destruction of metaphysics had opened its way to becoming science. The only problem Reinhold saw was that Kant had not sufficiently defined his revolution's main principle. In what name had Kant carried out his critique of pure reason? What was transcen-dental philosophy's highest principle, its Archimedean point? Kant gave us a critique of pure reason in order to found the metaphysics of nature, writes Reinhold,[24] but he never presented the foundations of his own philosophy. In order to convince those who have yet to adopt criticism, Reinhold argued that Kant's philosophy was in need of a *highest principle* from which all the prop-ositions of transcendental philosophy can be rigorously deduced. Reinhold claimed to follow the Kantian conception of science presented in the Archi-tectonic: "Whenever Kant speaks of philosophy as *science*, he demands *sys-tematic form*, i.e., the thoroughgoing unity of a manifold of cognitions under one principle."[25] If every science has its own principles, Kant's transcendental philosophy had yet to define its own. Reinhold writes: "As long as we have not reached this principle, there will be *philosophies*, but no *philosophy*."[26]

Reinhold called this philosophy, which was supposed to meditate on the foundations of philosophy, "elementary philosophy." His ambition was at first modest: it was supposed to found and justify Kant's critique of pure reason. But since it tried to be more "fundamental," it ended up replacing Kantianism and focusing on elementary philosophy.

Reinhold thus incited the new philosophy to reflect on its own foundations. One of his works of 1791 bears the name *On the Foundation of Philosophical Knowl-edge.* Philosophy's most important task, if it was to become a science, was to clarify it own principle (which would also be the principle of all knowledge). According to Reinhold, "elementary philosophy," which Kant had presupposed can be nothing other than a theory of the "faculty of representation." Rein-hold's first systematic work, written in 1789, was *An Essay Toward a New Theory of the Faculty of Representation.* Critical philosophy's greatest contribution was its claim that all relation to the world is done through our faculty of representa-tion: even the thing-in-itself belongs to the subject's faculty of representation. Elementary philosophy's principle could thus only consist in clarifying what Reinhold claimed to be the most elementary "fact" of our consciousness: all representation implies a relation to a subject and to an object. "Elementary phi-losophy" must start from this fact (*Tatsache*), which it cannot deduce, but which it must posit as absolutely first, as a fundamental principle, or better, as the fundamental principle of both knowledge and philosophy. Reinhold called this principle *par excellence*, the "principle of consciousness" (*Satz des Bewusstseins*):

> The concept of representation can be drawn from . . . an actual *fact*. This fact alone, *qua fact*, must ground the foundation of the elementary philosophy—for otherwise the foundation cannot rest, without circularity, on any philosophical demonstrable position. It is not through any inference of reason that we know *that in consciousness representation is distinguished through the subject from both object and subject and is referred to both*, but through simple *reflection* upon the actual fact of consciousness, that is, by ordering together what is present in it.[27]

Reinhold argues that this principle "does not need to be deduced from a principle of the science it founds" because elementary philosophy is "the ultimate source of scientific evidence and the source of its evidence lies outside of the scientific domain, in consciousness."[28] This principle, which is supposedly present "in *all* philosophical principles, cannot be a definition, nor have its terms defined, but must express a fact from which follows the original concept of representation as well as its only possible definition, consciousness."[29]

Reinhold's comments may seem outrageously hyperbolic, but they gave an important impulse to post-Kantian metaphysics. Reinhold confronted his contemporaries with the fact that philosophy *did not yet* have a principle. Its most important task, if it were to become a science, was therefore to explicate its foundations. Such a reflection would belong to elementary philosophy that would take its start from its highest principle—the principle of representation—which alone allows philosophy to become a system and act as a foundation for the other sciences. This was Reinhold's ambitious, albeit "elementary," program that he bequeathed to philosophy. Idealist metaphysics would then attempt to take up his challenge, and interpret the principle of philosophy in a more active, more original, and more complete way. In 1795, the young Schelling summed up Reinhold's contribution to contemporary philosophy by writing that although Reinhold had not solved the problem of philosophy, he had at least brought it into the clearest focus.[30]

Fichte and the Metaphysics of the I

Following Reinhold, the thinkers of German Idealism were convinced that Kant had never developed the system upon which his whole enterprise was supposedly founded, and which he had evoked in the architectonic of pure reason and his third *Critique*. Fichte sometimes speaks of Kant's "missing system,"[31] or the system he never presented, which Fichte's *Science of Knowledge* was supposed to finally present. Its rather austere title is perhaps emblematic of the direction Fichte took. But just as metaphysics had been the "sought after science" from Aristotle to Leibniz, so Fichte produced no canonical presentation of this science. In 1794, he presented its first and most illustrious outline enigmatically entitled *Grundlage der gesammten Wissenschaftslehre* (*Foundations of the Entire Science of Knowledge*). The title is ambiguous since it seems to refer to the *foundation* rather than to the *Science of Knowledge* itself, which remained a mere promise throughout his writings of the 1790s, and its final presentation was constantly deferred.

In fact, for Fichte, the "Science of Knowledge" is another name for philosophy.[32] His systematic and principial, and therefore metaphysical, ambition is obvious. His avowed goal is to express the fundamental principle of all philosophy, including Kantian philosophy, which was for him the highest state ever achieved by thought. But Kant, observes Fichte, "nowhere dealt with the foundation of *all* philosophy."[33] The expression betrays how the impetus for Fichte's work came from Reinhold, his predecessor in Jena whose elementary philosophy had promised such a foundation. Reinhold's philosophy was less a "first" philosophy in the metaphysical sense of the term, than the first philosophy as such since it was to be a reflection on the foundation of all philosophy. For Reinhold, such a philosophy could only be a "theory of the human faculty of representation" based on the idea—rather banal but nevertheless elementary—that all that is given—in fact, all that is—is given to us as representation. This was, according to Reinhold, the "first fact of consciousness."

The first philosophical writings of the young Fichte—who had become famous when it was revealed that he was the author of the *Critique of All Revelation*, published anonymously and commonly attributed to the venerable Kant—were his "personal meditations" on Reinhold's elementary philosophy. (These remained unpublished until recently when they were included in Fichte's *Complete Works*.[34]) In keeping with the project of recasting transcendentalism in light of the elementary philosophy, Fichte writes to Reinhold in the spring of 1795: "you, like Kant, have given humanity something it will always retain. He showed that one must begin with an investigation of the subject [i.e., the I]: you showed that the investigation must proceed from a single first principle. The truth which you have uttered is eternal."[35]

Fichte, however, also sought to address the objections to Reinhold's project made by Gottlob Ernst Shulze (1761–1833) in his *Aenesidemus or on the Foundations of the Elementary Philosophy presented by Mr. Professor Reinhold of Jena* (1792).

Aenesidemus was a Pyrrhonist, and therefore Skeptic, author of Antiquity who had doubted the notion of causality. Schulze sought to revive this skepticism and to turn it against Reinhold and Kant. What right did Kant have for applying causality to the things-in-themselves? What allows us to know whether Reinhold's principle is really the first? Does he not presuppose the principles of identity and contradiction?

Fichte answered Schulze's critique in a long review of the *Aenesidemus* published in the *Jenaer Allgemeine Literaturzeitung*, in which he mentions for the first time the *Tathandlung*.[36] As is the case with his *Science of Knowledge*, the expression, which is one of the most famous in Fichte's work, as well as in the history of metaphysics, is rather redundant. In German, the terms *Tat* and *Handlung* are synonymous. *Tat* means an action, and *Handlung* an activity. Translated literally, the idea of *Tathandlung* thus expresses the activity of an action. It only becomes meaningful if it is opposed to *Tatsache*, which Reinhold used to describe the supposedly first fact that was to be the principle of elementary philosophy. Schulze had argued that no fact can be an absolute point of departure. Every fact, presupposes some more original act (fact comes from the Latin *factum*, neuter *past* participle of *facere*, "to do"). Rather than start from a fact, which will always be secondary because it is posited by some other thing, why not begin, asks Fichte, from an absolutely primary act or "activity" such as a *Tathandlung*? Fichte's expression is emblematic of the revolutionary period when newly politically liberated citizens became aware of their power and rights. Fichte was thus the metaphysician of this emancipatory movement. The original activity consists, for him, in a pure act of self-positing, which is both subject and object of its activity. This self-positing is for Fichte the most elementary experience of the I. "The Science of Knowledge calls upon every person to reflect upon what he does when he says 'I.' According to the Science of Knowledge, what happens when one says 'I' is this: One supposes that one posits oneself, and that one posits oneself as subject-object."[37]

Now, this notion of activity, which is immediately obvious, has powerful metaphysical connotations. Aristotle had said that God was pure activity (*energeia*), whereas Leibniz spoke of the monad's "original activity."[38] In his *Grundlage* of 1794, Fichte elevated it to the level of first unconditioned principle (*erster, schlechthin unbedingter Grundsatz*):

Our task is to discover the primordial, absolutely unconditioned first principle of all human knowledge. This can be neither proved nor defined, it is to be an absolutely primary principle. It is intended to express that

Act [*Tathandlung*] which does not and cannot appear among the empirical
states of our consciousness, but rather lies at the basis of all consciousness
and alone makes it possible.[39]

In a rigorous *Science of Knowledge*, everything is deduced from this principle
that expresses an "original activity." It is in this way, says Fichte in a preface
written in 1798, that it can be called "metaphysics," but only if metaphysics is
not a "theory of the so-called things-in-themselves, but . . . a genetic deduction of what we find in our consciousness."[40] But, adds Fichte, the expression
metaphysics is inappropriate here. The *Science of Knowledge* is not metaphysics; it is even more fundamental. Metaphysics, he says, is supposed to explain
"the ordinary point of view of natural understanding." The critique (or the
Science of Knowledge) *goes beyond* metaphysics and attempts to explain it.[41]
There are therefore three distinct levels to consider here: the common understanding (or natural point of view), metaphysics, and critique (or the Science
of Knowledge). According to Fichte, Kant remained on the level of metaphysics, which seeks to explain the natural point of view, the one that admits of the
existence of things-in-themselves that are constituted independently from
consciousness. The *Science of Knowledge* is more reflective: it seeks to explain
the origin of these representations by deducing them from consciousness.

Since the Science of Knowledge aspires to a complete genetic explanation, it is more reflective than metaphysics, which is more concerned with
the natural point of view. This reflectivity determines the concept of the science itself: it is not a science that explains a certain phenomena (as metaphysics does), it is a scientific explanation of science itself, and therefore a "science
of knowledge." Fichte often explains what is meant here by science. Everyone
understands that it implies knowledge having absolute certitude and necessity, in a word, objective validity. But how to explain such a necessity and certitude, which can only lie in the I or consciousness? This reflective question
is one that neither common understanding nor science ever asks even though
they always presuppose it. Anyone who asks this question, which belongs to
the *Science of Knowledge*, "has thereby raised himself to the level of philosophy"
and "the aim of philosophy is to answer this question."[42] Philosophy must be
the *Science of Knowledge*, or it does not know what it is.

The *Science of Knowledge* thus radicalizes Kant's transcendental question:
By what right (*quid juris?*) is there something like scientific knowledge that
has universal validity? Kant showed, or so Fichte contends, that there can
be objective validity only for the subject or an I, which is the subject of science. Fichte's I is thus the heir to Kant's transcendental subject that sought to

anchor objectivity in the knowing subject. But the *Science of Knowledge* claims to be more systematic than the *Critique of Pure Reason*. By positing itself, it promises to start from an absolutely certain principle that allows all knowledge to be unified in a system. It is thus a principle in two important ways: not only is it the principle of science, and therefore of experience,[43] but it is also the principle of philosophy itself, understood as *Science of Knowledge*.

The most systematic exposition of these principles is in the 1794 *Grundlage*. If philosophy is to be rigorous, it must then start from an "absolutely unconditioned first principle. . . . [that] lies at the basis of all consciousness and makes it possible,"[44] the *Tathandlung*. What is the *Tathandlung* if not a radical self-positing of itself? The I is because it posits itself. Hence, Fichte's first principle: the I posits its own Being, or I = I (the I is the act of positing itself).

But the I does not exist alone. It is unthinkable without its opposite: the not-I, which must then also be posited by the I. Fichte thus arrives at his second principle: the I is opposed by the not-I.[45]

Thus the two main principles of the *Science of Knowledge* are the I and the not-I. But how is their relation to be thought without one canceling out the other? This is the birth of what can already be called "dialectic" thought, which tries to think the I and the not-I together without one annihilating the other.[46] The I and the not-I must therefore reciprocally limit each other. Now, the concept of limit, argues Fichte, includes that of divisibility. The I and the not-I must therefore be posited as divisible. Fichte thus arrives at his third major principle: *The "I" opposes in the "I" a divisible "not-I" to the divisible "I."* With great emphasis and little modesty, Fichte will say the following about this major principle:

> In the "I," I oppose a divisible "not-I" to the divisible "I." No philosophy goes further than this; but every thorough-going philosophy should go back to this point; and so far as it does so, it becomes a Science of Knowledge. Everything that is to emerge hereafter in the system of the human mind must be derivable from what we have established here.[47]

From this reciprocal determination of the I and the not-I, which is the basis for the *Science of Knowledge*, it is now possible to think the unity of the two main parts of philosophy. In theoretical philosophy, the I posits itself as determined by the not-I, and in practical philosophy, the I posits itself as determining the not-I.[48] Thus beneath the Kantian dualism of practical and theoretical philosophy a common and federating principle is discovered: the principle of the unity of the I and the not-I. This principle is posited as an irreducible requirement of the I, even if its realization amounts to an infinite aspiration (*unendliches Streben*), says Fichte using terms heralding Romanticism.

Yet, such a synthesis of the I and the not-I must be the work of the I, and even of the "absolute I," announces Fichte in an important text in which he claims to express the quintessence of Kant's critical philosophy. "Now the essence of the critical philosophy consists in this, that an absolute 'I' [*absolutes Ich*] is postulated as wholly unconditioned and incapable of determination by any higher thing; and if this philosophy is derived in due order from the above principle, it becomes Science of Knowledge."[49]

Now suddenly the I appears as an "absolute I"—quite an unprecedented promotion! The expression was to have a great future. But hadn't Fichte posited that the I was determined by the not-I, and was therefore determinable and far from absolute? Certainly, answers Fichte, but the I must at the very least recognize its *own* position in the not-I. The identity of the I with the not-I can thus be conceived as an idea or an ideal. If it is not yet realized, then so it must become. How? By the practical action of the I, which must make the not-I comply with the I. With this, Fichte's metaphysical reflections acquire not only a practical scope, but also a political and revolutionary one: the I is confronted with a world that resists it. But didn't the I posit the not-I? Isn't the I responsible for its imposed limits? To recognize this is to begin to overcome alienation. A world suffused with the rationality of the I then appears as a possible practical, even legal, goal.[50]

Fichte's ideas fascinated his contemporaries and launched the metaphysics of German Idealism, founded on the idea of an "absolute I" and understood as a thirst for freedom. The idea summed up the new spirit of Kantian philosophy and brought the latter to a level of systematization that Kant had not achieved. The metaphysical principles of the *Science of Knowledge* in a way gave a scientific basis to the spirit of the Enlightenment, such as Kant had understood it when he said that the *Aufklärung* [Enlightenment] was "human being's emergence from his self-incurred minority."[51] The concept of the not-I provided a striking rendering of the experience of *limitation* and finitude. But Fichte also exalted the human tendency—its infinite ambition (*unendliches Streben*)—to overcome its limitations, which can be made real through practical action. The philosophy of the future was not the old metaphysics, but a proud and rigorous Science of Knowledge and its first principle—the absolute I—became synonymous with freedom.[52]

The French Revolution was the first practical realization of the ideal of the identity between the I and the not-I, an event that Fichte hailed with great enthusiasm. The "subjects" finally started to overthrow the tyranny of the not-I. It is thus easy to understand how Friedrich Schlegel could write in 1794 that the three great events of his time were the French Revolution, Goethe's *Wilhelm Meister*, and Fichte's *Science of Knowledge*. From 1794 to 1799, Fichte was at the summit of his glory, he taught in Jena where his reputation was even greater than Goethe and Schiller's, who were also in Jena at the time. But Fichte's fame was short-lived. In 1799, he was forced to resign from the University of Jena after being accused of atheism (an accusation probably made for political motives). He then left for Berlin where he taught privately. The *Science of Knowledge* was finally presented in Berlin, but only to small circle of people. He did not become a professor again until 1810, when the University of Berlin was founded and he became the university's first rector.

The year 1799 was particularly difficult for Fichte. Not only did he have to leave Jena, but he was also severely criticized by Kant in the *Erlangen Literary Journal* (*Literatur Zeitung*) of January 11, 1799. It also became apparent that transcendental philosophy's torch had been passed on to the young Schelling whose philosophy of nature was based on a somewhat overt criticism of Fichte. All these wounds marked the proud Fichte and his philosophy even changed around 1800.

Certainly Fichte never renounced his earlier writings and always claimed his system had not changed.[53] But he never published the more speculative versions of his *Science of Knowledge*, which he kept for his audience in Berlin. He did publish some popular writings such as *The Vocation of Man* (1800) in which he started to place faith (*Glaube*) higher than knowledge (*Wissen*). Was it a religious turn aimed at countering the charges of atheism? The explanation seems incomplete. His pride wounded, Fichte never directly answered the infamous charges. Nevertheless, *The Vocation of Man* does contain some self-criticism in its critique of a project of the science of science. Can a science that seeks to understand itself lead to anything other than simulacra?

> You wanted to know about your knowledge. . . . What comes to be in and through knowledge is only knowledge. But all knowledge is only a depicting [*Alles Wissen aber ist nur Abbildung*], and in it something is always demanded which should correspond to the image. This demand can be satisfied by no knowledge, and a system of knowledge is necessarily a system of mere images, without any reality, meaning, and purpose.[54]

Science is the prisoner of its images and representations and cannot claim to reach Being itself or the absolute.

In fact, his *Science of Knowledge* of the 1800s dealt directly with the question of the absolute. Philosophy, still identified with the *Science of Knowledge*, cannot start from anything other than "absolute knowledge," but now such knowledge is shown to be that of Being itself, even of God himself. Fichte's contemporaries—or rather his thinning audience—were struck by this change in tone.[55] Fichte did not renounce his earlier ideas insofar as he remained committed to his fundamental intuition of the co-incidence of Being and thought,[56] which was thought in his early writings as the unity of subject and object. He obviously became increasingly concerned with answering his detractors who simply saw him as a philosopher of the I, which could not escape the level of subjective reflections.[57] Such criticism stemmed from the likes of Schelling and Hegel who spoke of a simple *Reflexionsphilosophie* with no objectivity or efficacy. Such attacks most probably led Fichte to insist on the unity of Being and thought as the characteristics of absolute knowledge. Unfortunately, his contemporaries did not know this elder Fichte, which has only been rediscovered in the last few decades.[58] For his contemporaries, he would always remain the philosopher of the 1794 *Grundlage* and the ultimate representative of what Schelling and Hegel reductively called "subjective idealism."

Schelling's Metaphysics of Identity

Schelling was German Idealism's intuitive genius, and perhaps its most metaphysical mind. He was also an extraordinarily precocious genius. He was only nineteen when he published his first philosophical essays: *On the Possibility of a Form of all Philosophy* (1794) and *Of the I as the Principle of Philosophy or the Unconditional in Human Knowledge* (1795).[59] In these essays, written rather quickly in 1794 to 1795—the *Grundlage* of the Science of Knowledge had just been published, Schelling avidly takes up Fichte's philosophy, transforms it, moves beyond it, and eventually develops his own system of philosophy. Or rather, one should say "his systems" since his "system" is reworked in a series drafts produced at a frenetic pace. After a series of attempts at a philosophy of nature published as essays between 1797 to 1799,[60] he published his *System of Transcendental Idealism* in 1800, and in 1801 the *Exposition of My System of Philosophy*, in which the "my" should be read as Schelling distancing himself from Fichte. Then, finally, in 1804 he published his *System of the Whole of Philosophy and the Philosophy of Nature in Particular*.

Schelling was only fifteen when he entered the legendary *Stift*, the protestant theological Seminary of the University of Tübingen where he became friends with two other geniuses, Hegel and Hölderlin, who were both five years older than he was. All three of the *Stift*'s three musketeers were training to be pastors, and first studied theology, but were rapidly influenced by their readings of Kant and Fichte. From then on, theology and the metaphysics on which it rests only made sense through the postulates and requirements of practical reason. The trio then together wrote a short project for a philosophical system, the paternity of which is varyingly attributed to each of them. Rediscovered at the beginning of the twentieth century, this fragmentary text called "The Earliest System-Program of German Idealism" opens with the promise of a new practical metaphysics:

> An *Ethics*. Since the whole of metaphysics falls for the future within *moral theory*—of which Kant with his pair of practical postulates has given only an *example*, and not *exhausted* it, this *Ethics* will be nothing less than a complete system of all Ideas or of all practical postulates (which is the same thing).[61]

But Fichte and Kant were not the only sources of this new metaphysics. Schelling, unlike Kant or Fichte, had a solid classical and philological education. Schelling's father was a pastor and a professor of the Old Testament and oriental languages at the Bebenhausen cloister not far from Tübingen. He gave his son lessons in Greek and Latin when Schelling was only ten years old. In 1792, Schelling presented his master's thesis written in Latin, *The Origin of Evil*.[62] In 1794, he wrote a commentary on the *Timaeus*, which has just been rediscovered.[63] The *Timaeus* continued to fascinate him: in 1797, he publishes *Ideas for a Philosophy of Nature*, and in 1798 he writes *On the World's Soul* (*Von der Weltseele*). Quite different from Kant and Fichte! The oldest metaphysics reappears out of its ancient sources.

In his commentary on the *Timaeus*, Schelling sees the demiurge's use of the ideas as an anticipation of Kant's transcendental subjectivity. But it is not Plato who is read through Kant, but rather Kant who is interpreted through Plato's philosophy of nature![64] Well before Kant, Plato had already understood that nature can only be understood through its intelligible substrate, "the world's soul." Thus as with transcendental philosophy, there is a correlation between nature and spirit, but here the Absolute is present in both. From then on, the identity between nature and spirit becomes the great *leitmotiv* of Schelling's philosophy of nature.

The idea for a philosophy of nature, which eventually became a critique of Fichte's subjectivism, was already heralded in the "The Earliest System-Program of German Idealism" of 1796 to 1797. In the "complete system of all ideas," which the new metaphysics promised to be, the "first idea is, of course, the representation *of my self*, as an absolutely free being." But this idea of freedom is already present in nature considered as pure self-deployment.

> Along with the free, self-conscious essence there stands forth—out of nothing—an entire *world* the one true and thinkable creation out of nothing.—Here I shall descend into the realms of physics; the question is this: how must a world be constituted for a moral being? I would like to give wings once more to our backward physics, that advances laboriously by experiments. Thus—if philosophy supplies ideas, and experience the data, we may at last come to have in essentials the physics that I look forward to for later times. It does not appear that our present-day physics can satisfy a creative spirit such as ours is or ought to be.[65]

Does nature not embody the first manifestation of freedom, or an I that is both subject and object of its activity? Fichte had masterfully developed the philosophy of the I and shown that nature can only be understood on the basis of its original activity. At first, the young Schelling's "physics" sought to complete Fichte's transcendentalism. But Schelling's insistence on the already-realized Absolute in nature was also a critique: Fichte remained a prisoner of a purely subjective form of idealism that did not escape the finite and never reaches the infinite promised by the idea of an *absolutes Ich* (absolute I). Since philosophy is the science that always begins with what is first, can it begin with anything other than the Absolute thought as auto-postulation? Only the absolute—the absolute already realized as nature—can be science's point of departure. Schelling is thus the first Idealist to start resolutely and consistently with the idea of a realized absolute. Fichte still thought the absolute as an exigency (*Aufgabe*) or as a task to be achieved through the practical action of the I. But if the absolute depended on human intervention, would this not degrade the autonomy and autarchy of the absolute I? Would not the infinite then depend on the finite?

The early Schelling, he of the 1794–1795 essays, still insisted on the idea that the absolute can only be thought as a self-positing I because the Fichtean I was thought as an original synthetic unity—that is, as the identity between the I and its other, of the I and nature, of subject and object. But since the absolute embodies the identity of subject and object for Schelling, it became irrelevant whether the point of departure is the subject or nature: the absolute operates in both. Although he maintained the Fichtean principle of the I,

Schelling quite early began to think this I in a Spinozist manner, as is testified in his letter to Hegel of February 4, 1795:

> I have, in the mean time, become Spinozist. . . . For Spinoza, the world (the object in its opposition to the subject) was everything. For me, it is the "I." The real difference between critical philosophy and dogmatic philosophy seems to me to be that the first starts from the absolute "I," which is as yet unconditioned by an object, and the second begins with the absolute object or the "not-I." Philosophy must necessarily start with the Unconditioned, and the only question is knowing what is this Unconditioned: whether it resides in the "I" or the "not-I." When this problem will be solved, all will be decided. For me, the supreme principle of all philosophy is the absolute "I," i.e., the "I" inasmuch as it is "I" and in which it is unconditioned by any object and is posited *freely.*[66]

Although Schelling still favored criticism, his Spinozism betrays the fact that he thought it may be legitimate to start from nature as well. Is not transcendental subjectivity originally at work in nature before being reflected by the consciousness of the I? Schelling writes to Fichte: is not the I the same as nature and "self-consciousness its greatest possibility"?[67] Must not nature become spirit before being deduced from the I?[68] For Fichte, as for Kant, nature was only a product of the subjective representation of the I, a simple not-I. For Schelling, however, nature appears as the "first I" because it already possesses its own subjectivity (*natura naturans*, nature "naturalizing" itself), as well as autonomy, finality, freedom and necessity, well before these categories become properties of the human I.

But Schelling did not renounce Kant or Fichte's transcendental philosophy as he developed his philosophy of nature (inspired by Spinoza and the *Timaeus*). In fact, he deduced the transcendental subject from the most primal subject: nature thought as an original manifestation of the I. Schelling thus still endorsed transcendental philosophy and still presented himself as an Idealist in his *System of Transcendental Idealism* (1800). Following Fichte, with whom he believed he can form an alliance, Schelling argued that the goal of philosophy is to uncover the conditions of the possibility of knowledge. Now all knowledge has a claim to truth, which must be understood as knowledge's adequate relation to its object, that is, the accord of subject and object, or, for Schelling, the accord of the I and nature.

For this accord to be possible, one must presuppose *a priori* the indissoluble unity of subject and object. Philosophy's, or science's, point of departure can therefore only be the *subject-object*, a first unity worthy of the term absolute. This level of thought is obviously that of philosophy. But there are two ways of raising non-philosophical consciousness to the level in which the unity of subject and object is revealed. Either, a *philosophy of nature*, which shows how the object is reflected in a subject, that is, how nature is "spiritualized," or, second, a *transcendental philosophy*, which deduces nature from the I by showing how an object is intertwined with the subject. Transcendental philosophy thus explains not only how the I posits the not-I, it also demonstrates the unity of the two: how the I recognizes itself in its own production.

But from a strictly *philosophical* perspective, the dichotomy of subject and object obviously does not really exist. Thus it makes *no difference* whether one starts from nature or the subject: In both cases the same result is achieved, namely, the unity of subject-object. In his 1800 *System of Transcendental Idealism*, Schelling therefore juxtaposes a Fichtean-inspired transcendental philosophy with his own philosophy of nature. But as we have already noted, Schelling begins with his philosophy of nature! Soon, he even does away with transcendental philosophy in the name of a philosophy of identity or indifference that has its most assured (and perhaps most caricatural and caricatured) expression in his 1801 *Exposition of My System*. Its title is certainly provocative since the system cannot belong to a particular individual, but only to philosophy itself. Schelling thus distances himself from Fichte and a merely transcendental philosophy.

In the *Exposition of My System*, Schelling proclaims that philosophy can only be a thought of the absolute or reason. Now, to be on the same level as reason is to abstract all distinctions between subject and object, and to immerse oneself in the true in-itself, or the absolute in which there is neither subject nor object. As the first paragraph of the 1801 *System* states, "I call *reason* absolute reason, or reason thought as complete indifference of subjective and objective [*totale Indifferenz des Subjektiven und Objektiven*]."[69] Reason is rational only if it encompasses everything and leaves nothing outside of itself. The § 2 insists on this point: "nothing is outside of reason, and everything is in it."[70] In reason's all-encompassing perspective, all "difference" disappears because reason is always identical to itself (§ 4). And he continues: in this system of identity, there is no distinction between the absolute and the thought of it. Such a (subjective, we might say) thought is never outside of reason because it would be fatal to a rational philosophy, all the more so since reason is thought "as the total indifference of subjective and objective" (§ 1). The Absolute's perspective thus turns subjectivity or the I, which claim to be outside reason, into a complete abstraction:

The thought of reason is possible for everyone. To reach this perspective, *one must abstract the one that thinks.* For the one that carries out this abstraction, reason immediately ceases to be something subjective, as it is commonly represented. But it cannot be itself thought as something objective since something that is objective, or thought, is only possible in opposition to the one that thinks, which is here completely abstracted. By this abstraction, therefore, it becomes the true *in-itself*, which leads to the point of indifference of the subjective and objective.[71]

This monist conception of the absolute, or reason, claims to be the only consistent way of thinking the Absolute. A thought that is distinct from its object cannot be on the absolute's level. All distinction between subject and object, or between the person thinking and his object, would introduce a limit or a scission in the absolute.

Therefore, one can speak of an *intellectual intuition* to explain the thought of the absolute. Although Kant had refused such an intuition, the early Fichte had sometimes used it to speak of the I's consciousness of itself and its activity.[72] But for Schelling, it is only an intuition of absolute identity and indifference. It is an intuition (Schelling sometimes speaks of *Ahndung* or presentiment) because it must be immediate. All mediation introduces a limit to the thought of the absolute. For a philosophy of identity such an intellectual intuition of the absolute is not so much *our* intuition of the absolute as the absolute's intuition of itself! And this intuition is not different from the absolute itself since in the absolute thinking and Being are the same.

Schelling was initially unwilling to call his thought metaphysics since it traditionally presented the absolute in a transcendent manner, which was completely inadequate for a philosophy of indifference. But insofar as his philosophy claimed a more adequate understanding of the absolute, it could not resist presenting itself as the "true metaphysics" as was the case in Schelling's 1804 new (!) *System of Philosophy in General.*[73] His statement of metaphysical faith reappears in a speech from 1807 "On the Essence of German Science." Science, in the emphatic sense it is given by German Idealism, finds itself identified with metaphysics understood as the capacity to grasp the many from the starting-point of the one and the one from the starting-point of the many.[74] Metaphysics is thus characterized by its sense of totality (*Sinn für Totalität*), in opposition to a mechanist and fragmented vision of the world.[75] It expresses a nation's soul (here the German nation then occupied by Napoleon's troops) and it is the source of all spiritual creation. Xavier Tilliette, who noted the emphatic use of metaphysics in the text, quotes Schelling's "winged words":

No matter what is said, all that is elevated and grand in the world happens because of something we may call metaphysics in its most general sense. Metaphysics has organically created the states and is what gives heart and soul to the human multitude, that is, makes it into a people. Metaphysics is what allows artists and poets to reproduce in sensible form the living sensation of eternal archetypes.[76]

But this vibrant and insightful speech was not followed up in Schelling's writings, which began to slow down and eventually practically stopped. The reason for this was most probably the publication of Hegel's *Phenomenology of Spirit* in 1807. Although Hegel, like Schelling, started from an already realized absolute, which he intended to work out in a *System of Philosophy*, the first part of which was the *Phenomenology of Spirit*, he also severely criticized Schelling's metaphysics of indifference on two major points. Hegel criticizes him for neglecting the very real differences that split the absolute apart. If one does not account for these differences, says Hegel in a passage that ruined their friendship, the absolute may appear as "the night in which . . . all the cows are black."[77] In the night of complete indifference when all is identical to everything—subject to object, thought to its object—nothing can be differentiated from anything else. If philosophy is to think the absolute, it must begin from the experience of difference, from conflict, and in a word, the scission that characterizes our reality and must be understood as a moment of the absolute.

Hegel also criticized Schelling for cavalierly ignoring the *concept* by exalting intellectual intuition. Philosophy unfounded on reason can only offer vain assurances that are worth the same as any other.[78] If philosophy seeks to *think* the absolute, the absolute must become a concept. Hegel thereby seems to see the absolute as the concept thinking itself. The later Schelling was increasingly weary of the concept's autarchy and took on Hegel's criticism by questioning Western philosophy's conceptual ambition with a passion that prefigures post-Idealist metaphysics.

The Later Schelling's Metaphysics

Schelling writes forgivingly to Hegel, on November 2 1807, to tell him he did not really believe the reference to the "night in which all cows are black" was aimed at him but rather at a prevalent misunderstanding of his ideas. Nevertheless, the comment undoubtedly hurt Schelling and probably led to a break in his work. Beginning in 1809, when his *Philosophical Investigations into the Essence of Human*

Freedom appeared, until his death in 1854, he published very little. He did, how-ever, continue teaching courses on revelation and mythology, the great muses of his youth. In 1810, he began work on an imposing manuscript on *The Ages of the World* (*Weltalter*) that was never completed although a few preliminary versions of it have been preserved.[79] It is in this period, around 1809 when Schelling was only thirty-four, that his second philosophy begins. Thus like Fichte, Schelling begins anew relatively early on in his career.

The 1809 essay on human freedom is one of Schelling's most metaphysi-cal essays.[80] In it, he takes on the metaphysical aporia of freedom in a system of identity. In a rational system in which everything appears to be prede-termined, little room seems to be left for freedom and the evil that follows from being free. Evil does exist however. So how is it to be explained? In the preface, Schelling writes that many people have misconstrued his ideas.[81] The system (of identity or indifference) seems to abolish all forms of free-dom. "May this study," writes Schelling, "strike down many prejudices and . . . much loose and shallow chatter."[82]

In order to speak of freedom in philosophy, one must show how it is inte-grated into the whole system. According to what Schelling calls an old but not forgotten legend, "the concept of freedom is in fact said to be incompatible with the concept of a system."[83] What a curious opinion, says Schelling, since freedom exists: everyone of us can feel it within ourselves. It must therefore somehow cohabitate with the rest of the world. The problem is thus not that of cohabitation, which is a fact, but of finding the system that allows one to think this possibility: "some system must exist, at least in the divine under-standing, with which freedom coexists."[84]

Schelling's argument is aimed at the opinion, which he attributes to Schle-gel but which is also that of Spinoza and the Stoics, that contends that any system of reason is a form of pantheism and is the equivalent of a form of fatalism. It is also a commonsensical position: if God is omnipotent, it is dif-ficult to understand how there can be something unconditioned outside of God like freedom, all the more so since all beings also depend on God by the act of continued creation.

The classic solution to this problem, proposed by Christianity, is that God created free beings, which he placed outside of himself, thus limiting his power. But this is not an adequate solution, says Schelling, since God would have thereby limited himself and this auto-limitation, which led to evil, means that God must have wanted evil, or even willingly caused it.

Schelling's solution is audacious and quite speculative. He claims to sal-vage freedom by saying that there is a difference *within God himself*—that is, a difference between his Being, or his essence (*Wesen*), and his ground (*Grund*). Schelling claims to draw his inspiration from Leibniz who had already used this distinction to understand the Trinity. Although the Son follows upon the Father understood as his *Grund* (ground, foundation), the Son's *Wesen*, his Being, or essence, is autonomous.[85] In German, unlike English, the term *Wesen* can have a concrete meaning when it is used to designate a being or beings (*un être ou un étant*): *ein schönes Wesen*, a good person. But it can also have a more abstract meaning, such as essence. Why distinguish ground (*Grund*) from essence (*Wesen*)? It is to recall, says Schelling, how essence (or Being) can subsist independently, but still depend on some ground other than itself. Its dependence (on some ground) need not abolish the essence's independence. Anything other would be surprising since the idea of a *Grund* implies that whatever follows from it exists independently.[86]

The relation of father to son provides a good example of this: the son depends on his father as his ground (*Grund*), but is nevertheless independent as to his Being (*Wesen*). This important "ontological difference" between the foundation (*Grund*) and Being (*Seyn*) was already included in the 1801 *Exposition of My System*,[87] but here it is directly applied to God!

With this distinction, it is possible to say that all things, all *Wesen*, follow from God as their ground. They follow from God as "emanations," which must be understood as an auto-revelation of God. Auto-revelation here means the beings emanating from God are, like him, free beings. Is there any better manifestation of God than freedom? Thus these beings exist distinctly, and therefore have an autonomous *Wesen*, even though they have their *Grund*, their *raison d'être*, in God.

Schelling thus hopes to have dispelled the charges of Spinozism. His pantheism does not exclude freedom insofar as *everything has its ground in God*. Rather, it is free will, says Schelling, which expresses the *essential Being* of God, as well as humankind's and nature as a whole conceived as free self-deployment. This leads him to his famous idea in his 1809 essay: "In the final and highest instance there is no other Being than will. Will is the primal Being."[88]

Freedom is then given a very precise meaning in the 1809 essay. In the real and living sense of the term, says Schelling, freedom is the faculty for doing good and evil.[89] Freedom now appears to be safe in Schelling's pantheism, but what is now the status of evil (on which he had first written in 1792)? Schelling sees evil as "the most deeply rooted problem of all the theory of freedom." And with it, the whole problem of theodicy is raised once again. Now, either evil really exists, in which case evil is posited in the infinite substance or original will and thereby "we ruin the concept of a being with supreme perfection"; or, evil is not real, as in Christian dogmatism that turns it into a *privatio boni*, in which case freedom is likewise denied.

To solve this dilemma, Schelling once again uses the distinction, "introduced by the philosophy of nature of our time," between "Being insofar as it exists [*Wesen*] and Being insofar as it is merely the ground [*Grund*] of existence."[90] The distinction not only allows a separation between God *and nature*, which follows from him, it also introduces a singular separation *within God himself*, namely, between his ground (*Grund*) and his existence (*Wesen*). As nothing exists before him, or outside of him, God contains within himself the ground of his existence (*Grund seiner Existenz*).[91] And yet, this ground, says Schelling, is not God in the absolute, but only his "ground." Schelling also calls this *Grund* God's nature, which, although inseparable from what he is, can be distinguished from his existence. Schelling here means *Existenz* in the etymological sense of the term, which has since been popularized by Heidegger. That is, "what springs from" (ἔκστασις, ἐξιστάμενον,[92] *being-outside-of-oneself*), what emerges from some ground (*Grund*) or a nature. God himself springs from a ground.

According to Schelling, this ontological distinction between God's ground and his existence explains the becoming of things and the emergence of evil. All existing things follow from their ground in God. Here, Schelling's argument becomes heretical. "In order to be divided from God, they must become from a ground different from God." Otherwise, they would themselves be God. They therefore emanate from what God is not: his "ground." This is "the only justified dualism," proclaims Schelling (who was deadly allergic to dualism), and then adds, this is the "system of the self-destruction and despair of reason."[93]

Divine generation can be described as a kind of nostalgia, or a "yearning the eternal One feels to give birth to itself."[94] And although aspiration implies will, adds Schelling, it is a will devoid of an understanding, and one that seeks, for this very reason, an understanding. And since creation is here understood as the self-revelation of God, then the world as we know it is an ordered cosmos. But beneath any order there always lurks some primal chaos that may reappear at any moment.[95] Order is thus never found in beginnings since its concept presupposes disorder or some initial anarchy. And, says Schelling, it is from this darkness that the understanding is born. Only God exists in full light because he exists out of himself.

The duality of ground and existence also applies to things, but unlike God, things have their ground (*Grund*) in God (even God's *Grund*) and not in themselves. Thus in creatures there is also will, but a blind will (*blinder Wille*) that also seeks the understanding. Schelling calls it the *Eigenwille der Kreatur*, which may be translated as "the self-will of creatures." Yet, in German, *Eigenwille* also means stubbornness and obstinacy. Here, the creatures' stubbornness consists in wanting to exist by themselves (or rather, on their own ground). Schelling then opposes the creatures' obstinacy with what he calls the *Universalwille*, the universal will.[96]

In humans, and only in humans, the *Eigenwille* can attain the level of *Universalwille*. The stubborn will can surpass itself and unite with the universal will of the whole. As with God, there are two principles in humans: the ground—principle of darkness—and that of light or spirit.[97] Although these two principles are united in God, their unity becomes disassociated in humans, a scission that explains the *possibility* of good and evil.

By raising themselves above nature, humans are individuals with personalities distinct from God. But "precisely the elevation of this will (*Eigenwille*) is evil,"[98] says Schelling, because will inverses the hierarchy of principles of the *Grund* and *Existenz* by elevating its dark side above the universal and eternal ground of things. Evil follows from this, but redemption is always possible "through restoration of separate and individual life into the being's inner glimpse of light."[99]

It is important to note, however, that it is not the distinction or separateness of humans that is evil, but only finitude's desire to be the center of Being. "Evil does not come from finitude in itself, but from finitude raised up to Being as a self [*Selbstsein*]."[100] Humans are torn by two tendencies: the divine principle that aspires to universality, and the principle of their ground that insists on its particularity. Schelling then writes a sentence that Heidegger loved: "the angst of living leads Man out of the center into which it was created."[101] As with Kant, Schelling, who refers to him explicitly, says this is *radical* evil. "Thus is the beginning of sin, that man transgresses from authentic Being into non-Being, from truth to lies, from light to darkness, in order to become a self-creating ground and, with the power of the center which he has within himself, to rule over all things."[102]

This cosmic drama presupposes the hierarchy of an order systematically arranged that is, in a way, the order of the philosophy of identity.[103] But the difference between *Grund* and *Existenz* has opened a breach in its placid identity. Before any order, says Schelling, there is first anarchy. But this is not all: the passage from anarchy to order describes a process that not only plays out in God, who is thought as auto-revelation, but is also present in the great "ages of the world." We can no longer claim, as Hegel did, that nothing happens in the philosophy of identity or the philosophy of the absolute. It is now eventful: the absolute is a necessarily historical becoming or self-revelation. The passage is essentially the passage of *Grund* to existence, of God rising above darkness and reaching the universal light through his victory over darkness, which is the victory of love or fully realized spirit. Yet just as light presupposes darkness, love also presupposes an original struggle.

Toward the end of his essay on the "foundation" of human freedom, Schelling says that the distinction between *Grund* and existence is perhaps less primary than had been suggested. Prior to the distinction between *Grund* and existence, there is an original ground, the (*Urgrund*), or a bottom-less abyss (*Ungrund*), says Schelling.[104] Before any foundation and any light is there not a bottom-less abyss (*Abgrund*)? What is this Being that precedes both the concept and light? Can the philosophy of the concept and light even think it?

Insofar as the original abyss is neither light nor pure thought, it resists conceptual thought. It is an "event" that can only be thought on its own terms because it is essentially a self-revelatory manifestation (*Selbstoffenbarung*). For it to be truly radical, philosophy must let what is prior to any concept speak. Schelling increasingly says that conceptual, or rational, thought is *negative*. It cannot escape it own intellectual products and cannot grasp what precedes or exceeds thought. Once again, Hegel is the target here: the concept can never account for itself and explain what gave rise to its emergence. Philosophy of the concept can at best hope to raise itself to its own limit (in which case it is an ascendant philosophy). But there may also be a *positive philosophy* that descends from this original Being—a pure event that exceeds thought and is akin to a historic revelation in the original sense of the term historic. Such a history would no longer pertain to reason itself,[105] as the latter can only think its own rationality, which it is unable to exceed.

The fundamental distinction between negative and positive philosophy was later systematized in the courses Schelling taught in Berlin during the 1840s following Hegel's death. Of particular importance here is his course on *The Philosophy of Revelation* (1842–1843),[106] which had been previously prepared by the critique of the (negative) philosophy of the concept in his *Munich Lectures* on modern philosophy in 1836 to 1837.[107] According to Schelling, the philosophy of the concept can never reach the level of effective existence (*Existenz*) or Being itself because the concept is always caught-up in its own fictions and thoughts devoid of any effective reality:

And since existence is always the positive, namely that which is posited, affirmed, asserted, then it had to then confess to being a purely negative philosophy, but precisely thereby had to leave space free outside itself for the philosophy which relates to existence, i.e. for the positive philosophy: it had to not present itself as the absolute philosophy, as the philosophy which leaves nothing outside itself.[108]

Positive philosophy, which becomes aware of what exceeds the concept, gives way to a "revelation" predating thought itself.[109] The later Schelling's positive philosophy took the surprising form of a *Philosophy of Revelation* or a *Philosophy of Mythology*. It was an immanent critique of systematic philosophies like his philosophy of identity. In these systems, thought only discovers in the object what is already in the subject. But how can one claim that the subject's products give access to Being itself? Had Kant not already rightly argued that Being was simply posited by thought and could not be grasped by the mind? Being, as something *posited*, cannot pertain to thought: it can only be taken up by a *positive* philosophy.[110]

Thus in the context of a positive philosophy, "metaphysics" unexpectedly becomes important. Indeed, it is now seen as an invitation to move *beyond* purely *logical* philosophy, which cannot escape the concept's immanence. In fact, "logic," was not the dominant part of classical philosophy; it was simply a propaedeutic leading to metaphysics—that is, to what is beyond logic. The traditional distinction between logic and metaphysics (which was the point of departure of Hegel's courses in Jena) corresponds to the distinction between negative and positive philosophy. Whereas the first can at best reach the level of genuine philosophy, only positive philosophy can achieve metaphysics' secret promise:

> Negative philosophy is simply a *philosophia ascendens* (rising from below) … and positive philosophy a *philosophia descendens* (descending from high to low). Together they bring philosophy full circle. One could easily bring this duality back … to the traditional division of theoretical philosophy into logic and metaphysics since the former is no more than a logic (logic of becoming) and all genuine metaphysics belongs to the other (positive philosophy).[111]

Hegel's Philosophy of Spirit

To think! Abstractly!—*Sauve qui peut!* Let those who can, save themselves. Even now I can hear a traitor, bought by the enemy, exclaim these words, denouncing this essay because it will deal with metaphysics. For *metaphysics* is a word, no less than *abstract*, and even *thinking* as well, from which everybody more or less runs away as from a man who has caught the plague.[112]

As with the other Idealists, Hegel generally used the term "metaphysics" to designate the old metaphysics, which he called the "metaphysics of the understanding" (*Verstandesmetaphysik*). He did however use it sometimes to designate the new system itself or his ambition to finally present the real *System of Philosophy*. *System der Philosophie* was the title he gave on the frontispiece of his 1807 work, which had a subtitle that read: "*First Part: Science of the Phenomenology of Spirit.*"

Like the young Schelling, Hegel was convinced philosophy can only be a system, the vocation of which is to think the Absolute. "Unless it is a system, a philosophy is not a scientific production."[113] *System of Philosophy* is therefore the only possible title for a philosophical work—a banal yet demanding title. Hegel was quite proud of his reputation of being the most systematic thinker in the history of metaphysics. It is therefore quite ironic that Hegel, unlike Schelling, never published a definitive version of his complete system. Other than important articles, such as *The Difference between Fichte's and Schelling's Systems of Philosophy* (1801) and *Faith and Knowledge* (1802), all written in Jena as a young man while editing with his friend Schelling the *Critical Journal of Philosophy* which discussed contemporary transcendental philosophy, Hegel only published four books during his lifetime:

- *Phenomenology of Spirit* (1807)
- *The Science of Logic* (three tomes; 1812, 1813, and 1816)
- *Principles of the Philosophy of Right* (1821)
- *Encyclopedia of Philosophical Sciences* (three editions: 1817, 1827, and 1830)

How do these books fit within Hegel's system? In 1807, the *Phenomenology* was supposed to be an "introduction" to the *System of Science*. Although calling it a "first part," as Hegel did in 1807, is appropriate, it is nevertheless misleading since, as he later acknowledged, the introduction to a science cannot be a part of the science itself. In fact, the *Science of Logic* was the real *first part* of the science itself (the *Phenomenology* acted as its didactic introduction). It was the first part because philosophy must always begin with a theory of thought. This task was so important to him that it is undoubtedly the section of his system that Hegel wrote with the most care. Besides logic, the system had two other parts: philosophy of nature and philosophy of spirit (the philosophy of right was part of the latter despite being published separately). Hegel was thus the first to anticipate the classical distinction between natural science (*Naturwissenschaft*) and the humanities (*Geisteswissenschaft*, literally, science of the spirit) that would reappear in the second half on the nineteenth century. The 1817 *Encyclopedia* followed the system's triadic division despite being a précis (*Grundriss*) for his audience in Heidelberg and Berlin. During his classes, his students used it as a manual that Hegel commented on with a mumbling voice and Swabian temper (and accent).[114] His commentaries were so important for any understanding of its arid text that the editors of the first posthumous edition of Hegel's works included notes taken by his students along with Hegel's own text. The result is a voluminous but highly informative work, often anecdotal and therefore easily accessible. But for this reason, unlike the *Phenomenology* or the *Logic*, it should not be considered as Hegel's own text. Since he died of cholera in 1831 at the age of sixty-one and since his system does not exist as such in his writings, we do not know whether Hegel ever intended to produce a mature version of his system. In this respect the contrast with Schelling is striking; Schelling continuously reformulated, even changed his system, and may have in the end doubted the very idea of a system.

For Hegel there can be only one system, although he did rework and modify it. There are therefore several versions of the one system with the same unique rational requirements, the definitive presentation of which, however, was always deferred.

And yet, in his first classes given in Jena, Hegel did not hesitate to call his system metaphysics. He was then teaching a course entitled *Logica et metaphysica*.[115] The class was required by the Wolffian *cursus*, still used in some regions of Germany, and divided theoretical philosophy into logic and metaphysics. Nevertheless, Hegel himself announced that his "System of Philosophy" (an obvious title!) would appear starting in 1804—the 1807 *Phenomenology* became its *de facto* first part (although it had not been mentioned in 1804). The system he promised was to have had three parts: Logic, Nature, and Metaphysics.[116] This threefold division of the philosophical sciences would later be replaced, in a later version of the system, by logic, philosophy of nature, and philosophy of spirit. Thus the only title that changed was metaphysics. It is therefore possible that his later "philosophy of spirit" replaced and achieved the metaphysics promised by his first systematic program and which he had already discussed in his classes in Jena under the title "Logic and Metaphysics" (at which time the philosophy of nature, then so important to Schelling, was missing).

The program for his triadic system (logic-nature-metaphysics) was then modified when Hegel began writing his *Phenomenology* and had the idea of beginning the system with an "introduction" (which was lacking in Schelling's "all or nothing" system, an absence Hegel may have criticized). The first clue of this change appears in the title of a class beginning in October 1806, at the time he was writing the *Phenomenology. Logicam et Metaphysicam sive philosophiam speculativam, praemissa Phaenomenologia mentis ex libri sui: System der Wissenschaft proxime proditura parte prima.*[117] His class on logic and metaphysics is now preceded by a *Phenomenology of Spirit* that corresponds to the first part of the book entitled *System of Science*, which was to be published shortly. The *Phenomenology*, soon to be the difficult if brilliant work of 1807, is now a propaedeutic to speculative philosophy, itself divided into logic and metaphysics (terms that will, as we shall see, end up merging together in *The Science of Logic*). But the most important division made in 1807 was of separating his *Phenomenology*, now understood as a propaedeutic, from the *Science* itself, which was to become the "second part" of his system. It is as though Hegel took up the Kantian division of critique and metaphysics (or speculative philosophy) for quite similar reasons. Before any "metaphysics," if one may even use the term, a propaedeutic is needed to explain how such a science is possible.

Another great irony of his system is that although Hegel never ceased to say that introductions and propaedeutics are useless in science (because they are extraneous to the system itself), he nevertheless wrote several prolegomena, prefaces, and forewords. Nobody will complain since these introductions are frequently easier to understand than the systems they introduce. It is therefore to the reader's benefit that Hegel carefully shows the way to reach the speculative level. Along with his pedagogical care (he was a high school principal for many years), Hegel also included a critique of Schelling's system, which had plunged the reader directly into a system that required an intellectual sacrifice because only intellectual intuition could guide the reader to his system's of absolute identity in which, as we have noted already, Hegel ironically claimed that all cows are black. The average reader has the right to demand a ladder to reach the level of science.

The Phenomenology of Spirit is such a ladder.[118] But the "phenomenalizing" of spirit (*Geist*), or its becoming-a-phenomenon *for* our consciousness, is also a subjective genitive: it is *spirit* that phenomenalizes *itself* for our consciousness. This can be further described using the analogy of ascending and descending paths that characterized the distinction between logic and metaphysics in School metaphysics, which Schelling used in his positive philosophy. The *Phenomenology* not only leads the individual in the *ascent* to the level of science by destroying mistaken opinions, but it also *lowers* spirit to the level of consciousness.

The idea of the spirit's "descent," which has obvious Christian origins,[119] is always the most important for Hegel: spirit cannot remain a purely abstract or mental reality, as it would then lack all effectivity (*Wirklichkeit*). Spirit is spirit only if it has an effect—that is, if it can completely suffuse reality and give it meaning. For this reason, Hegelian metaphysics is one of spirit: spirit is both its point of departure and its ultimate destination. The system's composition confirms this: science can only *start* with the *Phenomenology of Spirit*, and conclude with a philosophy of spirit, which grasps itself through philosophy. This is what Hegel's metaphysics sought to be: a phenomenology and a philosophy of spirit. It is the most essential characterization of the absolute which philosophy can think. "The absolute is Spirit; this is the highest definition of the absolute."[120]

But what does he mean by spirit? This is a very important question, to which his whole system is an answer. We may begin with a text drawn from the *Encyclopedia* where Hegel states that spirit is "the self-knowing, actual Idea."[121] It is obviously an "idea" since the ultimate principle of a system of philosophy must be rational: if reason does not exist, there is no philosophy. But the idea, posited as a point of departure (a bit like Plato's *hypothesis*), must also be *wirklich*—that is, it must be "effective," it must show and justify itself. We sometimes say in English that an idea "works" or "does not work." For Hegel, an idea "does not work" when it is abstract and pointless, and is of little interest. The idea—the principle of philosophy—must therefore show itself to be effective (*wirklich*) and, in fact, Hegel's whole "system" is nothing more that a large-scale demonstration of the idea's effectivity. As he says in one of his most famous texts: "what is rational is real, and what is real is rational."[122]

Although the expression shocked many people, for Hegel it simply expresses the presupposition of *all science*: all reality is rational and spirit can understand it. The principle of sufficient reason makes no other claim. But Hegel's expression is also a critique of overly abstract utopian rationality: reason that is not real, or unconcerned with being realized, is not rational....

Thus we must presuppose that reality is fundamentally rational and philosophy can systematically explicate its rationality. Contradictions are not a problem for Hegel: beneath every contradiction, every scission, lies a possible unity awaiting the integration of differences. But for Hegel, this rational unity does not erase differences or abolish contradictions, as is the case in a philosophy of identity. Hegel insists on this point: every scission is essential to unity. Spirit can only reach its truth by rediscovering itself in the absolute sundering. In order to achieve this intelligence of the absolute, consciousness must free itself of its limitations,[123] overcome the understanding's rigid opposition, and adopt reason's perspective (but can science have another?). The common consciousness must be shown that it can in fact raise itself to the level of reason; a maieutic task given to the *Phenomenology*.

For Hegel, an unrealized absolute, or one that avoids reality's contradictions, is not an absolute. Philosophy (or science) must therefore show not only that the real is rational, but also that the rational is already real. In this sense, spirit—which only recognizes itself in the absolute sundering—is the "realized idea" for Hegel. But to be worthy of the term spirit, the realized idea must also *know itself*, says Hegel. It must become conscious of itself—that is, of its importance in a system of philosophy. But one of the subtleties of his system is that, for Hegel, the idea can only become conscious of itself if it "realizes" itself in a confrontation with what is different from it. In order to establish itself as idea, the idea must prove itself. In so doing, the absolute becomes conscious of itself as spirit and as the meaning of all things.

But what "leads" Spirit—or the absolute seeking itself—to want to realize and become conscious of itself? Hegel's answer is clear and always the same: this movement's impulse is a desire for freedom. The spirit's essence or substance, says Hegel, is freedom.[124] He thus affirms his commitment to the metaphysics of freedom that had such an influence on German Idealism since Kant. But what does he mean when he says freedom is the essence of spirit? He answers by saying that spirit distinguishes itself from matter by its Being-by-itself, one could also say, by its "self-contained existence"[125] or *Bei-sich-selbst-Sein*, which is another name for freedom. "Now this is freedom, exactly. For if I am dependent (*abhängig*), my Being is referred to something else which I am not; I cannot exist independently of something external. I am free when, on the contrary, my existence depends upon myself."[126] Negatively, freedom means independence, and positively, it means auto-determination.

Yet, argues Hegel, this being-by-oneself that characterizes the spirit's freedom must also be self-consciousness (*Selbstbewusstsein*) because it is exactly what is meant by the expression "*being-by-oneself*" (*bei sich*). There is therefore no being-by-oneself without self-consciousness. But there are two moments to self-consciousness: the fact that I am conscious (*daß ich weiß*) and that of which I am conscious (*was ich weiß*). Obviously, in a fully realized consciousness of self both moments tend to merge together (*fallen zusammen*) because when spirit knows itself, it also knows *what it* is. However, adds Hegel, spirit must acquire this consciousness of what it is.[127] This is another way of saying that spirit is a process, a becoming, that leads to full self-consciousness and to the consciousness of itself as freedom. Thus Hegel will say, in his lectures on history, that world history—insofar as it wishes to be thought as a rational process; all its other aspects having little importance *for philosophy*—can and must be thought as "progress in the consciousness of freedom."[128] Freedom, says Hegel passionately, is "spirit's only goal" (*der einzige Zweck des Geistes*). It is the motor of history and the reason for all conflicts; all oppression in history is the history of the repression of freedom.[129]

Although the spirit's consciousness of itself as freedom can only be accomplished historically, it also has its place within the system. As we have seen, a system of philosophy must begin with logic, or the science of thought that leads to the idea, thought as the absolute idea (*die absolute Idee*) or as pure self-determination. Yet, this idea remains empty if it does not experience what is different from it—that is, nature. The passage from the *Logic* (the level of the abstract idea) to the philosophy of nature is its demonstration: first posited as the idea's other, nature then shows itself to be the idea's positing of itself inasmuch as nature's determinations appear as conceptual determinations.[130] But the idea does not become "conscious" of this integral determination until the end of the philosophy of nature when it literally "becomes" spirit—that is, when the animal (the last stage of the philosophy of nature) realizes its capacity for thought and becomes, in humans, a rational being endowed with reason and self-consciousness. Spirit is thus the realized idea that knows itself.

Hegel acknowledges that these expressions are rather curious for the common understanding. Phenomenology must therefore bring the common consciousness to conceive of a self-determining idea. Thus the *Phenomenology*'s pedagogical project is to lead the natural consciousness, level by level, until it becomes conscious of itself and reaches the level of absolute knowledge. What is this "absolute knowledge"? For Hegel, it is the level reached when consciousness no longer posits truth outside of itself, but recognizes itself as the source of all truth. The *Phenomenology*'s odyssey is the rather complex and repetitive tale—the common understanding always falls back on its old stupidities—of consciousness wishing to posit a "true reality" outside of itself, but then realizing it is simply a determination it had already posited.

To give but one example, "religion," which is the penultimate step of the *Phenomenology* (and of the philosophy of spirit in his system), does raise itself to the consideration of infinity, but it unfortunately posits this infinity outside of itself in a transcendent world distinct from the finite. Yet such a representation, argues Hegel, makes the infinite finite since it posits, on the one hand, the finite, and on the other, the infinite. It is a projection that pertains to the order of representation, legitimate for religion, but not for philosophy in which the idea can no longer use images and representations, but must understand itself only in the pure light of the concept. On the level of the concept, philosophy recognizes that true infinity resides in thought itself, which is able to transcend all finite determinations because they were all posited by thought in thought. From then on, nothing can escape the realm of thought conscious of its infinity, and the level of "absolute knowledge" is reached. The term "absolute" here denotes knowledge that solely depends on its self and knows itself (as in Fichte's *Science of Knowledge*): "the goal is spirit knowing what knowing is."[131] At the end of the *Phenomenology*, knowledge appears as a pure relation to itself, as the idea's knowledge of itself.

Hegel's argument is obviously in opposition to popular conceptions of knowledge that separate the act of knowing from what is known. That is why Hegel went through the trouble of writing the *Phenomenology of Spirit* before presenting his system. Since a system only pertains to reason—absolute reason—one must first elevate common consciousness to the level of absolute knowledge: knowledge of itself in which all objective determinations are revealed to be determinations of spirit knowing itself.

When the end of the *Phenomenology* is reached, "speculative philosophy" may then begin. During his stay in Jena, we know it was supposed to have a *logic* and a *metaphysics*. Yet, it was the *Logic* that appeared five years after the *Phenomenology*. The logic was supposed to belong to the ethereal level of pure thought where the idea determines itself and presupposes that consciousness with its desire to distinguish the idea from its object has been overcome. But Hegel preferred to churn out prefaces and introductions in order to prepare his readers for what awaits them...

The preface to the first edition (1812) and the first text of the *Logic*, proclaims that the science of logic will be what is normally called metaphysics, or speculative philosophy, a science that had supposedly been neglected until then.[132] From then on, speculative philosophy is no longer to contain both a logic *and* a metaphysics: logic (or what Hegel means by the term) now also includes metaphysics. This can be read as both a demotion and a promotion of metaphysical thought. Although metaphysics is thereby demoted ("humiliated" perhaps) since it is "replaced" by logic, it is also promoted since logic can only reveal its full meaning if it becomes the heir to the entire metaphysical tradition: metaphysics becomes logic, but logic also becomes metaphysics.

Such is the essence of Hegel's metaphysics: logic replaces metaphysics in order to better carry out its promise. Walter Schulz is correct in speaking of an *Aufhebung*, or a "sublation," of metaphysics in Hegel's writing.[133] This means that logic becomes the new foundation for metaphysics, now conscious of itself, which, in a way, leads to metaphysics' "suppression." But, asks Hegel, has metaphysical thought ever been anything other than a logic? On this,

Jacques Derrida is quite right in saying that Hegelianism "is the language of Western philosophy taking absolute possession of itself."[134]

In the preface to the 1812 *Logic*, Hegel notes that for the last twenty-five years, metaphysics has been "extirpated root and branch" (*mit Stumpf und Stiel ausgerottet*) and disappeared from the scientific world. Hegel says this nostalgically and quite obviously regrets its loss.[135] Not only is the most important part of speculative, and philosophical, thought thereby lost, so is "the spirit that contemplates its own pure essence" (*der mit seinem reinen Wesen sich beschäftigende Geist*). Where else can spirit become conscious of itself other than in its metaphysics? This situation led Hegel to say in a famous passage "a cultured people without any metaphysics is like a temple without a 'Holy of Holies.'"[136]

The expression is similar to what Kant had said about metaphysics as a natural disposition (*metaphysica naturalis*). Yet Hegel knew quite well that the decline of metaphysics was partially Kant's fault, or rather the fault of what Hegel calls quite correctly, Kant's "exoteric"[137] or popular doctrine that limits the understanding to the realm of possible experience. Empirical science and common sense then join together in destroying metaphysics and speculative thought. And yet, says Hegel, Kant was also the first to have turned metaphysics into logic.[138] He is most probably referring here to Kant's "transcendental logic" in which the conditions of objectivity were determined by the understanding's categories. A brilliant intuition, thinks Hegel, but one that is not devoid of problems. "Critical philosophy had, it is true, already turned metaphysics into logic but it ... was overawed by the object, and so the logical determinations were given an essentially subjective significance."[139] Although objectivity was thereby determined subjectively, the object still remained as a transcendent thing-in-itself unreachable by thought. What is the point of thinking if one cannot reach the object, asks Hegel ironically? The oldest metaphysics, he adds, had already recognized that the veritable Being of things was only expressed through thought.[140] Hegel is referring to Plato and Aristotle who long before acknowledged that the *eidos* belonged to both thought and Being.

In the first two books of his *Logic*, on the logic of Being and the logic of essence, Hegel follows the older, pre-Kantian, metaphysics. Indeed, his reference to Being and essence is quite obviously an allusion to the essential preoccupations of metaphysics starting with Parmenides, Plato and Aristotle, up to and including Spinoza and Leibniz. However, this "metaphysics" (which was in fact "logic" unaware of itself) believed it could identify all the objective determinations of things. The first two books of the *Logic* (which discuss Being and essence) are therefore entitled "objective logic." This logic, notes Hegel, can replace the older metaphysics. "The objective logic, then, takes the place of the former metaphysics which was intended to be the scientific construction of the world in terms of thoughts alone."[141] Objective logic, along with the metaphysics of the understanding, had naively forgotten that Being and essence were essentially determinations belonging to thought and the "subject." This discovery belongs to the subjective logic of the third and last book of Hegel's *Logic* called "Logic of the Concept." In it, thought finally reappropriates its essential determinations.

But subjective thought is no longer confronted with objects extraneously linked to the concept (as seemed to be the case for Kant). No, the determinations of thought are now autonomous in relation to the subject, or better, they are the new subject. In this speculative logic, the object's determinations are the idea's own determinations (*Fortbestimmungen*). This key term, *Fortbestimmungen*, is hard to translate into English. It literally designates the determinations that "lead the idea" from determination to determination. Logic had known for some time that a concept is defined by its determinations. Wolff had spoken of a concept's *essentialia*, or essential characteristics, that distinguish it from another concept. What Hegel is searching for here is the logic immanent to these determinations: how does one logically and necessarily pass from one determination to another? Thus there is "movement" in logic, a *Selbstbewegung*, or self-movement as Hegel calls it because it belongs to thought alone.[142]

But there is an important problem that the later Schelling underlined in his criticism. Is there really movement in thought? Can something really "move" a concept? And how does thought decide to posit nature as its other when it transitions from logic to the philosophy of nature?[143]

Hegel would have answered Schelling that only for the old metaphysics was there no "movement" in the realm of ideas. The metaphysics of the understanding (*Verstandesmetaphysik*) is one that conceives all determinations of thought (form and matter, finite and infinite, subject and object, and so on) as fixed, immutable, and impossible to transcend. Why transcend these determinations of the understanding? And how? Hegel answers: by recognizing that all determinations come from thought, that they have an origin (a historical or linguistic origin, we would say today, but for Hegel it was purely logical), and create each other. According to Hegel, the development of the idea obeys its own logic that is not linked to the person that *thinks it*, but is present whenever somebody tries to think in a rigorous manner.

Hegel's attitude toward the metaphysics of the understanding is ambivalent, like his attitude toward metaphysics in general, which is both "abolished" and "accomplished" by speculative logic. Insofar as it considers the understanding's determinations to be fixed and pertain to "objective Being," it must be overcome. But this does not mean that Hegel disdained it. The metaphysics of the understanding was worthy of praise because it had recognized how the power of thought is that of the concept and logic was essential to philosophy. Hegel underlines this point in his opposition to the philosophies of sentiment (*Gefühl*) and intuition that thrived around him in the wake of Romanticism. One can never overly defend the patient conceptual divisions honored by the metaphysics of the understanding against the concept's banishment from philosophy.[144] The older metaphysics was simply a bit naïve in thinking its conceptual determinations were "things" that had simply fallen from the sky.

This attitude, according to Hegel, belonged to the pre-Kantian metaphysics developed from Descartes to Wolff. As he says in the *Encyclopedia* (§ 26), this metaphysics was simply the first, albeit naïve (*unbefangen*), attitude toward objective thought,[145] which Kant had left behind when he recognized, at least in principle, that all conceptual determinations in fact belonged to the absolute subject or thought itself. Kant's only mistake was to have deprived these determinations of any objectivity, as if they were foreign to the things-in-themselves. Therefore, speculative logic radicalizes the Kantian identification of metaphysic with logic (all objective determinations follow from thought), but it also patiently takes up the divisions of the metaphysics of the understanding by showing how they result from the idea's progressive determination (*Fortbestimmung*). Metaphysics, or logic, thus merges with all the determinations of thought that the concept re-appropriates as it masters itself.

Hence the assessment given in the *Enyclopedia*:

> Metaphysics is nothing else [*nicht anderes*] but the entire range of the universal determinations of thought, as it were, the diamond net into which everything is brought and thereby first [*zuallererst*] made intelligible. Every educated consciousness [*jedes gebildete Bewußtsein*] has its metaphysics, an instinctive way of thinking, the absolute power within us of which we become master only when we make it in turn the object of our knowledge.[146]

But does Hegel not thereby limit metaphysics to the realm of logic and its formal determinations? For Hegel, it is more of a promotion than a limitation. His logicizing had "saved" metaphysics and brought it back to the scientific world from which it been banished for twenty-five years in the name of "common sense" and "empirical science." Like Kant, Hegel wished to oppose the prevalent indifference to metaphysics, harbor it and make it possible. And it is precisely the protection given to metaphysics that constitutes its real *Aufhebung*, or completion: metaphysics has become the logic of thought and no more (*nicht anderes*).

Although, in a way, he may be considered the "last metaphysician," Hegel was also the first to have considered metaphysics historically, and more importantly to have begun its "deconstruction." When he claims that metaphysics is nothing other than (*nicht anderes als*) the web (*Netz*), diamond or otherwise, formed by thought's determinations from which no understanding of reality can extricate itself, Hegel thereby unintentionally, and unbeknownst to his heirs, inaugurated a new logical conception of metaphysics. Metaphysics is no longer conceptual thought's quest to understand and a search for transcendence (in spirit, freedom, or Being); it is now defined as a conceptual network. Hegel's heirs have then silently taken up his logical conception of metaphysics. It appears in an infinitely less subtle way in the writings of August Comte, in neo-Kantianism and logical positivism, and even in the efforts to deconstruct the "logic of metaphysics" in the works of authors like Nietzsche, Heidegger and Derrida.

And yet, for the *young* Hegel, metaphysics was not limited to logic. It was to be the third part of his system, *after* logic and the philosophy of nature. The later Hegel would call this ultimate part of his system the "philosophy of spirit." The name is unsurprising since all his "metaphysics," even his philosophy, is one of spirit. Spirit, having finally "reached itself," now takes on three distinct forms. The first is *subjective spirit*, which takes an interest in the act of thought by recapitulating several steps of the *Phenomenology of Spirit*. The second is *objective spirit*, which is found in morality, mores, family structure and the institutions of state. The third is *absolute spirit*, or spirit finally freely revealed to itself. Hegel saw this at work in three domains: art, religion, and philosophy. As art, it embodies the sensible representation of the idea; as religion, it embodies a frequently transcendent representation of the idea; only as philosophy can it think the idea as the concept knowing itself. Spirit is called absolute in this last form because it is neither dependent on the sensible nor on any other representation and can grasp itself in the infinity of the concept. Philosophy of spirit, now fully conscious of itself, is the culmination of the system. Thus the young Hegel in Jena was not mistaken when he had conceived metaphysics as the third part of his triadic system (logic-nature-metaphysics). Although it was preserved in his later works, the reduction of metaphysics to logic was perhaps not Hegel's system last word.

When one says that all peoples and all civilized consciousness have their metaphysics (*"jedes gebildete Bewußtsein hat seine Metaphysik,"* *Encyclopedia*, § 246), is one only speaking of logic? Probably not. One is also speaking of one's culture, of one's conception of one's self, of institutions, philosophy, and one's ultimate aspirations. A further point must be mentioned: Hegel's *Encyclopedia of Philosophical Sciences* closes with a quotation, in Greek, taken from book XII of Aristotle's *Metaphysics*: spirit is a pure activity that thinks itself (*Metaphysics*, XII, 7). Hegel's solidarity with Aristotle is such that he does not even explain or comment the quotation that closes his system. This solidarity confirms that far from simply reducing metaphysics to logic, it is in Hegelian philosophy that metaphysical thought was fully achieved.

Post-Hegelian Metaphysics: A Primitive State or an Artistic Affair

We began the chapter by asking whether German Idealist thought was akin to metaphysics. The answer given by the German Idealists themselves is one of a calculated ambivalence. Certainly none of these authors presented their doctrine as metaphysics, which had become rather obsolete since Kant ("dogmatism," "metaphysics of the understanding," and so on), but keen observers will not fail to notice that their new systems (the *Wissenschaftslehre*, the system of identity, or the philosophy of spirit) perhaps appear to be the fulfillment of classical metaphysics.

The answer given by post-Idealist philosophy was much less ambiguous: Idealism was a return to the very metaphysics Kant had warned against. Post-Idealist thought thus proudly defined itself as anti-metaphysical, which really meant *anti-Hegelian*. The first wave of opponents came from the so-called Young, or Left, Hegelians, such as Feuerbach and Marx. They contested the idealist pretension of conceptually circumscribing reality, which they thought ignored concrete existence and social realities that must be "transformed" rather than simply understood. Despite Hegel's repeated denials, the idea, the concept, and the spirit were, according to the Young Hegelians, empty metaphysical abstractions unable to account for the realities of life. We may also include in the *anti-Idealist* reaction authors as diverse as Schopenhauer, even the later Schelling, Kierkegaard, and Nietzsche, all of whom were philosophical *outsiders*.[147] Their critiques of idealist metaphysics were also critiques of philosophy, which they had abandoned to its own ends since Hegel had brought it to its logical and systematic completion.

There was another, albeit more academic, reaction to the Hegelian completion of metaphysics that drew its inspiration from the growth of the exact sciences in the nineteenth century. As we all know, the nineteenth century was the century of science whose faith in progress replaced metaphysics. The triumph of science was confirmed by the Industrial Revolution and its uncontested feats of engineering. Science embodied the new "metaphysics" of the Industrial Revolution. This situation was difficult for philosophy since the terms "science" and "philosophy" had long been interchangeable, even in the nineteenth century (their synonymy was quite obvious to the Idealists). But now, with metaphysics banished from the scientific world, philosophy, which, from Plato to Hegel, had always understood itself with the aid of metaphysics, was in a state of crisis.

According to nineteenth century academic philosophy, Kant had firmly shown that metaphysics could not be a science (despite the titles of his books...). As German Idealism had been nothing more than a reiteration of classical metaphysics, philosophy's only available course was to embark on a "return to Kant," as Otto Liebmann famously stated in his 1865 work, *Kant and the Epigones*. This "return to Kant," which was eventually known as neo-Kantianism, is best represented by Hermann Cohen's work *The Kantian Theory of Experience* (1872). According to him, Kant criticized metaphysics in order to replace it with a reflection on the conditions of the possibility of experience, which was essentially that of the mathematical and physical sciences. Thus outclassed by science, philosophy could only survive as an epistemological inquiry into the *principles* of scientific knowledge. Only in such a role could metaphysics, as philosophy, continue to exist.

But by then the term was only of historical value, "metaphysics" described a bygone era in the history of philosophy. Most notably, Auguste Comte (1798–1857) distinguished three different stages in human history in his classes on positive philosophy given during Hegel's lifetime between 1826 and 1830.[148] The first stage was the "theological" stage (marked by supernatural explanations), followed by the "metaphysical" stage (which replaced supernatural explanations with abstractions), and finally the positive stage (in which science discovers the laws of observable phenomena). For Comte, metaphysics was at least worthy of not being described as purely theological (or "fetishist" in Comte's vocabulary), as well as "preparing" the way with its abstractions for the positive stage. Nevertheless, it belonged to a long-gone age and had no place in what Comte called the new "positivist catechism."

Wilhelm Dilthey, in the *Introduction to the Human Sciences* (1883), also saw metaphysics in a historical light.[149] Kant had defined the conditions for the objectivity of the mathematical and physical sciences, which had interested Hermann Cohen, but the human sciences had yet to receive their epistemological justification. What claims do these sciences have to objectivity? Without an epistemological foundation, they cannot escape being called subjective in contrast to the exact sciences of nature whose methodology had been justified by Kant. Dilthey's project of legitimizing the status of the human sciences took the Kantian form of a "Critique of Historical Reason." In German, the human sciences are called sciences of the spirit (*Geisteswissenschaften*). Obviously, spirit is not to be understood in the Idealist or metaphysical sense of the term; they are sciences of the spirit insofar as they pertain to spirit's manifestation in cultural, intellectual and artistic productions through which it seeks to understand itself. The sciences of the spirit are not metaphysical sciences, but "hermeneutic" disciplines because they attempt to understand the meaning inscribed in these objectivizations of spirit. His terminology (spirit, objectivization, exteriorization, etc.) is similar to Hegel's. Dilthey, who knew his Hegel, was aware of this, but he was also aware that all metaphysical ambitions were questionable in the age of science. The first part of the *Introduction to the Human Sciences*—the only one published—was devoted to a patient critique of metaphysical thought. There was only one reason for this: although knowledge must give up metaphysics, the sciences of the spirit perpetuate metaphysics's legacy as historical sciences of the spirit. The great naiveté of metaphysics was to have ignored the essential historicity of all intellectual productions. Whereas for Hegel, history confirmed the omnipotence of spirit and reason, for Dilthey, history becomes the impossibility of a *metaphysics* of the spirit.

This was a major turn of events. Whereas metaphysics had always been criticized for attempting to transcend experience, a new critique now appeared. Metaphysics is illusory because it seeks to transcend history. The great opposition is now metaphysics and historicism. Dilthey remained a Hegelian by recognizing that spirit can know itself only though history, but discarded the ideal of a completely transparent reality in the concept. However, as heirs to metaphysics, does this not call into question the human sciences' pretension of being objective? The question was one that Dilthey was unable to answer.

Although metaphysics was no longer considered a science in the positivist sense of the term, the "metaphysical need" remained. The desire for "understanding" of which Dilthey spoke carried on the legacy of Kant's *natural metaphysics*. But Dilthey's answers were only historical and therefore relative. Whereas Kant had sought the possibility of metaphysics *as science*, the nineteenth century's answers to the metaphysical need were largely developed outside of the scientific establishment, in art. Kant's *Critique of Pure Reason* and his destruction of metaphysics had also profoundly marked Arthur

Schopenhauer (1788–1860). Schopenhauer also spoke of a "metaphysical need," but one that can only survive on illusions,[150] hence his famous "pessimism." The philosopher must learn the art of living with the tragedy of existence by producing wisdom, as he did in his *Aphorisms on the Wisdom of Life*.[151] But his wisdom was not meant to lead to happiness: It was aimed at avoiding misfortune in a world of suffering.

Educated by the works of Schopenhauer and Wagner, the young Nietzsche exalted the virtues of a resolutely "tragic" vision of existence that he wished to discover in the oldest Greek thought. Completely oblivious to metaphysics, morality, and their hinterlands, the great tragic age (*das tragische Zeitalter*) of the Greeks lived comfortably with the tragic destiny of human nature. Nietzsche constantly rebuked later Greek and Christian morality for having imposed metaphysical ideals on human existence that turn it away from its condition. His philosophy sought to celebrate the love of destiny (*amor fati*) and hoped to free humans from moral and metaphysical fantasies. Nietzsche believed the greatest principles of existence could only be justified esthetically and sought to replace these fantasies with an artistic vision. The later Nietzsche saw quite clearly how art was suffused with a metaphysical dignity.[152] In an attempt at auto-criticism (1886) later appended to his *Birth of Tragedy* (1872), a work he said was "full of juvenile melancholy," Nietzsche himself spoke melancholically of his youthful work's "artists' metaphysics" (*Artistenmetaphysik*). Indeed, his new metaphysics showed how his idealization of the tragic age was really a tragic reaction to the collapse of metaphysics. Although the "free spirit," the *freie Geist* (!), which he made his own, seeks to liberate itself from metaphysical seduction, it will never do so completely. Nietzsche's first collection of aphorisms, *Human, All Too Human*, painfully acknowledges this fact in a passage that echoes what Kant had said of his "beloved" (*Geliebte*) metaphysics, which he was compelled to leave but to whom he always returned:

> How strong the metaphysical need is, and how hard nature makes it to bid
> it a final farewell, can be seen from the fact that even when the free spirit
> has divested himself of everything metaphysical the highest effects of art
> can easily set the metaphysical strings, which have so long been silent or
> indeed snapped apart, vibrating in sympathy. . . . If he becomes aware of
> being in this condition he feels a profound stab in the heart and sighs for
> the man who will lead him back to his lost love, whether she be called
> religion or metaphysics. It is in such moments that his intellectual probity
> is put to rest.[153]

The culmination of metaphysics in German Idealism thus provoked two resolutely anti-metaphysical reactions. On the one hand, the Young Hegelians
and the anti-idealists who condemned the abstract metaphysical concepts in
the name of concrete existence and esthetics; and on the other, neo-Kantianism
present in institutional philosophy that replaced metaphysics with epistemology. This anti-metaphysical movement lived on into the twentieth century in
two important philosophical schools of thought. First, Husserl's phenomenology whose "return to the things themselves" and his "Life-world" (*Lebenswelt*)
both connote strong anti-metaphysical leanings; and second, analytic philosophy that readily denounces metaphysical discourse as an abusive use of language to which its genuine philosophy is its therapy.

The latter is the conception of philosophy argued by Ludwig Wittgenstein
(1889–1951) in his *Tractatus Logico-Philosophicus* (1922). For him, the only reasonable
discourse is one that expresses what happens in the world in a propositional manner and thereby accounts for all that is. The *Tractatus's first* proposition claims,
"the world is all that happens" (*die Welt ist alles, was der Fall ist*, literally meaning
"what is the case"). The statement has an ambiguity to it in German that may be
purposeful. It states that *there is nothing more* than the observable world (an ontological statement on "what is": the world and no more). It also defines the Being
of the world as *all that happens in it* (statement that seeks to express the essence
of the world or of what is: the fact that things "happen"). In both cases, the statements are strongly metaphysical since they attempt to express the fundamental Being of things. Nonetheless, logical positivism, which drew inspiration from
Wittgenstein, hailed his work as a devastating critique, despite being unoriginal,
of all forms of metaphysics.[154] All discourse is "meaningless" or "metaphysical"
if it deals with something that cannot be observed in the world. The question
that may be asked of Wittgenstein is that of the status of his own discourse. Is
his discourse on meaning meaningful and why? Wittgenstein seems to have
acknowledged this difficulty by saying his statements were like a ladder that we
must throw away once we have climbed up it (*Tractatus* 6.54).

His avowal simply confirms that one may only overcome "metaphysics"—
itself a metaphysical gesture—in the name of another metaphysics. But the
metaphysics of logical positivism ("there is nothing more than this world and
what can be verified in it") is not the only one contained in the *Tractatus. There
are* also "things that cannot be put into words" but really exist (in the world).
Wittgenstein calls this inexpressible the "mystical,"[155] and says that it makes
itself "manifest" (6.522). But as soon he opens this door, Wittgenstein closes it
on the "seventh day" of the *Tractatus:* "what we cannot speak about we must
pass over in silence."

Heidegger will be the first to give new life to metaphysical thought. Metaphysics was the principal subject of his thought: it was its theme, its muse, its interlocutor and his staunchest opponent. But it was first of all his native land. Since he was destined for priesthood, he was first schooled in the strictest, most anti-modernist and anti-Kantian form of Thomist metaphysics. In his autobiographical texts, he admits being impressed by ontological treatises written by Carl Braig, his professor of dogmatics, and by Brentano's dissertation *On the Several Senses of Being in Aristotle*, which the Bishop of Freiburg, Konradin Gröber, had given him. His habilitation thesis (1916), supervised by the illustrious Heinrich Rickert, dealt with one of the most eminent medieval metaphysicians, Duns Scotus—although the text Heidegger studied has since been attributed to Thomas of Erfurt. During this period, Heidegger probably hoped to receive the chair in Catholic philosophy at the University of Freiburg. But in 1916, Edmund Husserl, the godfather of the phenomenological and anti-metaphysical thought, and a proponent of a return to the "Life-world" arrived in Freiburg. Husserl introduced him to new horizons, which at first seem completely compatible with his scholastic education. The cornerstone of phenomenology, the theory of intentionality, borrowed from Brentano comes straight from the Middle Ages. Heidegger, who then became Husserl's student and assistant, adopted phenomenology, but one of religious experience and of factical life. Unlike Husserl, however, who had first studied mathematics, Heidegger drew inspiration from rather unconventional authors such as Augustine, Luther, Dilthey, and Kierkegaard. He also read Aristotle, his great teacher, as the thinker of human existence's facticity, which medieval scholastics had completely obscured.[156] The hierarchical and ordered world of metaphysics had, according to Heidegger, hidden human finitude from itself. And, asks Heidegger, was scholastic metaphysics and its modern avatars (such as neo-Kantianism in its search for epistemological safety…) anything more than the veiling of human nature's worrisome facticity?

The two parts of the anti-Hegelian reaction thus marked Heidegger. Both phenomenology's need for concrete illustrations (as well as Kierkegaard's insistence on the decisions faced by existence), and neo-Kantianism's epistemological orientation influenced his discussion of the question of Being from the standpoint of human understanding. But Heidegger also sought to answer the great challenges that were historicism (Dilthey) and modern nihilism (Nietzsche). Is meaning possible in the age of relativism? The question was quite urgent for a thinker whose first concerns were religious.[157] Heidegger's answer consisted of a reviving of the question of Being, which was the foundation of metaphysics and remained presupposed by modernity. Did not modern nihilism depend on a particular intelligence of Being, which had been solidified by the metaphysical tradition?

Although his most important question came from metaphysics, namely, the question of Being, Heidegger hesitated to call his own work metaphysics. In truth, he only did so in 1928 to 1930 most notably in his lecture *What is Metaphysics?* and in his classes from the period, that is after the publication his masterpiece *Being and Time* (1927) in which he had used the term ontology rather than metaphysics. But insofar as his work sought to recall the priority of the question of Being for both science and existence, his ambition was undoubtedly metaphysical. However, starting in 1935, Heidegger began to give in to the temptation of distancing himself from metaphysics in the name of "another thought" that was to be nonmetaphysical. "Overcoming metaphysics" then became his philosophy's guide and greatly influenced his intellectual heirs. Let us now turn to his metaphysical and anti-metaphysical philosophy and examine its coherence.

CHAPTER 10

HEIDEGGER

The Resurrection of the Question of Being in the Name of Overcoming Metaphysics

The Project of a Destruction of the History of Ontology

Contemporary reflections on the revival, current importance and, paradoxically, the end of metaphysics owe much, if not everything, to the thought of Martin Heidegger. Heidegger is responsible for promoting the cause of metaphysics in the twentieth century because his essential project, begun in *Sein und Zeit* and carried on in the rest of his massive *oeuvre*, worked to revive the fundamental question of metaphysics: the question of Being. "This question had today been forgotten," proclaims the first line of *Being and Time*. But in order to revive the question, Heidegger says one must first perform a destruction of the history of ontology, or, as he will later claim, the destruction of the history of metaphysics, which increasingly emerged as the major obstacle to reviving the question of Being. For Heidegger metaphysics, or the attempted explanation of beings as a whole, obscures what is inexplicable, disconcerting and indeterminate in Being. We thereby also obscure our own radically temporal and uncontrollably brief experience of Being. We can only experience Being through the prism of time, or "in the transcendental horizon of time," as Heidegger says ironically since time weakens all "transcendental" pretensions, hence the title of his masterpiece, *Being and Time*. The symbiotic interrelation of Being and time had already been recognized by metaphysics which had *also* grasped Being through time.[1] But it did so, says Heidegger, in a very particular temporal perspective: constancy and permanence. Parmenides' permanent Being, Plato's *eidos*, Aristotle's substance, the medieval God, and the "human subject"—modernity's founding principle—all confirm this forgotten attitude toward time. Where does the privileged position given to permanence and timelessness come from? Why was Being systematically understood through a negation of time? Could the "meta-physical" deletion of time stem from the negation of the time that we are? Could the meta-physical expunging of time stem unnoticed from our own flight from the finitude of our being "there"? Indeed, for Heidegger our own Being is best summarized by his most important term *Dasein* ("being-there"), which in everyday German simply means existence (*existentia*). His use of this term was meant to draw attention to the temporal irruption, the "there" that I am, know and occupy. The term *Dasein* also underlines the fact I am there where there is *Being*. I inhabit a clearing where Being uncovers this "wonders of wonders," as Heidegger put it in *What is Metaphysics?*, namely, that there is something rather than nothing. He sees this as humanity's specific difference: Humans are open to Being, to the fact there are beings or things that are. *Dasein* is the place of what Heidegger calls the "ontological difference" between beings (*Seiende, l'étant*) and Being (*Sein, l'être*). Beyond beings that draw my attention and are available to me, "there is" Being and my own Being, both completely unavailable. For Heidegger, metaphysics, in its search for explanation determined by the principle of reason, remains on the level of beings, which can be grasped and understood only through the *eidos* or some other dominating perspective. It can never think of Being as the abyssal ground of all that is. Metaphysics had thus closed itself off from the mystery of Being, of the "there is." Hence the paradox: We may only think Being through a destruction of metaphysics.

Heidegger first presented his ambitious project in *Being and Time* as a destruction of the history of ontology. According to him, the idea of a destruction must not be understood in an exclusively negative sense. The German word for a negative destruction is *Zerstörung* or annihilation. Heidegger prefers the term *Destruktion*, which has a Latin origin and whose foremost meaning is certainly "destructive" but also cautiously implies the uncovering of metaphysics' "structures," which have remained important to this day. For Heidegger, destruction is positive and aimed at "today":[2] Our present must become aware of the metaphysical decisions that are its underpinnings in order to learn how to better ask the question of Being.

Although the project of a destruction of the history of ontology is a positive task, it is also meant to draw attention to the consequential decisions that have punctuated the history of metaphysics and fatally *concealed* the question of Being. What are these decisions? The most important one has to do with the relation of Being to time. The metaphysical tradition *also* understood Being from the perspective of time, but it did so unintentionally—that is, it was unaware that time guided its understanding of Being. Therefore, one of the most important tasks for this destruction is to show how the metaphysical tradition has been unknowingly determined by its understanding of Being as permanent presence (*Sein und Zeit*, 26).

The subtle term "destruction"—one must destroy the better to revive—thus conceals Heidegger's titanic ambition. Not only must it bring to light the connecting thread that has silently oriented the history of metaphysics, but Heidegger's book is also the first to think the relation of Being and time for itself on its native soil: *Dasein*. Only then can this link be grasped in an "authentic" or original way—that is, not through a derived, temporally infinite and reassuring idea, but rather from *Dasein*'s worrisome and radical finitude. Metaphysics, which understands true Being through the idea of permanence, thus rests on the flight from *Dasein*'s inexorable temporality. For Heidegger, only a resolute, lucid, or authentic *Dasein* can come to terms with its insurmountable mortality, which he calls its Being-towards-death.

"Being and Time" is therefore the subterranean theme of ontology, the essential relation that has sustained the history of metaphysics and even the history of humanity, a theme that Heidegger was the first to make perceptible.[3] The paradox is perhaps surprising to any friend of metaphysics, but it is nevertheless rigorous: it is impossible to resurrect the question of Being without "destroying" the history of ontology or metaphysics, the very tradition that has attempted to ask this question for two millennia.

The Twofold Priority of the Question of Being

Sein und Zeit's first sentence begins on the idea that Being has been forgotten—an idea that runs through the whole book—and closes by evoking metaphysics: "The question of Being has today been forgotten [even if] in our time we deem it progressive to give our approval to 'metaphysics' again [*wieder zu bejahen*]." Note that metaphysics is set off by quotation marks. Although Heidegger does not name any names, he is alluding to the rekindled interest in metaphysics found in the works of authors such as Georg Simmel and Nicolai Hartmann (who had just published his *Grundzüge einer Metaphysik der Erkenntnis*), and among

the neo-Kantians in the first decades of the twentieth century.[4] Their renewed
interest was a reaction to the generalized disfavor that had befallen metaphysics since Kant's *Critique of Pure Reason*. As we have already seen, the thinkers of
German Idealism had been quite reticent to call their philosophy metaphysics.
But for neo-Kantianism, Idealism had been a return to the worst kind of metaphysics. It was therefore in Kant's name, and in opposition to the post-Kantian
Idealists, that neo-Kantianism reaffirmed Kant's verdict that metaphysics
was obsolete. In so doing, neo-Kantianism believed it followed Kant's line by
arguing that philosophy could be nothing more than epistemology or a theory of knowledge. And yet, for several reasons the neo-Kantian reading started
to loose its luster in the wake of the First World War. On the one hand, second-
degree reflections on scientific methodology left the question of the orientation of human existence untouched. The ambient expressionism and the end of
the war—which had been abrupt for the Germans—amplified a prevalent feeling of disorientation.[5] A new philosophy of existence was sought in the works
of authors such as Kierkegaard, and later in those of Nietzsche and Jaspers.[6]
On the other hand, Kantian specialists had rediscovered how Kant had criticized traditional metaphysics in the name of another new metaphysics. He was
therefore not the unconditional adversary of all metaphysics, but the one who
had sought to brighten its future by opening it onto new rigorous horizons. As
for Hartmann, he sought to distance himself from the neo-Kantian epistemological idealism that argued all objects of knowledge were in fact constructions
of the mind. He sought to rehabilitate a certain understanding of the in-itself,
but within a theory of knowledge. For all these reasons, in this period the term
"metaphysics" had once again become respectable.

Nonetheless, the quotation marks setting off his reference to this new metaphysics illustrate the distance Heidegger wished to keep between himself and
this newly fashionable thinking.[7] He held that this popular metaphysics only
sought answers to questions arising from an obvious but vaguely-formulated
need for direction, which it aggravated by reinstating old solutions or expired
ideas (he was also thinking of the renewed interest in metaphysics within
Thomism, which had become the absolute reference for the Catholic Church
in the nineteenth century and later solidified in the wake of the crisis of mod-
ernism at the beginning of the twentieth century). Heidegger revived the
question of Being in 1927 because he sought a new and more radical point
of departure without laying claim to the term "metaphysics," preferring the
more neutral term "ontology."

The priority of the question of Being must be justified however, which he
does in the introduction to *Being and Time* entitled "The Necessity, Structure,

and Priority of the Question of Being." The title was provocative because the question of Being had been discredited since Kant. The *Critique of Pure Reason* had resolved that "pompous" ontology had to give way to the more modest project of an analytic of the determinations of our understanding. But, insists Heidegger, if ontology must indeed give way to an analytic, the new priority is now an analytic of our "*Dasein*" and our exposure to Being. Accordingly, *Being and Time* starts with an "analytic" of our being-there in order to better ask the question of Being.

For Heidegger, the priority of the question of Being is twofold: an ontological priority and an ontic priority. The *ontological priority* means that the question of Being claims priority in the order of knowledge (as was the case for Avicenna, Thomas, and Duns Scotus). Every science—every relation to beings—presupposes a certain comprehension of the Being (*Seinverständnis*) it studies: The Being studied by physics is not the one studied by chemistry or theology. According to Heidegger, philosophy is responsible for the ontological determinations belonging to a given type of knowledge's domain of objects. Although he inflects it is an ontological way, Heidegger's analysis here takes an epistemological turn that seemed obvious in this period, marked as it was by neo-Kantianism. Neo-Kantianism took science as a given and reconstructed its subjective and logical conditions of possibility. Heidegger defends the ontological priority of the question of Being in a similar way. Every science, he explains, pertains to a certain domain of beings. It employs fundamental concepts, which are themselves neither beings nor ontic, most often drawn from prescientific experience. They are rather the Being of such and such domain of beings, says Heidegger. The founding concepts of mathematics, of physics, or of the human sciences are thus derived from an ontological reflection. But these sciences, which are merely ontic, cannot themselves elucidate their own ontological concepts that circumscribe their domain of objects. Philosophy makes these clarifications and thereby becomes the "productive logic" of the positive sciences. *Sein und Zeit* thus ascribes an ambitious ontological and scientific primacy to philosophy since it must elaborate the specific ontologies on which rest the sciences of beings. Husserl spoke here of "regional" ontologies.

But the idea of regional ontologies that belong to each science does not exhaust the ontological ambition of philosophy. Every ontological explanation, such as the one philosophy must produce for the sciences, implies that the sense of Being has already been elucidated. The clarification of the sense of Being is therefore the primary task, which Heidegger calls "fundamental ontology." The *fundamental* sense of Being, presupposed by all regional sciences, must therefore be clarified if philosophy is to be devoted to Being. Heidegger's ontological project can thus be sketched out in a way that preserves something of the Scholastic hierarchy:

Ontic Sciences	Task: exploration of a domain of beings.
Ontologies	Task: elucidation of the fundamental concepts that circumscribe the way of being of these beings.
Fundamental Ontology	Task: clarification of the sense of Being as the "aprioristic condition of these ontologies."

But one must begin with *Dasein*'s understanding of Being in order to elucidate the fundamental sense of Being and clarify it conceptually (*Sein und Zeit*, 6). *Dasein* is not indifferent to the question of Being. Not only does it always have a vague understanding of Being, *Dasein* is also specifically distinguished by "the fact that, in its very Being, Being is an issue for it" (*Sein und Zeit*, 12). Heidegger calls this priority of Being for *Dasein* the *ontic priority*. The term means that the question (of the sense) of Being is not only a priority in the hierarchy of knowledge, it is also a priority for a specific *being* named *Dasein* that is ontically distinguished "by the fact that, in its very Being, Being is an issue for it" following the expression Heidegger had already used in his classes.[8] This priority is obviously informed by the care all individuals have for themselves, a care that will eventually come to summarize *Dasein* in §41. But care not only characterizes *Dasein* itself. Its careful concern is also responsible for *Dasein*'s flight from the question of its Being because the dizzying question that *Dasein* is for itself strikes deep into its most intimate parts so that it takes great care to rid itself of it, or better yet, to avoid it altogether. Therefore *Dasein* usually exists at a distance from itself. Heidegger speaks sometimes of a *Wegsein*, a being-elsewhere, a being far from oneself, in short, of *Dasein* slipping away, or that is not all "there."[9] *Dasein*'s forgetting of its own self is unquestionably a flight away from its temporality or its mortality. A flight into the inauthentic, believes Heidegger, since it thereby closes itself off from the condition of all *Dasein* from which all its projects are determined.

One can however ask what this primacy of the question of Being for *Dasein* has to do with the more general question of Being in classical metaphysics? Can one really identify the general question of Being with *Dasein*'s care for itself? Is it really the same question? Does Heidegger not merge Aristotle with Kierkegaard? What is the link he seeks in *Being and Time* between *Dasein*'s care and the more general question of the sense of Being, or, between the ontological primacy of Being (for science) and the ontic primacy (for each *Dasein*)?

In fact, the two are intimately linked. *Dasein* embodies the location of the understanding of Being, and is Heidegger's point of departure in *Being and Time*. *Dasein* is haunted by the care it has for its own Being because it knows it is racing towards its death, it is a *Sein-zum-Tode*. Before the *cogito sum*, it is the *sum moribundus* that embodies *Dasein*'s most fundamental certitude, says Heidegger at the end of a course of the summer semester 1925.[10] Therefore I am not a *res cogitans* that can be erected as *fundamentum inconcussum*, but rather a Being-towards-death. Obviously, this Being-towards-death is most often lived as flight, in an inauthentic manner whereby *Dasein* closes itself off from its genuine Being. But to speak of inauthenticity is also to imply that authenticity is at least possible.

Heidegger associates this lucid attitude towards death with a resolve or determination (*Ent-schlossenheit*). In Heidegger's German, *Entschlossenheit* literally designates the suppression (*ent-*) of the closing off of oneself from oneself (*Ver-schlossenheit*). A resolute and decided being confronted with its mortal condition can open itself to its Being-possible or to the possibilities of being that are stifled by its inauthenticity or its being-elsewhere (*Wegsein*). Heidegger is thus not far from Nietzsche's free spirit who is reconciled with its own destiny

Since all of *Dasein*'s understanding of Being is ruled by the cares taken to dissimulate its inevitable death, Heidegger can pass from the question of *Dasein*'s mortal Being to the question of Being in general. Heidegger sees the most eloquent illustration of this in *Dasein*'s tendency to understand Being in an a-temporal manner—that is, as permanent presence (as had been the case for all metaphysics). For *Dasein*, through which all understanding of Being must pass, true Being is therefore the always calmly present and enduring Being. Heidegger ceaselessly emphasized how this understanding of Being as permanent presence has lasted, from Parmenides to Hegel, throughout the history of Western metaphysics. But from what, asks Heidegger, does the importance of permanence stem if not from *Dasein*'s attempts to suppress its own temporality? The understanding of Being through time thus has its source in *Dasein* itself. And it is therefore *Dasein*'s relation to its Being (and to its temporality) that dictates its understanding of Being in general.

Heidegger's intention is to show how understanding Being as *permanent presence* stems from *Dasein*'s inauthentic relation to its temporality and its Being—that is, from the suppression of its most intimate temporality. Is another relation between *Dasein* and its Being possible? Must its irrefutable temporal presence as Being be ignored?

Thus there is a close link between the ontic priority of the question of Being for *Dasein* and the question of Being in metaphysics. *Being and Time*'s main thesis is that the history of ontology has silently understood Being as a permanent presence derived from *Dasein*'s inauthentic relation to its own temporality. Forgetting Being therefore belongs to both *Dasein* and to philosophy.

1. As *Dasein* flees its most intimate, most destabilizing, but most pressing question, it forgets about Being. *Sein und Zeit* thus seeks to remind *Dasein* of its most essential question, that of its Being.

2. This reminder is also aimed at awakening philosophy to itself since the question of Being is one it has willingly forgotten. This admission is especially important for modern philosophy, which since Descartes and Kant has turned away from Being and devoted itself to the knowing-subject. The modern obsession with epistemological certitude conceals *Dasein*'s fundamental uncertainty. But as Heidegger increasingly shows, this also applies to all metaphysics. Not only has the relation between Being and time never been thought on its own terms, but metaphysics has always favored beings (*Seiende*) over Being (*Sein*). This amounts to saying that metaphysics forgot the ontological difference between beings, which can be explained logically or theologically, and the event that is Being, which does not have a reason behind it. The emphasis on (present) beings and their essence erases the mystery of Being and its donation in time. Heidegger opposes this human and philosophical forgetting of the question of Being (or of its primacy), by lucidly and frankly restating the question of Being. All of Heidegger's thought—his metaphysics, perhaps—consists in reminding *Dasein*, and philosophy, of the elementary experience of Being that scares all certitude away.

Metaphysics: The Experience of Our Being Par Excellence (1929)

Shortly after publishing *Sein und Zeit*, Heidegger started to lay claim to the term "metaphysics," which he had previously associated with a philosophical trend. He did so in his classes and in the title of two important essays from 1929: *What is Metaphysics?* and *Kant and the Problem of Metaphysics*. Whereas he had previously preferred to speak of an analytic or an ontology of *Dasein*, he now began to speak of his project as the "metaphysics of *Dasein*."

In itself, the use of the term does not mark a radical shift in his work. To speak of metaphysics instead of ontology is a rather small change when the essential matter remains the question of Being. But Heidegger takes up the term "metaphysics" in 1929 because he associates it, quite rightly, with *Dasein* and philosophy's effort to "overcome" metaphysics. *Dasein* understands Being because it "moves beyond" the level of beings and is accordingly open to Being, its own and that of all things. This is the most basic sense Heidegger gives to transcendence and the thought of Being. Obviously, this transcendence must be understood ontologically rather than theologically.

While *Sein und Zeit* had already posited that Being was the "transcendent" pure and simple (*Sein und Zeit*, 38), with the 1929 essay "On the Essence of Ground"[11] he began to claim that transcendence had perhaps always been at the heart of the metaphysical élan. Even before then—in a class from the summer of 1927—Heidegger had argued that Plato may well have begun the "move beyond" beings with his *epekeina tes ousias*.[12] In this period Heidegger had no problem expressing his solidarity with Plato and the rest of metaphysical thought whose interrogations always extended beyond beings (*das Hinausfragen über das Seiende*). But Heidegger understood this as meaning that all metaphysics was called upon to think Being as what transcends beings. In the wake of the *epekeina tes ousias*, all good metaphysics had acknowledged the original primacy of ontological questions over any ontic knowledge. This intellectual solidarity then led Heidegger in 1928 to 1930, to present his own thought as the radicalization of metaphysics.

We may speak of Heidegger *radicalizing* metaphysics because he judged that traditional metaphysics had been inconsistent in thinking transcendence. Although metaphysics tried to move beyond the level of beings, Heidegger would later say, it always did so by better understanding "beingness," the *Seiendheit*—that is, what makes particular beings what they are. Heidegger thus increasingly saw Metaphysics as a thesis on what defines and constitutes beings (their "beingness"). The inquiry into beingness—which was not the path Heidegger took—can follow two possible courses.[13] Metaphysics can either inquire into the essential characteristics of beings as such (by identifying their essential categories: their *essentialia*, quiddity, definitions, and so on), or it can inquire into the *principle* of beings, their cause or reasons. This had already been sketched out in the *Phaedo*, where Plato had adumbrated metaphysics twofold aim:[14] What are beings, and what is their principle? With his usual genius, Plato had given a single answer to both questions. The idea is both the most real Being and the principle of all that is. But by "explaining" beings with the idea or some principle, metaphysics always remained on the level of beings without ever discovering Being itself. Since it never gets to the level of Being, the transcendence of beings is therefore not really transcendence, thought Heidegger. Quite obviously, Heidegger was seeking another type of transcendence: not one that rises from beings to their "principle," but one that awakens to Being itself.

Overcoming beings thus increasingly became overcoming metaphysics itself by better thinking its unthinkable, Being and bringing its essential movement, transcendence, into play. The 1929 essay *On the Essence of Ground* presents his program clearly and uses an expression that adumbrates how his radicalization will eventually lead to overcoming metaphysics itself. "A more radical and more universal conception of the essence of transcendence, however, necessarily entails a more originary elaboration [*ursprünglichere Ausarbeitung*] of the idea of ontology and thus of metaphysics."[15]

The whole logic behind the Heideggerian overcoming of metaphysics is contained in the idea of a "more originary elaboration of the idea of metaphysics." But is a *more originary* elaboration of metaphysics still metaphysics? In 1929, Heidegger seemed to think so since he forcefully lays claim to the term "metaphysics" in the name of a *more radical* conception of transcendence. And yet, this radicalization leads to the unthought ground of metaphysics,[16] the forgetting of Being. Strictly speaking, the thought that discovers the ground of metaphysics can no longer call itself metaphysics, as it is more of a "meta-metaphysics."

Nonetheless, Heidegger did use the intensely metaphysical concept of transcendence to develop his first concept of metaphysics. Heidegger's intention in 1929 was to grasp transcendence by its roots by speaking of *Dasein*, the transcendent, or excentric, being *par excellence*. This led him, in *Kant and the Problem of Metaphysics*,[17] to speak of the "metaphysics of *Dasein*." Understood according to its double genitive sense, it means metaphysics belongs to *Dasein* itself (subjective genitive) who unceasingly accomplishes it, and philosophy, understood as metaphysics, must thematize *Dasein* itself (objective genitive) in order to draw out its metaphysical structure. As *Dasein* is the preeminent metaphysical Being, the metaphysics of *Dasein* is the equivalent of a "metaphysics of metaphysics," to use Kant's expression that Heidegger liked to quote.[18] But again, is the metaphysics of metaphysics still metaphysics?[19] Is it not more appropriate to speak of meta-metaphysics?

Nevertheless, when he presented his ontology or metaphysics of *Dasein*, Heidegger had good reasons to think he was the first to have put a finger on the forgotten origin of metaphysics (the "transcendence of beings" that is the *Dasein*). This may explain the metaphysical euphoria of the period between 1928 and 1930. He soon renounced using the term "metaphysics," however, because he gradually became convinced that metaphysics was everything but the thought of Being. In its eagerness to explain beings, metaphysics had stopped paying attention to the mystery of Being.

The most important text for understanding the destiny of metaphysics in Heidegger's thought is the famous inaugural lecture *What is Metaphysics?* given on July 24, 1929 at University of Freiburg, a few months after the lecture "On The Essence of Ground," and the book on Kant. Once again—but for the last time—Heidegger lays claim to the title metaphysics by developing a metaphysical question (the first section is called "The Unfolding of a Metaphysical Inquiry"). But the very nature of his question reveals how he is beginning *to call metaphysics itself into question.* His inquiry into the nature of metaphysics led him increasingly to distance himself from metaphysics because he began to see clearly that it was a way of thinking aimed at objectifying and dominating beings and their principles, thereby avoiding the mystery of Being.

Nonetheless, his lecture conference's "metaphysical" aim is to open a direct, even stunning, access to Being through the experience of anxiety. Unlike his discussion of anxiety in *Sein und Zeit,* Heidegger here gives it an "ontological" sense. In *Sein und Zeit,* anxiety had been associated with *Dasein*'s encounter with its authentic being-in-the-world. As it discovers the emptiness of its everyday illusions, *Dasein*'s anxiety reveals, in a flash, its Being's nothingness as it awaits decision. Now, in the 1929 lecture conference, this nothingness becomes a radical ontological experience. Heidegger takes up *Sein und Zeit*'s idea—already expressed by Kierkegaard—that it is when faced with nothingness that one becomes ridden with anxiety. But now, the expression denotes the *nothingness of beings as such,* which become completely indifferent when they are caught-up in the vortex of anxiety.[20] In anxiety, beings provide no footing (*Halt*). But this experience also unveils what differentiates "beings" from nothingness, namely, that they are. Anxiety thus reveals something important about Being: there is something rather than nothing (as in Leibniz's famous expression with which Heidegger closes the lecture conference without any further explanation: "why is there something rather than nothing?"). By relativizing all merely ontic revelations and discoveries, anxiety discloses the flowering of Being in its storm.

In 1929, anxiety's disclosure of Being presents itself explicitly under the aegis of a metaphysical inquiry. And for a good reason: anxiety also reveals the metaphysical dimension of the fundamental event of one's Being. To the question "what is metaphysics?" the 1929 lecture conference answers: "Metaphysics is the fundamental event of our Being [*das Grundgeschehen im Dasein*]. It is our Being [*Dasein*] itself."[21] The reason for this is easy to understand: *Dasein,* which I am, or that I can be (here, in 1929, the cautious tone denotes how *Dasein* is most often concealed from itself and must be reclaimed), is the preeminent *ens metaphysicum.* The terms *Dasein* and metaphysics are thus almost equivalent: "Metaphysics is our *Dasein* itself."

Metaphysics is therefore rooted in our *Dasein*'s fundamental event (*Grundgeschehen*). The term *Geschehen* (event) will soon be given a new meaning: the event—even its mistakenness or errance—that is the *historical* realty of metaphysics. Its new meaning begins to appear in the 1929 lecture conference following the passage we have just discussed:

> Metaphysics is the fundamental event of in our *Dasein.* It is our *Dasein* itself. Because the truth of metaphysics dwells in this abyssal ground it stands in closest proximity to the constantly lurking possibility of deepest error.

Although metaphysics (or its "truth") inhabits the inmost depths of our *Dasein,* it is still in danger of radical errance. In a way, this possibility of missing out on the truth of metaphysics is a form of *Wegsein,* the fall from grace discussed in *Sein und Zeit.* Even though it may be married to Being, metaphysics can also overlook it and overlook it in a necessary way. Heidegger often spoke of this intimate cohabitation of truth and errancy, or greatness and decline.

Gradually, this errance comes to personify the history of Western metaphysics. But it does not entail a positivist conception of metaphysics in which it is an error from which we must liberate ourselves. Metaphysics, and the mark it has left on Western thought is not to be underestimated. For Heidegger, metaphysics embodies the "fundamental event," the *Grundgeschehen,* of the increasingly globalized Western world. It is therefore more than a discredited academic discipline belonging to a bygone era. Metaphysics is in an important way the very foundation of the present and what we are; it is the foundation of our *Dasein.*

Thus *What is Metaphysics?* argued that metaphysics was the fundamental event of our *Dasein,* of our exposure to Being. We could even borrow Kant's expression and speak of a natural metaphysics of *Dasein.* But for Heidegger, in his reflections on *Overcoming Metaphysics* from 1936 to 1946,[22] metaphysics remains fundamentally important because it has come to define our historical destiny, and our fatality (*Verhängnis*). This perspective becomes increasingly dominant in his class *Introduction to Metaphysics* from 1935 (published in 1953), which is, as Jean Wahl has noted, less an introduction to metaphysics than an attempt to escape from it.[23]

Whereas in 1929 it was the fundamental event of our *Dasein,* in 1935 metaphysics becomes the fundamental event of our planetary destiny.[24] Unfortunately it is difficult to follow the transformation of metaphysics in his work because after *What is Metaphysics?* and his numerous publications from the period between 1927 and 1929, Heidegger publishes nothing for several years. The next text to be published is his infamous 1933 *Rectoral Address* entitled "The Self-Assertion of the German University," which was more of a political text—and a sinister one at that—than a philosophical one. Between 1929 and 1933 (or 1935, the year of his class *Introduction to Metaphysics*), there is a gap in his scholarly writings. The classes that have since been published make up for the lack of published texts. But the silence of the period is itself meaningful since it also testifies to an even more radical reformulation of the question of Being,[25] which lead eventually to the 1935 class and the new beginning attempted in his *Contributions to Philosophy* of 1936 to 1938, published only recently. These writings testify to a more critical attitude toward metaphysics and the need for a new beginning in the "history of Being."

The Onto-Theo-Logical Constitution of Metaphysics

Although Heidegger's discussion of metaphysics became increasingly acute starting in the 1930s, the idea of a history of metaphysics that bore our destiny was not new to him. It was latent in the idea of the "history of ontology" that *Sein und Zeit* wished to "destroy" with its analytic of *Dasein* finally aware of its authentic temporality.

Obviously, the forgetting of Being, which opened *Sein und Zeit* had been understood as an inauthentic form of *Dasein's* temporality: by *forgetting* Being, *Dasein* closes itself off from its temporality. In order to correct its omission, Heidegger projected a philosophically and existentially frank and purposeful *reiteration* of the question of Being finally understood on the basis of time and finitude. Thus *Sein und Zeit's* promethean reaction to the forgetting of Being was also a reaction against the forgetting of temporality and the repression of finitude. Now the later Heidegger discovers that the reasons for this forgetting are perhaps deeper than he had previously thought: It is less a fact of the inauthentic *Dasein* than a historical consequence of metaphysics' destiny. The very constitution of "metaphysics" led to its forgetting of Being and its emphasis on beings that can be explained and managed. The "technical" understanding of beings coupled with a calculating conception of thought now became the cornerstone of metaphysics.

How did Heidegger develop this conception of metaphysics as the ancestor of modern technology (*Technik*)? As we have seen, during the period between 1929 and 1933 or 1935 when he gave the course *Introduction to Metaphysics*, Heidegger did not *publish* anything that we can use to understand the path leading from the metaphysical inquiry in *What is Metaphysics?* to his later resolute disaffection with metaphysics. Although we now have almost all the material from his classes given between 1929 and 1935,[26] the fact that they are lectures must not be forgotten. Most of these lectures on metaphysics are rather didactic in nature. In order to reframe better the question of Being, which remains his major leitmotiv, Heidegger frequently returned to the history and concept of metaphysics. The didactic and historical perspective of these texts is important. We should certainly not say of Heidegger what Hegel meanly said of Schelling, namely, that his philosophical education was *coram publico*. This historical perspective announces a gradual withdrawal from metaphysics and it is as though by explaining to his audience what metaphysics is and was, Heidegger discovers that it had probably never been able to ask its central question and had, in fact, done all it could to avoid doing so. Metaphysics would have been hampered by its own "structure," which led it to emphasize beings and the conditions of their possibility, thereby erasing all mention of the mystery of Being.

In the sketches Heidegger drew of the history of metaphysics, he often concentrated on the ambiguity of the object of metaphysics starting with Aristotle. The problem is a classic one: Being as Being can be either Being in its universality, or the principle of Being (or, "God"). Rather than defending an ontological (universal) or theological reading,[27] Heidegger simply takes stock of this duality, which he increasingly grasps as the "system" that corresponds to the onto-theo-logical constitution of metaphysics. According to Heidegger, the principial and the universal approaches are part of the same perspective of which the Thomist doctrine of the analogy of Being is its best expression. To think beings through their universality is also to think them in reference to a unique focal point that is their principle. And conversely, the search for a principle seeks to assure a mastery over beings reduced to an ultimate form of rationality.

Metaphysics' project is thus one of total rationality, but Heidegger increasingly asserted that this rationality is linked to an eradication of the finitude that the metaphysics of *Dasein* of 1929 had promised to reawaken.[28] But can Heidegger still lay claim to the term "metaphysics" if it is in its essence the most stubborn enemy of finitude? Heidegger had spoken of the metaphysics of *Dasein* in order to reformulate the question of Being on the basis of finitude. But had not this question been systematically and historically stifled by metaphysics? The issue comes to a head starting in the summer semester 1929 in his classes on the metaphysics of German Idealism.[29] Whereas Heidegger sees Kant as an ally insofar as Kant was the first to see the link between the understanding of Being and finitude, he stigmatizes Hegel's radical omission of finitude. Hegel's project, argues Heidegger, consists in "becoming master of finitude, of making it disappear, rather than elaborating on it."[30] His verdict on Hegel's metaphysics became Heidegger's definitive conclusion about metaphysics itself: metaphysics is no longer an inquiry into Being, but its greatest enemy.

Heidegger's course on Hegel from the winter semester 1930 to 1931 is important for understanding his new attitude toward metaphysics. In it, Heidegger summarizes Hegel's speculative position only to oppose and name it *onto-theo-logy*,[31] a name that will eventually come to characterize metaphysics as a whole. Heidegger explains the meaning of ontotheology, a expression that has since become an important philosophical concept: "By the expression 'ontotheology' we mean that the problem of the *on* [beings] is a logical matter aimed at the *teos* [the divine], which is already understood as belonging to 'logic.'"[32] All beings are governed *a priori* by the *logos*, which had become the common dominator of reality that makes its divinely ensured mastery possible. Heidegger, who sees this as just another attempt to tame beings and finitude, seeks another direction. For him, it is time rather than the *logos* or the concept that is the essential explanation of beings: "the direction of our path, which must cross Hegel's, is announced by the title 'Being and Time' that is, negatively, time—and *not the logos*."[33] Whereas Hegel's intention can be summarized by the title "ontotheology," Heidegger does not hesitate to speak of own project as *ontochrony*, where *chronos* (time) takes the place of *logos*.[34]

Here, in 1931, *ontochrony*, or the reduction of Being to time, directly opposes (Hegel's and increasingly all metaphysics') *ontotheology*, which seeks to submit Being to the theological and reassuring logical supremacy of the *logos*. One seeks to reinforce logic, the other to unsettle it (*erschüttern*).[35] For Heidegger, "the concept is not 'the master of time' [an expression taken from Hegel's *Encyclopedia*], rather time is the master of the concept," or the preeminent anti-concept since it is the absolute master.[36] The encounter between Hegel and Heidegger can be reduced to their understanding of Being. Whereas Hegel thinks Being as a function of infinity, for Heidegger "Being is finitude"[37] (*Sein is Endlichkeit*). The radicalization of finitude leads Heidegger's project to a history of Being that seeks to unsettle the principle of reason and overcome metaphysics.

As his thought moves from *Sein und Zeit* to the history of Being, Heidegger conserves one idea that allows us to better follow its shift, namely, that Being has always been understood as permanent presence. In *Being and Time*, Heidegger spoke of *Vorhandenheit*, or the subsisting being-present of beings by which they can be seen and grasped theoretically. And, in order to illustrate how *Dasein* is always interested in everyday beings that are part of its preoccupations, his ontology of *Dasein* had opposed beings as *Vorhandenheit* with beings as *Zuhandenheit*, or beings that are readily available as implements. Heidegger's intention was to show how the objectification of beings (the *Vorhandenheit*) is a conception of Being derived from the other (the *Zuhandenheit*), which, as readily available implements, implied *Dasein*'s immediate and preoccupied relation to Being.

Heidegger's secret objective in all this was to show how this presence of subsisting beings is derived from an inauthentic mode of *Dasein*'s temporality. In fact, in *Sein und Zeit*, the importance given to presence appeared as *Dasein*'s flight from its mortal and finite future, which only authentic *Dasein* can truly foresee. Starting in *Sein und Zeit*, Heidegger's explanation for why the concept of permanent presence was a "derived" one was meant as a judgment on the ontology of "substance" (*Substanzontologie*), or of *Vorhandenheit*, that had dominated the history of ontology. *Sein und Zeit* had intended to "destroy" this understanding of beings as permanent substance since it blocked the way for the question of Being, which can only be understood through time (but from which both *Vorhandenheit* and subsisting presence were silently derived).

Now, although all metaphysics—and not only Hegel's ontotheology—is governed by an understanding of beings as presence, or as *Vorhandenheit*, the forgetting of Being is no longer seen as accidental or only imputable to the inauthentic *Dasein*. It is essential to metaphysics. Unlike what had been announced in the first paragraphs of *Sein und Zeit*, a simple return to Plato and Aristotle cannot renew the question of Being. We must now learn to dispense with metaphysics in the name of "another" unnamed way of thinking that must take on the history of Being, which has determined the destiny of the West.

Obviously, the matter of the history of Being had preoccupied Heidegger for a long time, but now its philosophical radicalization led him not only to abandon the term "metaphysics," but also to oppose the entire history of metaphysics marked by its understanding of Being as permanent presence and as a subsisting given that may be dominated. Unlike the case in *Sein und Zeit*, the conception of Being as presence is now not only a product of inauthentic *Dasein* seeking the assurance of permanence, it is also "*the* power (*die Macht*) that today still sustains and dominates *all our* relations to beings as a whole."[38] Being as permanence can no longer be explained by *Dasein*'s decline, it is now the consequence of the historical destiny of the history of Being.

The Technological and Nihilist Completion of Metaphysics

Plato plays an important role in this history. Although Heidegger is obviously not the first to argue that Plato was the father of metaphysics, he does so in a new and dramatic way.[39] According to Heidegger, Plato did not launch metaphysical thought because he was the first to speak of a transcendent world, but rather by grasping it through the idea, he unwittingly interpreted Being in a "humanist" and "technological" way. This is the lesson of the famous allegory of the cave. According to Heidegger's reading of it, Plato tells us to turn away from beings such as they appear in the shadows of our caves and understand them, their purity and their logic, in light of the idea, which is only accessible to thought. Only the *eidos* can embody the reality of beings because it is stable and permanent. But to say that beings are *eidos* also favors one *viewpoint*. Indeed, the term *eidos* comes from the verb *idein* that means "to see" and "to know" (like it does in English). Thus, argues Heidegger, to consider beings in accordance with the idea means they are to be understood in relation to their "visibility" as though Being can only be defined by its capacity to be perceived. Plato, without realizing it, situated beings under the perspective of a "supervision" from which would be born metaphysics' demand for total explanation as well as modernity's most overt subjectivism and its strictly technical knowledge of beings.

As we have seen, starting with Hegel, metaphysics came to be defined by its "onto-theo-logical" constitution: It is only interested in beings (*onto*), which it unifies under a principle (*theo*) using the principle of reason (*logic*). And yet, says Heidegger, this onto-theo-logical reduction is only possible if beings are grasped through the εἶδος, which defines them through a perspective that imposes its conditions when apprehending them. Platonism, or metaphysics, thus becomes a form of "humanism." For Heidegger, the term means that since it gives a privileged position to its viewpoint on apparent beings, humanity construes itself as the ultimate reference point, or the "supervisor," of all beings. The essence of beings (the *eidos*) is thus solely derived from thought. In fact, in Plato's writings, the noetic realm, the *topos noetos*, which is the realm of true beings, is named after the thought (*nous*) that grasps it.

As Heidegger points out, Being is then only an empty shell devoid of meaning. Since we may only count on beings, Being becomes a mere reminder of what is imponderable. This metaphysical era in which Being can no longer be counted on is marked by the *nihil* of Being, or "nihilism," concludes Heidegger. Since Jacobi and Nietzsche, the expression generally signifies an absence of meaning ("God is dead") that characterizes our modern culture. But, says Heidegger, nihilism is really the ultimate consequence of the conception of Being that derives it meaning from the human point of view. Metaphysics' Platonism, by which Being is defined by its visibility, leads directly to modern "nihilism." Any meaning *superior* to humankind is impossible since metaphysics decreed that all meaning and value was a function of humans. But "value" here means what has value "for humankind." All value is value *for humans*, it is what "yields a return." The term "value," which has become popular in contemporary ethics, is in fact borrowed from nineteenth-century economic thinking.

Thus the relation to beings is only a technological or economic affair. This leads Heidegger to argue that our planetary technology is perhaps the fulfillment of the essence of metaphysics. Technology only considers beings through their utility and profitability: what is not technologically useful has no reason to be. Heidegger assures that he has nothing "against" technology, he simply notes how it regulates our relation to Being and is, in a way, our metaphysics. In the technological world, even the relation between humans and their god is a technical matter: God is but a resource used to appease certain needs by ensuring future permanence. This manufactured God is an idol: "to make gods for ourselves, is to despise gods,"[40] says Heidegger who prefers to wait for a god to arrive of his own accord like a burglar in the night.

Humanism, nihilism, and technology are for Heidegger modern terms for metaphysical thought as launched by Plato. From the moment when beings are only understood according to the idea that grounds them, when beings have become explicable by and for humans, technological domination dictates the only possible relation to beings.

But is this the only possible relation, asks Heidegger modestly? Is it not excessive to think that beings are really determined by humans? Perhaps the event of Being itself is lost in our voracious appetite for rationalization. We forget the awe-inspiring emergence of Being, which precedes the privilege given to beings. Thus technology, humanism, and nihilism confirm how metaphysics rests on the forgetting of Being.

Seeking *another* experience of Being, the later Heidegger sometimes turned to pre-Platonic and therefore pre-metaphysical authors in which he found a way of thinking that does not seek to dominate, but welcomes Being as it is given to us without any reason. He finds this way of thinking, for example, in Parmenides' simple expression "Being is," which makes a mockery of all explanations. By simply stating "Being is," Parmenides *Poem* did not impose any human determinations on it. Thus in the twilight of metaphysics, Heidegger hopes to rediscover something of the simplicity and serenity (*Gelassenheit*) of the first word on Being: "Being is" and no more. As can be seen in *A Dialogue on Language between a Japanese and an Inquirer*,[41] Heidegger also encountered this way of thinking in Eastern philosophy less marked by the hegemony of Western rationality.

The Unsettling of the Principle of Reason

In hopes of preparing *another* way of thinking that is more contemplative and attentive to the mystery of Being, the later Heidegger distanced himself from the metaphysical and technological need for explanation. He then began speaking of the idea of a *Satz vom Grund*, or a leap away from the principle of reason.

Satz vom Grund is the title of a course and of a book published in 1957, translated as *Principle of Reason* in English. In it, Heidegger deals with Leibniz's great "principle of reason" (that states, or dictates, that "nothing is without reason"), which he believes, for good reasons, summarizes the metaphysical project or Western rationality. But, asks Heidegger, was this principle itself founded? In German, to speak of *Satz* can imply that it is a *position* (a *Setzen*) or an affirmation that evades the explanation that the principle claims to require for all things: the principle is simply posited (*gesetzt*) in a phrase (*Satz*) as a decree devoid of any reason.

Heidegger begins by playing with the Latin rendering of the expression, *nihil est sine ratione*, which means, first, nothing is without reason. But it can also mean, says Heidegger, that the Nothing, or nothingness, has no reason: like Being, it "is" and has no need for any reason. Being thus not only marks the limit of the principle of reason, but it also reveals how metaphysics is buttressed by its need for rationality born to stifle the experience of Being or nothingness by pathetically affirming that "everything has a reason because reason had decided so!" Is this not a decree proclaimed by thought that encounters its limit in the experience of Being?

But *Satz* has other meanings that are also important. In music, the *Satz* is a symphonic movement: In German, one speaks of the first, second, or third *Satz*. This is important for the history of metaphysics: The *Satz vom Grund* corresponds to the first "movement" of the history of Being, the period of the *Grund*, its foundation. Therefore, prior to this moment, there could well have been another way of thinking less obsessed than ours with a search for foundations (hence his interest in the Presocratics). But more importantly, it also means that there could be, without us knowing how, a meditation less haunted by a need for complete rationalization that would follow upon metaphysics' interminable demise.[42] From this follows the last meaning of *Satz*: A *Satz* is also a leap. In German, when somebody is surprised and jumps, it is called a *Satz*. The *Satz vom Grund* is precisely this leaping back from the foundation (*weg vom Grund*). It announces a distancing and a release into a contemplative way of thinking and the "serenity" that comes from "equanimity" (*Gelassenheit*), which allows us finally to understand what the *Grund* and its rationality claim to be.[43] But this is not necessarily some sort of irrationalism, as the thought of the *Grund* would hasten to declare in a moment of hasty inquisitive agitation that confirms Heidegger's verdict on the end of metaphysical thought. Let us simply distance ourselves from this (modern and metaphysical) obsession with foundations, says Heidegger, and consider things with more restraint. Perhaps humankind does not measure up to the project of complete rationality and the mystery of the *there is*: Wow, there is something rather than nothing! What if what is unreasonable is the project of trying to completely explain beings as a whole with the consequent dependence on the human subject? The *Satz vom Grund*'s call for moderation and humility—so unsettling to the principle of reason—thus hopes to rediscover possibilities stifled by rationalism. It is a way of thinking that sees itself in Pascal's expression: "Let us then seek neither assurance nor stability."[44]

The Theological Scope of Heidegger's Overcoming of Metaphysics

If metaphysics is a form of nihilism and Heidegger hopes to prepare "another" way of thinking, then this "other" way of thinking must be a response to nihilism, and even an attempt to overcome it. But nihilism cannot be overcome by simply giving new "values" to humankind. Heidegger suggests that the greatest symptom of the forgetting of Being is perhaps the idea of values since it presupposes that what matters must depend on human evaluation. But if humans evaluate everything, on what then do they depend? What is their measure? (*was ist sein Maß?*), asks Heidegger in the wake of Hölderlin's verse: Is there a measure on earth? (*Giebt es auf Erden ein Maß?*). The question means both "where do they get their measure?" and "what holds humankind back when it gets beyond measure and reminds it that everything cannot be 'measured'?"

According to Heidegger, nihilism is the same as "the death of God" because a truly divine god cannot be grasped metaphysically. Can a god subject to our conditions truly be divine? For Heidegger, the god of metaphysics—the ultimate reason for the world—is an idol of human subjectivity that needs god only as its assurance (Descartes).

A divine god cannot show *itself* in a world where everything can be explained. So perhaps metaphysics is a form of a-theism, Heidegger concludes[45]—that is, a way of thinking that closes itself off from everything it is not as well as from the possibility of something completely different from it, such as a God yet to come. In this godless night, says Heidegger, only *another* way of thinking can sustain the possibility of an encounter between mortals and the divine.

Thus the idea that metaphysics forgot the question of Being does not refer to a theme unfortunately left out of metaphysics textbooks. It is a sign of our era's distress (*Not*) cut-off as it is from anything higher than itself. The theme of the forgotten question of Being points to this missing measure (*Maß*) and order. In a world where everything ultimately depends on humankind, the divine only remains as an answer to the very human need for explanation and solace. It is but a fabricated idol devoid of any divine loftiness. To think Being, Heidegger writes in the most personal manuscripts available, is to think the distress of the gods' divinity (*die Not der Gottschaft der Götter*)[46] and therefore to think a god that is still divine. It is often said that our era is one of disillusionment or of de-divinization. Heidegger speaks instead of *Gottesverlassenheit*, or an "abandonment" of the gods. This "abandonment" not only means that we no longer require gods, but that they have also left us to our own technological idols and no longer hold back our quest for dominance. According to Heidegger, the greatest symptom of this distress lies in the fact we do not acknowledge it as such since everything in our world works and is "under control." For this reason, he speaks of a distress at the absence of distress, or a forgetting of forgetting.

Thus the idea of the forgetting of Being emerges from a religious distress, in the widest and most unresolved sense of the term. Heidegger's aim is certainly not to palliate this distress (we are in a state where "only a god can save us"), but rather to feed it by crying out in the distress-less wilderness that the human condition is condemned to dereliction and cannot be saved by some technological solution, the only kind allowed today. This can be felt in Heidegger's heartfelt cry: "Interrogate Being! And in its silence—the birthplace of the word—answers the god. Search all beings, nowhere will you find a trace of god."

The passage is so troubling that one wonders whether it was read correctly. God is absent from the realm of beings, and a god can only speak to us through Being? And language is born in this way? Far from being a *hapax legomenon*, the quoted passage is one Heidegger often repeats in his manuscripts from the late 1930s.[47] In a world where the will to master beings has chassed away the imponderable, only another way of thinking Being can preserve the place vacated by the god of metaphysics.

Heidegger's ambition in his confrontation with metaphysics is not to overturn the destiny of Western thought since "anti-metaphysical activism" (so prevalent in modern times) would in a way perpetuate our technological and controlling relation to beings. For this reason, Heidegger eventually distanced himself from the project of "overcoming metaphysics," which had been his main concern since the late 1930s.[48] Metaphysics, even as the "non-thought" of Being, was an answer, concedes Heidegger, a first reaction to Being (at least!) since thought is now completely indifferent to Being. The last Heidegger sometimes saw the history of metaphysics as an event in the history of Being, which *because of its silence* still acknowledged something of the mystery of Being. Indeed, throughout the history of metaphysics, Being always remained veiled. And yet, this veiling, whispers Heidegger mystically, is perhaps itself a nod (*Wink*) from Being? In what way? Well, perhaps the veiling translates Being's withdrawal from metaphysics, or even a refusal (*Verweigerung*) to even enter it. What if the essence of Being was precisely this withdrawal as an opposition to metaphysics' domination?[49] Before becoming a forgotten thought, the absence of Being could be Being exempting itself from metaphysics, or better, "sheltering" itself in its refusal. These ideas are certainly very speculative and surely disturb all rational thought, but for Heidegger there is no real problem in this....

A Secretly Metaphysical Philosophy?

Heidegger's debate with metaphysics can often appear convoluted. Some of his texts are certainly cryptic. Some have even spoken maliciously of Heidegger's mythomania. But his fundamental experience of Being is rather simple, even elementary: There is Being, rather than nothing, and we are, but only for a time. For Heidegger, this experience was that of the first Greek thinkers: there is Being, which emerges and submerges us. But because of metaphysical thought's need for explanation and certitude, this fundamental marvel of nature (*physis*), which ceaselessly emerges and reemerges, is not experienced in all its stupefying simplicity. Every explanation is too late in the face of the mystery of Being. The greatest achievement of Heidegger's work on metaphysics is perhaps less the elaboration of a new and necessarily fumbling way of thinking Being than the destruction of the evidences of calculating reason. Insofar as he awakes our spirit to the mystery reason can never solve, Heidegger may well have led metaphysics to its greatest accomplishment, namely, astonishment in the face of Being, which towers over everything.

In fact, Heidegger's journey may have been more metaphysical than it appears at first glance. Was it not the enormous reservoir of metaphysics that gave him all his concepts: Being and beings, transcendence and foundation, essence, *logos* and *aletheia*? Heidegger may well have understood them in a different, "non-metaphysical," way, but what would have been his language without metaphysics? The rather forced construction of a metaphysics centered on technology may have stopped Heidegger from recognizing its true value.

Is it really true that metaphysics always aimed at a domination of beings reduced to pure subsistence? Of whom is Heidegger speaking when he thus stigmatizes metaphysical thought? It is as though he amalgamates Plato's idea of the Good with Descartes *res extensa*, which the *cogito* possessively masters, and projects onto the history of Western philosophy a Hegelian reading of metaphysics as the logic of thought.

But more fundamentally, when Heidegger only sees metaphysics as a way of using beings and their "technicization," is he not himself constructing a rather "technical" concept of metaphysics? What I mean is that Heidegger seems to conjure up metaphysics as a catch-all concept (onto-theo-logy fulfilled in technology), which he summarily applies to the whole history of metaphysics. Heidegger thus does to metaphysics what he never stopped criticizing it for doing: He creates a very objectifying logical and technical concept that drowns out the real voices of the metaphysical tradition.

Heidegger's secretly metaphysical *journey* allows us to put into perspective the rather technical concept of metaphysics he creates in his later philosophy. In 1916, at the end of his habilitation thesis on Duns Scotus,[50] he spoke of metaphysics as philosophy's indispensable "optic." In the wake of *Sein and Zeit*, he even presented himself as a metaphysical thinker since his inquiry sought to go beyond beings. In 1929, he was still conscious of reinvigorating the essential impetus for metaphysical thought, which was itself founded on our Being's metaphysical event, namely, our exposure to Being and its mystery. Although Heidegger did "criticize" metaphysics, he did so perhaps because it is not metaphysical enough, or not in tune with Being and ceased to marvel at its advent.

But is metaphysics not unceasingly born and reborn out of this astonishment, of which Heidegger was not the first, nor the last to speak? Has not the best metaphysics always sprung out of this wonder? Can we really claim that all the great thinkers in the history of metaphysics—Plato, Aristotle, Augustine, Avicenna, Duns Scotus, Thomas Aquinas, Suarez, Descartes, Spinoza, Leibniz, Kant, Fichte, Schelling, and Hegel—were "ontotheologists" and technicians of beings? Does not Heidegger seem to reduce our tradition to technical elements with his reductive concept of metaphysics?[51] We know that Heidegger grasped the era of technology as an enframing (*Gestell*) of beings as a whole. But is not his concept of metaphysics as enframing also an enframing of metaphysics itself, which deafens the voices of its tradition? And finally, is a thought that determines the bounds of finitude really a way of thinking that *ignores* finitude? As Hegel argued,[52] the real immoderation is perhaps to make finitude the new absolute with no possible opening onto transcendence.

Heidegger wished to think beyond metaphysics. But were his new beginning and his "leap" to another way of thinking really the best way? Did not his *leap* and his *other* beginning unwittingly remain technical in their deafness to the tradition and their impatient desire to end metaphysics?

At the end of one of his last texts, "Time and Being" (1962), Heidegger recognized that to think Being, and its advent, one must perhaps "cease all overcoming, and leave metaphysics to itself."[53] But in saying this, he certainly did not wish to pay homage to metaphysics! No indeed. Rather, what he meant to say was that the desire to overcome metaphysics is perhaps still in keeping with it. If we are to think differently, we must not only free ourselves from metaphysics, but also from the impulse to pass beyond it, to overcome it. But then, if we are to overcome the desire for this overcoming, we are certainly not free from the thought of overcoming!

What if metaphysics were precisely this idea of overcoming? Heideggerian thought would then be powerfully metaphysical. It certainly was metaphysical since it sought to reawaken the meaning of Being, of astonishment, in its transcendence of beings. And perhaps it was metaphysical in its very desire to overcome metaphysics. Had not metaphysics, since Parmenides and Plato, dreamt of transcending opinion? After all, the overcoming of *doxa* was done in the name of *another* possible way of thinking. But this was not the only metaphysical aspect of Heidegger's thought. His need for transcendence certainly seemed to sympathize with metaphysics: By trying to preserve the divinity of the divine in the midst of the distress caused by the forgetting of Being, was his thought not itself onto-*theo*-logical?

CHAPTER II

The Rediscovery of the History of Metaphysics

We asked ourselves earlier whether metaphysics had survived Kant and his critique. As far as Heidegger is concerned, the question need not be asked: His work unmistakably contributed to reopening the question of metaphysics. Whereas Kant essentially claimed that metaphysics belonged to the past and only the critical path remained open, Heidegger stated that although metaphysics is indeed part of our past, it also continues to influence the present in an important way.[1] Even the essence of modern utilitarianism and the essence of modern technology have metaphysical roots.

Like Kant, Heidegger sought to open the way for "another" way of thinking. More importantly however, he also made a new awareness of metaphysical thought possible. Although it is sometimes overlooked, it was Heidegger who brought the *history* of metaphysics to light. Before him, and for most of modernity, metaphysics had been no more than a type of philosophy that sought to pass beyond experience and which one could easily avoid by favoring, for example, the experimental sciences—a positivist and rather convenient concept of metaphysics that can be found in the works of Carnap and Habermas.[2]

And yet Heidegger showed that favoring experience in this way actually stems from a metaphysical decision. Even the claim that the only true reality is that of the so-called [!] sense experience is metaphysical because metaphysical thought, since Plato, has always limited reality to what can be overseen and regulated. Thus there is continuity between Plato and the most militant empiricism: in both cases, thought always decides what really is. And the separation of ancient metaphysics, founded on Being, from modern thought, resting on subjectivity, thereby disappears. Heidegger was also one of the first to show how the modern term "subject" was in fact the translation of an old concept taken from Greek ontology, *hupokeimenon* (the Latin *subjectum*). But the Greek term—and the Latin one for that matter—was never used to characterize the human perspective. It simply designated a substrate subsisting by itself, which lies (*keimenon*) at the foundation of a thing's determinations (thus we speak of a grammatical "subject"). Since human thought has now become the new foundation for the determinations of what is, the human subject must be included in the history of metaphysics.

The discovery of modern subjectivity's forgotten ontological foundations reaffirms the urgency of the question of Being not only for philosophy, but also for humankind itself. Giants such as Descartes and Kant attempted to do away with the question of Being and replace it with a more fundamental perspective that supposedly contained the determinations of all that is: an analytic of the *cogito* or of the pure understanding. Heidegger showed us ontology's destitution was in fact a substitution. What replaced the old "pompous" ontology was no less than the "metaphysics of subjectivity." The founding, permanent, and therefore true Being became thought. Although Descartes avoided the term ontology, he appropriately spoke of a new metaphysics or first philosophy. But the *cogito*'s metaphysical importance rested on its ontological importance, which stemmed from the reduction of Being to thought (*ens cogitatum*). Again it was Heidegger who showed how this masterful re-determination of Being by thought was preserved in Kant and Hegel's metaphysics and eventually reached it culmination in Nietzsche's understanding of Being as "will" and "value." By reducing Being to a value for a will to power, Nietzsche simply expressed the secret essence of metaphysical Platonism. Read from Heidegger's perspective, Nietzsche appears as the most consistent metaphysical thinker! But Nietzsche also recognized that if Being is reduced to will and value, which is then ratified by the dominion of technology—the only possible way of thinking that remains, then nihilism and the death of God are the inevitable destiny of the Western world.

Now a dramatic and far-reaching historical fresco, metaphysics has gained newfound relevance. Metaphysics is no longer a musty Scholastic discipline but "the fundamental event of our history" as Heidegger put it in *What is Metaphysics?*—an event the history of metaphysics never fully realized and ceaselessly concealed.

But might Heidegger have been mistaken? Is there another possible reading of the history of metaphysics? Heidegger's provocative account gave rise to new readings of the history of metaphysics and changed philosophy's relation to its history. The history of philosophy had previously been a doxographical affair devoted to the opinions of ancient philosophers and the history of problems. By recalling how the great thinkers in the history of metaphysics had determined our destiny and who we are, Heidegger taught us to see them as our contemporaries. He saw the greats both as adversaries who had contributed to concealing Being, and also as his allies when they let us catch sight of something like a fulguration of Being. The intensity of his work unmistakably showed how the history of philosophy is more than mere philological interpretation. Although other scholars sometimes confirmed his explications, his work was most often contested as a whole or in part. Other interpretations of the history of metaphysics and of its main authors have since appeared, most often as a response to Heidegger and to demonstrate another "structure" of metaphysical thought. It is impossible to give even a glimpse of all the readings and micro-debates that have since proliferated. Nevertheless, the essential point remains: since Heidegger there has been a regained interest in the metaphysics of Plato, Plotinus, Thomas, Duns Scotus, Descartes, Kant, Hegel, Schelling, and even Nietzsche. In a way, one can say that the history of metaphysics came into existence with Heidegger even when it is read in a very anti-Heideggerian way.

The Heideggerian rehabilitation of metaphysics also fueled attempts to reinstate metaphysics like those found in Christian existentialism. Heidegger's influence can be seen in Louis Lavelle's[3] (1883–1951) metaphysics, Emmanuel Mounier's[4] (1905–1950), or Gabriel Marcel's[5] (1889–1973) Personalism, as well as Jacques Maritain[6] (1882–1973) and Etienne Gilson's (1884–1978) neo-Thomism. Much like Heidegger, this movement sought to reintroduce the themes of Being and existence (terms that often meant the same thing) to philosophy, but by revitalizing the onto-theo-logical horizon of so-called classical metaphysics in an anti-modern and anti-Kantian way. Obviously, these authors were not Heideggerians (Heidegger was considered the "atheist" thinker, as is testified by his influence on Jean-Paul Sartre's work)—Gabriel Marcel even deliciously satirized Heidegger's jargon in one of his plays.[7] These reactive—and today rather forgotten—attempts at restoring metaphysics owed much to Heidegger's work. The resurgent[8] interest in metaphysics certainly began before Heidegger, the first lines of *Sein und Zeit* alluded to this, but the way Heidegger replaced epistemology and the theories of knowledge with ontology created an atmosphere in which Being and metaphysics were once again respectable themes and the voices of tradition could once again be heard.

However, as Jean-Paul Sartre's international success would show, it was less metaphysics as a discipline, which had remained rather shopworn and old-hat since Kant, than *ontology* that experienced regained interest. After a long eclipse, ontology not only became a stylish term, but also another name for philosophy. The long amnesia of Being seemed to be over. But it was a particular kind of ontology that reappeared, an ontology of "existence" and freedom.

The Rediscovery of the Metaphysics of Existence: From Gilson to Sartre

The father of the modern concept of existence is not Heidegger, but Søren Kierkegaard (1813–1855). Although unconcerned with metaphysics proper, his writings had such an important influence on Existentialism that Étienne Gilson devoted a whole chapter to him in his history of the question of Being.[9] In a way, Gilson was himself part of the rediscovery of existence that gave its name to the famous twentieth-century philosophical school: Existentialism. Even for an experienced historian such as Gilson, the term *existence* had a special, even magical, sound to it.

The term is striking, and eminently important. As we have seen, the word itself first means a projection, a spouting: *Exsistere* or *existare* means "to stand outside of" or "to spring out of." Thus Livy's expression: *si existat hodie ab inferis Lucurgus* ("if Lykurgus should rise from hell today"—with all the surprise this might entail). In Scholastic thought, the term meant that what "exists" comes from some source, a cause or *ex causis*, and can therefore be explained rationally. For Kierkegaard the case is a bit different, perhaps because of Schelling's influence: Existing does not designate an observable reality as much as an event, an active upheaval or outgrowth, which resists being grasped rationally. The term expresses the sudden appearance of humankind itself exposed to its Being—and therefore to its nothingness—and who is thereby confronted with a decision about its Being: "the Self is a relation which relates itself to its own self," writes Kierkegaard at the beginning of *Sickness unto Death.*[10]

Suspended above nothingness, existence is not a clearly defined reality, but a perpetual relation to self; in a word, anxiety awaiting resolution. As a Protestant preacher, Kierkegaard sought to remind individuals that their existential and religious choices decide the fate of their Being. His existential call was accompanied by a critique of conceptual philosophy, especially Hegel's, who was the Dane's sworn enemy. According to Kierkegaard, Hegel, by reducing reality to a universal and reassuring order, had sidestepped the fundamental human reality, its concrete existence and the individual—and in a way irrational—decisions it must make. Although Kierkegaard meant it as a systematic repudiation of philosophy itself, his critique had an important influence on twentieth-century philosophy.

It was not by chance that his influence was felt *after* the First World War. In Germany especially, the Great War had been experienced as the catastrophe of Western rationality. It seemed as though the civilization born out of the Enlightenment and its faith in reason had led to this butchery. In 1918, Oswald Spengler spoke famously of a *Decline of the West* underscoring the profound and widespread disillusionment with Western rational ideals.

In such a climate, the modern term "existence," which many forgot had been borrowed from medieval metaphysics, came to express the dereliction of human existence, abandoned to itself and confronted with its empty destiny. Not only was Existentialism born in these circumstances, but they are also important for Gilson's reading of the history of metaphysics. The two main points of Kierkegaard's concept of existence—the simple reminder of Being's irreducible facticity and the critique of the philosophy of the concept[11]—are also present in Gilson's conception of metaphysics. Influenced by Thomas Aquinas, who, he believed, was the only philosopher to have thought the unmotivated event of Being (or existence), Gilson accused all of Western metaphysics of only thinking the concept or essence—that is, only what can be grasped by thought. Hence the title of his remarkable work *l'Être et l'essence* published in 1948. Having always thought Being as essence, or as an "object," metaphysics "neutralized" what Gilson calls the "act of existing." The expression is certainly closer to Thomas than Kierkegaard, but it also meant for Gilson a pure "present in becoming" that marks the limit of conceptual metaphysics tied to object and essence. The emphasis put on essence, which Gilson associated with authors such as Aristotle and Suarez, led to forgetting existence and Being. As it has often been said, Gilson's critique is quite similar to Heidegger's,[12] with the notable difference that Gilson sees Thomas as the great exception in the forgetting of existence. Obviously Gilson's act of existing or *actus essendi* is not Heidegger's *Dasein*, but in both cases the importance given to existence is coupled with a critique of conceptual thinking that had fatally dominated the history of metaphysics.

Less interested in the history of metaphysics, but nevertheless a supporter of the existentialist critique of conceptual thought, Jean-Paul Sartre (1905–1980) was especially interested in human existence's state of dereliction, abandoned as it is to the absurdity of its condition. Since it was associated with the chimerical idea of supersensible transcendence, the term "metaphysics" is not part of Sartre's lexicon. However, as Dominique Janicaud has recalled, one of Sartre's first published texts, *La légende de la vérité*, appeared in an issue of the avant-garde journal *Bifur* in 1931 that also contained the first French translation of Heidegger's *What is Metaphysics?*[13] Sartre never spoke of this, but one cannot help thinking that he would only have had to read a couple pages from Heidegger's text—probably the first Sartre would have read—to realize how metaphysics is linked with the question of nothingness and the way it exists in humans as anxiety.

These themes reappear in his masterpiece, *Being and Nothingness* a title that betrays Heidegger omnipresence (the title of Sartre's opus, *L'Être et le Néant*, resembles the title given to the first French translation of *Being and Time, L'Être et le Temps*). But Heidegger, whose book had yet to be translated, appears therein as the philosopher of existence and historicity. Heidegger was Sartre's point of departure inasmuch he was seen as the "atheist" philosopher who had noted the decline of classical metaphysics[14] and placed human freedom, along with its heroic quest for authenticity, at the forefront of his work. Sartre did not take up the later Heidegger's discussion of metaphysics, which was less well known at the time, and concentrated instead on "human reality" in all its anxiety, now philosophy's primary given. Sartre, more than Heidegger or Jaspers, became the great exponent of Existentialism, which would eventually go beyond the bounds of academic philosophy and, following the end of the Second World War, influence Western culture as a whole. It became so dominant that it provoked a powerful counter-reaction starting in the 1960s when a proudly "anti-humanist" philosophy took the place of Sartre's humanist Existentialism on the French philosophical scene. In reaction to Sartre's philosophy, which believed that human freedom was a given,[15] Michel Foucault, who was influenced by the later Heidegger,[16] proposed in his book *The Order of Things* (1966) that humans were in fact a rather recent invention and one destined to disappear....

Historians of metaphysics, usually Thomists or Heideggerians, most often judge Sartre's contribution to metaphysics condescendingly. Sartre was certainly allergic to all forms of theological transcendence and gave different meanings to the terms "Being" and "nothingness," which Heidegger had already discussed. Whereas in *What is Metaphysics?*, nothingness denoted the nothingness of Being itself, for Sartre it meant the nothingness introduced into the world by the noisy eruption of individual humans refusing all determination. And "Being," in the title *Being and Nothingness*, was used to designate inert Being, which humans are not. Nevertheless, unlike many of imitators, Sartre read Heidegger in a productive manner. His aversion to metaphysics, the other side of his humanism, was a major influence on his time, as well as on a whole part of the history of metaphysics, the explication of the fundamental concepts of what is.

Sartre's work pertains much more to ontology than metaphysics however. The subtitle of *Being and Nothingness* announces an "essay on phenomenological ontology." As with ontology, the term "phenomenology," generally associated to the school of thought founded by Edmund Husserl and carried on by Heidegger, was then in vogue. It also had an anti-metaphysical side to it insofar as "phenomenology," according to Sartre, first means that one can only speak of phenomena such as they show themselves to our consciousness. Understood in this way, phenomenology also refers to Kant's phenomenalism and modern thought in general since both claim that consciousness only experiences phenomena and not the things-in-themselves. Sartre acknowledges this in the first line of his work: "modern thought realized considerable progress by reducing the existent to the series of appearances which manifest it." However, Sartre refuses the *idealism* of modern thought because for him Being cannot be completely *reduced* to something consciousness has constructed. He sees proof of this in a phenomenon that had greatly interested Husserl, namely, *intentionality*. Husserl used the term to recall that consciousness is always consciousness *of something* and is always oriented in a certain way. Consciousness is not a "psychic state" or an object of analysis: It is a project that strives for something.

According to Sartre, this definition of consciousness as intentionality can be understood in either of two ways. "Either we understand by this that consciousness is constitutive of the Being of its object [as in the idealist tradition], or it means that consciousness in its innermost nature is a relation to a transcendent Being."[17] Sartre declares himself in favor of the second, more realist reading of intentionality. He sees it as an "ontological proof" of the existence of Being in itself. The fact consciousness is always consciousness *of* something means consciousness always pertains "to a Being which it is not itself."[17]

For Sartre, this striving for "Being" is more dramatic than in Husserl and has a different meaning than in Heidegger. The title of the first section of

Being and Nothingness is "The Pursuit of Being." At first glance, one might think that Sartre's aim is, like Heidegger's, to resuscitate the "question of Being" so important for metaphysics. Such is not the case. Rather, the title means that consciousness seeks a "Being," which it will neither attain nor be. Consciousness is not a Being, but "nothingness," the negation of all Being.

Sartre calls this Being, which consciousness is not and cannot be unless it is in "bad faith," *Being-in-itself.* He encountered this term, which also belonged to medieval ontology, in his readings of Hegel influenced by Alexandre Kojève's lectures. It designates the Being that consciousness is not. Consciousness is, at best, "Being-*for-itself.*" Although Sartre is more interested in the "for-itself," the first hundred pages of *Being and Nothingness* are devoted to *Being-in-itself,* which transcends consciousness.

So what is Being-in-itself? As Sartre acknowledges, the question is difficult since Being-in-itself is defined by the fact that it does not have a self—that is, it is not conscious of its Being.[18] In fact, as Sartre says using a tautology similar to the one proclaimed by Parmenides, all that can be said of Being "in-itself" is that it is, it is in itself, and it is what it is:[19] Being "massive," "opaque," "full," even "filled with itself."[20] As "full positivity," this solid Being has no negation, no other, no consciousness, no distance, no depth, nor any freedom.

Sartre will even go so far as to say it eludes time itself:

> It is itself indefinitely and it exhausts itself in being. . . . It is, and when it gives way, one can not even say that it no longer is. Or, at least, a consciousness can be conscious of it no longer being, precisely because consciousness is temporal. But Being-in-itself does not exist as a lack there where it was; the full positivity of being is re-formed on its giving way. It was and at present other beings are: that is all.[21]

Sartre's atemporal Being-in-itself is the direct descendent of Descartes's *res extensa*, the Being of everything that is not consciousness.

But Sartre also follows Kant and Heidegger's lead: Time is no more than one of consciousness' intimate determinations. As an existent aware of its temporality, a human individual is a being "for-itself," and is therefore conscious of its Being's essential nothingness. But it is not really Being because it is characterized by the fact that it is nothing, the nothingness of being. Or, to use Sartre's classic expression: Consciousness "is what it is not and is not what it is."[22] It is "what it is not" because it is first defined by its future and its projects. It can always become other than what it is or what it appears to be. In a way, only as past can it be considered an in-itself since it cannot be changed. But its future remains blank and everything is permitted.[23] Consciousness is neither what it is, nor what it presently, or objectively, appears to be because it is not limited by its present determinations, which are contingent and can always be revoked. To say, for example, that a for-itself is a "lawyer," a "waiter," or a "communist" is to reduce it to an in-itself and disregard its freedom.

Although the for-itself can be characterized in opposition to the in-itself, it is more importantly a systematic capacity to negate, to always say "no": I am not such and such. It is through the for-itself, says Sartre famously, that nothingness enters the world.[24] Otherwise, the world would be pure positivity—that is, an array of essences completely subject to the principle of reason. The in-itself is only governed by freedom and its lack of definition is its definition. It is completely free of any determination and any essence that would reduce it to an in-itself. "Man is, indeed, a project which possesses a subjective life, instead of being a kind of moss, or a fungus or a cauliflower. Before that projection of the self nothing exists; not even in the heaven of intelligence: *Man will be what he purposes to be.*"[25]

Fungus, moss, and cauliflower, these are Sartre's models for the in-itself.... He seeks thereby to underline the fundamental difference that characterizes the "reign of freedom," to speak like Kant, instituted by the eruption of consciousness, pure nothingness in the "reign of Being." But this is not only the nothingness of freedom, it is also the nothingness of death that becomes conscious in humans: "consciousness is a being, the nature of which is to be conscious of the nothingness of its Being."[26] Hence, the anxiety of the for-itself that knows itself destined to nothingness and left adrift. When I am not anxious, I am stifling my anxiety that I am viscerally. I flee anxiety because I am anxiety.[27]

I flee what I "am" because I am in bad faith, says Sartre. When I seek tranquility or calmness, I am in fact seeking what I am not. This bad faith also leads me to hide from myself and from others. But bad faith is part of human finitude: Its opposite—sincerity or authenticity—is not really possible since it remains a project for the for-itself, which *can never coincide with its Being,* or with what it is. As Sartre clearly recognized, with respect to what I am, sincerity is a form of bad faith: "What then is sincerity except precisely a phenomenon of bad faith?"[28] Indeed, sincerity aspires to the coincidence of self with self, and hopes to turn myself into a thing, a "Being-in-itself," which I am not and cannot be.

Although freedom raises me above the in-itself and forever separates me from it, it is nevertheless a heavy burden, a burden that drives the human desire, constant and futile, to try to lighten the load, stop caring about its

Being and become a Being-in-itself. The for-itself suffers in a way from the "nostalgia" of Being, of Being-in-itself, which is unconscious of itself and its nothingness, and rests quietly unconcerned as an essence. It is a tragic nostalgia as absurd as existence itself. "Condemned to be free," humans are a "useless passion"[29]: "in life, a man commits himself, draws his own portrait and there is nothing but that portrait."[30]

Thus Sartre's "metaphysics" is quite different from Heidegger's. It does not await salvation, certainly not from "Being-in-itself," which has nothing to contribute. Free as we are, humans are not subjected to the dark history of metaphysics. The opposite is true, since this history is now over, humans can take stock of their freedom. One may therefore speak of Sartre's "metaphysics of freedom," but unlike Kant or Descartes, it rests on the inexistence of God: Since God does not exist, the only possible metaphysics or transcendence is that of freedom.

The Rediscovery of the Metaphysics of Language: From Gadamer to Derrida

Heidegger disliked Sartre's expression "we are precisely on a level where there is only human beings" because he saw it as a new expression of the "metaphysics of subjectivity." His sentiment was similar to the theologians who denounced the "drama of atheistic humanism," according to the expression of Father de Lubac. Heidegger preferred to say: "we are precisely in a situation where principally there is Being."[31] But he did say "we" are on this level, which could not be without us. Humankind thus remains the seat of the experience of Being, but unlike Sartre and perhaps in an attempt to distinguish himself from him, the later Heidegger removed humans from the center of Being. As a response to metaphysics' project of understanding Being centered on the human perspective and its values, Heidegger began to think Being as an event (*Ereignis*) that refuses (*Verweigerung*) all capture. Although the "refusal" of Being was not Sartre's "nothingness," it was nevertheless thought in relation to humans, since it sought to restrain the human desire for control. Heidegger always sought to prepare a new shelter *for humankind*. He was therefore not completely anti-humanist.[32]

Therefore, accusing Sartre of having "misread" Heidegger is perhaps a bit strong. After all, *Sein und Zeit* dealt only with Being insofar as it pertained to *Dasein*'s projects. But it is true that Sartre insisted less on the fact that it was a project *of Being*, than on the fact it was simply a project, and humankind, thrown into existence, was a being that could chose for itself.[33]

Keeping with the later Heidegger, we may now ask ourselves whether consciousness is really the master of its projects of understanding. Am I not "thrown" into projects of understanding before becoming their author? Hans-Georg Gadamer (1900–2002) emphasized the importance of "thrownness" in his masterpiece *Truth and Method* (1960). Although less well-known than Sartre, Gadamer had a profound impact on post-Heideggerian philosophy and opened ontological horizons unknown to the Existentialists. These new possibilities belong to a philosophy Gadamer called *hermeneutics.* Hermeneutics once designated the art of textual interpretation, the *ars interpretandi.* In *Being and Time,* Heidegger had taken up the term, which he had first encountered when studying biblical exegesis, and applied it to *Dasein* itself: prior to any textual interpretation, humans already interpret their world, interpret themselves and always already live within certain interpretations inherited from tradition. To put it briefly and to summarize hermeneutics and its pretension to universality: There is no Being without hermeneutics. Ontology is therefore necessarily hermeneutical.

The idea was not foreign to Sartre. Although he did not use the term "hermeneutics," Sartre was well aware that all understanding was part of a project. But for Sartre, this meant consciousness was forever able to define its own projects. Gadamer's hermeneutics draws a completely *different* conclusion from Heidegger's analysis: I am not the one that projects onto the world as much as I am projected into horizons of meaning that precede me. Whereas Sartre emphasized negation and the distance separating me from my historical constitution, Gadamer recalls how the facticity of human understanding can be grasped more appropriately by the fact that we belong, although perhaps unwittingly, to history:

> In fact history does not belong to us, we belong to history ... The focus of subjectivity is a distorting mirror. The self-awareness of the individual is only a flickering light in the closed circuit of historical life. That is why the prejudices of the individual, far more than its judgments, constitute the historical reality of its Being.[34]

Although the debate with Sartre was never crucial for Gadamer, Sartre's perspective is nevertheless present in an almost inverted form. Gadamer seems to replace the primacy of consciousness and projects with history's effective action on me (*Wirkungsgeschichte*). And consciousness (*Bewußtsein*), he says in an expression strangely similar to Marx, is "more Being than consciousness"[35]—that is, more opaque than transparent to itself. What it "is" depends less on its consciousness than on its historical determination. It is easy to see how some have associated him with what Paul Ricoeur called the "hermeneutics of suspicion" found in the works of Marx, Freud, Nietzsche and Structuralism, which also believed that consciousness was a "distorting mirror." However, Gadamer's hermeneutics, unlike the "hermeneutics of suspicion, does not claim to better understand and master consciousness' underlying mechanism by reducing it to a series of incorporated drives or forces and socioeconomic factors. It is precisely their scientism and its reductive aim that Gadamer sought to disavow when he recalls that understanding is produced by history's effective action and an encounter of traditions.

Gadamer liked to say that understanding is an *event*. His masterpiece was supposed to be called "understanding and event." The title means that understanding is less of a subjective operation than an event that takes hold of us and surprises us, like a work of art that grabs hold of us and carries us along. When we are "caught up" with a play, a piece of music, or a philosophy book, we neither control what is happening to us nor control ourselves, and we can only understand what is happening if we follow along. Understanding is an event rather than a moment of mastery. Therefore, says Gadamer, "understanding is not to be thought of so much as an action of one's subjectivity, but as the placing within an event of tradition, in which past and present are constantly fused." "This is what must be expressed in hermeneutical theory, which is far to dominated by the idea of a process, a method."[36] We are always too late, says Gadamer at the end of *Truth and Method*, when we try to explain what happens to us when we understand. And yet, it is nevertheless a truth experience.

In a time when all truth must supposedly rest on science, Gadamer's intention was to philosophically justify the hermeneutical experience of truth. Hence the title *Truth and Method*, understood to mean there is truth outside of and prior to method. Thus Gadamer's thought was unlike the hermeneutics of suspicion that sought to make consciousness transparent and deliver it from illusion. Gadamer saw the hermeneutics of suspicion's desire for transparency and emancipation from tradition as a symptom of the modern will toward domination that Heidegger's destruction of metaphysics had unmasked. But Gadamer did not endorse a form of historicism. He held that historicism (according to which "all truth is historical") or "relativism" also belongs to a technological way of thinking insofar as it seeks to explain truth by some relation to a historical constellation. Once again, this would be a reductive aim that would omit the truth of understanding. Gadamer's example is the work of art, which *transcends* its historical determination. Although it certainly does not escape history, the essential fact of a work of art is that it cannot be reduced to its history. Can we *understand* one of Plato's dialogues or one of Sophocles's plays by simply "situating" it within a historical context? Although it may take as its starting point the effective action that history has on us, understanding exceeds it by leading us to a higher level of knowledge. Hermeneutical truth allows us, up to a point, to transcend our finitude from which it springs.

Can we speak of metaphysics in the context of Gadamer's thought? As with most post-Heideggerians, Gadamer preferred to speak of *ontology*. Indeed, *Truth and Method* closes with a *universal ontology* grounded in language. For Gadamer, understanding is always imbued with language. In order to limit consciousness' pretensions to supremacy, Gadamer argued that understanding is less a subjective act than the "encounter of traditions." Now, as the last section of *Truth and Method* teaches us, this encounter has been grounded in language for time "out of mind"—that is, literally for time immemorial because consciousness is completely unaware of this foundation, which Western thought has stubbornly refused to acknowledge. Whereas for Heidegger, the forgetting of Being characterizes Western philosophy, for Gadamer it is rather *forgetting language*, or forgetting that language is thought's condition of possibility and its locus. Tradition always neglected language by subordinating it to thought as though thought in some way preexisted language. But, asks Gadamer, are thought and understanding even possible without language?

Hence his fundamental thesis: Language determines (the German says *bestimmt*: "gives a voice to") both the *process* (*Vollzug*) and the *object* (*Gegenstand*) of understanding. It determines the process inasmuch as all understanding strives to express itself with language and seeks the words to a given meaning. Classical philosophy would have spoken here of "conceptualization." But can any concept be produced without language? The *object* of understanding depends on language since what is understood can only be seen in the light of language. Obviously, one understands the world and other people, but this understanding can only be carried out within the imperceptible and immemorial element that is language.

But it is difficult, even impossible, to maintain the distinction between the *process* and the *object* of understanding. After all, can I really separate the object of my understanding from its wording? One may thus speak of a *fusion of understanding with what it understands* since the object can only be distinguished from its understanding by another act of understanding. The fusion between understanding and its object is founded by a more original foundation, namely, that of Being and the word. Being, or a thing, cannot be separated from language, from which it draws its voice and presence, and even its possible separation would require another language. Everything that can be understood is already on its way to language.

Gadamer's universal ontology can be summarized in the following simple, yet difficult, apothegm: "Being that can be understood is language."[37] It not only underlines that our *access* to Being is only possible through language (others had already said it before Gadamer), but also how Being is only given in language. Because of the original fusion of Being and word, it is impossible to distinguish Being from its presence in language. To refute Gadamer's linguistic ontology, a Being or an experience unrelated to linguistic intelligibility would have to be demonstrated.

Thus Being that I perceive or experience, even "silently," remains centered on language insofar as it is always experienced as such and such. Being is always already meaningful. Language even orients what cannot be said, or what supposedly transcends all discourse. To say (!) I do not have the necessary words to express something implicitly acknowledges that my words are unable to expresses what *must be said*. To use the most extreme example possible, to say no language will ever be able to express the suffering caused by the Holocaust, also says words are unable to express what I wish I could cry-out. Although I can only speak of the limits of language in the name of some other, perhaps impossible, language, I am still saying something, namely, the enormity of this tragic event is such that current discourse remains unfortunately unable to voice what must be said. The suffering I wish to express is obviously more than linguistic, but its understanding is necessarily tied to language. Gadamer's ontology thus draws out the universality of human understanding's linguistic locus.

Although Gadamer preferred to speak of ontology, he did state that as hermeneutics becomes aware of the universality of language it also leads us back to the questions of classical metaphysics (*führt uns in die Problemdimension der klassischen Metaphysik zurück*).[38] What he is vaguely alluding to is the medieval doctrine of transcendentals. Even though the reference may be unexpected, it admirably recognizes that metaphysics was once (unless it has always been) a science of the transcendentals or of the universal predicates of Being. What Gadamer finds fascinating in this doctrine is how the universal predicates are always *those of Being* and not those of knowledge or the subject. When one dealt with the Beautiful, the Good or the One, the concepts employed never pertained to thought, but rather to *Being itself*. This is important for Gadamer's universal ontology since he never conceives language as a subjective discourse, or as a thought *about* something. Language expresses first

and foremost the presence of Being in the mind in light of language's precedence over thought. The medieval doctrine preserved the original fusion and
unity of thought and Being which modern thought had disrupted by asserting
the opposition of subject and object that positioned thought in such a way that
it came to objectivize and dominate Being. Do we really master and possess
Being, and ourselves, with our concepts? Is it not rather Being that has always
shown itself through the forgotten light of language?

> This involves us, as was to be expected, in a number of questions with
> which philosophy has long been familiar. In metaphysics the concept of
> belonging refers to the transcendental relationship between Being and
> truth, which *conceives knowledge as an element of Being itself and not primarily
> as an attitude of the subject.* This involvement of knowledge in Being is the
> presupposition of all classical and medieval thought.[39]

Even though he does not speak of it very much, it is easy to understand
Gadamer's attraction to this metaphysics. A doctrine that recalls that thought
stems first from Being and its fusion with Being brought about through language gives greater importance to our understanding's finitude than one
developed "without language" and derived from the *cogito*'s self-proclaimed
independence from things. But is such a relation to Being even possible? No,
there must be language. Modern thought speaks a "language" that does not
acknowledge itself as such—the language of representation—imposed on
reality by the understanding. Despite its claims to the contrary, thought is not
autonomous in relation to Being, or to itself. It always presupposes the presence of reality, and its presence to itself, within the elusive horizon of language. This is also what Gadamer meant when he claimed consciousness was
"more Being than consciousness": Its Being is already shaped by language and
even more so than it thinks.

This metaphysics of our belonging to language and Being is, in its own
way, mindful of the limits of the "metaphysics of subjectivity" buttressed by
thought's project of dominating beings. Rather ironically, the inversion of
modern "transcendental" philosophy, founded on the subject's supremacy,
is carried out with the aid of medieval "transcendental" metaphysics. This
metaphysics, which was devoted to Being and knew practically nothing of the
"human subject," still believed that knowledge was not a matter of domination, but rather one of participation in Being and truth.[40]

Nevertheless, in *Truth and Method*, reflections on metaphysics are rare and
fleeting. It is as though Gadamer was wary of "rehabilitating" metaphysics

after Heidegger's destruction of it. That said, such reflections can be found at the *end* of his masterpiece and act as its conclusion, thus opening the possibility of another intelligence of metaphysics, and Being, than the one dominating Heidegger's writings.

Metaphysics appears in a much less discrete and admiring way in the work of another of Heidegger's heirs, Jacques Derrida (1930–2004). As was the case for Gadamer, Derrida's work is marked by language's underlying ubiquity. But Derrida's work is much closer to the hermeneutics of suspicion than Gadamer's, and asks whether language's precedence over thought, which it makes possible, is all that innocent. Is not a certain way of thinking, namely, metaphysics, tacitly imposed on all forms of intelligence and discourse? Although Derrida contributed to the "rediscovery of the metaphysics of language," he did so by paying close attention to the "language of metaphysics," which Heidegger had spoken of as a limit for the thought of Being in his *Letter on Humanism*.

For Derrida therefore metaphysics designates less a doctrine than a structure or a device regulating thought against which he vigilantly develops a deconstructive attitude inspired by the Heideggerian idea of destruction. It is as though he reads the same pages of *Sein und Zeit* as Gadamer but without the emphasis on *hermeneutics*, which he judges to be eminently suspicious since its aims to understand, decipher, and accordingly *appropriate* the other. Indeed, for Derrida, this aim of dominating or rendering intelligible is constitutive of metaphysical thought. His "imperialist," even bluntly political, conception of metaphysics identified with a hegemonic will founded on the repression of "difference" owes much to the later Heidegger.

For Heidegger, the essential difference was the one between Being (*Sein*) and beings (*Seiende*). As metaphysics became completely fixated on beings and transformed them into a technical resource available to the sovereign subject, it forgot how "Being" constitutes the abyssal ground of all beings. Metaphysics then appeared as an attempt to secure or seal off the abyss of the "original nothingness" discussed in *What is Metaphysics?*. By unsettling rationality and metaphysics, Heidegger had hoped to awake it to the abyss it seeks to conceal. This domination had been made possible by an intelligence of Being as permanent presence founded on the desire to occult our finite temporality and death. Although Derrida does take up the Heideggerian idea of a "repressive" metaphysics founded on the primacy of presence, he spontaneously associates it to Structuralism, which had strongly influenced his generation and claimed that the subject (which Sartre still exalted) was only the vehicle for linguistic and social structures. For Derrida however, Heidegger's perspective seemed more fundamental[41] since it revealed that presence is the metaphysical presupposition of any structure and thus its "arche-structure."

Derrida shows this using the doublet *signifier* and *signified* with which Ferdinand de Saussure had articulated his linguistics. For Derrida, it is a metaphysical distinction because the signifier, as signifier, is supposed to refer to the *presence* of the signified without it ever being given. When one tries to think the signified or the thing's "full" presence, one cannot escape from the realm of signs. The "meaning" itself is thus always differed by what Derrida calls 'différance,' which is a play on the double meaning of the French verb *différer* (to differ): The presence of the thing is supposedly "different" from the sign, but its presence is forever "differed." What Derrida deconstructs is, like Heidegger, the metaphysics of "presence" already at work in language itself from the moment all discourse gives the impression its meaning is "somewhere," or outside of discourse. What if all meaning simply stemmed from this metaphysics of presence?

Following Heidegger, Derrida argued that metaphysics emerges from forgetting difference, and more importantly from forgetting the différance that makes it possible. Although Derrida, like Gadamer, claims that this stems from forgetting language, he is much more of a structuralist than either Gadamer or Heidegger. Heidegger sought to deconstruct metaphysics and prepare the way for *another* way of thinking, less forgetful or more attentive to the truth of Being. Thus Heidegger seemingly presupposed something like the "meaning" or "truth" of Being—the equivalent of the complete and full presence of Being—which metaphysics had concealed. The early Derrida did not share this "belief" and judged it to be overly metaphysical. After all, was Heidegger not the one who had enabled the deconstruction of the fiction of presence? Derrida here claims to be more consistent than Heidegger. In passing from destruction to deconstruction, Derrida applies the razor-sharp blade of deconstruction to the question of Being and its unrealized preeminence. "And yet, are not the thought of the *meaning* or *truth* of Being, the determination of *différance* as the ontico-ontological difference, difference thought within the horizon of the question *of Being*, still intra-metaphysical effects of *différance*?"[42]

Heidegger's destruction of metaphysics was therefore not radical enough since he continued to ask the question of Being, which is different from beings, as though he sought its ultimate truth or meaning. But for Derrida, this ultimate truth, which cannot be ultimate since it fails to deliver any meaning, or any presence, is that of différance itself. This différance, as arche-structure, only designates "the movement according to which language, or any code, all system of referral in general, is constituted 'historically' as a web of differences."

"'Is constituted,' 'is produced,' 'is created,' 'movement,' 'historically,' etc., necessarily being understood beyond the metaphysical language in which they are retained, along with all their implications."[43]

Thus différance's arche-structure is "in a certain and very strange way 'older' than the ontological difference or than the truth of Being." More archaic, more subterranean, différance does not stem from the "history of Being." Derrida thereby reassesses what he calls the "Heideggerian hope," or "the quest for the proper word and unique name" of Being.[44]

Metaphysics thus depends here on subterranean structures. By subscribing to such a logical—and thereby quite modern—conception of metaphysics, Derrida follows Heidegger's lead and perhaps, in a more fundamental way, Hegel's lead as well. Hegel had indeed said metaphysics was nothing other than (*nichts anderes als*) "the entire range of the universal determinations of thought" and, so to speak, the "the diamond net into which everything is brought and thereby first made intelligible" (*Encyclopedia*, § 246). Hegel sought to radicalize the quest for intelligibility by making it transparent to itself. Derrida does something similar, but ends up deconstructing the idea of intelligibility, and reduces it to the game of différance. But is this structural intelligence of metaphysics emptied of all content and all experience,[45] not itself a highly technical way of grasping metaphysics?

Although Derrida takes all the necessary precautions to say one cannot become free of metaphysics since it would be another form of metaphysical hope, obviously Derrida's deconstruction, which tries to be more radical than Heidegger's, also wishes to be "less metaphysical." But why be less metaphysical? Well, because metaphysics rests on a fiction (the old hag "presence") and a form of repression. But the repression (of différance) stems from a structure or an arche-structure that Derrida (or Heidegger) was the first to bring to light. As with Heidegger, we may wonder whether the deconstruction of metaphysics is not unwittingly metaphysical. It is so since its method is archeological and its finality is ethical. Indeed, is not Derrida's approach, in its willingness to decode finally the arche-structure of all metaphysics, more metaphysical than metaphysics? Derrida would probably answer that in deconstructing a structure one is no longer subjected to it or at least one has learned to be wary of it. This was the case with Heidegger's attempt to think "the metaphysical event" in a *more original* way. His explanation of metaphysics was not metaphysical since it sought to look beyond its horizon by examining it in an objectivizing way. Metaphysics became its object, or its obsession, because metaphysics could only found its empire on the essential forgetting of Being and finitude.

For Derrida, the metaphysical "apparatus" must be considered with suspicion because it rests on a silent terror, that of the exclusion of otherness and difference.[46] The deconstruction of metaphysics is thus not deprived of any ethical purpose: It wishes to bring to light what the arche-structure of metaphysics conceals. But is this honorable emphasis on otherness and difference really anti-metaphysical? The author that allows us to see how it need not be the case is one that had an important impact on Derrida: Emmanuel Levinas.

The Rediscovery of the Metaphysics of Transcendence: Levinas

Metaphysics precedes Ontology.[47]

Whereas most post-Heideggerians preferred the term ontology to metaphysics, veiled in suspicion since Kant, the opposite is the case for Emmanuel Levinas (1905–1995). We saw in the Introduction that the history of metaphysics is oriented, to varying degrees, by the question of Being, ontology being the core of the metaphysical tree. It is this privileged place given to the question of Being, and ontology, which Levinas's metaphysical thought sought to call into question.

In 1951, Levinas published a short article in the *Revue de métaphysique et de morale* [*Journal of Metaphysics and Morals*—a very appropriate journal title in this case] entitled "Is Ontology Fundamental?"[48] The question implicitly singles out Heidegger and his project of a fundamental ontology as its target. Although this was the case, by taking on Heidegger's project Levinas was also seeking to upset the whole Western philosophical tradition founded on the primacy of ontology. Levinas's critique was subtle insofar as it agreed with Heidegger on many points, notably that the history of philosophy was really an ontology centered on a desire for intelligibility and domination, and that its history rested on an essential omission or repression. However, Levinas's point was to show that, despite his destruction of it, Heidegger had remained a part of the ontological tradition and had fallen victim to the same forgetting.

Levinas understood ontology, and its founding omission, in a particular way that was not necessarily foreign to Heidegger. For Levinas, to acknowledge that Western philosophy has "most often been an ontology" amounts to saying it had carried out "a reduction of the Other to the Same."[49] What Levinas meant was that behind all multiplicity and difference, philosophy, in its ontological orientation, always sought the figure of the same, an identical Being, an *eidos*, which gave it the supervisory viewpoint of an intelligence seeking to dominate its object. This sounds as if Levinas was repeating the Heideggerian critique of Platonism and it reduction of Being to the *eidos*. Yet, it is not the forgetting of Being of which Levinas speaks, but the forgetting of the Other. According to Levinas, the importance given to the Same inhabiting alterity, considered to be of negligible and upsetting significance, amounts to *neutralizing* the Other by depriving it of its voice and individuality.

> The neutralization of the Other who becomes a theme or an object—appearing, that is, taking its place in the light—is precisely this reduction to the Same. To know ontologically is to surprise in a being (*l'étant*) confronted that by which it is not this being (*l'étant*), this stranger, that by which it is somehow betrayed, surrenders, is given in the horizon in which it loses itself and appears, lays itself open to grasp, becomes concept. To know amounts to grasping Being out of nothing or reducing it to nothing, removing from it its alterity.[50]

"The work of ontology," says Levinas, "consists in apprehending the individual (which alone exists) not in its individuality, but in its generality."[51] Driven by its will to power and its "egoism"—its desire for knowledge or possession that seeks to reduce all alterity to the *ego*—ontology is transformed into first philosophy. Founded as it is on the primacy of the Same, it is necessarily impersonal and inhuman, taking no account of the Other's irreducible difference.

Ontology thus appears as "imperialist domination" and tyranny.[52] It is "opposed to justice, which involves obligations with regards to a being that refuses to give itself, the Other, who in this sense would be a being par excellence."[53] In order to combat its ontological imperialism, Levinas proposes a terminological inversion:[54] the primacy of the Same becomes that of the Other, and ontology's primacy is transferred to *ethics*, which he willingly calls *metaphysics*. For Levinas, all ontological thought is one of immanence, of the "same" present in all individuals, leveling over their differences. But *metaphysical* thought is one that discovers the transcendence of the "Other," which exceeds all my efforts to understand it.

By opposing ontology's totalitarianism, which attempts to reduce the Other to the same, the primacy given to ethics or metaphysics has its ground in the *irreducibility of the other*, or the immediate inescapable demand that emanates from it. One may object that the Other is only a general concept that personifies another figure of the Same. But this is not the case, answers Levinas. The Other is always a *face*, which can never be reduced to an idea I may have of it. "The way in which the Other presents itself, exceeding the idea of the Other in me, we here name *face*."[55] I am always faced with a face, which I cannot dominate. If I am called a subject it is in the feudal sense of the term. I am subjected to an other whose "hostage" I am. "A responsibility that obsesses, one that is an obsession, for the other besieges me, to the point where he makes me a *hostage*."[56]

The rehabilitation of ethics as first philosophy is coupled with a promotion of metaphysics, understood as thinking the radical transcendence of the Other in relation to me. It is hard to tell whether for Levinas this metaphysical transcendence belongs to another human or the divine. Nevertheless, the fusion of ethics and theology appears purposeful since in both cases it is a matter of the indefinable experience of Infinity. An infinity I cannot master and which has always already beckoned me when it commands: "Thou shall not kill." The call, which precedes the consciousness I have of myself, erupts like an "epiphany" of infinity since it never lets itself be reduced to the finite concept I have of it and exceeds any thought of finitude. Levinas liked to invoke Descartes who had founded his proof of the existence of God on the presence of the idea of infinity in me, which I could not have produced and is like a trace left in me by its transcendence.

As it exceeds the idea I have of it, the other does not let itself be integrated into any ontological totality, which always appears like a *violation* of the other's unity. Hence the title of Levinas's first major work *Totality and Infinity: An Essay on Exteriority*. Totality and infinity are for Levinas a dichotomy that corresponds to ontology and ethics, or immanence and metaphysics. Whereas Heidegger sought to revive the question of Being in the name of overcoming metaphysics, Levinas called for its opposite: One must revive metaphysics in the name of surpassing ontology.

Levinas's meditations inspired by the Hebraic tradition sought to thwart the purported "imperialism" of ontology's Hellenic tradition. It has led to a major rehabilitation of ethics in contemporary philosophy, which is a good thing. But what is less of a good thing is that it did so by employing "political" categories, and insinuations, that are not always obvious. Must the desire to *understand* somebody else necessarily be a form of totalitarianism? Perhaps not. Can we not see it instead as an attempt to do justice to the other's otherness? Nor is it certain whether metaphysics or ontology is a political matter. When Plato appealed to, against the Sophists, the evidence of a Being that can at least be intended by our thought, beyond the habits of partisanship, he revealed the universality of a thinking—that is, metaphysics, that could transcend politically motivated parties and contests.

On a more philosophical level, we may ask whether the primacy given to ethics is necessarily opposed to ontology. This is, again, far from obvious, and for two reasons. First, Levinas's ethics itself shares the philosophical pretension to universality by its use of terminology and dichotomies belonging to Western ontology. Thus Levinas thereby seeks to develop as metaphysics an ontology of the Other. Does the other not want to be understood in its own Being? If I am to answer the call of the other, am I not to distinguish its face from the one embodying the violence I must resist? Perhaps this totalitarianism stems less from ontology than from particularism that also has a face. Furthermore, Levinas obviously does not renounce the metaphysical, or theological, culmination of philosophy, which he reasserts more forcefully than Heidegger, Sartre, Gadamer, or Derrida. But what he did understand better than any other was that ethics always presupposes metaphysics.

CONCLUSION

The critics of metaphysics are certainly right on one thing: It has constituted, albeit discretely, the guiding thread of the entire Western tradition. The question is whether it really has to be jettisoned and why that would need to be the case. As this book has argued, there are, to begin with, many forms of metaphysics. The metaphysics one rejects is more often than not just one possibility amongst many and is always taken to task in the name of some other type of metaphysics. Plato is held to be the founder of metaphysics, with very good reasons, yet his theory of ideas was constantly challenged by Aristotle, another founding figure of metaphysics. If Descartes lambasted Aristotelian scholasticism, he did so while presenting his own *Metaphysical meditations* (1641). Kant, for his part, only called to question the possibilities of knowledge of pure reason in order to lay the groundwork of a new metaphysics.

This refreshing variety of metaphysical thinking is however not devoid of a common-core, without which it would make no sense to speak of metaphysics. This book hopes to have made the case that metaphysics is, in essence, the self-critical endeavor of the human mind to understand the whole of reality and its reasons, an undertaking which can indeed be seen to have supported the Western intellectual tradition. It is *self-critical* since metaphysicians have always corrected their predecessors and even their own previous attempts at coming to grips with the main features of our experience. It is nothing more than an *endeavor* since most of its thinkers were aware of the audacious nature of their undertaking and of the limits of language in their attempt to grasp "Being." Even the sheer object of this quest has relentlessly been disputed and one of the leading, often nagging questions of metaphysical thought has been about the nature of its object (Parmenides Being, Plato's ideas, Aristotle's Being as Being, Plotinus's One, Descartes's and Kant's *cogito*). Thankfully most metaphysicians provided compelling answers to this question, while raising a host of others in the process. It is the *human mind* that is at work here, so it relies on the entire range of its experience which is, in principle, open to everything which can be understood: It takes into account the senses, imagination, language, the mind, the sciences, the lessons of art and history, since nothing which the human spirit can encompass, and even that which exceeds it, is foreign to the metaphysical quest. Its hope is to help us *understand*. The human being is a *homo sapiens*, a knowing being which can sense things and seeks orientation. There is understanding and, hence, thinking in everything the human being accomplishes: it knows its way around, can sense where things are heading, what they mean and amount to, and this understanding can always be furthered, refined and revised. What we seek to understand is *reality*, what is, and metaphysics often, indeed constitutively reflects on the fact *that* things are and *why* they are how they are. We touch here two of the defining hallmarks of metaphysical thinking, namely, that it strives to understand the *whole* of reality and its *reasons*. By the nature of its query, metaphysics is oriented toward universality and reason.

Universality is by itself a major conquest of human reason. We do not only capture particular occurrences of phenomena through sense perception (what Aristotle called *aisthesis*), we are also endowed with memory, experience and can grasp overriding customs and principles. This is most evident in science, where laws and regularities are singled out. They need to be borne out by experience, and any *homo sapiens* will see that they do, but they help us understand better. It is a truism to recall that this quest for universality was first and foremost a requirement of metaphysical thinking in its effort to comprehend reality. In the meantime, it has become a most fruitful requirement in other domains such as human rights (which are still called, metaphysically enough, "principles"). Kant stressed this demand in ethics: a moral law, however one may want to construe it, aims at universality (the respect of particularity being one of those universal guidelines). Thus the metaphysical assumption: the more universal the perspective is, the more it aids us to understand our world and our experience.

Metaphysics also seeks for reasons, in the plural for it is far from certain that there is only one way of rationality. Pascal spoke of the reasons of the mind and those of the heart, and a *homo sapiens* is attuned to both. Ever since the Greeks reason has been recognized at three interrelated levels. 1) Reason was first understood as an order of the world ("objective reason", as some have called it), as the *nous* of Anaxagoras and Plato, or the *logos*, of Heraclitus and Stoicism, which rules the cosmos: this insight means that our reality is not ruled by sheer happenstance and incoherence, it displays, be it only in the harmony of the stars, a remarkable order which has never failed to spark philosophical astonishment. 2) Reason furthermore characterizes our (to be sure modest) ability to grasp, through our own reason, this rationality of the world. Reason points here to our capacity of thinking, which is so paramount that it distinguishes the human species as *homo sapiens* (whether this does justice to the cognitive capacities of other species, is another, important issue, yet one which human reason can certainly take on). 3) Reason finally serves to describe the argumentative manner in which our mind strives to account for the reason of the world. A rational argument is thus one that provides reasons which one can accept or challenge, but only if one has better reasons.

Is metaphysics as the effort to understand reality as a whole something which needs to be shelved? The more fundamental question is perhaps: can it and should it be? What are the basic criticisms leveled against metaphysical thought as such? They are less thorough and thought through than many seem to believe, since this criticism itself can only rest on reasons and a better grasp of reality as a whole.

Metaphysics is routinely denounced because it would be party to some transcendence, because of its "hegemonic" nature and because it would seek the grounds of things, which would make it blind to particularity, contingence and otherness. Is transcendence such a bad thing? Can one really think without going, to some extent, beyond experience and what is immediately given? The mere fact that we think by using intelligence and language makes us go beyond the immediately given and envision it in a more general outlook. To say that something is a danger, a beauty, a case of cancer or nonsense immediately raises it to the level of thinking. Metaphysics uses this natural transcendence of the human mind and language to argue that one only understands something when one sees it in a broader perspective. Can our experience be understood if one doesn't step back from the readily given and said? Is metaphysics so wrongheaded to urge us to raise our glance and to beware of too particularistic viewpoints? This is the basic sense of transcendence—that is, that one understands things better from a larger vantage point and even from a bird's eye view. As a case in point: Isn't the widespread attempt to "overcome" metaphysics itself an attempt to *transcend* (*meta*) a form of thought, which is alleged to be limited, in the hope of gaining one which is more radical? Metaphysics has never been practiced any other way.

The same must be said about the claim that metaphysics is condemned to thinking and abstract thought. It is true that abstractions are viewed with suspicion nowadays, but, aside from the fact that the notion of "abstractions" is in itself quite abstract, can one really think or go about one's experience without abstract thinking? As we have just seen, to think and to speak is to reach beyond the immediately given. Every sentence has something abstract about it by the mere fact that it brings together a subject and a predicate. A recitation of simple "concrete" things would sound like: table, book, lines, persons, green. This doesn't amount to anything meaningful. The fear of abstract thinking is the fear of thinking itself. The issue is not if one should think abstractly, one always does; it is whether the abstractions one uses are relevant or not. Those that are not are those that do not help us understand our reality. It is good metaphysics to avoid them and to offer better ones.

Can one fault metaphysics for being on the lookout for reasons, grounds, and foundations if one cannot provide reasons for not doing so? If one rails about the foundations put forward by metaphysics, or of a certain metaphysics, it can only be because one has come across more credible or fundamental ones. A metaphysics can only be replaced by one that pretends to be more cogent or more up to the requirement of metaphysical thinking itself.

More recent criticisms—which would have been unfathomable for the likes of Aristotle, Duns Scotus, or Leibniz—have accused metaphysics of being "violent" and blind to otherness. But where on Earth is the violence in the thinking of Being and its reasons? Isn't it this criticism itself that is extraordinarily violent in that it doesn't do justice to the human mind's hope of understanding reality? One should beware here of a concept of violence (or of "power") so vague that it looses any meaning. In the footsteps of Levinas, some have claimed that the violence would already reside in the thinking of "Being" (instead of the other or the Other). If we should refrain from privileging Being in philosophy, what other Being should we be thinking of? Metaphysics has shown that it is open here to a multitude of other candidates (but which in the long run only enable us to understand Being more acutely). Is there violence in the fact that metaphysics is geared towards the universal and thus ignores particularity? Again, particularity is itself a universal concept (like every concept). Should one ban universal thinking?

Is the universal perspective of metaphysics hostile to otherness? Otherness is also a metaphysical category, of which Plato eloquently spoke in his *Sophist*, Hegel in his *Logic*, and Lévinas in *Totality and Infinity*. When one argues that metaphysics is insensitive to otherness one assumes that otherness is always a good thing. Is that the case? The otherness of the good is the bad and that of peace is war, and one doesn't readily see why a premium should be put on them. Otherness *per se* is a prime example of an ill-advised and misleading abstraction. Of course there is alterity. The question is: *which* alterity should warrant attention? Here again, metaphysics has insightful answers. Its much-maligned transcendence is in itself a quest for an *other* and more just perspective on things.

On the whole, there have been two major inspirations in modern thought for the overcoming of metaphysics: Kant and Heidegger. The arguments of both have commanded all the attempts to go beyond metaphysics which have typified modern and postmodern thought. Both defend however rather different understandings of metaphysics and of the reasons why it should be discarded.

Kant generally understands metaphysics, in the pejorative sense (because he is also familiar with a more neutral and favorable notion of metaphysics, say, when he speaks of the metaphysical exposition of time and space in his first *Critique*, or more evidently still when he puts forward a metaphysics of morals), as a form of knowledge which would strive to go beyond experience. Kant follows here an understanding of metaphysics that equates it with a form of knowledge that would go *meta ta phusika*—that is, beyond the physical realm. One can speak here of a trans-empirical or "theological" understanding of metaphysics. One instantly sees why a metaphysics so defined is problematic: How can we experience that which goes beyond experience? Kant's criticizes metaphysics, as he construes it at least, because it wants to be a meta-physics. The simplicity of this argument was a factor in the success of his demanding *Critique of Pure Reason* and in the discredit into which metaphysics has fallen ever since. Mendelssohn spoke of Kant as the "*Alles Zermalmer*," the one who destroys everything, and Heine, in his writings on Germany, compared him to Robespierre and his "*Terrorismus*" (sic!).

It can be said that since Kant metaphysics has ceased to be a "science" in the strong sense of the word. One can doubt however whether it was ever recognized as a science in the rigorous sense: Plato fused his metaphysical insights with mythical and poetic elements, Descartes spoke with disdain of scholastic metaphysics, the Empiricists never cared much for metaphysics, and the claims of metaphysics have ritually been met with skepticism, if not scorn, throughout its history. The criticism of metaphysics is not exactly the newest kid on the block.

Yet Kant's simple and forceful argument did not keep him from practicing metaphysics. If he inquires about the conditions of possibility of metaphysics, it is in order to put forward the prolegomena to a credible metaphysics. He himself delivered a metaphysics of nature, in his *Critique of Pure Reason* of 1781 as well as in his *First Metaphysical Principles of Nature* of 1786, to say nothing of his posthumous work (his very readable *Opus postumum*). More importantly perhaps, he wrote the *Groundwork to a Metaphysics of Morals* (1785) and a *Metaphysics of Morals* in 1797. Was his focus only on the morals and not chiefly on their metaphysics? To say the least, metaphysics was thus "possible" according to Kant. We have shown here that metaphysics is a feasible project for Kant when it contents itself with establishing the *a priori* conditions of our experience. Kant's argument is subtle and has often been misunderstood. His answer remains linked to experience (the foundation of any knowledge), thus seeming to respect his censure of every form of trans-empirical cognition, but it transgresses de facto this limit, as his successors recognized, by reflecting on the *a priori* conditions of this experience: the categories and principles of pure understanding in theoretical knowledge, and the categorical imperative to action in the metaphysics of morals, which is buttressed by the postulates of practical reason. In both instances, Kant has obviously no qualms about speaking of metaphysics since he published metaphysical principles of nature and a metaphysics of morals. But how is this metaphysical knowledge possible, one can ask? For Kant, in what has been named a "transcendental" argument, it is justified since without these principles we could not make sense of our experience. Kant thus confirms that one cannot supersede metaphysics without having another, more compelling metaphysics to offer. In the process, Kant's metaphysics ends up answering some of the most traditional queries of metaphysical thinking. As has been recalled in this book, metaphysics, in its universal and ontological perspective, reflects on Being as Being, and in its more theological outlook, on the transcendent principle of reality. If Kant's answer to the question of *metaphysica generalis* about the universal attributes of phenomena can be found in the Analytics of his *Critique of Pure Reason*, in his metaphysics of practical reason Kant sets forth a defensible solution to the basic expectation of *metaphysica specialis* and rational theology, that of a believable proof of the existence of God and the immortality of the soul. If Kant is the worst enemy or the Robespierre of metaphysics, it doesn't need friends since its gravediggers are its best midwives.

Heidegger's understanding and criticism of metaphysics go in a different direction, even if he is most familiar with Kant's project. His significant bone of contention is not whether a trans-empirical form of knowledge is possible, but whether the metaphysical tradition can raise the question of Being. To this question, Heidegger's opus suggests at least two answers, which differ somewhat from one another. In *Being and Time* (1927), *Kant and the Problem of Metaphysics* (1929), as well as in *What is Metaphysics?* (1929), Heidegger still seems to believe that it is possible to ask and reawaken the question of Being under the heading of a "metaphysics," but only if metaphysics becomes a reflection on the temporal condition of our understanding of Being. The metaphysics Heidegger is after is what he calls in 1929 a "metaphysics of *Dasein*,"—that is, an ontological account of the being that we are and which comprehends Being in a temporal fashion because it is itself a mortal being to the core, so much so in fact that this being tends to understand, as a form of compensation as it were, Being in general through the prism of permanence, stability, and a-temporality. This nontemporal understanding of Being would have dominated the Western tradition, from Parmenides to Descartes and Nietzsche. In other words, the Heidegger of the late 1920s argues that a metaphysics of Being is possible, indeed called for, but only on the more sweeping basis of an ontology of our finite and temporal *Dasein*.

The later Heidegger abandoned however this hope of reawakening the question of Being under the patronage of metaphysics, which increasingly came to be viewed with suspicion. Heidegger indeed turned into an ardent adversary of metaphysical thinking on the grounds that it would be chronically incapable of thinking Being.

Metaphysics is here invested with a new, unheard of meaning. It is not, as in Kant's famous criticism, the name of an alleged trans-physical science of realities which would be inaccessible to our experience, it is defined as a manner of thinking that would have characterized the West but whose extension would now be planetary: metaphysics is understood as an attempt to explain the entirety of Being out of its ultimate foundations in order to render it available, malleable, and disposable by human thought. Metaphysics is here the contrary of a thinking of Being, since Being, Heidegger contends with an impressive mixture of poetry, mysticism and sound argument, is "without reason" (*sine ratione*): It simply is—that is, it emerges in the open. Heidegger relies here on the Greek etymology of nature (*phusis*) as sheer appearing or unfolding (*phuein*). According to him, the entire regimen of metaphysical thinking would have striven, since Plato, to obfuscate this gratuitous, but unsettling self-unfolding of Being. Metaphysics appears here as an imperial and indeed "violent" form of thinking which would attempt to dominate Being by explaining it out of some cause which reason would construct to satisfy its needs. Hence the rush to reason (and universality) which would be emblematic of metaphysics and scientific knowledge as such. In this rational frenzy, metaphysics would do away with the mystery of the emergence of Being with a view to securing man's dominion on the world of beings, which metaphysics would reduce to mere "resources" (*Bestand*) at the disposal of any human project (there are thus "natural" and "human resources"). This metaphysical imperium would usher in the era of modern technology where what is deemed worthy of being is only that which fits into a human project of domination. In this, Heidegger sighs, Being is forgotten, since it is only beings that can be dominated. Salvation can thus only come from another, more meditative beginning of thinking which would relinquish this will to master and explain Being. It would of course leave behind metaphysics since it would have been the worst enemy of the thinking of Being Heidegger is after. But one is tempted to ask, is that really the case?

To be sure, this understanding of metaphysics as the forgetting of Being which is conducive to modern technology is miles away from Kant's notion of metaphysics. There are family resemblances in both criticisms in that Heidegger attacks the metaphysical obsession with a-temporality to return to what is for him the basic experience, that of the temporal event of our *Dasein*. But Kant, or the positivists who followed him, would have never recognized his criticism in Heidegger's, who, for his part, would have claimed to be far more radical than Kant.

One thing appears striking in Heidegger's settling of accounts with metaphysics: For a thinking that wants to do away with the metaphysical urge to explain, Heidegger ends up explaining quite a lot. On the one hand, he claims to rise for the first time to consciousness the secret plot of the entire Western tradition, honorably summed up under the heading of metaphysics (one could say that the quiet and somewhat off the beaten path discipline of metaphysics never asked for this much, but will readily take that as a compliment). On the other, it aims to prepare an entirely new beginning for thought, which would transcend (*meta* all over again) metaphysical thinking and on which our redemption would depend. In plain language, Heidegger faults metaphysics for being too rationalistic, but with powerful reasons of his own.

Metaphysics has been for him too rational in wanting to provide reasons for Being, about which Heidegger assumes it escapes rationality (but how can one know this? and: is it so sure?). Heidegger thus believes he is the first to think Being as such which metaphysics would have overlooked or suppressed. But is metaphysics really foreign to the thought of Being? It takes a special kind of hubris to claim it is. Didn't Aristotle initiate metaphysical thinking when he spoke of a science of Being as Being, underlining that it is "something we constantly seek after" (*zetoumènè*)? Did it not find a first approximation in Parmenides' tautological thinking of Being and in Plato's insight into the beauty of the *eidos* as the true Being which eludes our mortal grasp? In this regard, it was perhaps the Heidegger of 1929 who was more consequent when he presented his own thinking as a "metaphysics of *Dasein*". In his effort to return to the forgotten ground of metaphysics, Heidegger would appear to be, as has been argued here, a metaphysical thinker to the core.

The later Heidegger stigmatizes metaphysical thinking for being onto-theo-logical. Three threads are here woven into one another: (1) It would aim at universal Being and not the event of Being; (2) it would seek a theological foundation for this universal Being instead of liberating itself from the hold of beings; and (3) it would follow the logic of human reason rather than listen to the stammering of Being in a few chosen words of the archaic Greek language like *aletheia*, *physis* and *logos*. But doesn't Heidegger's own thinking towards Being obey this very same onto-theo-logical bend? It is ontological itself in that it also hopes to think the *whole* of Being as a "temporal event" (*Ereignis*). It is "theological" in its hope against hope to prepare the readiness for the advent of something Sacred in the night of the forgetfulness of Being, and it is deeply logical in that it invents an entirely new vocabulary for the happening or *Ereignis* of Being, which one doesn't disparage in the least when one observes, rightly, that it is most poetical and mystical. In the end, Heidegger, like Kant, only seeks to overcome metaphysics to think more thoroughly its two highest objects, Being and the Divine, the jewels of *metaphysica generalis* and *metaphysica specialis*.

It is to be regretted that the countless heirs of Kant and Heidegger, in modern and contemporary philosophy, did not recognize, for the most part, the thoroughly metaphysical nature of their critical confrontations with the metaphysical tradition. In each case, metaphysics was taken to task in the name of a more lucid and radical metaphysics. Both can thus only be rightly appraised when one sees them against the backdrop of the metaphysical tradition, to which they belong and which they carried further.

This metaphysical endeavor came to the fore when Parmenides raised Being to the level of thinking: Being and thinking are the same, he said at the beginning of metaphysics. Plato seized upon this insight when he recognized that reason can glimpse true Being when it is arrested by the splendor of the *eidos*—that is, the order, symmetry and harmony—which shines through the world of our experience. Thinking then, unmistakably but humbly, becomes aware that this world of ours is not only guided by the random whims of fortune and chance, which can hardly guide anything. They testify to some good that rules our world and our action and which we strive to understand when we think metaphysically.

ABBREVIATIONS

AK: Königlich Preussischen Akademie der Wissenschaften ed. *Kants gesammelte Schriften.* 29 vols., 4 parts (Berlin: Georg Reiner, 1900–).

AT: Charles Adam and Paul Tannery, eds. *Œuvres de Descartes* (*Descartes' Works*). 11 vols. (Paris: Vrin, 1971 [1897–1913]).

DK: Hermann Diels and Walther Kranz, eds. *Die Fragmente der Vorsokratiker* (*Presocratic Fragments*). 3 vols. (Berlin: Weidmansche Buchhandlung, 1922, 1934 [1903]).

GA: *Gesamtausgabe* (*Complete Works*) refers to either:
Martin Heidegger. 4 parts, 102 vols. (Frankfurt: Klosstermann, 1975–).
Johann Gottlieb Fichte. 4 parts, 40 vols., R. Lauth, H. Jacob et al., eds. (Stuttgart: Frommann-Holzboog, 1962–).

GW: Hans-Georg Gadamer. *Gesammelte Werke* (*Works*). 10 vols. (Tübingen: Mohr Siebeck, 1985–1995).

SW: *Sämmtliche Werke* (*Complete Works*) refers to either:
Johann Gottlieb Fichte. 8 vols., J. H. Fichte, ed. (Berlin: De Gruyter, 1971 [1834–1835]).
Friedrich Wilhelm Joseph Schelling. 2 parts, 14 vols. F. K. A. Schelling, ed. (Stuttgart: Cotta, 1856–1861).

Note on References

In addition to giving the page number when quoting a translation, I have included the original notation. Thus, for Plato, I also use the canonical notation (Stephanus) found in the margins of all translations. For Aristotle, I use Bekker's. For Augustine I refer, parenthetically following the reference to the translation, to the book number followed by chapter and section. For *Critique of Pure Reason*, I give the reference to the original pagination of the first two editions (A and B) found in the margins of all translations. And for *Being and Time*, I provide the original pagination of *Sein und Zeit* found in all translations.

Preface

1. See Luc Brisson, "Un si long anonymat," in *La métaphysique: Son histoire, sa critique, ses enjeux*, ed. Jean-Marc Narbonne and Luc Langlois (Paris/Québec: Vrin/ PUL, 1999), 43.

2. Two modern thinkers of note, both influenced by Heidegger, have made this connection between metaphysics and violence: Jacques Derrida, "Violence and Metaphysics," in his book *Writing and Difference* (1967), trans. A. Bass (Chicago: University of Chicago Press, 1978) and Gianni Vattimo, "Metaphysics and Violence," in ed. Santiago Zabala, *Weakening Philosophy* (Montreal: McGill-Queen's University Press, 2007), 400–421.

Introduction

1. Gottfried Wilhelm Leibniz, "Principles of Nature and Grace based on Reason (1714)" in *Philosophical Essays*, ed. Roger Ariew and Daniel Garber (Indianapolis, IN: Hackett, 1982), 209–210. "So far we have just spoken as simple *physicists*; now we must rise to *metaphysics*, by making use of the *great principle*, little used, commonly,

that nothing takes place without sufficient reason, that is, that nothing happens without it being possible for someone who knows enough things to give a reason sufficient to determine why it is so and so and not otherwise. Assuming this principle, the first question we have the right to ask will be, *why is there something rather than nothing?*".

2. See Pierre Aubenque, *Le problème de l'être chez Aristote* (Paris: Presses Universitaires de France, 1964), 23–24. This tradition is based on the account given by Strabo (c. 63 BCE–19 CE) and Plutarch (c. 46–120 CE), which is particularly worthy of attention since it is almost contemporaneous with Andronicus's editing of the manuscripts. According to this account, Aristotle's manuscripts initially belonged to Theophrastus, his disciple and successor at the head of the Peripatetic school. In his will, written in 288 BCE, Theophratus gave all his manuscripts, including Aristotle's, to his co-disciple, Neleus of Scepsis. Neleus then brought all the manuscripts to Scepsis, near Troy. His heirs were rather ignorant however, and left them in a cellar for some two hundred years. In the first century BCE, their descendants supposedly sold the texts to a bibliophile, Apellicon of Teos, who brought them to Athens. Then following the invasion of Athens in 86 BCE, the Roman general Sulla brought them to Rome as booty. Andronicus's teacher, the grammarian Tyrannion of Amisus, bought the manuscripts and first edited them in 60 BCE. This account is often judged skeptically, but some eminent scholars of the ancient world do think there is some truth to it. See Ingemar Düring, *Aristoteles: Darstellung und Interpretation seines Denkens* (Heidelberg, Germany: Carl Winter Verlag, 1966), 40; ed. Helmut Flashar, *Grundriss der Geschichte der Philosophie, Ueberwegs: Antike 3: Ältere Akademis-Aristoteles-Peripatos* (Basel, Germany: Schwabe Verlag, 1983), 191 ff.; and more recently, Yvon Lafrance, "Une nouvelle histoire de la philosophie grecque," in *Dialogue*, 38 (1999): 859–860.

3. See Helmut Flashar, ed., *Grundriss der Geschichte der Philosophie, Ueberwegs: Antike 3: Ältere Akademis-Aristoteles-Peripatos,* § 10, 192.

4. Immanuel Kant, *Vorlesungen Kants über Metaphysik aus drei Semstern,* ed. S. Hirzel (Leipzig, 1894), 186.

5. Aristotle, *Metaphysics,* 1003 a 21–26; trans. William D. Ross in *The Complete Works of Aristotle,* 2 vols., ed. Jonathan Barnes (Princeton: Princeton University Press, 1984), 2:1584.

6. Pierre Hadot, *Qu'est-ce que la philosophie antique?* (Paris: Gallimard, 1995); *La philosophie comme manière de vivre,* interviews with Jeannie Carlier and Arnold I. Davidson (Paris: Albin Michel, 2001).

7. Saint Augustine of Hippo, *Confessions,* trans. Francis J. Sheed (Indianapolis, IN: Hackett, 2006 [1993]), 217 (X, 33, 50): "Thou in whose eyes I have become a

question to myself: and that is my infirmity." The original Latin reads: "*Tu autem, 'domine deus meus, exaudi, respice' et vide et 'miserere et sana me,' in cuius oculis mihi quæstio factus sum, et ipse est languor meus.*"

1. Parmenides: The Evidence of Being

1. The English translations of Parmenides' *Poem* used here are the following: Denis O'Brien in *Études sur Parménide*, 2 vols., Pierre Aubenque, ed. (Paris: Vrin, 1987), I:4–80—referred to as O'Brien; Leonardo Tarán, *Parmenides. A Text with Translation, Commentary, and Critical Essays* (Princeton: Princeton University Press, 1965), 7–172—referred to as Tarán. We will always quote the fragment (frag.) followed by the verse (v.). For more on the context and its philosophical significance, see Rémi Brague, "La vraisemblance du faux (Parménides, frag. 1, v. 31–32)" in *Études sur Parménide* (Paris: Vrin, 1987), 1:52.

2. Aristotle, *Metaphysics*, A, 6, 987 b 3, Xenophon, *Memorabilia*, Book 1, chapter 1, § 11–15.

3. Aristotle, 3, 983 b 17–27; trans. Jonathan Barnes in *Early Greek Philosophy*, Jonathan Barnes, ed. (London: Penguin, 1987), 63.

4. Ibid., "But as to the number and form of this sort of principle, they do not all agree."

5. Using the best of the philological knowledge of his time, Martin Heidegger wrote an important text entitled "Anaximander's Saying (1946)" in *Off the Beaten Track*, trans. Julian Young and Kenneth Haynes (Cambridge: Cambridge University Press, 2002), 242–281. However, few specialists of classical antiquity saw this as a serious philological interpretation of Anaximander because Heidegger drew heavily on the resources of his own philosophy. Nevertheless, he is probably correct in seeing it as the first expression of Western philosophy.

6. Trans. Jonathan Barnes, *Early Greek Philosophy*, 74–75.

7. On these testimonials see David Gallop, *Parmenides of Elea: A Text and Translation with an Introduction* (Toronto: University of Toronto Press, 1984), 105 (DK I, 2, 218).

8. See Yvon Lafrance, "Le sujet du poème de Parménides : L'être ou l'univers?," *Elenchos*, 20 (1999): 271; see also Simplicius's later testimonial (6th century), in Gallop, *Parmenides of Elea*, 109 (DK, I, 14, 220). Yvon Lafrance ("Le sujet du poème de Parménides") also evokes Galen's testimonial (2nd century CE) according to whom all (!) the Ancients entitled their works "On Nature" (*Peri phuseôs*). One wonders what was then the point of giving titles to their texts. Again, one suspects Aristotle's influence.

9. The most influential reading of this type, which is also a classic introduction to Presocratic thought, is John Burnett's *Early Greek Philosophy* (Cleveland, NY: Meridian, 1957 [1930]), 169–196.

10. On this see Eric A. Havelock, "Preliteracy and the Presocratics" in *The Literate Revolution in Greece and Its Cultural Consequences* (Princeton: Princeton University Press, 1982), 234 ff.

11. See Saint Augustine of Hippo, *The Confessions*, trans. Francis J. Sheed (Indianapolis, IN: Hackett, 2006 [1993]), 97–98 (VI, 3, 3).

12. The problem of the spoken word and writing dominate Plato's *Phaedrus*. See the commentary by Luc Brisson, *Phèdre* (Paris: Garnier-Flammarion, 1989).

13. See fragment B 17 (DK, I: 244; Taràn, 171: "On the right, boys; on the left, girls." See also O'Brien, 65).

14. See Hans-Georg Gadamer, "Parmenides oder das Diesseits des Seins," in GW, vol. 7: *Griechische Philosophie III: Plato im Dialog* (Tübingen, Germany: Mohr Siebeck, 1991), 3–31. Karl Reinhart, *Parmenides und die Geschichte der griechischen Philosophie* (Bonn: Cohen, 1916), 66, also insisted on the fact that the discourse on Being was the goddess's.

15. Parmenides, DK, I, 1, 2 (Taràn, 8).

16. Ibid., frag. B 1, v. 9–10 (O'Brien, 4; Taràn, 8).

17. Ibid., frag. 1, v. 12–23 (O'Brien, 5–6; Taràn, 8–9).

18. Ibid., frag. 1, v. 22–28 (O'Brien, 6–7; Taràn, 9).

19. On the fragility of destiny in Greek culture see Martha Nussbaum, *The Fragility of Goodness, Luck, and Ethics in Greek Tragedy and Philosophy* (Cambridge: Cambridge University Press, 1986). This fragility can be opposed to the modern attitude that seeks to control everything, even the uncontrollable: time, health, happiness, and way of life.

20. Parmenides, frag. 1, v. 28–32 (O'Brien, 7–8—modified; Taràn, 9).

21. The first to have seen this was Karl Reinhart, *Parmenides und die Geschichte der griechischen Philosophie*, 36 ff. Reinhart also showed how the Sophist Gorgias took up these three ways. Reinhart's interpretation was followed by Uvo Hölscher in his edition of Parmenides, *Vom Wesen des Seienden: Die Fragmente* (Frankfurt: Suhrkamp, 1969).

22. Simplicius's text speaks (frag. 1, v. 28) of a "well-rounded truth" (*eupethéos*). O'Brien, suspicious of a platonic transformation, follows an older version of the text that goes back to Plutarch, Clement of Alexandria, and Sextus Empiricus, which speaks of "persuasive" truth (*eupeithéos*) or one that leads to conviction.

23. See Pierre Aubenque, "Syntaxe et sémantique de l'être," in *Études sur Parménide*, II:III.

24. This is rather uncommon in everyday English, and examples are hard to come by. But one can nevertheless imagine waking up one morning to a newspaper

headline that reads: "It is over, the war is over." The "it," left undetermined in the first clause, builds up the tension that is resolved in the next clause when we learn it refers to the "war."

25. Pierre Aubenque, II:110: "*Estin* [it is] is the assertion of Being, and not, as the traditional interpretation claims, an assertion on Being or beings. Parmenides' thesis is not a thesis *on* Being, but the *thesis* of Being, the positing of Being."

26. Parmenides, frag. 8, v. 2–4 (O'Brien, 34; Tarán, 85).

27. Ibid., frag. 8, v. 7 (Tarán, 85)—modified translation.

28. Ibid., frag. 8, v. 9–10.

29. See Denis O'Brien's analysis "L'Être et l'éternité," in *Études sur Parmenide*, II:135–162.

30. He was not the first, however. Ernst Hoffman in *Die Sprache und die archaische Logik* (Tübingen: Mohr Siebeck, 1925), 9–10, had already identified the importance given to permanence. Since then the connection between Being and permanence in Parmenides' *Poem* has been much discussed. See also the more recent study by Catherine Collobert, *L'être de Parménide, ou le refus du temps* (Paris: Kimé, 1993).

31. Parmenides, frag. 2, v. 6 (O'Brien, 17).

32. Ibid., frag. 2, v. 1–8 (O'Brien, 16–17; Tarán, 32)—modified translation.

33. Ibid., frag. 8, v. 38–41 (O'Brien, 42; Tarán, 86)—modified translation.

34. Ibid., frag. 7, v. 4–5 (Tarán, 73).

35. Ernst Hoffman, *Die Sprache und die archaische Logik* (1925), 10 ff. See also Pierre Aubenque, "Syntaxe et sémantique de l'être," II:119: "The word *glossa* is used here pejoratively. It seems to designate idle chatter, *glossolalia*, that is opposed to the goddess's (true) discourse [*rhèthenta*: passive aorist participle of *legein*] and the logos she urges her disciple to adopt." The difference is further emphasized at the end of the goddess's discourse: "Here I end my trustworthy discourse [*piston logon*] and my thought concerning truth [*alètheiès*]. From now on, learn the opinions [*doxas*] of mortals, listening to the deceptive order of my words [*epeôn*]" (Parmenides, frag. 8, v. 50–52; Tarán, 86)—modified translation.

36. Parmenides, DK I, 6, 1, 232 (Tarán, 54, O'Brien, 24)—modified translation. See also DK I, 8, 8 ff. (236, Tarán, 85); "Not from Nonbeing shall I allow you to say or to think, for it is not possible to say or to think that it is not."

37. See Pierre Aubenque, "Syntaxe et sémantique de l'être," 2:129.

38. See the title of Yvon Lafrance's article, "Le sujet du poème de Parménide: L'être ou l'univers? [Le Subject of Parmenides' *Poem*: Being or the universe?]," 265–308.

39. Parmenides, frag. 7 (Tarán, 73)—translation modified.

40. See also Barnes, *Early Greek Philosophy*, 155–156 (DK I, 25, 253).

41. "Socrates" recognized this in Plato's *Parmenides* (128 a, trans. Francis M. Cornford in *The Collected Dialogues of Plato* [Princeton: Princeton University Press,

1989] 922): "You [Parmenides] assert in your poem, that Being is one, and for this you advance admirable proofs. Zeno, for his part, asserts that it is not a plurality, and he too has many weighty proofs to bring forward. You assert unity; he asserts no plurality."—modified translation.

42. On Leucippus, see DK II:2.

43. Plato, *Symposium*, 208 c 1 and 203 d 8 (on Eros).

44. DK 68 A 9 (II, 220); see Michael J. O'Brien's translation of Protagoras's fragments in Rosamund Kent Sprague, ed., *The Older Sophists: A complete translation by several hands of the fragments in die Fragmente der Vorsockratiker,* ed. Diels-Kranz (Indianapolis, IN: Hackett, 2001 [1972]), 6.

45. DK II:229; *The Older Sophists,* 20.

46. Theaetetus, 152 a, trans. Francis M. Cornford. Protagoras's thesis also appears in the *Cratylus,* 385 e–386 a.

47. 152 a, trans. Cornford.

48. According to Saint Eusebius's testimony in *Preparation of the Gospel,* see *The Older Sophists,* 20 (DK II:229–230).

49. Plato (*Pheadrus,* 267 c 6) tells us Protagoras wrote a treatise on the correctness of words (*orthoepeia*), called *Correct Diction.*

50. According to Apollodorus's testimony cited by Diogenes Laertius, *The Older Sophists,* trans. G. Kennedy, 35 (DK II, 238). On Gorgias, see the entry by Michel Narcy in the third volume of *Dictionnaire des philosophes antiques,* 4 vols., ed. Richard Goulet (Paris: CNRS, 2000).

51. See *The Older Sophists,* 42 ff. (DK II, 242 ff.).

52. Ibid., 45 (DK II, 244–245). A different version of the same idea appears in Plato's *Parmenides* (135 a): there are numerous problems related to the existence of the ideas, but even if they do exist, they are perhaps unknowable by human nature.

53. Ibid., 46 (DK II, 245): *ouk ara to on phroneitai tai katalambanetai.*

54. Ibid., 46—translation modified for fluency.

55. Barbara Cassin gave a good description of the relation between the Eleatics and the Sophists in her entry on Gorgias in *Dictionnaire des philosophes* (Paris: Albin Michel, 1998), 628: "The three theses of Gorgias's treatise: 'nothing is'; 'if it is, it is unknowable'; 'if it is and if it is knowable, it cannot be demonstrated' only make sense in the perspective of Parmenides' *Poem* and the thought of Being and nature, which begins the philosophical tradition. Gorgias uses the force of identity and the logical constraint of non-contradiction to make all identity, all identification of a subject with the verb 'to be,' as well as all predicative structure, impossible. He replaces Parmenides' word with the autonomous act of discourse. His audacity is the culmination of the Sophists' power."

2. Plato: The Hypothesis of the Idea

1. Harold Cherniss has gone as far as to doubt the authenticity of these accounts; see *Aristotle's Criticism of Plato and the Academy* (New York: Russell & Russell, 1962 [1944]) and *The Riddle of the Early Academy* (New York: Russell & Russell, 1962 [1945]). Hans Joachim Krämer later contested his arguments in *Arete bei Platon und Aristoteles* (Heidelberg: Winter 1959), which set off the debate of the last fifty years on Plato's "unwritten doctrines." Unfortunately, Harold Cherniss (1904–1987) never responded.

2. On this, see Konrad Gaiser, *Protreptik und Paranäse bei Platon* (Stuttgart, Germany, 1955). It is this interest for the protreptic character of Plato's writings that led the Tübingen school (Krämer, Gaiser, Szlezak, Reale) to take an interest in the testimonials about Plato's oral teachings and notice how they essentially agree with the dialogues. See also Konrad Graiser, *Platons ungeschriebene Lehre* (Stuttgart, Germany: Klett, 1963); John N. Findlay, *Plato: The Written and Unwritten Doctrines* (London: Routledge & Kegan Paul, 1974). Monique Dixaut, *Le naturel philosophique: Essai sur les dialogues de Platon* (Paris: Les Belles Lettres/Vrin, 1985), has shown how there is no firm doctrine in the Platonic dialogues, but one should not conclude from this that Plato did not have a doctrine or a fundamental idea.

3. This is the title to Thomas Szlezak's best-known book on the subject: *Reading Plato*, trans. Graham Zanker (London: Routledge, 1999).

4. The *Theaetetus* (176 b) uses the famous expression *homoiosis theô*, an effort at "becoming like divinity." Plato, like Parmenides, does acknowledge, however, that for humans it can only be an effort, a striving for wisdom, which the term *philosophia,* love of wisdom, summarizes quite well. The gods do not philosophize (*Symposium*, 204 a).

5. The relation between the two is hard to discern when one stubbornly makes Plato out to be the proponent of (abstract) ideas and Aristotle the proponent of (materialized) forms when, in fact, both use the term εἶδος.

6. It is an example that Plato uses frequently, in part, because the term εἶδος in Greek also designates beauty, something that is often forgotten even though it has its equivalent in classical Latin: *species*.

7. Darwin's idea of an evolution of species was therefore revolutionary, and heretical, but it still presupposes that a thing's real Being is contained in its εἶδος.

8. *Symposium*, 210 e–211 d, trans. M. Joyce in *Collected Dialogues of Plato*, ed. Edith Hamilton and Huntington Cairns (Princeton: Princeton University Press, 1989), 562–563—modified translation for fluency.

9. *Phaedo*, 76 d: "We are always talking about them" (*ha truloumen aei*) in the sense of our mouths are always full of ideas.

10. Paul Natorp, *Plato's Theory of Ideas: An Introduction to Idealism*, trans. Vasilis Politis and John Connolly (Sankt Augustin: Academia, 2004).

11. Léon Robin claims "Technically, what is called a hypothesis does not imply the idea of a conjecture, as in our modern use of the term. 'Thesis' may be better because it implies a position that is the basis for subsequent thought." On this, see his French translation of the *Phaedo* in *Platon: Œuvres Complètes*, 2 vols. (Paris: Gallimard, coll. "Bibliothèque de la Pléiade," 1950), II:1377. For Yvon Lafrance, the Platonic notion of the *hypothesis* "is closer to the modern sense of the term 'hypothesis,' implying a supposition or conjecture." See Yvon Lafrance, *Pour interpréter Platon II: La ligne en République VI, 509 d–511 e. Le texte et son histoire*, (Montreal: Bellarmin, coll. "Noesis," 1994), 306.

12. *Phaedo*, 100 c–d, trans. Hugh Tredennick in *Plato: The Collected Dialogues*, 81–82.

13. See Stanley Rosen, "Remarks on Nietzsche's Platonism," in *The Quarrel Between Philosophy and Poetry: Studies in Ancient Thought* (London; Routledge, 1988), 199: "But the Ideas of Socrates, as he tells us in the *Phaedo* [100, a–d], are the 'strongest hypotheses' and the 'safest response' that we can make about the natures of things." He also says: "The Ideas are silent paradigms of what eludes discourse even as regulating it" (202).

14. The *Sophist* (especially 254 a, but starting from 253 b) also states that the thought of Being belongs to the dialectician, or the philosopher: "And the Philosopher, always holding converse through reason with the idea of Being, is also dark from excess of light; for the souls of the many have no eye which can endure the vision of the divine," trans. Benjamin Jowett in *The Dialogues of Plato*, 4th ed., 4 vols. (Oxford: Clarendon, 1953 [1871]), III:408.

15. See Étienne Gilson, *L'Être et l'essence* (Paris: Vrin, 1962 [1948]), 27. Unfortunately the English translation makes no reference to the *vere ens* when discussing this point, see Étienne Gilson, *Being and some Philosophers*, 2nd ed. (Toronto: Pontifical Institute of Medieval Studies, 1952 [1948]), 10.

16. *Republic*, 476 a–b, trans. Paul Shorey in *The Collected Dialogues of Plato*, 715.

17. Ibid., 525 d; see also 525 b–c: "It is also befitting, then, Glaucon, that this branch of learning should be prescribed by law and that we should induce those who are to share the highest functions of state to enter upon that study of calculation and take hold of it, not as amateurs, but to follow it up until they attain to the contemplation of the nature of number, by pure thought, not for the purpose of buying and selling, as if they were preparing to be merchants or hucksters, but for the uses of war and for facilitating the conversion of the soul itself from the world of generation to truth and Being [*ep'aletheias te kai ousian*]," trans. Shorey—modified for fluency.

18. On the relation between originals and images, even in the passages where Plato does not make it explicit, see Yvon Lafrance, *Pour interpréter Platon II*, 348 ff.

19. I here use Yvon Lafrance's translation in *Pour interpréter Platon II*, 402: "The expression describes the epistemic state of normal humans for whom knowledge depends on visible and sensible things. . . . The dialectician's role is therefore to unmask, so to speak, this sensible credence and expose its 'fallibility.'"

20. In accordance with *Republic*, 511 d 8. See Yvon Lafrance, *Pour interpréter Platon II*, 398: "When constructing a graphic representation of the Line, the term *anôtatô* obliges us to construct a vertical line and not a horizontal one, as do Chambry and other commentators."

21. Yvon Lafrance, *Pour interpréter Platon II*, 393, translates *dianoia* as "dianoetic" thought (but he also uses the neologism "discursion") and *nous* as "noetic thought."

22. Later in 533 c, Plato says the nonhypothetical is a principle [*archè*] that represents the goal of dialectics. "The dialectic method [*hè dialektikè methodos*] alone rises to the principle [*ep'autèn archèn*] which is above hypotheses, converting and gently leading the eye of the soul [*to tès psyches omma*] out of the barbarous slough of ignorance into the light of the upper world, with the help of the sciences which we have been describing" (trans. Jowett in *The Dialogues of Plato*, II:91)—modified translation.

23. See Yvon Lafarance, *Pour interpréter Platon II*, 308.

24. See ibid., 368—Our translation from the French.

25. See *Republic*, 511 c 4–7: "You mean to distinguish the realm of Being and the intelligible, which is contemplated by the power of dialectics, as something truer and more exact than the object of the so-called sciences whose assumptions are hypotheses" (trans. Paul Shorey in *Collected Dialogues of Plato*, 746)—modified to keep with the point being made.

26. On this see the articles by H. Krämer, "EPEKEINA TYS OUSIAS. *Zu Platon, Politeia 509 B*" in *Archiv für Philosophie*, 51 (1969): 1–30; and "*Die Idee des Guten. Sonnen- und Liniengleichnis*" (Buch VI, 504 a–511 e) in Otfried Höffe ed., *Platon, Politeia* (Berlin: Akademie Verlag, 1997), 179–203.

27. *Republic*, 508 e, trans. Shorey—modified.

28. Ibid., 509 b.

29. On this reading that rejects the idea of an ontological transcendence (thought to be overly Neoplatonic) of the idea of the Good, see Luc Brisson, *Lectures de Platon* (Paris: Vrin, 2000), 85: "But the transcendence of the Good is not absolute, it is qualified. It surpasses other realities' *ousia* not in-itself, but by its dignity and its power like a king who surpasses his subjects in dignity and power even though he remains human."

30. See Francis M. Cornford's remark in *Plato and Parmenides: Parmenides' Way of Truth and Plato's Parmenides*, 2nd ed. (London: Routledge & Kegan Paul, 1939),

132: "Whereas you can ask the reason for a thing's existence and the answer will be that it exists for the sake of its goodness, you cannot ask for a reason for goodness; the good is an end in itself."

31. On this, see Luc Brisson, *Le même et l'autre dans la structure ontologique du Timée de Platon* 1st ed., (Paris: Klincksieck, 1974), 2nd ed. (Sankt-Augustin: Academia Verlag, 1994).

32. On the question of the divine in Plato, see Pierre Hadot, *Qu'est-ce que la philosophie antique* (Paris: Gallimard, 1995), 344: "The divine [in Plato] is something vague, which includes entities on different levels, such as the Good, the ideas, the Divine Intellect, the mythical artisan, the Demiurge, and finally the soul of the world."

33. *Republic*, VI, 507 b, trans. Shorey.

34. In the beginning of the *Parmenides* (129 b), the idea of the One is also said to be a great principle: "All things are one by having a share in unity and at the same time many by sharing in plurality." See Hans Joachim Krämer, "EPEKEINA TYS OUSIAS. Zu Platon, *Politeia, 509 b*".

35. See Aristotle, *Physics*, 203 a 15; *Metaphysics*, 987 b 20–27.

36. See *Timaeus*, 29 a (trans. Jowett in *The Collected Dialogues of Plato*, 1162): "If the world be indeed fair and the artificer good, it is manifest that he must have looked to that which is eternal."

37. See Aristotle, *Metaphysics*, A, 6; *Physics*, 203 a 10.

3. Aristotle: The Horizons of First Philosophy

1. See Luc Brisson, "Un si long anonymat" in *La métaphysique: Son histoire, sa critique, ses enjeux*, ed. Jean-Marc Narbonne and Luc Langlois (Paris/Quebec: Vrin/PUL, 1999), 37–60.

2. The first to insist on this point were Paul Moraux in *Les listes anciennes des ouvrages d'Aristote* (Louvain, Belgium: Nauwelaerts, 1951) (who showed that in the oldest catalogues, the "*meta ta phusika*" writings were not inserted after the *Physics* but after the works on "mathematics"!) and Hans Reiner, "Die Enstehung und ursprüngliche Bedeutung des Names Metaphysik" in *Zeitschrift für philosophische Forschung*, 8 (1954): 210–237 (who argues the unlikely possibility—but one we cannot reject—that Aristotle was aware of the title). See also Pierre Aubenque, *Le problème de l'être chez Aristote* (Paris: PUF, 1964), 29; and Luc Brisson, "Un si long anonymat," 45. Ingemar Düring in *Aristoteles: Darstellung und Interpretation seines Denkens* (Heidelberg, Germany: Carl Winter Verlag, 1966), 287 and 592, views these interpretations skeptically and defends the traditional reading according to which the term only had a bibliographical function.

3. See Pierre Aubenque, *Le problème de l'être chez Aristote*, 32.

4. See Luc Brisson ("Un si long anonymat," 45) who cites the testimony given by Alexander of Aphrodisias (second to third century CE; *Metaphysics*, 171, 5–7: "The science that is the object of the inquiry and that is proposed here is wisdom or the theological science which Aristotle entitles metaphysics because it comes after physics in the order relative to us") and Asclepius of Tralles (fifth century CE; *Metaphysics* 1, 19–20: "The work is called "metaphysics" [*meta ta physika*] because, after discussing physical realities, Aristotle then discusses the science of divine things.").

5. On this, see the title of Vianney Décaries's work, which represents Aristotelian studies so well (as well as metaphysics, and even philosophy itself insofar as its object is never self-evident), *L'objet de la métaphysique d'Aristote* [The Object of Aristotle's Metaphysics] (Paris: Vrin, 1961). See also the recent studies, in French, on this question: Annick Julien, *Eidos et ousia. De l'unité théorique de la Métaphysique d'Aristote* (Paris: Klincksieck, 1999) and Annick Stevens, *L'ontologie d'Aristote au carrefour du logique et du réel* (Paris: Vrin, 2000).

6. *Metaphysics*, A, 9, 992 b 18–20. Pierre Aubenque has noted that the critique of the idea of a science of Being belongs to the anti-Platonic polemic (confirmed by the context of *Metaphysics*, A, 9). According to Aubenque (*Le problème de l'être chez Aristote*, 207), the polemic dates from the beginning of Aristotle's career: "The idea that *there is no unique science of Being or of the Good* characterizes the anti-Patonic polemic, which can logically be dated to the beginning of Aristotle's career." The reason being that Aristotle would have (later?) argued for the existence, and even the preeminence of a science of Being in *Metaphysics*, Γ and Z.

7. Other than *Metaphysics*, A, see *Metaphysics*, D, 2, which is similar to *Physics*, II, 3.

8. *Timaeus* 69 a, trans. Benjamin Jowett in *Collected Dialogues of Plato* (Princeton: Princeton University Press, 1989 [1961]), 1192.

9. Luc Brisson, in his translation, says: "I use material (*matériau*) to translate *khôra* since the latter is not only "in which" becoming takes place, but "of which" sensible things are made." See *Timée/Critias*, trans. Luc Brisson (Paris: Garnier-Flammarion, 1992), 12.

10. See *Physics*, II, 3, 195 a 22 ff.

11. See *Metaphysics*, A, 3, 983 a 27.

12. *Physics*, II, 3, 194 b 33, trans. R. P. Hardy and R. K. Gaye in *The Complete Works of Aristotle: the Revised Oxford Translation*, 2 vols., ed. Jonathan Barnes (Princeton: Princeton University Press, 1984), I:332.

13. See *Metaphysics*, XII, 10, 1075 b 9. Aristotle does, however, follow Anaxagoras's lead in the *Physics* when he says that the latter was right to call spirit,

which acts as a principle of movement, an impassive principle (*Physics*, VIII, 5, 256 b 25).

14. *Metaphysics*, A, 6, 988 a 9. See Emilio Berti, "Origine et originalité de la métaphysique aristotélicienne," *Archiv für Geschichte der Philosophie*, 63 (1981): 241 ff.

15. See *Physics*, II, 3.

16. As Pierre Aubenque says: "Every science must demonstrate a property (τι) on a subject (περί τι / *peri ti*) using principles (ἔκ τινων / *ek tinôn*)." See Pierre Aubenque, *Le problème de l'être chez Aristote*, 216.

17. *Metaphysics*, A, 9, 992 b 18.

18. Pierre Aubenque, *Le problème de l'être chez Aristote*, 207.

19. As Joseph Owens has exhaustively shown in *The Doctrine of Being in the Aristotelian "Metaphysics"* (Toronto: Toronto University Press, 1963 [1951]), 48: "No one in ancient times […] doubted that the Primary Philosophy and 'Theology' were one for Aristotle. On into the twelfth century "Being qua Being" was quoted with the Being of the separate entities, the divine and separate and immobile Being. During the Christian Middle Ages, on the other hand, and down to the beginning of the Modern era, the Aristotelian formula 'Being qua Being' was interpreted as *ens commune* in a sense opposed to the divine Being."

20. See in particular *Metaphysics*, Γ, I, 1003 a 31: "Therefore it is of Being as Being that we must grasp the first causes," trans. William D. Ross in *The Complete Works of Aristotle: The Revised Oxford Translation*, II:1584. See also the beginning of *Metaphysics*, E, 1025 b 3–4: "We are seeking the principles and the causes of things that are, and obviously of Beings *as* Beings," trans. Ross, II:1619—modified translation.

21. We must therefore preserve the original text in 1026 a 14 and reject Schwegler's correction (separated, *chôrista*, instead of "not separated," *achôrista*, a correction Jaeger and Tricot adopt), which assigns objects "separate" from matter to physics, that is, objects existing autonomously (which would be nonsensical). On this see Vianney Décarie, "La physique porte-t-elle sur des 'non-séparés'?" in *Revue des sciences philosophiques et théologiques*, 38 (1954):465–468, also in *Études aristotéliciennes: Métaphysique et théologie* (Paris: Vrin-Reprise, 1985), 7–9.

22. *Metaphysics*, E, I, 1026 a 24–32; trans. W. D. Ross in *The Complete Works Aristotle*, II: 1620—modified translation.

23. See Hans Joachim Krämer, *Der Ursprung der Geistesmetaphysik* (Amsterdam: B. R. Grüner, 1964, 1967), 141: "*Im Bericht der akademischen* στοχεῖον-*Metaphysik ist nämlich die Wissenschaft von der Transzendenz und ihren* ἀρκαι *und* στοχεῖα *zugleich die Grundwissenshaft alles Seienden überhaupt, weil die Prinzipien alles Seiende in strenger Seinsableitung aus sich entlassen.*" (Freely translated: "In the domain of the metaphysics of the elements [that constitute beings], the science of transcendence, of

its principles and elements, is also the fundamental science of all Being in general because all beings are derived from these principles in a strict ontological manner.") See also Günther Patzig, "Theologie und Ontologie in der 'Metaphysik' des Aristoteles" in *Kant-Studien*, 52 (1964):185–205, especially 191: "First philosophy is a particular form of theology because it is also universal ontology." It is probably because of first philosophy's universality that Aristotle also discusses the principle of noncontradiction in book Γ. Since first philosophy inquires into the universal principles of Being, it must also inquire into the universal principles of thought.

24. See Martin Heidegger, "The Onto-Theo-Logical Constitution of Metaphysics," in *Identity and Difference*, trans. Joan Stambaugh (New York: Harper & Row, 1969), 42–74.

25. The text of *Metaphysics*, K, 7, 1064 b 10 repeats the text of *Metaphysics*, E.

26. In his famous article "Thema und Disposition der aristotelischen Metaphysik," in *Philosophische Monatshefte* (1888):37–65, 540–574.

27. See Ingemar Düring, *Aristoteles: Darstellung und Interpretation seines Denkens*, 117: "*Sonst hat Aristoteles den Ausdruck* θεολογική *weiter nie ernsthaft gebraucht. Der Name war ein zufälliger Einfall, parenthetisch motiviert, und hat kein Spur in seinem Schriften oder denen seiner Nachfolger hinterlassen*" ("Aristotle never seriously used the term *theologikè* anywhere else. The term was the product of sudden inspiration that belongs to a parenthesis and left no trace in any of his other writings nor in those of his successors."). Düring concludes that it is time we abandon the idea of Aristotelian theology ("*Mir scheint es, daß Zeit gekommen ist, den Ausdruck 'die Theologie des Aristotles' aufzugeben oder ihm wenigstens den ihm zukommenden anspruchslosen Platz zuzuweisen: er war ein bloßer Einfall, als Aristoteles ein Wort suchte, um die schöne Dreizahl zu erreichen.*").

28. See Werner Jaeger, *Aristoteles: Grundlegung einer Geschichte seiner Entwicklung* (Berlin: Weidmannsche Buchhandlung, 1966 [1923]), 198.

29. See *Metaphysics*, Δ, 7, 1017 a 7; E, 2, 1026 b 33.

30. *Categories*, 5, 2 a 11–19, trans. J. L. Ackrill in *The Complete Works of Aristotle*, I: 4. See also *Metaphysics*, Δ, 8 on the meanings of substance but without the distinction between primary and secondary substances.

31. On true Being, see Charles. H. Kahn, *The Verb "Be" in Ancient Greek* (Dordrecht, Netherlands: Reidel, 1973).

32. *On Sophistical Refutations*, 5, 167 a 2. In his book, *Being and Some Philosophers*, 2nd ed. (Toronto: Pontifical Institute of Medieval Studies, 1952 [1948]), Étienne Gilson argues the Greeks were less interested in the act of being, the *esse*, than the fact that it was something (τι) or a *quid*. The thought of Being (or of existence) is, according to him, the prerogative of Christian thought

and Thomism in particular. In an argument that parallels Heidegger's, but was most probably conceived independently, Gilson thus states that Greek thought is characterized by the forgetting of Being, in the sense of existence or the act of being.

33. *Metaphysics*, Z, 1, 1028 a 10, trans. William D. Ross, 1623.

34. *Metaphysics*, Z, 1, 1028, b 3, trans. William D. Ross, 1624.

35. See Ingemar Düring (*Aristoteles: Darstellung und Interpretation seines Denkens*, 96), who notes that Plato only uses the expression *kata olou* (*Meno*, 77 a, "in general"), and even then, only once.

36. See *Metaphysics*, Z, 3, 1029 a 30, where he clearly rejects the possibility of the *sunholon*, which later commentators would not always emphasize: "The substance compounded of both, i.e., of matter and form may be dismissed; for it is posterior and its nature is obvious."

37. See Richard Bodéüs, *Aristotle and the Theology of the Living Immortals*, trans. Jan Edward Garrett (Albany: SUNY Press, 2000), 76 ff. and 199 ff. Plato was the first to use the term *theologia* (*Republic*, 379 a).

38. See also *Physics*, VIII, 256 a 29; 257 a 8 ff.

39. Theophrastus (371–288 BCE), *Metaphysics*, trans. W. D. Ross and F. H. Fobes (Hildesheim, Germany: Georg Olms, 1967), 5 a 17 ff. (7 ff.). Hans Krämer's solution (in *Der Ursprung der Geistesmetaphysik*) is well known, but it is only a conjecture: The prime movers are the object of the first prime movers' thought.

40. Philipp Merlan has brilliantly drawn attention to their numerous similarities, see "Aristotle's Unmoved Movers," *Traditio*, 4 (1946):1–30.

41. *Metaphysics*, XII, 7, 1072 b 24: "If, then, God is always in that joyful state in which we are sometimes, this compels our wonder; and if in a better this compels it yet more. And God *is* in a better state."

42. See Hans-Georg Gadamer, "Parmenides oder das Diesseits des Seins," in *Griechische Philosophie II: Plato im Dialog*, GW, VII:281: "*So bin ich zu der paradoxen Folgerung gekommen, daß der von Aristoteles behauptete ontologische* χωρισμός *der Ideen einem Plato unterstellt worden ist, der nur einen methodischen Chorismos kannte. Der ontologische Chorismos ist dagegen eine Lehre des Aristoteles und nicht des Plato. Er hat den Gott von der physischen Bewegungswelt in der Weise getrennt, die er im Buch* Λ *der 'Metaphysik' entwickelt.*" "I thus came to the paradoxical conclusion that Aristotle wrongly attributed an ontological *chorismos* to Plato's ideas when the latter only argued for a methodological *chorismos*. The ontological *chorismos* is, in fact, Aristotle's doctrine and not Plato's. It was Aristotle who separated God from the physical world of movement, as he did in book Λ of the 'Metaphysics.'" See, 215 and 404 ff. See also *The Idea of the Good in Platonic-Aristotelian Philosophy*, trans. P. Christopher Smith (New Haven: Yale University Press, 1986).

4. The Last Summit of Classical Metaphysics: The Neoplatonic Eruption

1. See Hans Joachim Krämer, *Platonismus und hellenistische Philosophie* (Berlin: Walter de Gruyter, 1971), 18. See also Ingemar Düring, *Aristoteles: Darstellung und Interpretation seines Denkens* (Heidelberg, Germany: Carl Winter Verlag, 1966), 117. Düring claims that the Aristotelian division of sciences has been highly exaggerated. It was only with the Stoics, thus after Aristotle, that the division was systematized and became an end in itself. See Anthony A. Long and David N. Sedley, eds., *The Hellenistic Philosophers*, 2 vols. (New York: Cambridge University Press, 1987), I:160 ff.

2. See Hans Krämer, *Der Ursprung der Geistmetaphysik* (Amsterdam: P. Schippers, 1964), 11. On the Stoic ontology, see the fragments collected by Anthony Long and David Sedley, *The Hellenistic Philosophers*, I:162–182.

3. Plotinus, *The Enneads*, VI, 9, 5. We shall use Arthur H. Armstrong's translation in Plotinus, *The Enneads in Six Volumes* (Cambridge, MA: Harvard University Press, The Loeb Classical Library, 1966). Unless otherwise indicated, we shall refer to Porphyry's classification: volume, ennead, and section.

4. See Hans Krämer, *Der Ursprung der Geistmetaphysik*, 292: "*Plotin versteht sich als Erneuerer und Interpret des Philosophie Platons und nicht weiter.*" (Plotinus saw himself as a reviver and interpreter of Plato's philosophy, and no more.)

5. Porphyry, "On the Life of Plotinus and the Order of his Books," in *The Enneads*, trans. A. H. Armstrong, 6 vols. (Cambridge: Harvard University Press, 1966), I:3.

6. See the introduction to Plotinus, *Treatise 25*, II, 5 in Jean-Marc Narbonne's translation (Paris: Cerf, 1998), 18.

7. *Enneads*, VI, 9: "*Treatise 9*" is the chronologically ninth treatise (of 54). VI, 9 means it is the final treatise of Porphyry's compilation and therefore the apex.

8. Plotinus, *Treatise 9* (*Enneads*, VI, 9, 1), trans. Armstrong.

9. Hypostasis literally means standing (*stasis*) under (*hypo*) the One. Although Plotinus does use the term *hypostasis*, many translators prefer using the term *existence*, which gives a modern feel to Neoplatonism. See Pierre Hadot's warning in his translation in *Traité 50 (Enneads, III, 5)*, (Paris, Cerf, 1990), 24: "One must not use the expression 'the three hypostases' since Plotinus never used it to…summarize his doctrine. For Plotinus, the word *hypostasis* generally means 'existence' or the 'substantial product' of a transcendental reality. It is not used in a technical way to designate the Good, the Spirit, and the soul. The title of *Treatise 10* (*Enneads*, V, 1) 'On the Three Hypostases' does not square with Plotinus's use of the term and was probably given by Porphyry." Jean-Michel Narbonne concurs in his translation

of *Treatise 25* (*Enneads*, II, 5) (Paris: Cerf, 1998), 61. But does this not mean that we claim to understand Plotinus better than Porphyry who knew him?

10. Plotinus, *Enneads*, V, 2, trans. Arthur H. Armstrong: "the One, perfect because it seeks nothing, has nothing, and needs nothing, overflows, as it were, and its superabundance makes something other than itself."

11. *Enneads*, VI, 9, 3.

12. Ibid., V, 3, 12.

13. Ibid., VI, 9, 4.

14. Ibid., 9, 9.

15. Ibid., V, 3, 17.

16. On this "separation," see *Enneads*, III, 7. Augustine later took up the notion in his *Confessions*, see Saint Augustine of Hippo, *The Confessions*, 2nd ed., trans. Francis J. Sheed (Indianapolis, IN: Hackett, 2006 [1993]), 255 (Book XI, Chapter 29, Section 39). See also *On the Trinity*, IX, 1.

17. See "Fragment du commentaire de Porphyre sur 'Sur le Parmenide,'" in Pierre Hadot, *Porphyre et Victorinus*, 2 vols. (Paris: Études augustiniennes, 1968), II: 104–105. See also Pierre Hadot's comments, I:252, 248.

18. See Alain de Libera, *La philosophie médiévale* (Paris: PUF, 1993), 248 ff.

19. See James J. O'Donnell, "Augustine: His Time and Lives," in *The Cambridge Companion to Augustine*, ed. Eleonore Stump and Norman Kretzmann (Cambridge: Cambridge University Press, 2001), 10.

20. Augustine was not as well versed in Aristotle's works. In his *Confessions* (IV, 16, 29), Augustine admits being put off by the dryness of the *Categories*. He seems not to have known Aristotle's *Metaphysics*. In fact, Aristotle's writings had the reputation of being quite difficult to understand. (See Augustine's *On the Profit of Believing*, 6, 13: "*libros Aristotelis reconditos et obscuros.*")

21. See James O'Donnell, "Augustine the African": "Thus at age thirty, Augustine had won the most visible academic chair in the Latin world." (The text is quoted from the one that can be found on the following Web site http://www9. georgetown.edu/faculty/jod/augustine/) The site also contains O'Donnell's commentary on the *Confessions* first published in 1992: *Augustine: Confessions*, 3 vols. (Oxford, UK: Clarendon, 1992). It will be used in the following.

22. See Saint Augustine of Hippo, *Against the Academicians and the Teacher*, trans. Peter King (Indianapolis: Hackett, 1995); *On Order*, trans. Silvano Borrusco (South Bend, IN: St. Augustine, 2007); *Soliloquies and the Immorality of the Soul*, trans. Gerard Watson (Warminster, PA: Aris & Phillips, 1990); "The Happy Life," in *Augustine of Hippo: Selected Writings*, ed. Mary T. Clark (Mahwah, NJ: Pauline, 1984), 163–194.

23. *Confessions*, trans. Francis J. Sheed, 211 (X, 29, 40).

24. See James J. O'Donnell's commentary on 7.1.1. (*Augustine: The Confessions*, II: 394): "The immutability of God can scarcely be called a Christian doctrine, insofar as there is little explicit Christian scripture to warrant such an assertion. . . . The challenge for any Christian doctrine of immutability, of course, is that there is plenty of evidence that God is mutable—if the Old Testament is to be read literally. . . . A. does not hesitate to credit the Platonists with seeing the link between immutability and a correct notion of God as bodiless."

25. See O'Donnell, commentary on 7.9.13 (*Augustine: The Confessions*, II:413) "The present passage has been the focus of every debate in the present century over the meaning of A.'s intellectual autobiography. What books of the Platonists did he read? What effect did they have upon him—in 386 and later? As heirs of generations of patient investigation, we can discuss those questions with greater precision than ever, but they continue to elude decisive, and universally acclaimed, answer."

26. *Confessions*, 126 (VII, 9, 13). Translation modified.

27. Ibid., 127 (VII, 9, 14): "but I did not find that the *word became flesh and dwelt among us.*"

28. See O'Donnell, *Augustine: Confessions*, 413, at 7.9.13: "Central to A.'s presentation of the doctrines of the Platonists, he employs a rhetorical device that has gone comparatively unattended. He does not quote or paraphrase the Platonic books themselves (thereby making their identification difficult), but he quotes the *ipsissima verba* of Christian scripture as though they offered a fair summary of contents of an non-Christian philosophical work; incidentally the device allows close comparison of the doctrines of Platonists and Christians. He has already employed the device, in his last account of reading a philosophical classic, the *Hortensius* (at 3.4.8 quoting Col. 2. 8–9 . . .). The syncretism he makes is one that seemed obvious at the time."

29. *Confessions*, 128 (VII, 10, 16): "*admonitus redire ad memetipsum.*"

30. Ibid., 128–29 (VII, 10, 16)—translation modified. See also *Enneads*, I, 6 and 9; V, 3.

31. Ibid., 129 (VII, 11, 17): "*Et inspexi cetera infra te et vidi nec omnino esse nec omnino non esse: esse quidem, quoniam abs te sunt, non esse autem, quoniam id quod es non sunt. Id enim vere est quod incommutabiliter manet.*"

32. On God understood as *Idipsum*, "being itself," see the insightful note in French edition of Augustine's complete works, *Œuvres*, 85 vols. (Paris: Desclée, De Brouwer, Bibliothèque augustinienne, 1941–), XIV:550–552.

33. *Confessions*, 255 (XI, 29, 39), translation modified. See also *The City of God against the Pagans*, trans. R. W. Dyson (Cambridge: Cambridge University Press, 1998), IX, 17, 382: "the soul of man is unlike that incorporeal and immutable and

eternal Being in proportion as it longs for temporal and mutable things . . . and so to remedy this condition of separation from God, a mediator is indeed needed."

34. On this transition and Augustine's appropriation of Platonism, see Joachim Ritter, *Mundus intelligibilis. Eine Untersuchtung zur Aufnahme und Umwandlung der neuplatonischen Ontologie bei Augustinus* [A study on Augustine's revival and transformation of Neoplatonic ontology] (Frankfurt, Germany: Klosstermann, 2001 [1937]).

35. *The City of God*, 382 (IX, 17): "*Fugiendum est igitru ad carissimam patriam, et ibi pater et ibi omnia. Quæ igitur, inquit, classis aut fuga? Similem Deo fieri.*" On this, see François Joseph Thonnard's note, "Sur une citation de Plotin" in *Œuvres*, 34: 614–616. He recalls that although "*similem deo fieri*" (become like God) is not in Plotinus's text (*Enneads*, I, 6, 8), it is not foreign to his thought, which echoes a famous passage from Plato's *Theaetetus* (176 a) on the *homoiôsis theô*, becoming equal to the divine.

5. Metaphysics and Theology in the Middle Ages

1. For example, see Descartes's famous letters to Mersenne of 11 November 1640 (qtd. in Jean-Luc Marion, *On Descartes' Metaphysical Prism*, trans. Jeffrey L. Kosky, [Chicago: University of Chicago Press, 1999], 32): "Yesterday, I sent my *Metaphysics* to M. de Zuytlichem [Huygens] to post to you [. . .]"; "I am finally sending to you my work on metaphysics, which I have not yet put a title on, so that I can make you its godfather and leave the baptism to you." I cannot think of any medieval author who spoke in this way of "his" metaphysics.

2. See Jean-Luc Marion, "La science toujours recherchée et toujours manquante," in *La métaphysique: Son histoire, sa critique ses enjeux*, ed. Jean-Marc Narbonne and Luc Langlois (Paris/Québec: Vrin/PUL, 1999), 21—freely translated from the French.

3. See Luc Brisson, "Aristotélisme," in *La philosophie grecque*, ed. Monique Canto-Sperber (Paris: PUF, 1997), 688.

4. On the history of the *translatio studiorum*, see Alain de Libera, *La philosophie médiévale* (Paris: PUF, 1993), as well as Luc Brisson's excellent work on the transmission of Plato's and Aristotle's philosophy in *La philosophie grecque*.

5. On God as *principium*, see Saint Augustine of Hippo, *The Trinity*, trans. Edmund Hill in *The Works of Saint Augustine: A translation for the 21st century*, 35 vols., ed. John Rotelle (New York: New City, 1990–), V: 198 (Book V, Chapter 3).

6. See Alain de Libera, *La philosophie médiévale*, 249.

7. Ibid.

8. See Ludger Honnefelder, "Transzendence oder transzendental: über die Möglichkeit von Metaphysics," in *Philosophisches Jahrbuch*, 91 (1985): 275.

9. See Alain de Libera, *La philosophie médiévale*, 323—freely translated from the original French.

10. For more on medieval metaphysics, see the works of Etienne Gilson, particularily *L'Être et l'essence*, 2nd ed. (Paris: Vrin, 1962 [1948]) partially translated into English as *Being and Some Philosophers*, 2nd ed. (Toronto: Pontifical Institute of Medieval Studies, 1952 [1948]), but also Paul Wilpert, ed., *Die Metaphysik im Mittelalter: Ihr Ursprung und ihre Bedeutung* (Berlin: Walter de Gruyter, 1963); Albert Zimmermann, *Ontologie oder Metaphysik? Die Diskussion über den Gegenstand der Metaphysik im 13. und 14. Jahrhundert* (Louvain, Belgium: Peeters, 1998 [1965]); Alain De Libera, "Genèse et structure des métaphysiques médiévales," in *La métaphysique: Son histoire, sa critique, ses enjeux*, ed. Jean-Marc Narbonne and Luc Langlois (Paris/Québec: Vrin/PUL, 1999), 159–181; Jean-François Courtine, *Suarez et le système de la métaphysique* (Paris: PUF, 1990); Ludger Honnefelder, *Ens inquantum ens: Der Begriff des Seienden als solchen als Gegenstand der Metaphysik nach der Lehre des Johannes Duns Scotus* (Münster: Aschendorff, 1979) and *Scientia transcendens: Die formale Bestimmung der Seiendheit und Realität in der Metaphysik des Mittelalters und der Neuzeit (Duns Scotus, Suárez, Wolff, Kant, Peirce)* (Hamburg, Germany: Meiner, 1990); Jan A. Aersten and Andreas Speer, eds., *Was ist Philosophie im Mittelalter?* (Berlin: de Gruyter, 1998).

11. On the Latin word *fides*, see the article in Alfred Ernout and Antoine Meillet, ed., *Dictionnaire étymmologique de la langue latine: histoire des mots*, 4th ed. (Paris: Klincksieck, 1959), 233: "The root [of *fido*] is the same as the Greek *peithomai* 'I trust'" The word became important for Romans law: "solemn commitment, guarantee, oath"; hence "good faith, loyalty, trust given to one's word," etc. Somebody who is not worthy of *fidus* is *"perfidus"*, perfidious, unfaithful. See also Rudolf Bultmann's article on *pisteuô* in Gerhard Kittel and Gerhard Friedrich eds., *Theological Dictionary of the New Testament*, 10 vols. (Grand Rapids, MI: Eerdmans, 1964–1976), VI:203–228.

12. On curiosity, see the third part of Hans Blumenberg's book, *The Legitimacy of the Modern Age*, trans. Robert M. Wallace (Cambridge, MA: MIT Press, 1983).

13. Tertullian, *Apology*, trans. T. R. Glover (Cambridge, MA: Harvard University Press, 1960), see chap. XVII and XLIX.

14. See Alain De Libera, *La philosophie médiévale*, 5: "Justinian's decision can be easily explained. The Emperor's principal objective was to unify the empire, and religious unity was essential and indispensable for imperial politics."

15. Ibid.

16. See *Metaphysics*, 993 b 20: "philosophy should be called knowledge of truth" (ἐπιστήμη τῆς ἀληθείας / *episteme tès aletheias*).

17. See the excellent commentary annexed to Bernard Pautrat's translation: Anselm de Cantorbery, *Proslogion: Allocution sur l'existence de Dieu* (Paris: Garnier-Flammarion, 1993).

18. Anselm, "Proslogion" in *Basic Writings*, trans. Thomas Williams (Indianapolis, IN: Hackett, 2007), 81.

19. Anselm, *Proslogion*, 82—translation modified for clarity.

20. Ibid.—translation modified.

21. Étienne Gilson, *La philosophie au Moyen Age*, 2 vols. (Paris: Petite Bibliothèque Payot, 1976 [1922, 1944]), I:246.

22. See Jean-Luc Marion, "Is the Argument Ontological? The Anselmian Proof and the Two Demonstrations of the Existence of God in the *Meditations*," in *Cartesian Questions: Method and Metaphysics*, trans. Jean-Luc Marion and Jeffrey L. Kosky (Chicago: University of Chicago Press, 1999), 145–146.

23. This is what Étienne Gilson does in *La philosophie au Moyen Âge*, I:249: "An idea of God exist in my mind: this is enough."

24. Jean-Luc Marion, "Is the Argument Ontological? The Anselmian Proof and the Two Demonstrations of the Existence of God in the *Meditations*," in *Cartesian Questions: Method and Metaphysics*, 146.

25. But a monk named Gaunilon also contested the argument during Anselm's lifetime. See Étienne Gilson, *La philosophie au Moyen Âge*, I:246: "Gaunilon argued that one cannot derive something's actual existence from its existence in one's mind. That a thing exists as an object of thought does not mean it actually exists, it simply means that one can conceive of it. There are a number of imaginary, or impossible, objects that despite existing in the mind certainly have no existence outside of one's mind."

26. Alain De Libera, *La philosophie médiévale*, I:116. See also Alain de Libera, "Genèse et structure des métaphysiques médiévales," in *La métaphysique: Son histoire, sa critique, ses enjeux*, 165: "What is normally called 'metaphysics' in the history of medieval thought starts with appearance of the Arab peripatetic corpus. This includes the question of its subject: Being as Being (*ens inquantum ens*), as Avicenna argues (in which case *philosophia prima sive scientia divina* must prove God's existence), or substance and the principles of substances, as Averroes argues (in which case physics must demonstrate God's existence as a Prime Mover, rather than the Avicennian God, who is the first agent of Being as Being)."

27. Jean Pierre Langelier, "Avicenne, le savant épicurien," *Le Devoir*, July 29 2000.

28. A term Avicenna will use to describe knowledge of "what is after nature." *The Metaphysics of The Healing*, trans. Michael E. Marmura (Provo: Brigham Young University Press, 2005), Book I, Chapter 3, 18. Note that the Arabic text appears on the facing page.

29. See Luc Brisson, *La métaphysique: Son histoire, sa critique, ses enjeux*, 43; Alain de Libera, "Genèse et structure...," 162.

30. See George Anawati's preface to his authoritative French translation, *La métaphysique du Shifa*, 2 vols. (Paris: Vrin, 1978), I:12 ff.

31. An English translation exists under the title *The Metaphysics of Avicenna: A Critical Translation-Commentary and Analysis of the Fundamental Arguments in Avicenna's* Metaphysica *in the* Danish Nama-i 'ala'i *(The Book of the Scientific Knowledge)*, trans. Parviz Morewedge (London: Routledge & Kegan Paul, 1973).

32. See George Anawati, *La métaphysique du Shifa*, I:25—our translation from the French.

33. See Alain de Libera, *La philosophie médiévale*, 113: "It was Avicenna who introduced the West to Aristotelian thought, and even to philosophy itself."

34. The biography was inserted at the beginning of the Latin version during the Middle Ages. See George Anawati, "Preface," in *Métaphysique du Shifa*, 62.

35. See Anawati, *Métaphysique du Shifa*, I:12 and the Latin edition, *Avicenna Latinus: Liber de Philosophia prima sive scientia divina*, 3 vols., ed. Simone van Riet (Louvain/Leiden: Peeters/Brill, 1977), I:1.

36. Anawati, *Métaphysique du Shifa*, I:12.

37. In the West, but also in the Arab world, Aristotle was understood through the "Book of Causes" (*Liber de causis*) then attributed to Aristotle. We now know it was written by an Arab author inspired by Proclus's *Elements of Theology*. The *Liber de causis* was one of the most commented books during the Middle Ages and had an important effect on the way Aristotle's metaphysics was understood. For an English translation, see *The Book of Causes*, trans. Dennis J. Brand (Milwaukee: Marquette University Press, 1984). See also Henri-Dominique Saffrey, "L'état actuel des recherches sur le *Liber de causis* comme source de la métaphysique au Moyen Âge," in *Die Metaphysik im Mittelater: Ihr Ursprung und ihr Bedeutung*, Paul Wilpert, ed. (Berlin: Walter de Gruyter, 1963), 267–281; Alain de Libera, *La philosophie médiévale*, 78 ff.; Cristina D'Ancona Costa, *Recherches sur le* Liber de causis (Paris: Vrin, 1995).

38. See Albert Zimmermann, *Ontologie oder Metaphysik? Die Diskussion über den Gegenstand der Metaphysik im 13. und 14. Jahrhundert*, 144: "*In Avicennas Metaphysik finden die mittelalterlichen Philosophen das eigentliche Vorbild für eine systematische Untersuchung der Frage, was das Subjekt dieser Wissenschaft sei*" ("Medieval philosophers found in Avicenna's metaphysics their model for dealing systematically with the question of the object of metaphysics.").

39. Avicenna, *The Metaphysics of the Healing*, I, 1, 3. *Avicenna Latinus*, I, 1, 5. The idea a science's subject is already admitted by the science is found in Aristotle's *Posterior Analytics* (I, 10, 76 b 11–16).

40. Although the English translation uses the expression "existent inasmuch as it is an existent," we follow Dr. Grondin, who refers to the Latin translation ("*ens, inquantum est ens*"), and says Being as Being (*l'être en tant qu'être*).

41. See Alain de Libera, *La philosophie médiévale*, I:115: "He is the first to define the object (the Latin *subjectum*) of metaphysics as 'Being as Being' rather than God, even though, this is the crux of his argument, metaphysics must demonstrate his existence." See Albert Zimmermann, *Ontologie oder Metaphysik?*, 148, who recalls, following Joseph Owens (see chap. 3, note 19), that Avicenna is also the first author for whom "Being as Being" does not designate the Supreme, theological, being, but Being in all its ontological amplitude.

42. Avicenna, *The Metaphysics of the Healing*, I, 2, 9. *Avicenna Latinus*, I, 2, 12: "*Igitur ostensum est tibi ex his omnibus quod ens, inquantum est ens, est commune omnibus his et quod ipsum debi poni subiectum huius magisterii.*"

43. Avicenna, *Metaphysics of the Healing*, I, 2, 10. *Avicenna Latinus*, I, 2, 13: "*Ideo primum subiectum huius scientiæ est ens; et ea quæ inquirit sunt consequentia ens, inquantum est ens sine condicione.*"

44. Avicenna, *Metaphysics of the Healing*, I, 2, 10. *Avicenna Latinus*, I, 2, 13: "*Quorum quædam sunt ei quasi species, ut substantia, quantitas et qualitas, quoniam esse non eget dividi in alia priusquam in ista, sicut substantia eget dividi in alia antequam perveniat ad dividendum in hominem et non hominem.*"

45. Avicenna, *Metaphysics of the Healing*, I, 5, 22. *Avicenna Latinus*, I, 5, 29: "*Dicemus igitur quod res et ens et necesse talia sunt quod statim imprimuntur in anima prima impressione.*"

46. Avicenna, *The Metaphysics of the Healing*, I, 5, 24. *Avicenna Latinus*, I, 5, 31. See Alain de Libera's insightful explanations in *La querelle des universaux* (Paris: Seuil, 1996), 186, 316.

47. Avicenna, *The Metaphysics of the Healing*, I, 5, 27 ff. *Avicenna Latinus*, I, 5, 34.

48. Avicenna, *The Metaphysics of the Healing*, I, 5, 28. *Avicenna Latinus*, I, 5, 36.

49. Avicenna, *The Metaphysics of the Healing*, I, 7, 38. *Avicenna Latinus*, I, 7, 47: "*Eius autem quod est possibile esse, iam manifesta est ex hoc proprietas, scilicet quia ipsum necessario eget alio quod faciat illud esse in effectu.*" On what follows, see Ulrich Rudolf, "La preuve de l'existence de Dieu chez Avicenne et dans la théologie musulmane," in *Langages et philosophie: Hommages à Jean Jolivet*, ed. Alain de Libera, Abdelali Elamrani-Jamal and Alain Galonnier (Paris: Vrin, 1997), 339–346.

50. Avicenna, *The Metaphysics of the Healing*, VIII, 4, 276: "Hence, there is no quiddity for necessary Being other than it being necessary Being. And this is the thing's Being [*al-anniyya*]—translation modified.

51. Avicenna, *The Metaphysics of the Healing*, VIII, 4, 273–274; *Avicenna Latinus*, VIII, 4, 343.

52. See Ulrich Rudolf, "La preuve de l'existence de Dieu chez Avicenne et dans la théologie musulmane," 343.

53. Avicenna, *The Metaphysics of the Healing*, IX, 1, 306 ff; *Avicenna Latinus*, IX, 1, 380.

54. Ibid., *The Metaphysics of the Healing*, VIII, 6, 287; *Avicenna Latinus*, VIII, 6, 358. Thomas Aquinas will contest this idea and assert that God also knows singular objects (*Summa Contra Gentiles*, chap. 65) and even base objects (chap. 70).

55. Ibid., *The Metaphysics of the Healing*, VIII, 7, 291; *Avicenna Latinus*, VIII, 7, 101. See also IX, 4, 330–331 (*Avicenna Latinus*, IX, 4, 406): "The separated intellects are numerically many. Therefore, they do not come into existence from the first simultaneously; but it must be the case that the highest of them is the first existent proceeding from Him, followed successively by one intellect after another. Because there is beneath each intellect a sphere with its matter and its form, which is the soul, and also an intellect below it, there is beneath each intellect three things in existence. [...] Thus, there necessarily follows from the first intellect, inasmuch as it intellectually apprehends the First, the existence of an intellect beneath it. Inasmuch as it intellectually apprehends itself, there follows from it the existence of the form of the outermost sphere and its perfection—namely the soul."

56. Avicenna, *The Metaphysics of the Healing*, IX, 3, 325; *Avicenna Latinus*, IX, 3, 401.

57. Averroes, *The Decisive Treatise: Determining the Connection Between the Law and Wisdom*, trans. Charles E. Butterworth (Provo: Brigham Young University, 2001).

58. See Averroes, *Grand Commentaire de la métaphysique, livre Beta*, trans. Laurence Bauloye (Paris: Vrin, 2002). See also Zimmermann, *Ontologie oder Metaphysik?*, 152 ff.

59. Ibid.

60. See Alain de Libera, *Averroès et l'averroïsme* (Paris: PUF, 1991), 24: "Everything that is mobile has a mover, he says, and it is moved insofar as it is its potential, but a mover moves by being an act. Although a mover may stop moving, it remains mobile insofar as it conserves the ability to move even though it is not moving. If we say the universe's ultimate motor moves occasionally, there must be necessarily some other motor prior to it. If we suppose that this other motor also moves intermittently, the same applies to it as did on the first case. Therefore, either we must continue in this way for infinity, or we must admit the existence of some other motor that is neither moved and nor moves by essence or by accident. This motor would be eternal and so would be what it moves. Ibn Rushd continues: 'if, in fact, at a given moment it was only potentially moved by this supposed eternal mover, there would be some other mover prior to it. As soon as we know there is an eternal movement to celestial bodies, we must conclude that this eternal movement is the celestial movement, whose motor is eternal and whose existence has already been demonstrated (see *Physics*, VIII, 256 a 13).'"

61. Alain de Libera, *Averroès et l'averroïsme*, 153.

62. Ibid., 27: "For a philosopher such a Ibn Rushd, God always created the universe. To say he created it at a given moment implies the appearance in him of a cause that would have provoked this creation."

63. See Étienne Gilson, *l'Être et l'essence*, 84 (the passage is omitted in the English translation): "We do not have general presentation of what would have been a 'thomistic philosophy' written by Saint Thomas himself. But its main theses are encountered in his theological writings, where the historian can see them at work." See also Olivier Boulnois, "Quand commence l'ontothéologie? Aristote, Thomas d'Aquin et Duns Scotus," in *Revue thomiste*, 95 (1995): 101: "All of Thomas's efforts were directed towards theology. For him, metaphysics is only a program given in a few definitions of science (especially in his commentary on Boethius' *De Trinitate*) and by his commentary on Aristotle. He never develops his own metaphysics. We may even say: he does not give to metaphysics the status of a rigorous science, it is a science in a general sense. A rigorous science is founded upon unequivocal concepts. But, as Thomas emphasizes, beings are not unequivocal. Metaphysics only uses such terms and therefore it can be a science only in the general sense of the term."

64. Saint Thomas Aquinas, *Summa Theologiae*, trans. by English Dominicans (New York: Christian Classics, 1981). We shall quote it by referring to Question (q.) follow by Article (art.).

65. Aquinas, *Summa Theologiae*, I, q. 1, art. 7: "But in this science, the treatment is mainly about God; for it is called theology, as treating of God [*sermo de Deo*]. Therefore God is the object of this science."

66. Ibid., art. 5.

67. Saint Thomas Aquinas, *Summa Contra Gentiles*, trans. by English Dominicans (London: Burns, Oates, & Washbourne, 1934).

68. Saint Thomas Aquinas, *Commentary on the Metaphysics of Aristotle*, trans. John P. Rowan (Chicago: Henry Regnery, 1961), 1–2. See also Suzanne Mansion, "L'intélligibilité métaphysique d'après le *Proemium* du commentaire de saint Thomas à la métaphysique d'Aristote," in *Rivista di filosofia neo-scolastica*, 70 (1978):49–62; and Jean-François Courtine, *Suarez et le système de la métaphysique* (Paris: PUF, 1990), 31–99. Étienne Gilson also uses this text to introduce Thomas in *L'Être et l'essence*, 82 ff; *Being and some Philosophers*, 154 ff.

69. Saint Thomas Aquinas, *Commentary on the Metaphysics of Aristotle*, trans. John P. Rowan (Chicago: Henry Regnery Company, 1961), 1.

70. See Olivier Boulnois, "Quand commence l'ontothéologie?" 100.

71. See, for example, *Summa Theologiae*, I, q. 2, art. 1, *Utrum Deus esse, sit per se notum*. "Whether the proposition 'God exists' is self-evident?"

72. Saint Thomas Aquinas, *Summa Theologiae*, I, q. 2, art. 1.

73. Ibid., art. 3.

74. Saint Thomas Aquinas, *On Being and Essence*, 2nd ed., trans. Armand Maurer (Toronto: Pontifical Institute of Medieval Studies, 1968), 61. See Saint Augustine, *On the Trinity*, trans. Edmund Hill in *The Works of Saint Augustine*, V: 190 (V, II, 3): "And who can be more than he that said to his servant, '*I am who I am*' . . . thus only that which not only does not but also absolutely cannot change deserves without qualification to be said really and truly to be." (*"Et quis magis est, quam ille qui dixit famulo suo Moysi: 'ego sum qui sum'. . . ; ac per hoc illud solum quod non tantum non mutatur, verum etiam mutari omnino non potest, sine scrupulo occurrit quod verissime dicatur esse."*).

75. Étienne Gilson, *L'Être et l'essence*, 107; *Being and some Philosophers*, 172–173. We translate the original French.

76. *Summa Contra Gentiles*, 53 ff.; *Summa Theologiae* I, q. 3, art. 4.

77. See Étienne Gilson's note on the term *existentia* in *L'Être et l'essence*, 344 ff (this appendix is not in the English translation). The verb *existere* is a classic. Its meaning comes across quite well in the following passage from Livy (*History of Rome*, XXXIX, 37, 3): "*Si existat hodie ab inferis Lucurgus, gaudeat ruinis eorum*" ("if Lycurgus should rise form the dead today"). Descartes will have no qualms speaking of God's *existere* (notably in the title of his third Meditation: "*De Deo, quod existat*"), without any after thought, of course, but this existence also "emerges" from something, namely the *cogito*.

78. See Jean-François Courtine, *Suarez et le système de la métaphysique*, 55. One may distinguish the Latin meaning of *existentia* from the emphatic sense it have been given in the twentieth century's "philosophies of existence," such as those of Heidegger, Jaspers and Sartre. For Heidegger, the term existence, which we may write with a hyphen ("ex-sist"), characterizes human nature, which can retreat away from the world of beings, of things that are, and be exposed to Being, the "wonders of wonders, that is, that there is something rather than nothing."

79. Even if Albert Magnus attributes it to Avicenna.

80. See Duns Scotus, "Man's Natural Knowledge of God," in *Philosophical Writings*, trans. Allan Wolter (Indianapolis, IN: Hackett, 1987), 13–33. On the life and work of Duns Scotus see the Introduction in *Philosophical Writings* (xiii–xxx); see also Ludger Honnefelder, *La métaphysique comme science transcendantale* (Paris: PUF, 2002), 19 ff.

81. Jean-François Courtine, *Suarez et le système de la métaphysique*, 139—our translation from the original French.

82. Ibid., 139–140—our translation from the original French.

83. See the text quoted by Courtine, *Suarez et le système de la métaphysique*, 148: "*Igitur Metaphysica transcendens est tota prior scientia divina, et ita essent quatuor scientiæ speculative, una transcendens, et aliæ tres speciales.*"

84. Courtine, *Suarez et le système de la métaphysique*, 152–153; Albert Zimmermann, *Ontologie oder Metaphysik?*, 327: Ludger Honnefelder, *La métaphysique comme science transcendentale*, 76.

85. See Duns Scotus, "Man's Natural Knowledge of God," in *Philosophical Writings*, 13–33; See also Ludger Honnefelder, *Ens in quantum ens: Der Begriff des Seienden als solchen als Gegenstand der Metaphysik nach der Lehre des Johannes Duns Scotus* (Münster, Germany: Aschendorft, 1979), 396–405; *Scientia transcendens: Die formale Bestimmung der Seienheit und Realität in der Metaphysik des Mittelalters und Neuzeit (Duns Scotus, Suárez, Wolff, Kant, Peirce)*, (Hamburg, Germany: Meiner, 1990); "Transzendent oder transzendental: über dir Möglichkeit von Metaphysik" in *Philosophische Jahrbuch*, 91 (1985): 273–290.

86. Duns Scotus, "Man's Natural Knowledge of God," 20 (*Ordinatio* I, 3, 26).

87. Duns Scotus, "Concerning Metaphysics," in *Philosophical Writings*, 4.

88. Quoted in Étienne Gilson, *Being and Some Philosophers*, 88–89 (*L'Être et l'essence*, 134).

89. Étienne Gilson, *L'Être et l'essence*, 135 (*Being and some Philosophers*, 89). See also Ludger Honnefelder, *La métaphysique comme science transcendentale*, 77.

90. Gilson, *L'Être et l'essence*, 136; Honnefelder, *La métaphysique comme science transcendentale*, 54.

91. The distinction was already present in the little-known author, François de Marchia, which Albert Zimmermann emphasizes (*Ontologie oder Metaphysik?*, 358 ff.). He also includes a manuscript of Marchia's (84–100) with the following important passage: "*Quod duplex est metaphysica, quædam communis, et quædam propria sive particularis. Et secundum hoc dico, quod subjectum metaphysicæ [communis] est res communis ad omnes res primæ intentionis, non secundum quod est contracta ad rem determinati generis nec substantiæ simplicis nec quantitatis nec causarum ultimarum nec ad rem abstractam vel non abstractam, sed ut est res communis ad omnes res primæ intentionis. Subjectum vero metaphysicæ particularis est res separata a materia secundum essentiam et secundum rationem.*"

92. See Jean-François Courtine, *Suarez et le système de la métaphysique*, 331 (who remarks that Suarez still uses the couple *communis-particularis*, 334.)

93. See Courtine, *Suarez et le système de la métaphysique*, 415.

94. Ibid., 453.

95. See also what Martin Heidegger says in the first paragraph of *Kant and the Problem of Metaphysics* (1926); most recent English translation: *Kant and the Problem of Metaphysics*, trans. Richard Taft (Bloomington: Indiana University Press, 1997).

96. See Courtine, *Suarez et le système de la métaphysique*, 335 (on the first book of Suarez's *Disputationes*): "The *Disputationes*' task, in their first part, is therefore to present and explicate the *universalissima ratio entis*, that is, the meaning of Being, the properties and principles that are beyond all specific or generic differences and common to all beings." The pages of Courtine's book on "transcendental" philosophy are very helpful for understanding transcendental thought and its ontological orientation.

97. On the importance of efficient causality and the rejection of final causes implied by Ockham's position, see André Muralt, "La causalité divine et le primat de l'efficience chez Guillaume d'Occam," in *Historia philosophiæ medii oevi. Festschrift für Kurt Flasch*, 2 vols. (Amsterdam: B.R. Grüner, 1991), II: 744–769.

98. See the second part of Hans Blumenberg, *The Legitimacy of the Modern Age*, trans. Robert M. Wallace (Cambridge, MA: MIT Press, 1983).

99. See Alain De Libera, *La philosophie médiévale*, 438. See also his book *La querelle des universaux* (Paris: PUF, 1997).

100. See Alain De Libera, *La philosophie médiévale*, 440 ff.

101. See Jean-François Courtine, *Suarez et le système de la métaphysique*, 460 ff.

102. See ibid., 449.

6. Descartes: First Philosophy According to the *Cogito*

1. See Jean-François Courtine, *Suarez et le système de la métaphysique*, (Paris: PUF, 1990), 410, 449, 454.

2. Johannes Clauberg, *Elementa philosophiæ sive Ontosophia* (Gronigen, 1647). See Jean-Luc Marion, "Descartes et l'onto-théologie," in *Bulletin de la Société française de philosophie*, Séance du 24 avril 1982, 154.

3. Jean-Luc Marion, *On Descartes' Metaphysical Prism: The Constitution and Limits of Onto-Theo-Logy in Cartesian Thought*, trans. Jeffrey L. Kosky (Chicago: University of Chicago Press, 1999), 67, 72–73. See also, "Descartes et l'onto-théologie," 123.

4. Jean-Luc Marion, "Descartes et l'onto-théologie," 120.

5. In the following we are indebted to the work of Jean-Luc Marion: *Descartes's Grey Ontology: Cartesian Science and Aristotelian Thought in the Regulae* (South Bend: St. Augustine's Press, 2004); *Sur la théologie blanche de Descartes* (Paris: PUF, 1981); *On Descartes' Metaphysical Prism: The Constitution and Limits of Onto-Theo-Logy in Cartesian Thought*, trans. Jeffrey L. Kosky (Chicago: University of Chicago Press, 1999); *Cartesian Questions: Method and Metaphysics*, trans. Jean-Luc Marion and Jeffrey L. Kosky (Chicago: Chicago University Press, 1999); *On the Ego and on*

God: Further Cartesian Questions, trans. Christina M. Gschwandtner (New York: Fordham University Press, 2007).

6. René Descartes, *Letters to Mersenne of 11 November 1630*, qtd. in *On Descartes' Metaphysical Prism*, trans. Jeffrey L. Kosky, 32.

7. René Descartes, "Meditations on First Philosophy," in *Discourse on Method and Meditations on First Philosophy*, 4th ed., trans. Donald A. Cress (Indianapolis/ Cambridge: Hackett Publishing, 1998), 52 (AT: VII, 9).

8. On this, see Manfred Riedel, "Grund und Abgrund der Sujektivität. Nach-cartesianische Meditationen," in *Hören auf die Sprache: Die akroamtische Dimension der Hermeneutik* (Frankfurt, Germany: Suhrkamp, 1990), 19; François Guéry, "Descartes et la 'méditation': Ce que méditer veut dire," in *Revue philosophique de la France et de l'étranger*, no. 2 (2000), 170–74. Pierre Hadot in *Qu'est-ce que la philosophie antique?* (Paris: Gallimard, 1995), 396, recalls that Descartes's meditations are in keeping with the ancient tradition of spiritual exercises.

9. René Descartes, "Meditations on First Philosophy," 59 (AT: VII, 17).

10. Ibid., 60 (AT: VII, 18).

11. Ibid., 59 (AT: VII, 18).

12. See for example the third "Meditations on First Philosophy," 73 (AT, VII: 39) and "Third Objections," in *Meditations on First Philosophy*, trans. Michael Moriarty (Oxford: Oxford University Press, 2008), 115–116 (AT, IX:143).

13. René Descartes, "Meditations on First Philosophy," 60: "*ac prudentiæ est nunquam illis plane confidere qui nos vel semel deceperunt.*"

14. Ibid., 60 (AT, VII:18).

15. Ibid., 60 (AT, VII:19). Saint Augustine in *On the Trinity* had already used similar arguments to refute the arguments of the skeptics who claimed that nothing could be known for certain. Augustine answers by saying that even if one is insane, dreaming, or wrong, one can be certain of being alive. See *On the Trinity*, trans. Edmund Hill in *The Works of Saint Augustine*, 35 vols., ed. John Rotelle (New York: New City, 1990-), V:412 (Book XV, Chapter 21): "*certum est etiam eum qui fallitur vivere.*"

16. Descartes, "Meditations on First Philosophy," 61 (AT, VII:21).

17. Ibid., 62 (AT, VII:22).

18. A very Augustinian moment, See *On the Trinity*, trans. Edmund Hill, V: 296–297 (X, 10, 14): "If the mind doubts, it wishes to be certain" ("*Si dubitat, certus esse vult; si dubitat, cogitat; si dubitat, scit se nescire; si dubitat, judicat non se temere consentire oportere. Quisque igitur aliunde dubitat, de his omnibus dubitare non debet: quæ si non essent, de ulla re dubitare non posset.*")

19. Descartes, "Meditations on First Philosophy," 63 (AT, VII:23–24).

20. Ibid., 63 (AT, VII:24).

21. The idea of an *inconcussum* truth is often associated with Descartes, but it can also be found in Augustine. See *On the Trinity*, IX, 11: "*ipsa vero forma inconcussæ ac stabilis veritatis...*" (the idea of an unshakable and stable truth).

22. Descartes, "Meditations on First Philosophy," 63–64 (AT, VII:24)—translation modified.

23. Ibid., 64 (AT, VII:25).

24. See also the letter-preface to the "Principes de la philosophie" in *Œuvres de Descartes*, ed. Charles Adam and Paul Tannery (Paris: Vrin, 1970–), vol. IX, part 2, 10 : "I took the being or existence of this thought as the first principle."

25. See Jean-Luc Marion, *Being Given: Toward a Phenomenology of Givenness*, trans. Jeffrey L. Kosky (Stanford: Stanford University Press, 2002), 274–275: "I am, not first because I think myself (according to the identity formula *ego cogito, ego sum*), but because an other (or others, I don't yet know) intervenes first (since I am only 'also, *etiam*') in order to deceive me, that is to say, to persuade me that I am myself deceived, since he is deceiving me." "The certain ego, as first truth, is therefore not a first authority—not so much because it would depend on the supposed 'veracity' of the existing God (here it is a question of neither one nor the other), but because it results from its original interlocution by what deceives it, persuades it, and therefore thinks it." "The ego thinks itself, but after the fact."

26. Descartes, "Meditations on First Philosophy," 65 (AT, VII:26).

27. Ibid., 65 (AT, VII:27).

28. See Jean-Luc Marion, "Descartes et l'onto-théologie," 165.

29. On this, see Jean-Luc Marion, *On Descartes' Metaphysical Prism*, 90–103: "The First Pronouncement about the Being of Beings: *cogitatio*."

30. Ibid., 92.

31. On this, see Jean-Luc Marion, "The General Rule of Truth in the Third Meditation," in *On the Ego and on God: Further Cartesian Questions*, trans. Christina M. Gschwandtner (New York: Fordham University Press, 2007), 42–62.

32. René Descartes, "Meditations on First Philosophy," 59 (AT, VII:17).

33. Ibid., 70 (AT, VII:35).

34. Jean-Luc Marion, *On the Ego and on God: Further Cartesian Questions*, trans. Christina M. Gschwandtner, 43.

35. Ibid., 64.

36. Descartes, "Meditations on First Philosophy," 70 (AT, VII:35).

37. Ibid., 70 (AT, VII:35–36).

38. Ibid., 71 (AT, VII:36).

39. As Ludger Honnefelder notes, the notion of an *ens infinitum* was important for Duns Scotus as well. See Ludger Honnenfelder, *La métaphysique comme*

science transcendentale (Paris: PUF, 2002), 70. The importance of infinity for divine intelligence goes back to Plotinus, *Enneads*, III, 7, 5 and III, 8, 8. "Therefore, too, it is unbounded (*apeiron*) in this way and, if anything comes from it, there is no dim-inution, neither of what comes from it, because it, too, is all things (*panta*)." (See also *Enn.*, III, 7, 5).

40. Descartes, "Meditations on First Philosophy," 73 (AT, VII:40).

41. Ibid. In the nineteenth century, Ludwig Feuerbach will argue the contrary, namely that infinity is in fact the negation of the finite.

42. Jean-Luc Marion, *On the Ego and on God*, 172.

43. Descartes, "Meditations on First Philosophy," 74 (AT, VII:42).

44. Ibid., 80 (AT, VII:52).

45. Because Descartes never uses the term *veracitas* (Jean-Luc Marion, *On the Ego and on God*, 43)

46. See René Decartes "Sixth Reply," in *Meditations on First Philosophy*, trans. Michael Moriarty (Oxford: Oxford University Press, 2008), 204 (AT, IX:230): "As for an atheist's science, it is easy to show that he can know nothing with any certainty and assurance; since, as I have already said, the less powerful the sup-posed source of the atheist's Being, the more reason he will have to doubt, since his nature may be so imperfect he will be in error even when something appears most evident to him. Only the recognition of a truthful God can rid him of his doubt." Translation modified.

47. See Jean-Luc Marion, *On Descartes' Metaphysical Prism*, 121. See also Marion, "Descartes et l'onto-théologie," 150.

48. René Decartes, "Fourth Objection," in *Meditations on First Philosophy*, trans. Michael Moriarty, 137 (AT, IX:166): "I have only one final reservation: how can the author avoid arguing in a circle, when he says we know for certain that the things we clearly and distinctly perceive are true, only because God exists. But we can only be certain God exists, because this is clearly and distinctly perceived by us. Therefore before we can be certain God exists, we must be certain, that whatever is clearly and distinctly perceived by us is true."

49. On the Descartes's twofold legacy, see Jean-Luc Marion, *On Descartes' Metaphysical Prism*, 125 ff. See also Paul Ricoeur, *Oneself as Another*, trans. Kathleen Blamey (Chicago: Chicago University Press, 1992), 10 ff.

50. Nicolas Malebranche (1638–1715), the author of *Recherches de la vérité* (1674, 3 vols.), argues the occasionalist argument according to which all knowledge, any intellectual act implies God's intervention. When I see a material body, for exam-ple, it is God that puts the idea in my mind (since body and soul are not con-nected). Everything depends on God, and vision comes from God. This God is

therefore "all Being." On the accusation of Spinozism leveled at Malebranche, see Marion, *On the Ego and on God: Further Cartesian Questions*, 179.

7. Spinoza and Leibniz: The Metaphysics of Simplicity and Integral Rationality

1. Baruch de Spinoza, "Treatise on the Emendation of the Intellect," in *Collected Works of Spinoza*, 2 vols., trans. Edwin Curley (Princeton: Princeton University Press, 1985), I:7. *Ethics*, trans. Edwin Curley (London: Penguin, 1996), part IV, Proposition 28, 129: "Knowledge of God is the mind's greatest good; its greatest virtue is to know God." ("*summum mentis bonum est Dei cognition & summa mentis virtus Deum cognoscere*").

2. Spinoza, "Treatise on the Emendation of the Intellect," 10.

3. Ibid., 41.

4. Ibid., 34.

5. Baruch de Spinoza, "Short Treatise on God, Man, and his Well-Being," in *Collected Works of Spinoza*, I:61.

6. Ibid., I:62.

7. See Jean-Luc Marion, *On the Ego and on God: Further Cartesian Questions*, trans. Christina M. Gschwandtner (New York: Fordham University Press, 2007), 178.

8. Baruch de Spinoza, *Ethics*, IV, Preface, 114: "*Æternum namque illud, & infinitum Ens, quod Deum, seu Naturam appellamus, eadem, qua existit, necessitate agit. . . . Ratio igitur, seu causa, cur Deus, seu Natura agit, & cur existit, una, eademque est.*"

9. Spinoza, *Ethics*, I, Appendix, 25; see I, Proposition XV: "*Quicquid est, in Deo est, & nihil sine Deo esse, neque concipi potest.*"

10. Spinoza, "Metaphysical Thoughts," in *Collected Works of Spinoza*, I:299, 315. He may have been introduced to the distinction by Marini, *Exercitationes Metaphysicæ* (1615), 44, 49. On this see, Spinoza, *Œuvres*, 4 vols. trans. Charles Appuhn (Paris: Garnier-Flammarion, 1964–66), I:434.

11. Ibid., I:302; on the positing of God as "necessary Being," see *Ethics*, I, Proposition XI, 7 ff.

12. Ibid., I:324.

13. Spinoza, *Ethics*, I, Proposition XX, 16.

14. Spinoza, "Metaphysical Thoughts," respectively I:299, 324.

15. Gottfried Wilhelm Leibniz, *New Essays on Human Understanding*, trans. Peter Remnant and Jonathan Bennett (Cambridge: Cambridge University Press, 1981), Book IV, chapter 8, 430. See also Leibniz, "De primae philosophiae Emendatione, et de Notione Substantiae," in *Die philosophische Schriften*, 7 vols., ed. C. I. Gerhardt (Hildesheim, Germany: Georg Olms, 1996), V:468: "And nobody

will be surprised if the queen of the sciences that we know as first philosophy and which Aristotle called the desired science (*zetouménè*), still remains today an elusive science." The original Latin reads: "*Unde nemo mirari debet, scientiam illam principem, quae Primae Philosophiae nomine venit et Aristoteli desiderata seu quaesita, adhuc inter quaerenda mansisse.*"

16. Gottfried Wilhelm Leibniz, "Discourse on Metaphysics (1686)," in *Philosophical Essays*, trans. and ed. Roger Ariew and Daniel Garber (Indianapolis, IN: Hackett, 1989), § 11, 43.

17. This is the case for early writings on *De summa rerum*, see Gottfried Wilhelm Leibniz, *De summa rerum: Metaphysical papers, 1675–1676*, trans. George H. R. Parkinson (New Haven: Yale University Press, 1992).

18. See Johann Gottlieb Fichte, "Second Introduction to the Science of Knowledge," in *Science of Knowledge*, trans. Peter Heath and John Lachs (Cambridge: Cambridge University Press, 1982), 82–83. Fichte insisted on the difference between the spirit and the word because he believed he was expressing the spirit of Kantian philosophy while seemingly neglecting its word. On this, see my article, "Fichte and Leibniz," in *Fichte: Historical Context/Contemporary Controversies* (Atlantic Highlands, NJ: Humanities Press International, 1994), 181–190.

19. See Gottfried Wilhelm Leibniz, "Discourse on Metaphysics," 51. The idea will later be taken up by Kant who will ascribe these principles, along with the causes of appearances, to our understanding.

20. Baruch de Spinoza, *Ethics* III, proposition VI: "Each thing, a far as it can by its own power, strives to persevere in its Being" (*unaquæque res, quantum in se est, in suo esse perseverare conatur*).

21. Gottfried Wilhelm Leibniz, "A New System of the Nature and Communication of Substances, and of the Union of the Soul and Body (1695)," in *Philosophical Essays*, 139: "I perceived that considering *extended mass* alone was not sufficient, and that it was necessary, in addition, to make use of the notion of *force*, which is very intelligible, despite the fact that it belongs in the domain of metaphysics.... Hence, it was necessary to restore, and, as it were, to rehabilitate the *substantial forms* which are in such disrepute today.... I found then that their nature consists in force, and that from this there follows something analogous to sensation and appetite."

22. Ibid., 139.

23. Leibniz, "The Principles of Philosophy, or, the Monadology," in *Philosophical Essays*, § 3, 213.

24. Ibid., § 9.

25. Ibid., § 19.

26. Ibid., § 32.

27. Ibid., § 38. Leibniz uses a similar expression elsewhere. See *Die Philoso-phische Schriften*, VII:289: "This necessary Being is the reason for the existence of things and we usually call with the name God [*est scilicet ens illud ultima Rerum, et uno vocabulo solet appellari DEUS*]." Dr. Grondin uses the French trans-lation in Leibniz, *Recherches générales sur l'analyse des notion et vérités. 24 thèse métaphysiques et autres textes logiques et métaphysiques*, trans. Emmanuel Cattin (Paris: PUF, 1998), 466.

28. Ibid., § 44.

29. Ibid., § 48.

30. Ibid., § 53.

31. Voltaire, *Traité de métaphysique*, written in 1734, was not published until 1784 when it appeared in the posthumous edition of his works. It was heavily influ-enced by the philosophy of John Locke.

8. Kant: Metaphysics Turned Critical

1. Immanuel Kant, "Inquiry Concerning the Distinctness of the Principles of Natural Theology and Morality," in *Theoretical Philosophy (1755–1770)*, trans. David Walford (Cambridge: Cambridge University Press, 1992), 255 (AK II: 283).

2. Immanuel Kant, *Critique of Pure Reason*, A 850; B 878. We shall refer in the fol-lowing to two translations: Norman Kemp Smith (London: MacMillan and Co., 1933), 664; Paul Guyer and Allan W. Wood (Cambridge: Cambridge University Press, 1998), 700.

3. Ibid., *Critique of Pure Reason*, A ix. Kemp Smith, 8; Guyer and Wood, 99.

4. Ibid., *Critique of Pure Reason*, A x. Kemp Smith, 8; Guyer and Wood, 100.

5. Ibid., *Critique of Pure Reason*, B 21. Kemp Smith, 56; Guyer and Wood, 147.

6. Ibid., *Critique of Pure Reason*, A 798; B 826. Kemp Smith, 631; Guyer and Wood, 673.

7. Ibid., *Critique of Pure Reason*, B 22. Kemp Smith, 57; Guyer and Wood, 148.

8. Ibid., *Critique of Pure Reason*, A 832; B 860. Kemp Smith, 653; Guyer and Wood, 691.

9. Ibid., *Critique of Pure Reason*, A 836; B 864. Kemp Smith, 655; Guyer and Wood, 693.

10. Ibid., *Critique of Pure Reason*, A xii. Kemp Smith, 9; Guyer and Wood, 101.

11. Ibid., *Critique of Pure Reason*, A xii. Kemp Smith, 9; Guyer and Wood, 101.

12. See Kant's famous confession in *Prolegomena to any Future Metaphysics that will be able to come forward as Science*, trans. James W. Ellington (Indianapolis, IN:

Hackett, 1977), 5 (AK IV:260): "I openly confess that my remembering David Hume was the very thing which many years ago first interrupted my dogmatic slumber."

13. Immanuel Kant, *Critique of Pure Reason,* A xx. Kemp Smith, 14; Guyer and Wood, 104.

14. Ibid., *Critique of Pure Reason,* B 113. Kemp Smith, 118; Guyer and Wood, 216.

15. Ibid., *Critique of Pure Reason,* B 113. Kemp Smith, 118; Guyer and Wood, 216.

16. Ibid., *Critique of Pure Reason,* A 125. Kemp Smith, 147; Guyer and Wood, 241.

17. Ibid.,*Critique of Pure Reason,* A 246; B 303. Kemp Smith, 264; Guyer and Wood, 344–345.

18. See the Academy edition of Kant's complete works, vol. AK XXVIII:1, 1 ("*die Wissenschaft von den allgemeinen [generalium] Prädikaten aller Dinge.*").

19. Immanuel Kant, *Lectures on Metaphysics,* trans. Karl Ameriks and Steve Naragon (Cambridge: Cambridge University Press, 1997), 309 (AK 28:542).

20. Immanuel Kant, *Critique of Pure Reason,* A xx–xxi. Kemp Smith, 13–14; Guyer and Wood, 104–105.

21. Ibid., *Critique of Pure Reason,* A 12; B 26. Kemp Smith, 59; Guyer and Wood, 149–150.

22. Immanuel Kant, "Dreams of a Spirit-Seer Elucidated by Dreams of Metaphysics," in *Theoretical Philosophy (1755–1770),* 354: "Metaphysics is a science of the *limits of human reason.* A small country always has a long frontier; it is hence, in general, more important for it to be thoroughly acquainted with its possessions, and to secure its power over them, than blindly to launch on campaigns of conquest. Thus, the second advantage of metaphysics is at once the least known and the most important, although it is also an advantage which is only attained at a fairly late stage and after long experience."

23. Immanuel Kant, *Critique of Pure Reason,* A xix–xx. Kemp Smith, 13; Guyer and Wood, 104.

24. This is a very paradoxical expression since theoretical metaphysics, if it is possible, can only pertain to the *a priori* legislation at work within nature itself. See for example the title of Herbert J. Paton's classic work: *Kant's Metaphysic of Experience,* 2 vols. (London: Allen & Unwin, 1965 [1936]).

25. Immanuel Kant, *Critique of Pure Reason,* A 797; B 825. Kemp Smith, 631; Guyer and Wood, 673.

26. Immanuel Kant, *Groundwork of the Metaphysics of Morals,* trans. Mary Gregor (Cambridge: Cambridge University Press, 1997), 57 ff. (AK IV:452 ff.).

27. Ibid., 58 (AK IV:454).

28. Ibid., 45 (AK IV:438).

29. Ibid., 59 (AK IV:455).

30. Ibid., 62 (AK IV:458).

31. Immanuel Kant, *Critique of Pure Reason*, A 12; B 26. Kemp Smith, 59; Guyer and Wood, 133.

32. On this, see my article "La conclusion de la Critique de la Raison Pure," in *Kant-Studien*, 81 (1990): 129–144.

33. Immanuel Kant, *Critique of Pure Reason*, A 796; B 824. Kemp Smith, 630; Guyer and Wood, 672.

34. Ibid., *Critique of Pure Reason*, A 797; B 825. Kemp Smith, 630; Guyer and Wood, 673.

35. The expression is of Augustinian origin. See Saint Augustine of Hippo, "Divine Providence and the Problem of Evil," trans. Robert P. Russell in *The Happy Life; Answer to the Sceptics; Divine Providence and the Problem of Evil*, ed. Ludwig Schopp (New York; Cima, 1948), 324 (*De Ordine*, Book II, Chapter 47): "The science of philosophy has already adopted this knowledge [of the One] and has discovered in it nothing more than what unity is, but in a manner far more profound and sublime [than mathematics, which have just been discussed]. To philosophy pertains a twofold question: the first treats of the soul; the second of God [*una de anima, altera de Deo*] [which for Kant are also the two great objects of metaphysics]. The first makes us know ourselves; the second our origin. The former is the more delightful to us [*dulcior*]; the latter, more precious [*charior*]. The former makes us fit for a happy life [*illa nos dignos beata vita*]; the latter renders us happy [*beatos hæc facit*]. The first is for beginners; the latter, for the well instructed. This is the order of wisdom's branches of study by which one becomes competent to grasp the order of things [*per que fit quisque idoneus ad intelligendum ordinem rerum*] and to discern two worlds and the very Author of the universe [*id est ad dignoscendos duos mundos et ipsum, parentem universitatis*]."

36. Immanuel Kant, *Critique of Pure Reason*, A 805; B 833. Kemp Smith, 636; Guyer and Wood, 677. "For all hoping is directed to happiness, and stands in the same relation to the practical and the law of morality as knowing and the law of nature to the theoretical knowledge of things."

37. Ibid., *Critique of Pure Reason*, A 809; B 837. Kemp Smith, 638; Guyer and Wood, 679.

38. Ibid., *Critique of Pure Reason*, A 809; B 837. Kemp Smith, 638; Guyer and Wood, 679.

39. Ibid., *Critique of Pure Reason*, A 810; B 838. Kemp Smith, 639; Guyer and Wood, 680.

40. On the motif of elevation above an animal state, which for Kant justifies the admission of an intelligible world, see my article: "La phénoménologie de la loi morale," in Francois Duscheneau and Claude Piché ed., *Kant actuel*, Volume

d'études kantiennes en homage posthume à Pierre Laberge (Paris/Montreal: Vrin/Bellarmin, 2000), 51–65.

41. Immanuel Kant, *Critique of Pure Reason,* A 810; B 838. Kemp Smith, 639; Guyer and Wood, 680.

42. Bernard Carnois, *La cohérence de la doctrine kantienne de la liberté* (Paris: Seuil, 1976).

43. Immanuel Kant, *Critique of Pure Reason,* A 830–831; B 859–860. Kemp Smith, 651; Guyer and Wood, 690.

44. Ibid., *Critique of Pure Reason,* A 592; B 620. Kemp Smith, 500; Guyer and Wood, 563.

45. Ibid., *Critique of Pure Reason,* A 598; B 627. Kemp Smith, 504; Guyer and Wood, 567.

46. Ibid., *Critique of Pure Reason,* A 598; B 627. Kemp Smith, 504; Guyer and Wood, 567.

47. Ibid., *Critique of Pure Reason,* A 599; B 628. Kemp Smith, 505; Guyer and Wood, 567.

9. Metaphysics After Kant?

1. Immanuel Kant, *Critique of Pure Reason,* B xxii, trans. Norman Kemp Smith (London: MacMillan, 1933), 25; trans. Guyer and Wood (Cambridge: Cambridge University Press, 1998), 113.

2. Immanuel Kant, *Prolegomena to any Future Metaphysics that will be able to come forward as Science,* trans. James W. Ellington (Indianapolis, IN: Hackett, 1977), 23.

3. See Dieter Heinrich and Rolf-Peter Hortsmann, ed., *Metaphysik nach Kant?* Stuttgarter Hegel-Kongress 1987 (Stuttgart, Germany: Klett-Cotta, 1988).

4. See Immanuel Kant, "Declaration on Fichte's *Wissenschaftslehre,* August 7 1799," in *Correspondence,* ed. Arnulf Zweig (Cambridge: Cambridge University Press, 1999), 559–560 (AK 12, 370–371). In his declaration, Kant states that he opposes "metaphysics, as defined according to *Fichtean* principles."

5. Otto Liebmann, *Kant und die Epigonen, Eine kritische Abhandlung* (Stuttgart, Germany: C. Scholber, 1865).

6. Johann Gottlieb Fichte, "The First Introduction to the Science of Knowledge," in *The Science of Knowledge,* ed. and trans., Peter Heath and John Lachs (Cambridge: Cambridge University Press, 1982), 16 (SW, I:434).

7. Johann Gottlieb Fichte, "Foundation of the Entire Science of Knowledge (1794)," in *The Science of Knowledge,* 251–252 (SW, I:285–286). We will return to this.

8. Immanuel Kant, *Critique of Pure Reason*, B 25. Kemp Smith, 59; Guyer and Wood, 149.

9. Ibid., *Critique of Pure Reason*, A 634; B 662. Kemp Smith, 527; Guyer and Wood, 585.

10. Ibid., *Critique of Pure Reason*, A xxi. Kemp Smith, 14; Guyer and Wood, 104–105.

11. Ibid., *Critique of Pure Reason*, A 832; B 860. Kemp Smith, 653; Guyer and Wood, 691.

12. Ibid., *Critique of Pure Reason*, A 838; B 866. Kemp Smith, 657; Guyer and Wood, 694.

13. Ibid., *Critique of Pure Reason*, A 838; B 866. Kemp Smith, 657; Guyer and Wood, 694.

14. Johann Gottlieb Fichte, "Second Introduction to the Science of Knowledge," in *The Science of Knowledge*, 52 (SW, I:480).

15. Friedrich Heinrich Jacobi, "On Transcendental Idealism," in *The Main Philosophical Writings and the Novel Allwill*, ed. George Di Giovanni (Montreal: McGill-Queens Press, 1994).

16. Ibid., 337–338.

17. On this, see my article, "De Kant à Fichte," in *Proceedings: Sixth International Kant Congress* (1985), ed. G. Funke and T. Seebohm (Washington, DC: The University Press of America, 1989), 471–492.

18. See Johann Gottlieb Fichte, GA, part 4, I: 188: "*Wie kommt aber jemand auf ein Ding an sich, das für ihn nicht da ist? Vernünftige Wesen reden also von etwas, das auf die Vorstellung keiner Vernunft bezogen werden soll; indem sie aber davon sprechen, wird ja eine Vorstellung darauf bezogen; welches ein Widerspruch ist. Ist also vom Dinge an sich die Rede, so verlange ich, daß van allem Bewustsein und aller Vernunft abstrahiert, und doch etwas vernünftiges darüber gesagt werde. Dieß ist ein Widerspruch, ein völliger reiner Widerspruch. Das Postulat des Dings an sich kann man also nennen das Postulat der reinen Unvernunft.*" And, 190: "*Kant geht mit dem Dinge an sich noch zu schonend um, und dieß mag der Grund sein, warum er nicht recht verstanden worden. Kritischer Philosoph ist der, der ganz davon überzeugt ist, daß der Gedanke eines Dinges an sich ganz Unvernunft ist.*"

19. Johann Gottlieb Fichte, "First Introduction to the Science of Knowledge," in *The Science of Knowledge*, 10 (SW, I:428).

20. Johann Gottlieb Fichte, "Foundations of the Entire Science of Knowledge (1794)," in *The Science of Knowledge*, 252 (SW, I:286).

21. See Johann Gottlieb Fichte, "Concerning the Concept of *Wissenschaftslehre* or, of so-called 'Philosophy,'" in *Fichte: Early Philosophical Writings*, ed. Daniel Breazeale (Ithaca/London: Cornell University Press, 1988), 97 (SW, I:32): "metaphysics itself, which does not have to be a theory of the so-called things-in-themselves, but may be a genetic deduction of what we find in our consciousness."

22. See Karl Leonhard Reinhold, *Letter on the Kantian Philosophy*, ed. Karl Ameriks (Cambridge: Cambridge University Press, 2005). In the following, Jean Grondin uses the biographical information in the introduction to the French translation *Philosophie élémentaire*, trans. François-Xavier Chenet (Paris: Vrin, 1989), 11.

23. His first class had some 400 students in attendance, as many as Schiller. In 1794, he had 600 students at a time when the University of Jena only had some 860 students. See François-Xavier Chenet, *Philosophie élémentaire*, 11.

24. Karl Leonhard Reinhold, "The Foundation of Philosophical Knowledge," in *Between Kant and Hegel: Texts in the Development of post-Kantian Idealism*, trans. George Di Giovanni (Indianapolis, IN: Hackett, 2000), 66, 85.

25. Ibid., 87.

26. Karl Leonhard Reinhold, *Über das Fundament des philosophischen Wissens* (Hamburg, Germany: Meiner, 1978 [1791]), 12. Translator's note: unfortunately, this passage from Reinhold's "The Foundation of Philosophical Knowledge" has not been translated into English. Jean Grondin uses the French translation in *Philosophie élémentaire*, 197.

27. Karl Leonhard Reinhold, "The Foundation of Philosophical Knowledge," 70. Reinhold then continues: "The concept of *representation, inasmuch as it lies at the foundation* of the proposition just stated, is *immediately* drawn from consciousness; as such it is entirely *simple* and incapable of analysis. Its source is an *actual fact* which is suited to yield the *last* possible foundation for all explanation precisely because, *qua fact*, it admits of no explanation but is itself self-explanatory. No definition of *representation* is therefore possible. The principles of consciousness, far from being a *definition*, qualifies rather as the *first principle* of all philosophy precisely because it presents a concept that does not allow definition; it is not itself the highest among possible definitions, yet it makes that highest definition possible in the first place."

28. Karl Leonhard Reinhold, *Beiträge zur Berichtigung bisheriger Missverständnisse der Philosophen*, 2 vols. (Jena, 1790–1794), I:282. Grondin refers to the French in *Philosophie élémentaire*, 148.

29. Ibid., (Jena, 1794), II:417; *Philosophie élémentaire*, 176.

30. Friedrich Wilhelm Schelling, "On the I as Principle of Philosophy, or On the Unconditional in Human Knowledge," in *The Unconditional in Human Knowledge*, trans. Fritz Marti (London: Associated University Presses, 1980), 81 (SW, I:176).

31. Johann Gottlieb Fichte, "Second Introduction to the Science of Knowledge," in *The Science of Knowledge*, 51 (SW, I:478): "Now I am very well aware that

Kant by no means *established* a system of the aforementioned kind; for in that case the present author would have saved himself the trouble and chosen some other branch of human knowledge as the science of his labors. *I* am aware that he by no means *proved* the categories he set up to be conditions of self-consciousness, but merely said that they were so. . . . However, I think I also know with equal certainty that *Kant envisaged* such a system; that everything that he actually propounds consists of fragments and consequences of such a system, and that his claims have sense and coherence only on this assumption." See also the course Fichte gave between 1796 and 1799 published as *Foundations of Transcendental Philosophy: Wissenschaftslehre Novo Methodo*, trans. Daniel Breazeale (Ithaca: Cornell University Press, 1992), 79: "Kant, however, constructed no system."

32. See the title of Fichte's 1794 essay: "Concerning the Concept of *Wissenschaftslehre* or, of so-called 'Philosophy,'" in *Fichte: Early Philosophical Writings*, 94–135.

33. Johann Gottlieb Fichte, "Second Introduction to the Science of Knowledge," in *The Science of Knowledge*, 46 (SW, I:472).

34. Johann Gottlieb Fichte, "Eigene Meditationen über Elementarphilosophie," in GA, part 2, III: 21–266. This has yet to be translated into English. Jean Grondin uses the French translation: *Méditations personnelles sur la philosophie élémentaire*, trans. Isabelle Thomas-Fogiel (Paris: Vrin, 1999). See also K. L. Reinhold, *Le principe de conscience: Nouvelle présentation des moments principaux de la philosophie élémentaire*, trans. Jean-François Goubet (Paris: L'Harmattan, 1999). On Reinhold's important influence on the young Fichte see Rainer Lauth, "Genèse du 'Fondement de toute doctrine de la science' de Fichte à partir de ses '*Méditations personnelles sur l'Elementarphilosophie*,'" in *Archives de philosophie*, 34 (1971): 51–79; see also, "La conception de la philosophie cartésienne par Reinhold au début du XIXe siècle. Ses conséquences pour le développement de la philosophie allemande," in *Les études philosophiques* (Longeuil, France: Le Préambule, 1985), 191–204.

35. Fichte, "Letter to Reinhold, March–April 1795," in *Fichte: Early Philosophical Writings*, trans. Daniel Breazeale, 384.

36. Johann Gottlieb Fichte. "Review of *Aenesidemus*," in *Fichte: Early Philosophical Writings*, 59–77 (*SW*, I: 8). See also Friedrich Wilhelm Schelling, *System of Transcendental Idealism* (1800), trans. P. Heath (Charlottesville: University Press of Virginia, 1978), 28 ff.

37. Johann Gottlieb Fichte, *Foundations of Transcendental Philosophy: Wissenschaftslehre Novo Methodo*, 82.

38. See Gottfried Wilhelm Leibniz, "A New System of Nature and Communication of Substances, and the Union of the Soul and the Body (1695)," in

Philosophical Essays, trans. Roger Ariew and Daniel Garber (Indianapolis, IN: Hackett, 1989), 139.

39. Johann Gottlieb Fichte, "Foundations of the Entire Science of Knowledge (1794)," in *The Science of Knowledge*, 93 (SW, I:91).

40. Johann Gottlieb Fichte, "Concerning the Concept of *Wissenschaftslehre* or, of so-called 'Philosophy,'" in *Fichte: Early Philosophical Writings*, 97 (SW, I:32).

41. Ibid., 97: "Critique is itself not metaphysics, but lies beyond metaphysics. It is related to metaphysics in exactly the same way that metaphysics is related to the ordinary point of view of natural understanding. Metaphysics explains the ordinary point of view, and metaphysics is itself explained by critique." One could think that Fichte inverts the foundational relation that Kant had established between critique and metaphysics, in which the former makes the later possible. In fact, Fichte radicalizes Kant's position: critique founds metaphysics because it is necessarily more fundamental and more radical. His position is not always rigorously maintained. In his courses in metaphysics and logic from 1797, Fichte sometimes implies that the Science of Knowledge and Metaphysics were synonymous (GA, part 4, II:76). See also his letter to Schelling (September 10, 1799) in F. W. J. Schelling, *Briefe und Dokumente*, 3 vols., ed. Horst Fuhrman (Bonn: Bouvier Verlag, 1973), II:187: "In my use of language, the term Science of Knowledge does not mean logic, but only transcendental philosophy or metaphysics."

42. Johann Gottlieb Fichte, *Foundations of Transcendental Philosophy*: Wissenschaftslehre Novo Methodo, 78.

43. Johann Gottlieb Fichte, "First Introduction to the Science of Knowledge," in *The Science of Knowledge*, 22–23 (SW, I:442).

44. Johann Gottlieb Fichte, "Foundations of the Entire Science of Knowledge (1794)," in *The Science of Knowledge*, 93 (SW, I:91).

45. Ibid., 104–105 (SW, I:104).

46. Ibid., 107–108 (SW, I:108).

47. Ibid., in *The Science of Knowledge*, 110 (SW, I: 110). "*über diese Erkenntniss hinaus geht keine Philosophie; aber bis zu ihr zurückgehen soll jede gründliche Philosophie; und so wie sie es thut, wird sie Wissenshaftslehre. Alles was von nun an im Systeme des menschlichen Geistes vorkommen soll, muss sich aus dem Aufgestellten ableiten lassen.*"

48. Ibid., 217 (SW, I:246).

49. Ibid., 117 (SW, I:119). Schelling will adopt the expression "absolute 'I,'" see Friedrich Wilhelm Joseph Schelling, "Of the I as Principle of Philosophy, or On the Unconditional in Human Knowledge," in *The Unconditional in Human Knowledge*, trans. Fritz Marti (London: Associated University Presses, 1980), 75.

50. See, Johann Gottlieb Fichte, *Foundations of Natural Right*, ed. Frederick Neuhouser, trans. Michael Baur (Cambridge: Cambridge University Press, 2000).

51. Immanuel Kant, "An Answer to the Question: What is Enlightenment?" in *Practical Philosophy*, trans. Mary J. Gregor (Cambridg: Cambridge University Press, 1996), 17. See also Immanuel Kant, "Idea for a Universal History with a Cosmopolitan Purpose (1784)," trans. Allen W. Wood in *Anthropology, History, and Education*, ed. Günter Zöller (Cambridge: Cambridge University Press, 2007), 117.

52. See also Jean-Christophe Goddard, ed., *Fichte: Le Moi et la liberté* (Paris: PUF, 2000).

53. See the preface to the second edition of the *Foundations of the Science of Knowledge* (1801), SW, I:85.

54. Johann Gottlieb Fichte, *The Vocation of Man*, trans. Peter Peuss (Indianapolis, IN: Hackett, 1987), 64–65 (SW, II:246).

55. See the testimonial left by a Norwegian student, Christian Oersted, dating from February 16, 1802 (quoted in the preface to the 1801–1802 exposition of his philosophy in GA, part 2, VI:114): "*Du siehst leicht, daß er jetzt ganz neue Ausdrücke wählt: daß aber sein System dasselbe ist wie vorher, behaupt er selbst.*" ["You can easily see that Fichte now uses completely new expressions, but he says his system remains the same."]

56. Claudio Cesa, *Fichte et l'idealismo trascendentale* (Bologna: Il Mulino, 1992), 153.

57. Johann Gottlieb Fichte, *Darstellung der Wissenschaftslehre* (1801), SW, II:1–163.

58. See W. Janke, *Fichte: Sein und Reflexion* (Berlin: De Gruyter, 1970); Johannes Brachtendorf, *Fichtes Lehre vom Sein: Eine kritische Darstellung der Wissenschaftslehren von 1794, 1798/199 und 1812* (Paderborn, Germany: Schöning, 1995).

59. See F. W. J. Schelling, *The Unconditional in Human Knowledge*, trans. Fritz Marti (London: Associated University Presses, 1980).

60. *Ideas for a Philosophy of Nature: As Introduction to the Study of this Science* (1797), trans. E. E. Harris and P. Heath (Cambridge: Cambridge University Press, 1988). *First Outline of a System of the Philosophy of Nature* (1799), trans. Keith P. Peterson (Albany: SUNY Press, 2004); "Introduction to the Outline of a System of the Philosophy of Nature," in *First Outline of a System of the Philosophy of Nature* (1799), trans. Keith P. Peterson, 193–232.

61. "The Earliest System-Program of German Idealism," in *The Hegel Reader*, ed. Stephen Houlgate (Malden, MA: Blackwell, 1998), 28.

62. F. W. J. Schelling, *De malorum origine* (1792), Latin text with German translation in Schelling, *Werke, Historisch-kritische Ausgabe*, 18 vols., ed. W. G. Jacobs, J. Jantzen, and W. Schieche (Stuttgart, Germany: Frommann-Holzboog, 1976),

I:47–181. The complete title speaks of an "Attempt at a critical and philosophical interpretation of the oldest philosophical thesis in *Genesis* chap. 3: on the Origin of Evil." His interpretation was inspired by Kant's "Radical Evil" published in 1792. The question of evil reappears in Schelling's famous essay on human freedom (1809).

63. F. W. J. Schelling, *Timaeus* (1794), ed. Harmut Buchner (Stuttgart, Germany: Frommann-Holzboog, 1994). It is important to note that Schelling was fascinated by the *Timaeus* throughout his career. See, for example, his course from 1841 to 1842 on *Philosophy of Revelation*, SW, XIII:100.

64. See Rüdiger Bubner, "La découverte de Platon par Schelling," in *Images de Platon et lectures de ses œuvres. Les interprétations de Platon à travers les siècles*, ed. A. Nescheke-Hentschke (Louvain, Belgium: Peeters, 1997), 257–282. In his important essay, Bubner cites a manuscript written when Schelling was very young, which to my knowledge has yet to be published, entitled *Ways of Seeing of the Ancient World on Different Questions, Colligated from Homer, Plato, etc.* Written in August 1792, the text precedes the emergence of Fichte's idealism. Its first part is called "On the Poets, the Prophets, the Poets Inspiration, Enthusiasm, Theopneustia, and Divine Action on Man in General according to Plato." Schelling draws inspiration from Plato's *Ion*, which discusses the poets' divine inspiration. The young Schelling generalizes the idea of "divine favor" (*theia moira, Ion*, 534 c): he associates it to "the profound intellection of the world beyond all human theory," a divine favor that is present "in all productions of the human understanding."

65. "The Earliest System-Program of German Idealism," in *The Hegel Reader*, 28.

66. F. W. J. Schelling, "Letter to Hegel February 4, 1795," in *Briefe und Dokumente*, II: 65—our trans. See also, "On the Possibility of a Form of all Philosophy," in *The Unconditioned in Human Knowledge*, 41–42: "the question whether philosophy is possible at all places us within the domain of that first science, which could be called propaedeutic of philosophy (*philosophia prima*), or, better yet, theory (science) of all science, archscience, or science *kat'exochen*, since it is the condition of all the other sciences."

67. See F. W. J. Schelling, "Letter to Fichte, 19 November 1800," in *Briefe und Dokumente*, II:295 and 297.

68. F. W. J. Schelling "Universal Deduction of the Dynamic Process," in *Zeitschrift für speculative Physik*, vol. 1 (1800), § 63 (SW, IV:75–78): "Philosophy of nature gives a physical explanation of idealism and demonstrates how it *must* spring from nature." Jean Grondin refers to the French translation in *Fichte/Schelling Correspondance*, trans. Myriam Bienenstock (Paris: PUF, 1991), 149.

69. F. W. J. Schelling, *Darstellung meines Systems*, SW, IV:114, § 1. Unfortunately, it has yet to be translated into English. Jean Grondin uses the French translation: *Exposition de mon système de la philosophie*, trans. Emmanuel Cattin (Paris: Vrin, 2000).

70. Ibid., *Darstellung meines Systems*, SW, IV:115, § 2.

71. Ibid., § 1.

72. On this, see Xavier Tillette, *L'intuition intellectuel de Kant à Hegel* (Paris: Vrin, 1995).

73. F. W. J. Schelling, "System of Philosophy in General and of the Philosophy of Nature in particular," in *Idealism and the Endgame of Theory*, trans. Thomas Pfau (Albany: SUNY Press, 1994), 141–194. Unfortunately, this translation only covers the first part of Schelling's text. See SW, I:6, 224: "It is with these phrases that universal philosophy ends. With them, the universal foundation of all rational science or real metaphysics is given." ("... *mit denselben ist die allgemeine Grundlange aller Vernunftwissenschaft oder aller wahren Metaphysik gegeben.*")

74. F. W. J. Schelling, "Über das Wesen der deutschen Wissenschaft," SW, VIII:1–18, here, 9.

75. Ibid., SW, VIII:9.

76. Ibid., SW, VIII:9. Translation modified.

77. Georg Wilhelm Hegel, *Phenomenology of Spirit*, trans. Arnold V. Miller (Oxford: Oxford University Press, 1977), 9.

78. Ibid., 49: "*ein trockenes Versichern.*"

79. F. W. J. Schelling, *The Ages of the World*, trans. Jason M. Wirth (Albany: SUNY Press, 2000).

80. F. W. J. Schelling, *Philosophical Investigations into the Essence of Human Freedom*, trans. Jeff Love and Johannes Shmidt (Albany: SUNY Press, 2006).

81. Ibid., 4–5 (SW, VII:333).

82. Ibid., 5 (SW, VII:335): "*manches lose und seichte Geschwätz von der anderen Seite niederschlagen.*"

83. Ibid., 9 (SW, VII:336).

84. Ibid., 9 (SW, VII:337). Translation modified.

85. Ibid., 17–18 (SW, VII:346).

86. Ibid.

87. F. W. J. Schelling, *Darstellung meines Systems*, SW, IV:130, § 35: "Nothing particular has the ground for its existence in itself. Otherwise, Being would be derived from its existence." (*Nichts Einzelnes hat den Grund seines Daseyns in sich selbst. Denn sonst müsste da Seyn aus seine Wesen erfolgen*). Jacques Rivelaygue, "Schelling: Du système à la critique," in *Leçons de métaphysique allemande*, 2 vols. (Paris: Grasset), I:378.

See F. W. J. Schelling, "Philosophical Letter on Dogmatism and Criticism," in *The Unconditional in Human Knowledge*, 175: "If there *is* a God he can only be *because* he is. His existence and his essence must be identical."

88. F. W. J. Schelling, *Philosophical Investigations into the Essence of Human Freedom*, 21 (SW, VII:350). Heidegger used this passage to claim that for Schelling Being is Will (which would express the hidden essence of metaphysics). Yet, the will, as it is discussed here, is the God's primal Being.

89. Ibid., 22–23 (SW, VII:352).

90. Ibid., 27 (SW, VII:357). Translation modified.

91. Ibid.

92. See Plato, *Phaedrus*, 249 c–d. See Jean-François Courtine, *Suarez et le système de la métaphysique* (Paris: Garnier-Flammarion, 1990), 192.

93. F. W. J. Schelling, *Philosophical Investigations into the Essence of Human Freedom*, 24 (SW, VII:353). Translation modified.

94. Ibid., 28 (SW, VII:359). On the Plotinian motifs in Schelling's work, see Xavier Tillette, "Vision plotinienne et intuition schellingnienne," in *L'Absolu et la philosophie* (Paris: PUF, 1987), 59–80.

95. Ibid., 29 (SW, VII:359). ("*aber immer liegt noch im Grunde das Regellose, als könnte es einmal wieder durchbrechen.*")

96. Ibid., 33 (SW, VII:363). "*Das Prinzip, sofern es aus dem Grunde stammt und dunkel ist, ist der Eigenwille der Kreature.… Diesem Eigenwillen der Kreatur steht er Universalwille entgegen, der jenen gebraucht und als bloßes Werkzeug sich unterordnet.*"

97. Ibid., 32–33 (SW, VII:363): "*Im Menschen ist die ganze Macht des finstern Prinzips und in ebendemselben zugleich die ganze Kraft des Lichtes.*"

98. Ibid., 34 (SW, VII:365).

99. Ibid., 35 (SW, VII:365).

100. Ibid., 38 (SW, VII:371): ". . . *aus der zum Selbstsein erhobenen Endlichkeit.*"

101. Ibid., 47 (SW, VII:381): "*Die Angst des Lebens selbst treibt den Meschen aus dem Zentrum in das erschaffen worden ist.*"

102. Ibid., 55 (SW, VII:390).

103. See Xavier Tillette, *L'Absolu et la philosophie*, 167: "It is still on the uniform monochromatic ground of Indifference that a grand historical philosophy is now revealed, and the eclipse of serene Identity is reflected by an increase of insatisfaction and constructive will."

104. F. W. J. Schelling, *Philosophical Investigations into the Essence of Human Freedom*, 68 (SW, VII:406): "*es muß vor allem Grund und vor allem Existierenden, also überhaupt vor aller Dualität, ein Wesen sein; wie können wir anders nennen als den Urgrund oder vielmehr* Ungrund?" See (SW, VII:407): "*Das Wesen des Grundes wie das des*

Existierenden kann nur das vor *allem Grunde Vorhergehende sein, also das schlechthin betrachtete Absolute, der Ungrund.*" Shelling's emphasis.

105. On the distinction between negative and positive philosophy, see the chapter on Schelling in my book: *Kant et le problème de la philosophie: l'a priori* (Paris: Vrin, 1999), 138–142.

106. Unfortunately, this course has yet to be translated into English.

107. See the translator's preface to the French translation: *Contribution à l'histoire de la philosophie (Leçons de Munich)*, trans. J.-F. Marquette (Paris: PUF, 1983), 6–7.

108. F. W. J. Schelling, *On the History of Modern Philosophy*, trans. Andrew Bowie (Cambridge: Cambridge University Press, 1994), 133 (SW, X:14).

109. *Philosophie der Offenbarung*, SW, XIII:161: "What is simply existing, which is nothing but existing, is precisely what reduces thought, what silences it and defeats reason. Thought always pertains to what is possible, to possibility." Translation modified.

110. Ibid., XIII:163: "Kant calls the unconditioned necessity of Being that precedes all thought, 'human reason's abyss'. I quote these words because they translate Kant's feeling for the sublime in Being that precedes all thought, to which we have substituted Being. Being is certainly still the beginning of philosophy, but only as a moment of philosophy. However, this incontrovertible way of thinking that reaches into the depths of human reason pertains to *the* Being that is *prior* to all thought." Translation modified.

111. Ibid., XIII:151 n. Translation modified.

112. Georg Wilhelm Friedrich Hegel, "Who Thinks Abstractly," in *Hegel: Texts and Commentary*, trans. Walter Kaufmann (Garden City, NY: Anchor, 1966), 114. "*Denken, Abstrakt?—Sauve qui peut! Rette sich, wer kann!—So höre ich schon einen vom Feinde erkauften Verräter ausrufen, der diesen Aufsatz dafür ausschreit, daß hier von Metaphysik die Rede sein werde. Denn Metaphysik ist das Wort, wie abstrakt und beinahe auch Denken ist das Wort, vor dem jeder mehr oder minder wie vor einem mit der Pest behafteten davonläuft.*" *Werke*, Theorie-Werkausgabe, 20 vols., ed. Eva Moldenhauer and Karl Marcus Michel (Frankfurt, Germany: Suhrkamp, 1970), II:575.

113. G. W. F. Hegel, *Encyclopedia of the Philosophical Sciences*, 3 vols., trans. William Wallace and A. V. Miller (Oxford: Oxford University Press, 1970–1975), I:20, § 14. (*Werke*, VIII:53).

114. See Herbert Schnädelbach, ed., *Hegels Enzyklopädie der philosophischen Wissenschaften: Ein Kommentar zum Systemgrundriss.* (Frankfurt, Germany: Suhrkamp, 2000), 11.

115. See G. W. F. Hegel, *The Jena System, 1804–5: Logic and Metaphysics*, trans. John W. Burbidge and George di Giovanni (Montreal: McGill-Queen's Press, 1986); "Hegel's *First Philosophy of Spirit* (being part III of the 'System of Speculative

Philosophy' of 1803/04)," trans. H. S. Harris in *System of Ethical Life (1802/3) and First Philosophy of Spirit (part III of the System of Speculative Philosophy 1803/4)* (Albany: SUNY Press, 1979), 187–266.

116. See the preface to Jean-Pierre Labarrière's translation of Hegel's *Phenomenology of Spirit* (Paris: Gallimard, 1993), 11.

117. G. W. F. Hegel, *Phenoménologie de l'esprit*, trans. Jean-Pierre Labarrière (Paris: Gallimard, 1993), 16.

118. G. W. F. Hegel, *Phenomenology of Spirit*, trans. Arnold V. Miller (Oxford: Oxford University Press, 1977), 15.

119. See Herbert Schädelbach, *Hegel zur Einfürhrung* (Hamburg, Germany: Junius, 1999).

120. G. W. F. Hegel, *Encyclopedia of the Philosophical Sciences*, 3 vols., trans. William Wallace and A. V. Miller (Oxford: Oxford University Press, 1970–1975), III:19, § 384 (*Zusatz*). Translation modified. See also Hegel, *Lectures on the History of Philosophy*, 3 vols., trans. E. S. Haldane (Lincoln: University of Nebraska Press, 1995 [1892–96]), 1:108.

121. Hegel, *Encyclopedia of the Philosophical Sciences*, III:§ 379–381: "*die sich selbst wissende wirkliche Idee.*"

122. See the preface to Hegel's *Philosophy of Right*, and the *Encyclopedia*, I § 6.

123. G. W. F. Hegel, "The Difference between Fichte's and Schelling's System of Philosophy: The Need for Philosophy," in *The Hegel Reader*, 43.

124. See *Encyclopedia of the Philosophical Sciences*, III:§ 382.

125. G. W. F. Hegel, *The Philosophy of History*, trans. J. Sibree (Mineaola, NY: Dover, 1956), 17.

126. Ibid., 17: "*Dies eben ist die Freiheit, denn wenn ich abhängig bin, so beziehe ich mich auf ein Anderes, das ich nicht bin; ich kann nicht sein ohne ein Äußeres; frei bin ich, wenn ich bei mir selbst bin.*"

127. Ibid., 17: "*er* [Spirit] *ist zugleich die Tätigkeit, zu sich zu kommen und so sich hervorzubringen, sich zu dem zu machen, was er an sich ist.*"

128. Ibid., 18.

129. Obviously, the struggle for freedom is not the only factor at work in history. Hegel does not deny this. He knows that history is the theater of great passions without which nothing happens. Freedom is simply history's essence, that is, what is brought out when one considers it philosophically, or in a rational perspective.

130. See Wolfgang Neuser, "Die Naturphilosophie," in *Hegels Enzyklopädie der philosophischen Wissenschaften: Ein Kommentar zum Systemgrundriss.* ed. Herbert Schnädelbach, 144.

131. G. W. F. Hegel, *The Phenomenology of Spirit*, 17.

132. G. W. F. Hegel, *The Science of Logic*, trans. Arnold V. Miller (Atlantic Highlands, NJ: Humanities Press International, 1989), 27: "*die logische Wissenschaft, welche die eigentliche Metaphysik oder reine spekulative Philosophie ausmacht, hat sich bisher sehr vernachlässigt gesehen.*"

133. See Walter Schulze, "Hegel und das Problem der Aufhebung der Metaphysik," in *Martin Heidegger zum siebzigsten Geburtstag*, ed. G. Neske (Pfullingen: Neske, 1976), 176.

134. Jacques Derrida, "Violence and Metaphysics: An Essay on the Thought of Emmanuel Levinas," in *Writing and Difference*, trans. Allan Bass (Chicago: University of Chicago Press, 1978), 119–120.

135. See Jean-Marc Lardic, "Hegel et la métaphysique wolfienne," in *Archives de philosophie*, 65 (2002): 16.

136. G. W. F. Hegel, *The Science of Logic*, 25: "*ein gebildetes Volk ohne Metaphysik* [is] *wie ein Tempel ohne Allerheiligstes.*"

137. Ibid., 25.

138. Ibid., 51.

139. Ibid., 51.

140. Ibid., 45.

141. Ibid., 63. Translation modified.

142. Ibid., 28.

143. F. W. J. Schelling, *On the History of Modern Philosophy*, 134–163.

144. See G. W. F. Hegel, *The Phenomenology of Spirit*, 18: "The activity of dissolution is the power and work of the understanding, the most astonishing and mightiest of powers, or rather the absolute power" ("*die Tätigkeit des Scheidens ist die Kraft und Arbeit der Verstandes, der wundersamsten und größten oder vielmehr der absoluten Macht.*")

145. See G. W. F. Hegel, *Encyclopedia of the Philosophical Sciences*, I:47 ff., § 26.

146. Ibid., II:11, § 246 (*Zusatz*): "*Denn Metaphysik heißt nichts anderes, als der Umfang der allgemeinen Denkbestimmungen, gleichsam das diamentene Netz, in das wir allen Stoff bringen und dadurch erst verständlich machen. Jedes gebildete Bewußtsein hat seine Metaphysik, das instinctartige Denken, die absolute Macht in uns, über die wir nur Meister werden, wenn wir sie selbst zum Gegenstand unserer Erkenntnis machen.*" On the accord between logic and metaphysics, see also *Encyclopedia of the Philosophical Sciences*, I:§ 24.

147. On this, see Karl Löwith, *From Hegel to Nietzsche: The Revolution in Nineteenth Century Thought*, trans. David E. Green (Garden City, NY: Doubleday, 1964).

148. Auguste Comte, *The Positive Philosophy of Auguste Comte*, 2 vols., trans. Harriet Martineau (Bristol: Thoemmes, 2001); *Catechism of Positive Religion*, trans. Richard Congreve (Clifton: A.M. Kelley, 1973); see also *August Comte and Positivism: The Essential Writings*, ed. Gertrud Lenzer (New Brunswick, NJ: Transaction, 1998).

149. Wilhelm Dilthey, *Introduction to the Human Sciences*, ed. Rudolph A. Makkreel and Frithjof Rodi (Princeton: Princeton University Press, 1989); *The Formation of the Historical World in the Human Sciences*, ed. Rudolph A. Makkreel and Frithjof Rodi (Princeton: Princeton University Press, 2002).

150. Arthur Schopenhauer, *The World as Will and Representation*, 2 vols. trans. E. F. Payne (New York: Dover, 1969), II:§ 17, 160–187.

151. Arthur Schopenhauer, "Aphorisms on the Wisdom of Life," in *Pererga and Paralipomena*, 2 vols., trans E. F. J. Payne (Oxford: Oxford University Press, 2000), I:311–520.

152. Friedrich Nietzsche, "The Birth of Tragedy," in *Friedrich Nietzsche: sämtliche Werke, Kritische Studienausgabe*, 15 vols., ed. Giorgio Colli and Mazzino Montinari (Berlin: Walter de Gruyter, 1967–77), I:13. On the Nietzschean critique of metaphysics, see Ingeborg Heidemann, "Nietzsche Kritik der Metaphysik," in *Kant-Studien*, 52 (1961–1962): 507–543; and Mihailo Djuric, *Nietzsche und die Metaphysik* (Berlin: de Gruyter, 1985).

153. Friedrich Nietzsche, *Human, all too Human: A Book for Free Spirits* (1878), trans. R. J. Hollingdale (Cambridge: Cambridge University Press, 1996), § 153, 82. On Kant's expression see *Critique of Pure Reason*, A 850; B 878 (Kemp Smith, 664; Guyer and Wood, 700).

154. Rudolph Carnap, "The Elimination of Metaphysics through Logical Analysis of Language," in *Logical Positivism*, Alfred Jules Ayer ed. (Glencoe, UK: The Free Press, 1959), 60–81; "Überwindung der Metaphysik durch logische Analyse der Sprache," in *Erkenntnis* 2 (1931), 219–241. On Carnap, see Alfred Jules Ayer, *Language, Truth and Logic* (London: Gollancz, 1936). See also, Franco Volpi, "Wittgenstein et Heidegger: Le dépassement de la métaphysique entre philosophie analytique et philosophie continentale" in *La métaphysique: Son histoire, sa critique, ses enjeux*, ed. Jean-Marc Narbonne et Luc Langlois (Paris/Québec: Vrin/PUL, 1999), 61–89.

155. On the *Tractatus* and metaphysics, see Jean Greisch, *Le buisson ardent et les lumières de la raison: L'invention de la philosophie de la religion*, 3 vols. (Paris: Cerf, 2002-2004), I:397, 404.

156. Martin Heidegger, *Phenomenological Interpretations of Aristotle: Initiation to Phenomenological Research*, trans. Richard Rojcewicz (Bloomington: Indiana University Press, 2001).

157. See Hans-Georg Gadamer, *Heidegger's Ways*, trans. John W. Stanley (Albany: SUNY Press, 1994), 167 ff.

10. Heidegger: The Resurrection of the Question of Being in the Name of Overcoming Metaphysics

1. On this, see my article: "Le sens du titre *Être et Temps*," in *L'horizon herméneutique de la pensée contemporaine* (Paris: Vrin, 1993), 17–35.

2. Martin Heidegger, *Sein und Zeit* (1927), 22. In the following, we will quote *Sein und Zeit* according to its original pagination found in Heidegger's *Complete Works* (GA, vol. II) and in the margins of all English translations.

3. This is why Heidegger distinguishes the reflection on "Being and time" from the modest book that takes up this reflection. See Martin Heidegger, *Schelling's Treatise on the Essence of Human Freedom*, trans. Joan Stambaugh (Athens: Ohio University Press, 1985), 189; *Schellings Abhandlung über das Wesen der menschlichen Freiheit* (Tübingen, Germany: Niemeyer, 1971), 229.

4. See Gerhardt Funke, "Die Wendung zur Metaphysik im Neukantianismus des 20. Jahrhunderts," in *Actes du Congrès d'Ottawa sur Kant dans les traditions anglo-américaine et continentale*, ed. Pierre Laberge, François Duscheneau, and Bryan E. Morrisey (Ottawa: Editions de L'Université d'Ottawa, 1974), 36–76. See also Gerd Haeffner's excellent book on the concept of metaphysics in Heidegger's work, *Heideggers Begriff des Metaphysik*, 2nd ed. (Munich: Johannes Verlag, 1981), 24, 132, that refers to books by Peter Wust, *Die Auferstehung der Metaphysik* (Leipzig, Germany: Meiner, 1920), Georg Simmel, *Lebensanschauung: vier metaphysische Kapitel* (München, Germany: Duncker und Humblot, 1918), Max Wundt, *Kant als Metaphysiker: ein beitrag zur geschichte der deutschen philosophie im 18. jahrhundert* (Hildesheim, Germany: Georg Olms, 1984 [1924]), and Nicolai Hartmann, *Grundzüge einer Metaphysik der Erkenntnis* (Berlin: Vereinigung wissenschaftlicher Verleger, 1921). Max Scheler also increasingly spoke of metaphysics in his last essays.

5. On the crisis of Western civilization at the end of First World War, see my book, *Hans-Georg Gadamer: A biography*, trans. Joel Weinsheimer (New Haven: Yale University Press, 2003), 56 ff.

6. The third volume of Karl Jaspers's *Philosophy*, is simply called "Metaphysics." See Karl Jaspers, *Philosophy*, 3 vols, trans. E. B. Ashton (Chicago: University of Chicago Press, 1969–1971).

7. In the first phrase of his habilitation conference on "The Concept of Time in History" (1915), Heidegger spoke of the "metaphysical tendency [*Drang*] of his contemporaries who did not wish to remain on level of a theory of knowledge" (GA, I:357). In his course from the summer of 1929 (GA, XVIII:21–23), he also discussed

this "disposition" to metaphysics (*die heutige Bereitschaft zur Metaphysik*). Nevertheless, Heidegger did himself sometimes display his own passion for metaphysics. In the end of his habilitation thesis (1916) on Duns Scotus, he says, without any warning—his thesis dealt with questions of logic—that philosophy cannot dispense, in the long run, with its authentic focus, namely "metaphysics" (GA, I:348)! Similarly, in the Introduction to *What is Metaphysics?*, Heidegger cites, in the original French, Descartes' famous text in which he compares philosophy to "a tree: the roots are metaphysics, the trunk is physics, and the branches that issue from trunk are all the other sciences" (GA, IX:361, also quoted in GA, LXVII:95); see "Introduction to 'What is Metaphysics?'" in *Pathmarks*, trans. Walter Kaufmann (Cambridge: Cambridge University Press, 1980, 277). These texts testify to his lasting fascination for the questions of metaphysics despite the changes and transformations in his philosophy. It was, in fact, more of a love-hate relation. Passionate as he was about the question of Being, he ceaselessly criticized metaphysics because it failed to ask its essential question, as if metaphysics had been unable to be sufficiently metaphysical.

8. Martin Heidegger, GA, XX:405; GA, XXI:220

9. See ibid., GA, XXIX:30, 95 ff.; GA, LXV:323. See also GA, LXVI:219–20.

10. Ibid., GA, XX:437.

11. See Martin Heidegger, "On the Essence of Ground," trans. William McNeill, in *Pathmarks*, 97–135.

12. Martin Heidegger, *The Basic Problems of Phenomenology*, trans. Albert Hofstadter (Bloomington: Indiana University Press, 1982), 283-6 (GA, XXIV:400–405).

13. See ibid.,GA, IX:443.

14. See Ludger Honnefelder, "Transzendent oder transzendental: über die Möglichkeit von Metaphysik," in *Philosophisches Jahrbuch*, no. 91 (1985), 273–290.

15. Martin Heidegger, "On the Essence of Ground," 109–110 (*Vom Wesen des Grundes*, 1929: GA, IX:138).

16. In the 1949 "Introduction to 'What is Metaphysics?'" Heidegger spoke of a *Rückgang in den Grund der Metaphysik*, a return to the foundation of metaphysics.

17. This is the title of the last chapter of the book: "The Metaphysics of *Dasein*," See Martin Heidegger, *Kant and the Problem of Metaphysics*, trans. James Churchill (Bloomington: Indiana University Press, 1962), 239 ff. (GA, III:231).

18. Ibid., 238 (GA, III:230).

19. Ibid., in his reflections from 1938–1939, published after his death (GA, LXVII: 68), Heidegger saw the idea of a "metaphysics of metaphysics" as a relapse (*Rückfall*) back to the way of thinking that had to be overcome if one is to draw near to

Being. He says the same about transcendence (GA, LXVII:63): "Despite the originary interpretation of *Da-sein*, to maintain the concept of transcendence is to relapse back into metaphysics."

20. Martin Heidegger, "What is Metaphysics," trans. David Ferell Krell in *Pathmarks*, 88–89 (GA, IX:111).

21. Ibid., 96 (GA, IX:120). Translation modified.

22. Martin Heidegger, "Overcoming Metaphysics," in *The End of Philosophy*, trans. Joan Stambaugh (Chicago: University of Chicago Press, 2003 [1973]), 90 (*Vorträge und Aufsätze* [Pfullingen: Neske, 1954], 73): "Metaphysics is in all [!] its forms and all [!] its historical stages a unique, but perhaps [this must never be forgotten!] necessary, fate of the West [*das notwendige Verhangnis des Abendländes*] and the precondition of its planetary dominance." The meaning of this "fate" must be well understood. It does not designate a blind *fatum* as much as our civilization's increasingly entrenched attitude (which, unlike a *fatum*, can be stopped, or at the very least "lessened"). See the comments by Dominique Janicaud in his article "Phénoménologie et métaphysique," in *La métaphysique, Son histoire, sa critique, ses enjeux*, ed. Jean-Marc Narbonne et Luc Langlois (Paris/Québec: Vrin/PUL, 1999), 123: "Ever since Nietzsche and following the later Heidegger, metaphysics can no longer only be considered as either a corpus or as a *project*, it is also a *destiny*. What is meant by this? Certainly not a *fatum* imposed massively or mechanically. One must understand that western thought's intimate propensity for a rational mastery of things and beings (*êtres*) has propelled our history in a way that escapes our individual will and control, and has led to science and technology's conquest of the world and the cosmos. Does this uncover the hidden truth of metaphysics, or is it thereby travestied?"

23. Jean Wahl, *Vers la fin de l'ontologie: Études sur l'Introduction à la métaphysique par Heidegger* (Paris, 1956), 4 (qtd. in G. Haeffner, *Heideggers Begriff der Metaphysik* (Munchen: Johannes Berchmas Verlag, 1981), 137. Heidegger himself underlined the ambiguity of the title in the 1935 course (GA, XL:22).

24. See his course from the summer of 1930 (GA, XXXI:115): "Similarly, the book called *Being and Time* is not what is decisive. What is important is for the reader to become attentive to the fundamental event of western metaphysics [*das Grundgeschehen der abendländischen Metaphysik*], the metaphysics of our *Dasein*, an event that books cannot determine and before which we can only give way." The text is perhaps ambiguous since it maintains the identity of the metaphysics of our *Dasein* with the event that is western metaphysics. But the identity is nevertheless rigorously established since our *Dasein* is caught up in the event of Western metaphysics.

25. Otto Pöggeler dates the "essential" crisis to 1929. See Otto Pöggeler, "Die Krise des phänomenologie Philosophiebegriffs (1929)" in *Phänomenologie im Wiederstreit* (Frankfort: Auhrkamp, 1989), 255–276.

26. Martin Heidegger, GA, XXVII, XXVIII, XXIX–XXX, XXXI, XXXII, XXXIII, XXXIV, XXXVI–XXXVII. Only the course from summer 1932 is still missing (GA, XXXV: The Beginning of Western Philosophy: Anaximander and Parmenides). A new beginning can be seen in the summer semester 1934 (GA, XXXVIII) when Heidegger gives for the first time a course on the essence of language, which proposes to "invert logic." A new beginning is confirmed by his courses on Hölderlin in the following winter semester (GA, XXXIX; 1934–1935) and his course on the *Introduction to Metaphysics* (GA, XL) from the summer 1935, which we have since 1953. It is also important to recall that Heidegger wrote a self-critique (still unpublished) of *Sein und Zeit* around 1932. On this, see Joan Stambaugh, "Heidegger," in *Phenomenology: Dialogues and Bridges* (Albany: SUNY Press, 1982), 7. Perhaps this self-critique (which will probably be published in the fourth section of the GA) led to the idea of a new beginning.

27. Immanuel Kant was the first to use the term ontotheology in the *Critique of Pure Reason* (A 632; B 660), where he used it to designate the demonstration of God's existence by concepts. On this see, Dieter Heinrich, *Die ontologische Gottesbeweis*, 2nd ed. (Tübingen, Germany: Mohr Siebeck, 1960), 1. For Heidegger, the term signifies the complicity of ontology and theology (see for example GA, IX: 443). We shall see that such a concept of ontotheology appears in Heidegger's works as early as 1930–31 in his course on Hegel (GA, XXXII:140).

28. On this see Heidegger's course from the summer semester 1929 (GA, XXVIII:40): "The Foundation of Metaphysics as the Metaphysics of Dasein."

29. On this, see my article "Der deutsche Idealismus und Heideggers Verschärfung des Problems der Metaphysik nach *Sein und Zeit*," in *Heideggers Zwiegespräch mit dem deutschen Idealismus*, ed. H. Seubert (Cologne, Germany: Bohlau Verlag, Collegium Hermeneuticum Band 7, 2003), 41–57.

30. Martin Heidegger, GA, XXVIII:47 (*der Endlichkeit Herr werden, sie zum Verschwinden zu bringen, statt umgekehrt sie auszuarbeiten*). See also the course from the winter semester 1930–1931 on Hegel (GA, XXXII, 209), in which the opposition between Idealism and *Sein und Zeit*'s project is stated clearly: "the claim that the essence of Being is time asserts precisely the opposite of what Hegel wished to show in all his philosophy."

31. Ibid., 141.

32. Ibid., 142.

33. Ibid., 143.

34. Ibid., 144. As is confirmed in his posthumous reflections found in GA, LXVII:95 (*Metaphysics and Nihilism*), the use of the term ontochrony belonged to the 1930–1931 period, or so he writes in 1938–1939. In these reflections from 1938–1939, Heidegger seeks to play down his *opposition* to the *logos* in order to emphasize better the radical *difference* of his inquiry into Being. Nevertheless, his opposition to the metaphysics of the *logos*, which, in 1930–1931, he believed culminates in Hegel's philosophy, leads him to attempt a new beginning.

35. Ibid., GA, XXXVIII:8.

36. Ibid., GA, XXXII:144. One must not forget that Hegel had already said this in the last chapter of the *Phenomenology*, which discusses absolute knowledge. Heidegger, however, reads the chapter on the basis of the idea that time is "erased" (*getilgt*) by the absolute's knowledge of itself.

37. Ibid., GA, XXXII:145.

38. Martin Heidegger, *Introduction to Metaphysics*, trans. Gregory Fried and Richard Polt (New Haven: Yale University Press, 2000), 217. *Einführung in die Metaphysik* (Tübingen, Germany: Niemeyer, 1952), 154 (GA, XL:211).

39. See Martin Heidegger, "Plato's Doctrine of Truth," trans. Thomas Sheehan in *Pathmarks*, 155–182.

40. Martin Heidegger, GA, LXVII:17.

41. See Martin Heidegger, *On the Way to Language*, trans. Peter D. Hertz (San Francisco: Harper & Row, 1971), 1–54.

42. See Heidegger's essay "Science and Reflection," (*Wissenschaft und Besinnung*) in *The Question Concerning Technology and Other Essays*, trans. William Lovitt (New York: Harper & Row, 1977). *Besinnung* is also the title of an important volume of Heidegger's posthumous works (GA, LXVI) that follows the *Beiträge* (GA, LXV).

43. See Martin Heidegger, *Discourse on Thinking*, trans. John Anderson (New York: Harper & Row, 1966).

44. Quoted in Martin Heidegger, GA, LXVII:103.

45. Martin Heidegger, "Nietzsche's Word: 'God is Dead,'" in *Off the Beaten Track*, trans. Julian Young and Kenneth Hayes (Cambridge: Cambridge University Press, 2002). *Holzwege* (Frankfurt, Germany: Klostermann, 1950), 240–242; see also GA, LIV:166.

46. Martin Heidegger, GA, LXVI:255–256.

47. Ibid., GA, LXVI: 353: "*Frage das Seyn! Und in dessen Stille, als dem Anfang des Wortes, antwortet der Gott. Alles Seiende mögt ihr durchstreifen, nirgends zeigt sich die Spur des Gottes.*" The same expression appears in GA, LXIX:31, 105, 211; see also 214, 221.

48. The expression "Overcoming Metaphysics" is the title of an important essay and the title of a voluminous manuscript from 1938–1939 (GA, LXVII). See "Overcoming Metaphysics," in *The End of Philosophy*, trans. Joan Stambaugh, 84–110.

49. Martin Heidegger, GA, LXVII:220: "What if the restraint [of Being] was a refusal [*Verweigerung*]?"

50. Ibid., GA, I:348.

51. Paul Ricoeur, *The Rule of Metaphor: the Creation of Meaning in Language*, trans. Robert Czerny, Kathleen McLaughlin and John Costello (New York/London: Rouletdge, 2003 [1977]), 368: "It seems to me time to deny oneself the convenience, which has become a laziness in thinking, of lumping the whole of Western thought together under a single word, metaphysics." See also Jean Greisch, *Le Cogito herméneutique*, (Paris: Vrin, 2000), 16.

52. Georg Wilhelm Friedrich Hegel, *Encyclopedia of the Philosophical Sciences*, 3 vols., trans. William Wallace and Arnold V. Miller (Oxford: Oxford University Press, 1970-1975), III:§ 386 (*Werke*, X: 35).

53. Martin Heidegger, *Time and Being*, trans. Joan Stambaugh (New York: Harper & Row, 1972), 24. *Zur Sache des Denkens* (Tübingen, Germany: Niemeyer, 1969), 25.

11. On Metaphysics Since Heidegger

1. See Martin Heidegger, "Overcoming Metaphysics," in *The End of Philosophy*, trans. Joan Stambaugh (Chicago: University of Chicago Press, 2003 [1973]), 85 (*Vorträge und Aufsätze*, 67): "The past does not exclude, but rather includes, the fact that metaphysics is now for the first time beginning its unconditional rule." When Heidegger speaks of "overcoming metaphysics," the expression must also be understood as an subjective genitive, as Dominique Janicaud recalls in *La métaphysique à la limite* (Paris: PUF, 1983), 15, 16: metaphysics "overcomes" itself (literally, it wriggles itself through, *über-winden*) into the essence of technic.

2. Jürgen Habermas, *Postmetaphysical Thinking: Philosophical Essays*, trans. William Mark Hohengarten (Cambridge, MA: MIT Press, 1992).

3. See Louis Lavelle, *La dialectique de l'éternel présent* (1900); *De l'être* (Paris: F. Alcan, 1928).

4. Emmanuel Mounier was the founder of the journal *Savoir*; see his small work in the collection "Que sais-je" on *Personnalism* (Paris: PUF, 1950).

5. Gabriel Marcel, *Being and Having*, trans. Katharine Farrer (Westminster: Dacre Press, 1949); or *Being and Having: an Existentialist Diary* (New York: Harper & Row, 1965); see in French: *Être et Avoir*, 2 vols. (Paris: Aubier, 1968).

6. Jacques Maritain, *A Preface to Metaphysics: Seven Lectures on Being* (Freeport, NY: Books for Libraries Press, 1971). See also *An Essay on Christian Philosophy*, trans. Edward H. Flannery (New York: Philosophical Library, 1955). On the history of neothomism, see the important acticle by Emmanuel Tourpe,

"Thomas et la modernité. Un point de vue spéculatif sur l'histoire de la métaphysique thomiste," in *Revue des sciences philosophiques et théologiques*, 85 (2001): 433–460.

7. Gabriel Marcel, *La dimension Florestan* (Paris: Plon, 1958). See also Dominique Janicaud, *Heidegger en France*, 2 vols. (Paris: Albin Michel, 2001), I:137 ff.

8. One of its most importance inspirations, in France, was Joseph Maréchal (1878–1944). See Joseph Maréchal, *Le point de départ de la métaphysique. Leçons sur le développement historique et théorique du problème de la connaissance*, 5 vols. (Brussels: éditions Universelles, 1944).

9. Étienne Gilson, *L'Être et l'essence* 2nd ed. (Paris: Vrin, 1962 [1948]), chap. 8, 223–247: "Existence against Philosophy." Unfortunately this chapter is not included in the English translation.

10. Søren Kierkegaard, *Sickness unto Death: A Christian Psychological Exposition of Upbuilding and Awakening*, trans. Howard V. Hong and Edna H. Hong (Princeton: Princeton University Press, 1980), 15. "The self is a relation which relates itself to its own self or is the relation's relating itself to itself in the relation; the self is not the relation but is the relation's relating itself to itself."—translation modified. One must obviously distinguish the concept of existence in *Sein und Zeit* from the meaning given to it in *The Letter on Humanism* (see *Pathmarks* [Cambridge: Cambridge University Press, 1998], 248 ff., 260 ff.) where *ex-sistere* designates the "site" of *Dasein* outside of beings, its transcendence of beings and its exposure to Being. The 1929 to 1930 course prepared the transition when it began by saying (GA, XXIX/XXX, 531): "*Es ist das Seiende ureigener Art, das aufgebrochen ist zu dem Sein, das wir Da-sein nennen, zu dem Seienden, von dem wir sagen, daß es existiert, d.h. ex-sistit, im Wesen seines Seins ein Heraustreten aus sich selbst ist, ohne sich doch zu verlassen.*"

11. We must not forget that Jacques Maritain's teacher, Henri Bergson (1859–1941), had already emphasized the limit of conceptual thought. According to Bergson, the concept can only lead to analytical and exterior knowledge of things. Only intuition can allow us to delve into the core of things themselves. He identified intuitive knowledge with metaphysics. See, Henri Bergson, *An Introduction to Metaphysics*, trans. T. E. Hulme (New York: The Liberal Arts Press, 1955), 28–29: "Just in so far as abstract ideas can render service to analysis, that is, to the scientific study of the object in its relation to other objects, so far are they incapable of replacing intuition, that is, the metaphysical investigation of what is essential and unique in the object."

12. On this, see Jean-François Courtine, "Différence métaphysique et différence ontologique (À propos du débat Gilson-Heidegger qui n'aura pas lieu)," in

Heidegger et la Phénoménologie (Paris: Vrin, 1990), 33–53. Since the two thinkers were contemporaries, it is hard to say whether Heidegger influenced Gilson or not.

13. See Dominique Janicaud, *Heidegger en France*, 2 vols. (Paris: Albin Michel, 2001), I:41, 59.

14. On the shock of his meeting with Heidegger, see Dominique Janicaud, *Heidegger en France*, I:56.

15. Jean-Paul Sartre, *Existentialism and Humanism*, trans. Philip Mairet (London: Methuen, 1948), 24: "existentialism, in our sense of the word, is a doctrine that does render human life possible; a doctrine, also, which affirms that every truth and every action imply both an environment and a human subjectivity"; "the effect of existentialism is that it puts every man in possession of himself as he is, and places the entire responsibility for his existence squarely on his shoulders." (29). Heidegger immediately answered Sartre in his *Letter on Humanism* (1946) and said that Being was the essential matter and not man.

16. As Dominique Janicaud recalls in "Heidegger und Jean-Paul Sartre. Anerkennung und Abweisung," in *Heidegger-Handbuch*, ed. Dieter Thomä (Stuttgart, Germany: Metzler Verlag, 2003), 416.

17. Jean-Paul Sartre, *Being and Nothingness*, trans. Hazel E. Barnes (London: Routledge, 2003), 16.

18. Ibid., 100: "The term in-itself, which we have borrowed from tradition to designate the transcending Being, is inaccurate. At the limit of coincidence with itself, in fact, the self vanishes to give place to identical Being. The *self* does not belong to Being-in-itself."

19. Ibid., 22: "Being is. Being is in-itself. Being is what it is. These are the three characteristics which the preliminary examination of the phenomena of Being allows us to assign to the Being of phenomena."

20. Ibid., 20 ff.

21. Ibid., 22.

22. Ibid., 94.

23. Ibid., 88.

24. Ibid., 48.

25. Sartre, *Existentialism and Humanism*, 28. Translation modified.

26. Sartre, *Being and Nothingness*, 70.

27. Ibid., 67–68.

28. Ibid., 81–83, 85 ff. See Juliette Simont, "Jean-Paul Sartre," in *Dictionnaire des philosophes* (Paris: Albin Michel, 1998), 1354: "*Being and Nothingness*, a treatise on freedom, is also a scathing exploration of the ways consciousness tries to avoid grasping itself as freedom. The root of refusal of freedom is bad faith, or inauthenticity."

29. Sartre, *Existentialism and Humanism*, 34; *Being and Nothingness*, 636.

30. Sartre, *Existentialism and Humanism*, 42. See also the excellent biography by Annie Cohen-Solal, *Sartre 1905–1980* (Paris Gallimard, 1985), 427. But is human freedom the same everywhere? One day Simone de Beauvoir asked Sartre: "So, what kind of freedom do women have in a harem, for example?" Sartre answered begrudgingly: "Well, one is more free than the others, but yes, the margin is quite small." (Cohen-Solal, *Sartre 1905–1980*, 353.)

31. Martin Heidegger, "Letter on Humanism," trans. Frank A. Capuzzi, in *Pathmarks*, 254 (GA, IX:331).

32. Gerhard Krüger more than anybody else criticized his humanization of Being, see Gerhard Krüger, "Martin Heidegger und der Humanismus," in *Theologische Rundschau* (1950): 148–178.

33. Sartre, *Existentialism and Humanism*, 29.

34. Hans-Georg Gadamer. *Truth and Method*, trans. Garrett Barden and John Cumming (New York: Seabury, 1975), 245 (GW, I:281).

35. Hans-Georg Gadamer, GW, II:247: "*mehr Sein als Bewußtsein.*"

36. Ibid., 258 (GW, I:295). On Gadamer's critique of the instrumental conception of understanding, see Jean Grondin, *The Philosophy of Gadamer*, trans. Kathryn Plant (Montreal: McGill-Queen's Press, 2003).

37. Ibid., 432 (GW, I:478).

38. Ibid., 417–418 (GW, I:464).

39. Ibid., 416 (GW, I:462). Translation modified.

40. This was also the main idea behind Gadamer's work on Plato. He sought to oppose Heidegger's reading, which had always turned Plato into the precursor of "metaphysics" and its hegemonic attitude.

41. See Jacques Derrida, "Structure, Sign and Play in the Discourse of the Human Sciences," in *Writing and Difference*, trans. Alan Bass (Chicago: University of Chicago Press, 1978) 279–280. See also "Violence and Metaphysics: an Essay on the Philosophy of Emmanuel Levinas," in *Writing and Difference*, 134: "If the meaning of Being always has been determined by philosophy as presence, then the *question of* Being, posed on the basis of the transcendental horizon of time (first stage, in *Being and Time*) is the first tremor of the philosophical security, as it is of self-confident presence."

42. Jacques Derrida, "Différance," in *Margins of Philosophy*, trans. Alan Bass (Chicago: University of Chicago Press, 1982), 22.

43. Ibid., 12.

44. Ibid., 27.

45. See Jacques Derrida, *Of Grammatology*, trans. Gayatri Chakravorty Spivak (Baltimore: Johns Hopkins University Press, 1997), 60: "As for the concept, it is

most unwieldy here. Like all the notions I am using here, it belongs to the history of metaphysics and we can only use it under erasure. '*Experience*' has always designated the relation to some presence, whether it takes the form of consciousness of not."

46. See Jacques Derrida, *Monolingualism of the Other or, the Prosthesis of Origin*, trans. Patrick Mensah (Stanford: Stanford University Press, 1998), 23: "inside languages there is a terror, soft, discrete or glaring; that is our subject."

47. Title of the fourth chapter of *Totality and Infinity, an Essay on Exteriority*, trans. Alphonso Lingis (Pittsburg, PA: Duquesne University Press, 1969).

48. Republished in English as Emmanuel Levinas, "Is Ontology Fundamental?' in *Entre nous: On Thinking of the Other*, trans. Michael B. Smith and Barbara Harshaw (New York: Columbia University Press, 1998), 1–12.

49. Emmanuel Levinas, *Totality and Infinity: An Essay on Exteriority*, 43.

50. Ibid., 43–44.

51. Ibid., 44.

52. Ibid., 47.

53. Ibid., 45.

54. Ibid., 47.

55. Ibid., 50.

56. Emmanuel Levinas, "God on the Basis of Ethics," in *God, Death and Time*, trans. Bettina Bergo (Stanford: Stanford University Press, 2000), 138.

The best introduction to metaphysics comes from reading and rereading its greatest works. With this in mind and instead of an erudite bibliography, which would span the entire history of philosophy, here is an approximate list of the most important texts that have marked the history of metaphysics, and Western philosophy, from Antiquity to the present day. The list is kept to its most succinct expression in order to encourage readers to discover the metaphysical tradition for themselves. The reader should note that the main works that make up the history of metaphysics are few in number and rarely voluminous. We have included the editions used in this translation, but the reader should note, however, that in many cases numerous other editions and translations are available and sometimes easier to find.

PARMENIDES (FIFTH CENTURY BCE)

"Parmenides' Poem." Trans. Denis O'Brien. In *Études sur Parmenide.* 2 vols. Ed. Pierre Aubenque. Paris: Vrin, 1987, I:4–80.

Parmenides: A Text with Translation, Commentary, and Critical Essays. Trans. Leonardo Tarán. Princeton: Princeton University Press, 1965, 7–172.

PLATO (428 TO 347 BCE)

Collected Dialogues of Plato. Ed. Edith Hamilton and Huntington Cairns. Princeton: Princeton University Press, 1989 [1961].

Many other translations are available in paperback. We recommend reading: *The Symposium, The Phaedo, The Meno, The Phaedrus*, and the *Republic*. See also *The Sophist, The Parmenides, The Timaeus*, and *The Philebus*, all important for the history of ontology.

ARISTOTLE (385 TO 322 BCE)

"Metaphysics." Trans. William D. Ross. In *The Complete Works of Aristotle: The Revised Oxford Translation*. 2 vols. Ed. Jonathan Barnes. Princeton: Princeton University Press, 1984, II:1552–1728.

"Physics." Trans. R. P. Hardie and R. K. Gake. In *The Complete Works of Aristotle: The Revised Oxford Translation*. 2 vols. Ed. Jonathan Barnes. Princeton: Princeton University Press, 1984, II:315–446.

THEOPHRASTUS (371 TO 288 BCE)

Metaphysics. Trans. William D. Ross and Francis H. Fobes. Hildesheim, Germany: Georg Olms, 1967.

On Hellenistic philosophy, see *The Hellenistic Philosophers*. 2 vols. Ed. Anthony A. Long and David N. Sedley. New York: Cambridge University Press, 1987.

PLOTINUS (205 TO 270 CE)

The Enneads. Trans. Arthur H. Armstrong. 6 vols. Cambridge, MA: Harvard University Press, 1966.

SAINT AUGUSTINE OF HIPPO (354 TO 430)

The Confessions. Trans. Francis J. Sheed. Indianapolis, IN: Hackett, 2006 (1993).

Rotelle, John, ed. *The Works of Saint Augustine: A translation for the 21st century*. 3 parts, 35 vols. New York: New City, 1990–. When completed the series will contain all of Augustine's works including books (part 1), letters (part 2), and homilies (part 3).

SAINT ANSELM (1033 TO 1109)

"Proslogion." Trans. Thomas Williams. In *Basic Writings*. Indianapolis, IN: Hackett, 2007, 75–98.

AVICENNA (IBN SINA, 980 TO 1037)

The Metaphysics of The Healing. Trans. Michael E. Marmura. Provo: Brigham Young University Press, 2005.

The Metaphysics of Avicenna: A critical translation-commentary and analysis of the fundamental arguments in Avicenna's Metaphysica *in the* Danish Nama-i 'ala'i *(The Book of the Scientific Knowledge).* Trans. Parviz Morewedge. London: Routledge & Kegan Paul, 1973.

AVERROES (IBN RUSHD, 1126 TO 1198)

The Decisive Treatise: Determining the Connection Between the Law and Wisdom. Trans. Charles E. Butterworth. Provo: Brigham Young University, 2001.

SAINT THOMAS AQUINAS (1225 TO 1274)

On Being and Essence. Trans. Armand Maurer. Toronto: Pontifical Institute of Medieval Studies, 1968.

Summa Contra Gentiles. Trans. English Dominicans. London: Burns, Oates, and Washbourne, 1934.

Summa Theologiae. Trans. English Dominicans. New York: Christian Classics, 1981.

Commentary on the Metaphysics of Aristotle. Trans. John P. Rowan. Chicago: Henry Regnery, 1961.

The Division and Methods of the Sciences, Questions V–VI of the Commentary on Boethius' De Trinitate. Trans. Armand Maurer, 4th ed. Toronto: Pontifical Institute of Mediaeval Studies, 1986.

DUNS SCOTUS (C. 1265 TO 1308)

"Concerning Metaphysics." Trans. Allan Wolter. In *Philosophical Writings.* Indianapolis, IN: Hackett, 1987, 1–12.

"Man's Natural Knowledge of God." Trans. Allan Wolter in *Philosophical Writings.* Indianapolis, IN: Hackett, 1987, 13–33.

DESCARTES, RENÉ (1596 TO 1650)

Discourse on Method and Meditations on First Philosophy. Trans. Ronald A. Cress, 4th ed. Indianapolis, IN: Hackett, 1998.

Meditations, Objections, and Replies. Trans. Roger Ariew and Donald Cress. Indianapolis, IN: Hackett, 2006.

SPINOZA, BARUCH (1632 TO 1677)

Ethics. Trans. Edwin Curley. London: Penguin, 1994.

"Treatise on the Emendation of the Intellect." In *Collected Works of Spinoza.* 2 vols. Trans. Edwin Curley. Princeton: Princeton University Press, 1985, I:6–45.

"Short Treatise on God, Man, and his Well-Being." In *Collected Works of Spinoza.* 2 vols. Trans. Edwin Curley. Princeton: Princeton University Press, 1985, I:53–156.

"Metaphysical Thoughts." In *Collected Works of Spinoza.* 2 vols. Trans. by Edwin Curley. Princeton: Princeton University Press, 1985, I:299–346.

LEIBNIZ, GOTTFRIED WILHELM (1646–1716)

"Discourse on Metaphysics." In *Philosophical Essays.* Trans. Roger Ariew and Daniel Garber. Indianapolis, IN: Hackett, 1989, 35–68.

New Essays on Human Understanding, trans. Peter Remnant and Jonathan Bennett. Cambridge: Cambridge University Press, 1981.

"The Principles of Philosophy, or, the Monadology." In *Philosophical Essays.* Trans. by Roger Ariew and Daniel Garber. Indianapolis, IN: Hackett, 1989, 213–224.

KANT, IMMANUEL (1724 TO 1804)

"Inquiry Concerning the Distinctness of the Principles of Natural Theology and Morality." In *Theoretical Philosophy (1755–1770).* Trans. David Walford. Cambridge/New York: Cambridge University Press, 1992, 247–286.

"Dreams of a Spirit-Seer Elucidated by Dreams of Metaphysics." In *Theoretical Philosophy (1755–1770).* Trans. David Walford. Cambridge: Cambridge University Press, 1992, 305–360.

Critique of Pure Reason. Trans. Norman Kemp Smith. London: MacMillan, 1933.

Critique of Pure Reason. Trans. Paul Guyer and Allan W. Wood. Cambridge: Cambridge University Press, 1998.

Prolegomena to any Future Metaphysics that will be able to come forward as Science. Trans. James W. Ellington. Indianapolis, IN: Hackett, 1977.

Groundwork of the Metaphysics of Morals. Trans. Mary Gregor. Cambridge: Cambridge University Press, 1997.

Critique of Practical Reason. Trans. Mary Gregor. New York: Cambridge University Press, 1997.

Lectures on Metaphysics. Ed. Karl Ameriks and Steve Naragon. New York: Cambridge University Press, 1997.

FICHTE, JOHANN GOTTLIEB (1762 TO 1814)

Early Philosophical Writings. Trans. Daniel Breazeale. Ithaca: Cornell University Press, 1988.

Science of Knowledge. Trans. Peter Heath and John Lachs. Cambridge: Cambridge University Press, 1982.

Foundations of Transcendental Philosophy: Wissenschaftslehre Novo Methodo. Trans. Daniel Breazeale. Ithaca: Cornell University Press, 1992.

The Vocation of Man. Trans. Peter Preuss. Indianapolis, IN: Hackett, 1987.

SCHELLING, FRIEDRICH WILHELM JOSEPH (1775 TO 1854)

Ideas for a Philosophy of Nature: As Introduction to the Study of this Science (1797). Trans. E. E. Harris and P. Heath. Cambridge: Cambridge University Press, 1988.

First Outline of a System of the Philosophy of Nature (1799). Trans. Keith P. Peterson. Albany: SUNY Press, 2004.

System of Transcendental Idealism. Trans. Peter Heath. Charlottesville: University Press of Virginia, 1978.

The Unconditional in Human Knowledge. Trans. Fritz Marti. London: Associated University Presses, 1980.

Philosophical Investigations into the Essence of Human Freedom. Trans. Jeff Love and Johannes Shmidt. Albany: SUNY Press, 2006.

On the History of Modern Philosophy. Trans. Andrew Bowie. Cambridge: Cambridge University Press, 1994.

HEGEL, GEORG WILHELM FRIEDRICH (1770 TO 1831)

Phenomenology of Spirit. Trans. Arnold V. Miller. Oxford: Oxford University Press, 1977.

The Science of Logic. Trans. Arnold V. Miller. Atlantic Highlands, NJ: Humanities Press International, 1989.

Encyclopedia of the Philosophical Sciences. 3 vols. Trans. William Wallace and Arnold V. Miller. Oxford: Oxford University Press, 1970–1975.

System of Ethical Life (1802/3) and first Philosophy of spirit (part III of the System of speculative philosophy 1803/4). Ed. Henry S. Harris and Thomas M. Knox. Albany: SUNY Press, 1979.

The Jena System, 1804–5: Logic and Metaphysics. Trans. John W. Burbidge and George di Giovanni. Montréal: McGill-Queen's Press, 1986.

The Hegel Reader. Ed. Stephen Houlgate. Malden, MA: Blackwell, 1998.

KIERKEGAARD, SØREN (1813 TO 1855)

Either/or. Trans. David F. Swenson. Princeton: Princeton University Press, 1971.

Repetition and Philosophical Crumbs. Trans. M. G. Piety. Oxford: Oxford University Press, 2009.

Stages on Life's way: Studies by Various Persons. Trans. Howard V. Hong and Edna H. Hong. Princeton: Princeton University Press, 1988.

The Sickness unto Death: A Christian Psychological Exposition for Upbuilding and Awakening. Trans. Howard V. Hong and Edna H. Hong. Princeton: Princeton University Press, 1980.

NIETZSCHE, FRIEDRICH (1844 TO 1900)

The Birth of Tragedy and The Case of Wagner. Trans. Walter Kaufmann. New York: Vintage Books, 1967.

Human, all too Human: A Book for Free Spirits. Trans. R. J. Hollingdale. Cambridge: Cambridge University Press, 1996.

The Gay Science. Trans. Walter Kaufmann. New York: Random House, 1974.

Thus Spoke Zarathustra. Trans. R. Hollingdale. New York: Penguin Books, 2003 (1969).

Twilight of the Idols and *The Anti-Christ.* Trans. R. J. Hollingdale. London: Penguin, 1990.

On the Genealogy of Morals and Ecce Homo. Trans. Walter Kaufmann. New York: Vintage Books, 1989.

BERGSON, HENRI (1859 TO 1941)

Creative Evolution. Trans. Arthur Mitchell. New York: Palgrave Macmillan, 2007.

An Introduction to Metaphysics. Trans. T. E. Hulme. New York: The Liberal Arts Press, 1955.

HUSSERL, EDMUND (1859 TO 1938)

The Idea of Phenomenology. Trans. Lee Hardy. Dordrecht/Boston: Kluwer, 1999.

Ideas Pertaining to a Pure Phenomenology and to a Phenomenological Philosophy. 3 vols. Trans. Fred Kersten. Dordrecht, Netherlands: Kluwer, 1980–1989.

JASPERS, KARL (1883 TO 1969)

Philosophy. 3 vols. Trans. E. B. Ashton. Chicago: University of Chicago Press, 1969–1971. Especially volume III, "Metaphysics."

HEIDEGGER, MARTIN (1889 TO 1976)

Being and Time. Trans. John Macquarrie and Edward Robinson. San Francisco: Harper & Row, 1962.

Kant and the Problem of Metaphysics. Trans. Richard Taft. Bloomington: Indiana University Press, 1997.

"What is Metaphysics?" Trans. David Farell Krell. In *Pathmarks*. Ed. William McNeil. New York: Cambridge University Press, 1998, 82–96.

WITTGENSTEIN, LUDWIG (1889 TO 1951)

Tractatus Logico-Philosophicus. Trans. David F. Pears and B. F. McGuinness. New York: Routledge, 1961.

SARTRE, JEAN-PAUL (1905 TO 1980)

Being and Nothingness. Trans. Hazel E. Barnes. London: Routledge, 2003.

Existentialism and Humanism. Trans. Philip Mairet. London: Methuen, 1948.

GADAMER, HANS-GEORG (1900 TO 2002)

Truth and Method. Trans. Garrett Barden and John Cumming. New York: Seabury, 1975.

Grondin, Jean, *The Philosophy of Gadamer.* Trans. Kathryn Plant. Montréal: McGill-Queen's Press, 2003.

LEVINAS, EMMANUEL (1905 TO 1995)

Totality and Infinity: An Essay on Exteriority. Trans. Alphonso Lingis. Pittsburgh, PA: Duquesne University Press, 2007.

Otherwise than Being: or, Beyond Essence. Trans. Alphonso Lingis. Boston: Kluwer, 1981.

Entre nous: On Thinking of the Other. Trans. Michael B. Smith and Barbara Harshaw. New York: Columbia University Press, 1998.

DERRIDA, JACQUES (1930 TO 2004)

"Speech and Phenomena" and other Essays On Husserl's Theory of Signs. Trans. David B. Allison. Evanston: North Western University Press, 1973.

Of Grammatology. Trans. Gayatri Chakravorty Spivak. Baltimore: Johns Hopkins University Press, 1997.

Writing and Difference. Trans. Alan Bass. London: Routledge, 2001.

Margins of Philosophy. Trans. Alan Bass. Chicago: University of Chicago Press, 1982.

Psyche: Inventions of the Other. 2 vols. Ed. Peggy Kamuf and Elizabeth Rotenberg. Stanford: Stanford University Press, 2007–2008.

Printed in the USA
CPSIA information can be obtained
at www.ICGtesting.com
JSHW021318300924
70779JS00002B/21